FOUR

GREEK AUTHORS

EXTRACTS FROM
HOMER, ANTIPHON, EURIPIDES AND THUCYDIDES

Edited with Introduction,
Notes and Vocabulary by
E.C. KENNEDY

Bristol Classical Press

First published by Macmillan Education Ltd in 1968

This edition published in 1996 by
Bristol Classical Press
an imprint of
Gerald Duckworth & Co. Ltd
61 Frith Street
London W1D 3JL
e-mail: inquiries@duckworth-publishers.co.uk
Website: www.ducknet.co.uk

Reprinted 1997, 2000

A catalogue record for this book is available
from the British Library

ISBN 1-85399-501-0

Printed in Great Britain by
Booksprint

1003461606

Contents

List of Illustrations

The two drawings are taken from *A Companion to Homer* edited by
Alan J. B. Wace and Frank H. Stubbings

Preface

NEARLY all elementary school texts of Greek authors now available — and the number is decreasing as editions are allowed to go out of print — were produced in the nineteenth century, when boys began Greek at an earlier age and spent more time on it than is now possible. Many of the older books are therefore too hard for modern boys and girls, who need more help in the explanation of difficulties and a full vocabulary. The publishers deserve gratitude from teachers and learners of Greek for so generously continuing to publish elementary editions of authors at a time when the number of students of the language is so small.

I have chosen extracts from four Greek authors which I hope will be considered interesting. They are 'The Contest of the Bow', *Odyssey* XXI, in which Odysseus returns home after twenty years' absence to confront the suitors who are pestering his wife; most of 'The Murder of Herodes' by Antiphon, the speech for the defence in a real murder trial; 'Scenes from Euripides' *Ion*', a romantic melodrama in which a mother tries to kill the child whom she abandoned in infancy and which ends happily with a recognition scene; and Thucydides' 'Siege of Plataea', which describes the siege of the city, the escape by night of half the beleagured garrison, and the eventual massacre of the rest. If this is all the Greek that some pupils are going to read, I hope that they will enjoy the contents of this book.

The text of Homer and of Thucydides are those of W. B. Stanford and E. C. Marchant respectively in Macmillan's Classical Series; of Euripides, the Oxford Classical Text by Gilbert Murray, by kind permission of the Clarendon Press; and of Antiphon, the Teubner text by T. Thalheim. For Homer I have consulted editions of the *Odyssey* by W. W. Merry and W. B. Stanford, *A Companion to Homer* by A. J. B. Wace and F. H. Stubbings, and S. H. Butcher and A. Lang's translation: for Antiphon, the Loeb translation by K. J. Maidment, and Kathleen Freeman's 'Murder of Herodes', and R. C. Jebb's edition of part of the speech; for Euripides, editions by F. A. Paley and A. S. Owen, and the translation by E. P. Coleridge; and for Thucydides, editions of Books II and III by Marchant, and translations by B. Jowett, R. Crawley, and C. F. Smith in the Loeb series. I am grateful to my former colleague at Malvern, Mr. J. T. Hart, for reading through the Introductions and making some valuable suggestions.

E. C. KENNEDY

Malvern
March 1967

HOMER

Greece and the Aegean

Introduction

NOTHING whatever is known about the life of Homer. The ancient Greeks believed that he was the author of both the *Iliad* and the *Odyssey*, that he was blind, and that he was born and lived in one of the Ionian cities (Greek colonies) on the west coast of Asia Minor, perhaps Colophon or Smyrna, at some time between the ninth and seventh centuries or even earlier; much of this may well be true. But European scholars for more than a century after A.D. 1795 believed that both poems were made up of a number of separate 'lays', composed by different poets in about the tenth century B.C., of whom one man, 'Homer', produced the largest part; these lays were combined into the two epics several centuries later by an editor or editors, after the invention of writing. Different versions of this view were held by the 'Analysts', as those who believed in a multiple authorship are called, until about 1920, when the 'Unitarians', who believed in a single author, began to hold the field again.

Recent research into the folk-poetry of modern Yugoslavia and Russia shows that 'oral' epics can be produced by a poet who cannot read or write but who composes extempore, assisted by a prodigious memory stocked with a large number of poetic 'formulas' that are as it were the bare bones of his art and give him a basis on which to build an original poem. This suggests that in ancient Greece successive generations of 'bards' were able to chant (in hexameter verse) to the music of the lyre poems about the Heroic Age in which they lived or which preceded them by anything up to five centuries. They had at their disposal the 'formulas', consisting of a noun and an adjective, or a longer phrase, or a whole line or even a group of lines, that were the common stock of all bards, by the aid of which they could compose a poem on any subject required by their audience, of a length to suit the occasion, in a rich man's palace or at a festival or at any meeting of the people in the market-place. They would not always produce the same version of their own story but might improve on it or expand it at will. One of the last and incomparably the greatest of these bards was Homer, who used the formulas and themes of his predecessors to produce in due course nearly the whole of his two epics; but by his supreme art in arranging and describing events and in his drawing of character he combined the disconnected stories of the two legends into coherent and artistic poems. Epics of such great length that were composed and retained in the memory of the poet without being written down would naturally contain some inconsistencies that his audience would not notice, for it would take him several days to recite the whole of one poem on a special occasion, without wearying himself and his listeners. The strange thing is that there are not more inconsistencies, though no doubt some have been removed by editors.

The traditional date of the Fall of Troy is 1184, but modern archaeology has now put it some fifty years earlier, between 1250 and 1230. Its captors were the Achaeans, or Mycenaean Greeks, so called because the centre of their civilisation and empire was Mycenae in the north-eastern Peloponnese, of which by tradition Agamemnon was king at the time of the Trojan War. Mycenaean supremacy in

Greece and the Aegean lasted from *c.* 1550 (all these dates are very uncertain) until the end of the Bronze Age in *c.* 1100. Knossos in Crete with its wonderful Minoan art became subject to Mycenae in *c.* 1500 and was destroyed a century later. The recent decipherment of the Linear B tablets, of which many have been found at Knossos (fifteenth century) and at Pylos in the south-western Peloponnese and a few at Mycenae (late thirteenth century) show that the Mycenaeans spoke Greek and could write in a 'syllabary', in which signs represent syllables, but not in an alphabetic script. Linear B was used only by court scribes to keep records of palace property and stores, not for literature, and the princes and people of the Mycenaean period could not read or write.

The Iron Age of Greece started in *c.* 1100, when the 'Dorian Invaders' from the north overran the whole country, including Mycenae, and began a Dark Age that lasted for three centuries during which the culture, art, and luxury of Mycenaeans, and the Linear B script, were forgotten. But the bards who had entertained the Achaean heroes at their banquets with tales of the Trojan War and earlier legends of Greece, and their successors, continued to produce their songs during the Dark Age and the centuries that followed, each one using the formulas and themes of his predecessor and, if he could, improving on the poems and the technique of oral composition, until the time of Homer and later. Homer's life cannot be dated with any accuracy, but any time from 800 to 660 is possible, the last seventy years of that period being the more likely. Writing as we know it began in Greece in *c.* 750 and Homer himself probably could not write, though his poems may have been written down during his lifetime, possibly even at his dictation — though it must be made clear again that all these dates and suggestions are conjectural. He was an Ionian Greek and used the Ionic and Aeolic dialects (from north-eastern Asia Minor) and a few Arcado-Cyprian and Attic forms, and even traces of Mycenaean Greek. (Attic Greek is the dialect in whch nearly all the classical authors, who mostly lived at Athens in Attica, wrote.) It is not certain whether Homer composed both the *Iliad* and the *Odyssey*. Some scholars think that he was the author of the *Iliad* and that another great poet, a generation later, produced the *Odyssey;* others believe, as the ancient Greeks themselves believed, that the same man composed both poems, the *Iliad* in the prime of life and the *Odyssey* in old age, because the similarities in the treatment of the two epics are more striking than the differences.

The theme of the *Iliad* is 'The Wrath of Achilles', caused by an affront offered him by Agamemnon at Troy during the last and tenth year of the war, and the events that followed. The *Odyssey* describes the adventures of Odysseus, son of Laertes and king of Ithaca, an island off the south-western coast of Greece, during his ten years' wanderings after the fall of Troy, where he fought with great courage and cunning.

Books I–IV describe affairs in Ithaca in the twentieth year after Odysseus' departure for Troy, when he is now believed to be dead. His faithful wife Penelope is being wooed by many of the island princes, who behave with the greatest insolence in the palace. She put them off for a time by pretending to be weaving a funeral robe for Laertes, but each night she unwove what she had woven in the day, until they discovered the trick and insisted on her choosing a new husband. Her son Telemachus goes to the mainland in search of news of Odysseus, and the suitors plan to murder him on his return. Books V–VIII contain the adventures of Odysseus, who is released by the goddess Calypso after being detained by her for seven years on the island of Ogygia. He makes a raft and reaches the land of the Phaeacians (perhaps the modern Corfu), where he is found cast up on the shore by King Alcinous' charming daughter Nausicaa and is entertained at court by her father.

In Books IX–XII Odysseus tells Alcinous of his adventures since leaving Troy, his visit to the land of the Lotus-eaters, his escape from the terrible Cyclops, Polyphemus, and from the cannibal Laestrygonians, and his stay for a year with the witch Circe on the island of Aeaea, where his comrades were turned into swine until he restored them to human shape with the aid of a magic herb. Circe advised him to consult the seer Tiresias in the Underworld, where he spoke to many of his dead friends and to his mother. He then evaded the Sirens, who tried to lure him on to the rocks with their sweet singing, passed between Scylla and Charybdis (the Straits of Messina), and after more adventures reached Calypso's island as the sole survivor of all his fleet.

In Books XIII–XVI Odysseus is sent back to Ithaca by Alcinous, is given the appearance of an old beggar by Athena, and learns from the faithful swineherd Eumaeus about the shameful conduct of the suitors. Telemachus escapes the suitors' ambush, returns home, and is told by the beggar that he is really Odysseus; together father and son plan to destroy the suitors. In Books XVII–XX Odysseus goes to his palace and is recognised by his old dog Argus, who dies of joy immediately afterwards, is insulted by the goat-herd Melanthius and by Antinous, the leader of the suitors, and defeats another beggar, Irus, in a fight. A maidservant and the suitor Eurymachus insult Odysseus, who is later recognised by his old nurse Eurycleia when she sees an old boar-scar on his thigh. Penelope in despair announces her intention of marrying the suitor who on the next day can string Odysseus' great bow and shoot an arrow through the sockets of twelve axeheads placed in a row. Next morning Zeus sends a good omen to Odysseus, who is insulted again by Melanthius and a suitor, and a fugitive seer called Theoclymenus has a vision of the death of the suitors, though they merely laugh at him and drive him out.

In Books XXI–XXIV none of the suitors can string the bow, but Odysseus easily does it and shoots an arrow through the axeheads. He then shoots down Antinous, and with the help of Telemachus, Eumaeus, and the faithful oxherd Philaetius, to both of whom he has previously revealed himself, kills all the suitors and hangs the twelve maidservants who have been consorting with them. Penelope refuses to believe that he is really Odysseus, but is at last convinced by his knowledge of the strange construction of their bedstead, and Odysseus goes to visit his father Laertes. The kinsfolk of the slain suitors come to the palace to get revenge and are reconciled to Odysseus by Athena in the nick of time.

THE HOMERIC HEXAMETER

The *Iliad* and the *Odyssey* were written (but originally composed 'orally') in dactylic hexameters consisting of a line of six metrical 'feet', of which the first four can be either a 'dactyl' ($- \cup \cup$) or a 'spondee' ($- -$), the fifth is usually a dactyl, and the sixth always a spondee or a 'trochee' (– ∪). There is always a break between two words in the third or/ and the fourth foot, which binds together the two halves of the line and makes them into a rhythmic whole; this break is called a 'caesura', and when it comes after the first syllable of a foot it is called a 'strong' caesura, when after the first short syllable of a dactyl it is called a 'weak' caesura. The scheme of the hexameter is as follows, with the caesuras marked with a double line.

$$— \cup \cup \ \Big|\!— \cup \cup \ \Big|\!—\ \Big\|\ \cup \cup \ \Big|\!—\ \Big\|\ \cup \cup \ \Big|\!— \cup \cup \ \Big|\!—\ \overset{\cup}{—}$$
$$—\ —\ \Big|\!—\ —\ \Big|\!—\ \Big\|\ —\ \Big|\!—\ \Big\|\ —\ \Big|\ $$

Here is a line (4) containing five dactyls, with a weak caesura in the third foot:

ἐν μεγά- | ροις 'Οδυ- | σῆος ‖ά- | έθλια | καὶ φόνου | ἀρχήν.

Here is a rare form (15) containing six spondees, with a strong caesura in the third foot:

τὼ δ' ἐν | Μεσσή- | νη ‖ ξυμ- | βλήτην | ἀλλή- | λοιϊν

Here is one (9) containing four dactyls and two spondees, with a strong caesura in the third foot:

ἔσχατον | ἔνθαδέ | οἱ ‖ κει- | μήλια τοῖο ἄ- | νακτος

A short vowel can be 'elided' before a following vowel and not pronounced or written at all, as in τὼ δ' ἐν (15), and sometimes a diphthong is elided, like φαίνετ' ἀέθλον (73), where φαίνετ' = φαίνεται. A long vowel or diphthong is often pronounced as though it were short before another vowel, like καὶ φόνου ἀρχήν (4).

Complete 'hiatus', when two vowels come together, can occur without any shortening of a long vowel and without elision, as in ᾧ ἔνι οἴκῳ (27), where there is hiatus between ᾧ and ἔνι but not between ἔνι and οἴκῳ, which is an apparent case of hiatus very frequently found. This is due to the influence of an old Greek letter called 'digamma' because its shape, ⊦, is like two capital gammas; it was pronounced like our *w* and fell out of use soon after Homer's time. Thus in 9 οἱ and ἄνακτος were originally ⊦οι and ⊦άνακτος, pronounced 'woi' and 'wanaktos', so that the preceding vowels were not elided. Traces of the lost digamma can be seen in a comparison of Greek with cognate languages, e.g. ⊦οῖνος, Latin *vinum*, English 'wine'; ⊦έσπερος Latin *vesper*; ⊦έργον, English 'work'. But the effect of digamma is sometimes neglected and the preceding vowel is elided in the ordinary way. When two vowels come together in a word without forming a diphthong they are sometimes pronounced as one long syllable, by the process called 'synizesis', 'binding together', as in 277, θεοειδέα, where -έα is pronounced as one long syllable.

Vowels that are naturally short generally form a long syllable before two consonants or an initial ρ, and are sometimes pronounced as though they were long at the end of a word when followed by a word beginning with λ, μ, ν, or σ, as in 56, κλαῖε μά |λα λιγέ|ως. Lengthening sometimes also occurs in the first syllable of a foot, as in 208,

ἤλυθον | εἰκόσ- | τῳ ‖ ἔτε- | ϊ ‖ ἐς | πάτριδα | γαῖαν

where there are three irregularities of scansion in ἔτεϊ ἐς. The first is that ἔτεϊ is pronounced as three syllables instead of the usual two (∪ –); the second is that the short ι of the same word is lengthened in the first syllable of the fourth foot; and the third is that there is hiatus between ἔτεϊ and the following vowel in ἐς. But there is no hiatus between εἰκόστῳ and ἔτεϊ because ἔτεϊ originally began with a digamma, Ϝέτεϊ. Homer thus uses great freedom in altering the 'quantity' of words to suit the metre. Such irregularities will generally be mentioned in the notes the first time that they occur in the book, with a reference to these pages; after the first time they will be taken for granted because in Greek all elisions are marked by apostrophes in the text, so that there is usually little difficulty in scanning Homeric hexameters. Irregularities that are not obvious, like fifth-foot spondees or instances of 'synizesis', will be mentioned in the notes whenever they occur. Nothing will be said in the Introduction about Homeric forms of grammar that often affect the quantity of words, because all Homeric irregularities appear in the Vocabulary after the normal Attic use of the words. Some rules for the length of Greek Syllables are given on page 66.

The Contest of the Bow

ODYSSEY XXI

1–41 Athena suggests to Penelope that she should bring out her husband Odysseus' bow and the iron axes for the suitors' contest. The previous history of the bow, which was given to Odysseus by his friend Iphitus, is related.

Τῇ δ' ἄρ' ἐπὶ φρεσὶ θῆκε θεὰ γλαυκῶπις Ἀθήνη,
κούρῃ Ἰκαρίοιο, περίφρονι Πηνελοπείῃ,
τόξον μνηστήρεσσι θέμεν πολιόν τε σίδηρον
ἐν μεγάροις Ὀδυσῆος, ἀέθλια καὶ φόνου ἀρχήν.
κλίμακα δ' ὑψηλὴν προσεβήσετο οἷο δόμοιο,   5
εἵλετο δὲ κληῖδ' εὐκαμπέα χειρὶ παχείῃ
καλὴν χαλκείην· κώπη δ' ἐλέφαντος ἐπῆεν.
βῆ δ' ἴμεναι θάλαμόνδε σὺν ἀμφιπόλοισι γυναιξὶν
ἔσχατον· ἔνθα δέ οἱ κειμήλια κεῖτο ἄνακτος,
χαλκός τε χρυσός τε πολύκμητός τε σίδηρος.   10
ἔνθα δὲ τόξον κεῖτο παλίντονον ἠδὲ φαρέτρη
ἰοδόκος, πολλοὶ δ' ἔνεσαν στονόεντες ὀϊστοί,
δῶρα τά οἱ ξεῖνος Λακεδαίμονι δῶκε τυχήσας
Ἴφιτος Εὐρυτίδης, ἐπιείκελος ἀθανάτοισι.
τὼ δ' ἐν Μεσσήνῃ ξυμβλήτην ἀλλήλοιϊν   15
οἴκῳ ἐν Ὀρτιλόχοιο δαΐφρονος. ἦ τοι Ὀδυσσεὺς
ἦλθε μετὰ χρεῖος, τό ῥά οἱ πᾶς δῆμος ὄφελλε·
μῆλα γὰρ ἐξ Ἰθάκης Μεσσήνιοι ἄνδρες ἄειραν
νηυσὶ πολυκλήϊσι τριηκόσι' ἠδὲ νομῆας.
τῶν ἕνεκ' ἐξεσίην πολλὴν ὁδὸν ἦλθεν Ὀδυσσεὺς   20
παιδνὸς ἐών· πρὸ γὰρ ἧκε πατὴρ ἄλλοι τε γέροντες.

Ἴφιτος αὖθ' ἵππους διζήμενος, αἵ οἱ ὅλοντο
δώδεκα θήλειαι, ὑπὸ δ' ἡμίονοι ταλαεργοί·
αἵ δή οἱ καὶ ἔπειτα φόνος καὶ μοῖρα γένοντο,
ἐπεὶ δὴ Διὸς υἱὸν ἀφίκετο καρτερόθυμον,   25
φῶθ' Ἡρακλῆα, μεγάλων ἐπιίστορα ἔργων,
ὅς μιν ξεῖνον ἐόντα κατέκτανεν ᾧ ἐνὶ οἴκῳ,
σχέτλιος, οὐδὲ θεῶν ὄπιν αἰδέσατ' οὐδὲ τράπεζαν,
τὴν ἥν οἱ παρέθηκεν· ἔπειτα δὲ πέφνε καὶ αὐτόν,
ἵππους δ' αὐτὸς ἔχε κρατερώνυχας ἐν μεγάροισι.   30
τὰς ἐρέων Ὀδυσῆϊ συνήντετο, δῶκε δὲ τόξον,
τὸ πρὶν μέν ῥ' ἐφόρει μέγας Εὔρυτος, αὐτὰρ ὁ παιδὶ
κάλλιπ' ἀποθνήσκων ἐν δώμασιν ὑψηλοῖσι.
τῷ δ' Ὀδυσεὺς ξίφος ὀξὺ καὶ ἄλκιμον ἔγχος ἔδωκεν,
ἀρχὴν ξεινοσύνης προσκηδέος. οὐδὲ τραπέζῃ   35
γνώτην ἀλλήλων· πρὶν γὰρ Διὸς υἱὸς ἔπεφνεν
Ἴφιτον Εὐρυτίδην, ἐπιείκελον ἀθανάτοισιν,
ὅς οἱ τόξον ἔδωκε. τὸ δ' οὔ ποτε δῖος Ὀδυσσεὺς
ἐρχόμενος πόλεμόνδε μελαινάων ἐπὶ νηῶν
ᾑρεῖτ', ἀλλ' αὐτοῦ μνῆμα ξείνοιο φίλοιο
κέσκετ' ἐνὶ μεγάροισι, φόρει δέ μιν ἧς ἐπὶ γαίης.   40

42-79 *Penelope goes to the treasure-chamber and weeps over the bow. She brings it and some arrows and the war-gear of Odysseus down to the hall, where she tells the suitors that she will marry the one who can string the bow and shoot an arrow through twelve axes.*

Ἡ δ' ὅτε δὴ θάλαμον τὸν ἀφίκετο δῖα γυναικῶν,
οὐδόν τε δρύϊνον προσεβήσετο, τόν ποτε τέκτων
ξέσσεν ἐπισταμένως καὶ ἐπὶ στάθμην ἴθυνεν,
ἐν δὲ σταθμοὺς ἄρσε, θύρας δ' ἐπέθηκε φαεινάς·   45
αὐτίκ' ἄρ' ἥ γ' ἱμάντα θοῶς ἀπέλυσε κορώνης,
ἐν δὲ κληῖδ' ἧκε, θυρέων δ' ἀνέκοπτεν ὀχῆας

ἄντα τιτυσκομένη· τὰ δ' ἀνέβραχεν ἠΰτε ταῦρος
βοσκόμενος λειμῶνι· τόσσ' ἔβραχε καλὰ θύρετρα
πληγέντα κληῖδι, πετάσθησαν δέ οἱ ὦκα.   50
ἡ δ' ἄρ' ἐφ' ὑψηλῆς σανίδος βῆ· ἔνθα δὲ χηλοὶ
ἕστασαν, ἐν δ' ἄρα τῇσι θυώδεα εἵματ' ἔκειτο.
ἔνθεν ὀρεξαμένη ἀπὸ πασσάλου αἴνυτο τόξον
αὐτῷ γωρυτῷ, ὅς οἱ περίκειτο φαεινός.
ἑζομένη δὲ κατ' αὖθι, φίλοις ἐπὶ γούνασι θεῖσα,   55
κλαῖε μάλα λιγέως, ἐκ δ' ᾗρεε τόξον ἄνακτος.
ἡ δ' ἐπεὶ οὖν τάρφθη πολυδακρύτοιο γόοιο,
βῆ ῥ' ἴμεναι μέγαρόνδε μετὰ μνηστῆρας ἀγαυοὺς
τόξον ἔχουσ' ἐν χειρὶ παλίντονον ἠδὲ φαρέτρην
ἰοδόκον· πολλοὶ δ' ἔνεσαν στονόεντες ὀϊστοί.   60
τῇ δ' ἄρ' ἅμ' ἀμφίπολοι φέρον ὄγκιον, ἔνθα σίδηρος
κεῖτο πολὺς καὶ χαλκός, ἀέθλια τοῖο ἄνακτος.
ἡ δ' ὅτε δὴ μνηστῆρας ἀφίκετο δῖα γυναικῶν,
στῆ ῥα παρὰ σταθμὸν τέγεος πύκα ποιητοῖο
ἄντα παρειάων σχομένη λιπαρὰ κρήδεμνα.   65
ἀμφίπολος δ' ἄρα οἱ κεδνὴ ἑκάτερθε παρέστη.
αὐτίκα δὲ μνηστῆρσι μετηύδα καὶ φάτο μῦθον·
" κέκλυτέ μεν, μνηστῆρες ἀγήνορες, οἳ τόδε δῶμα
ἐχράετ' ἐσθιέμεν καὶ πινέμεν ἐμμενὲς αἰεὶ
ἀνδρὸς ἀποιχομένοιο πολὺν χρόνον· οὐδέ τιν' ἄλλην   70
μύθου ποιήσασθαι ἐπισχεσίην ἐδύνασθε,
ἀλλ' ἐμὲ ἱέμενοι γῆμαι θέσθαι τε γυναῖκα.
ἀλλ' ἄγετε, μνηστῆρες, ἐπεὶ τόδε φαίνετ' ἄεθλον·
θήσω γὰρ μέγα τόξον Ὀδυσσῆς θείοιο·
ὃς δέ κε ῥηΐτατ' ἐντανύσῃ βιὸν ἐν παλάμῃσι   75
καὶ διοϊστεύσῃ πελέκεων δυοκαίδεκα πάντων,
τῷ κεν ἅμ' ἑσποίμην νοσφισσαμένη τόδε δῶμα
κουρίδιον, μάλα καλόν, ἐνίπλειον βιότοιο,
τοῦ ποτε μεμνήσεσθαι ὀΐομαι ἔν περ ὀνείρῳ."

80–117 Eumaeus and the oxherd shed tears as they set out the axes, and Antinous rebukes them for causing even more sorrow to their mistress. Telemachus laughs at the thought that his mother will marry one of the suitors, and urges them to begin the contest, in which he also will try his skill.

Ὣς φάτο, καί ῥ' Εὔμαιον ἀνώγει, δῖον ὑφορβόν,   80
τόξον μνηστήρεσσι θέμεν πολιόν τε σίδηρον.
δακρύσας δ' Εὔμαιος ἐδέξατο καὶ κατέθηκε·
κλαῖε δὲ βουκόλος ἄλλοθ', ἐπεὶ ἴδε τόξον ἄνακτος.
Ἀντίνοος δ' ἐνένιπεν ἔπος τ' ἔφατ' ἔκ τ' ὀνόμαζε·
" νήπιοι ἀγροιῶται, ἐφημέρια φρονέοντες!   85
ἆ δειλώ, τί νυ δάκρυ κατείβετον ἠδὲ γυναικὶ
θυμὸν ἐνὶ στήθεσσιν ὀρίνετον; ἧ τε καὶ ἄλλως
κεῖται ἐν ἄλγεσι θυμός, ἐπεὶ φίλον ὤλεσ' ἀκοίτην.
ἀλλ' ἀκέων δαίνυσθε καθήμενοι, ἠὲ θύραζε
κλαίετον ἐξελθόντε, κατ' αὐτόθι τόξα λιπόντε   90
μνηστήρεσσιν ἄεθλον ἀάατον· οὐ γὰρ ὀΐω
ῥηϊδίως τόδε τόξον ἐΰξοον ἐντανύεσθαι.
οὐ γάρ τις μέτα τοῖος ἀνὴρ ἐν τοῖσδεσι πᾶσιν
οἷος Ὀδυσσεὺς ἔσκεν· ἐγὼ δέ μιν αὐτὸς ὄπωπα —
καὶ γὰρ μνήμων εἰμί — πάϊς δ' ἔτι νήπιος ἦα."   95
Ὣς φάτο· τῷ δ' ἄρα θυμὸς ἐνὶ στήθεσσιν ἐώλπει
νευρὴν ἐντανύειν διοϊστεύσειν τε σιδήρου.
ἦ τοι ὀϊστοῦ γε πρῶτος γεύσεσθαι ἔμελλεν
ἐκ χειρῶν Ὀδυσῆος ἀμύμονος, ὃν τότ' ἀτίμα
ἥμενος ἐν μεγάροις, ἐπὶ δ' ὄρνυε πάντας ἑταίρους.   100
τοῖσι δὲ καὶ μετέειφ' ἱερὴ ἲς Τηλεμάχοιο·
" ὢ πόποι, ἦ μάλα με Ζεὺς ἄφρονα θῆκε Κρονίων·
μήτηρ μέν μοί φησι φίλη, πινυτή περ ἐοῦσα,
ἄλλῳ ἅμ' ἕψεσθαι νοσφισσαμένη τόδε δῶμα·
αὐτὰρ ἐγὼ γελόω καὶ τέρπομαι ἄφρονι θυμῷ.   105
ἀλλ' ἄγετε, μνηστῆρες, ἐπεὶ τόδε φαίνετ' ἄεθλον,
οἵη νῦν οὐκ ἔστι γυνὴ κατ' Ἀχαιΐδα γαῖαν,

οὔτε Πύλου ἱερῆς οὔτ' Ἄργεος οὔτε Μυκήνης·
οὔτ' αὐτῆς Ἰθάκης οὔτ' ἠπείροιο μελαίνης·
καὶ δ' αὐτοὶ τόδε ἴστε· τί με χρὴ μητέρος αἴνου;   110
ἀλλ' ἄγε μὴ μύνῃσι παρέλκετε μηδ' ἔτι τόξου
δηρὸν ἀποτρωπᾶσθε τανυστύος, ὄφρα ἴδωμεν.
καὶ δέ κεν αὐτὸς ἐγὼ τοῦ τόξου πειρησαίμην·
εἰ δέ κεν ἐντανύσω διοϊστεύσω τε σιδήρου,
οὔ κέ μοι ἀχνυμένῳ τάδε δώματα πότνια μήτηρ   115
λείποι ἅμ' ἄλλῳ ἰοῦσ', ὅτ' ἐγὼ κατόπισθε λιποίμην
οἷός τ' ἤδη πατρὸς ἀέθλια κάλ' ἀνελέσθαι."

118–162 Telemachus sets up the axes in line on the floor of the hall and nearly strings the bow himself, but is stopped by a sign from Odysseus. Leodes fails in his attempt, and foretells ill luck for the suitors, who must leave Penelope to a better man.

Ἦ καὶ ἀπ' ὤμοιϊν χλαῖναν θέτο φοινικόεσσαν
ὀρθὸς ἀναΐξας, ἀπὸ δὲ ξίφος ὀξὺ θέτ' ὤμων.
πρῶτον μὲν πελέκεας στῆσεν, διὰ τάφρον ὀρύξας   120
πᾶσι μίαν μακρήν, καὶ ἐπὶ στάθμην ἴθυνεν,
ἀμφὶ δὲ γαῖαν ἔναξε· τάφος δ' ἔλε πάντας ἰδόντας,
ὡς εὐκόσμως στῆσε· πάρος δ' οὔ πώ ποτ' ὀπώπει.
στῆ δ' ἄρ' ἐπ' οὐδὸν ἰὼν καὶ τόξου πειρήτιζε.
τρὶς μέν μιν πελέμιξεν ἐρύσσασθαι μενεαίνων,   125
τρὶς δὲ μεθῆκε βίης, ἐπιελπόμενος τό γε θυμῷ
νευρὴν ἐντανύειν διοϊστεύσειν τε σιδήρου.
καί νύ κε δή ῥ' ἐτάνυσσε βίῃ τὸ τέταρτον ἀνέλκων,
ἀλλ' Ὀδυσεὺς ἀνένευε καὶ ἔσχεθεν ἱέμενόν περ.
τοῖς δ' αὖτις μετέειφ' ἱερὴ ἲς Τηλεμάχοιο·   130
"ὦ πόποι, ἦ καὶ ἔπειτα κακός τ' ἔσομαι καὶ ἄκικυς,
ἠὲ νεώτερός εἰμι καὶ οὔ πω χερσὶ πέποιθα
ἄνδρ' ἀπαμύνασθαι, ὅτε τις πρότερος χαλεπήνῃ.

ἀλλ' ἄγεθ', οἵ περ ἐμεῖο βίῃ προφερέστεροί ἐστε,
τόξου πειρήσασθε, καὶ ἐκτελέωμεν ἄεθλον." 135
  Ὣς εἰπὼν τόξον μὲν ἀπὸ ἕο θῆκε χαμᾶζε,
κλίνας κολλητῇσιν ἐϋξέστῃς σανίδεσσιν,
αὐτοῦ δ' ὠκὺ βέλος καλῇ προσέκλινε κορώνῃ·
ἂψ δ' αὖτις κατ' ἄρ' ἕζετ' ἐπὶ θρόνου ἔνθεν ἀνέστη.
τοῖσιν δ' Ἀντίνοος μετέφη, Εὐπείθεος υἱός· 140
" ὄρνυσθ' ἐξείης ἐπιδέξια πάντες ἑταῖροι,
ἀρξάμενοι τοῦ χώρου ὅθεν τέ περ οἰνοχοεύει."
  Ὣς ἔφατ' Ἀντίνοος· τοῖσιν δ' ἐπιήνδανε μῦθος.
Ληώδης δὲ πρῶτος ἀνίστατο, Οἴνοπος υἱός,
ὅ σφι θυοσκόος ἔσκε, παρὰ κρητῆρα δὲ καλὸν 145
ἷζε μυχοίτατος αἰεί· ἀτασθαλίαι δέ οἱ οἴῳ
ἐχθραὶ ἔσαν, πᾶσιν δὲ νεμέσσα μνηστήρεσσιν·
ὅς ῥα τότε πρῶτος τόξον λάβε καὶ βέλος ὠκύ.
στῆ δ' ἄρ' ἐπ' οὐδὸν ἰὼν καὶ τόξου πειρήτιζεν,
οὐδέ μιν ἐντάνυσε· πρὶν γὰρ κάμε χεῖρας ἀνέλκων 150
ἀτρίπτους ἁπαλάς· μετὰ δὲ μνηστῆρσιν ἔειπεν·
" ὦ φίλοι, οὐ μὲν ἐγὼ τανύω, λαβέτω δὲ καὶ ἄλλος.
πολλοὺς γὰρ τόδε τόξον ἀριστῆας κεκαδήσει
θυμοῦ καὶ ψυχῆς, ἐπεὶ ἦ πολὺ φέρτερόν ἐστι
τεθνάμεν ἢ ζώοντας ἁμαρτεῖν, οὗ θ' ἕνεκ' αἰεὶ 155
ἐνθάδ' ὁμιλέομεν ποτιδέγμενοι ἤματα πάντα.
νῦν μέν τις καὶ ἔλπετ' ἐνὶ φρεσὶν ἠδὲ μενοινᾷ
γῆμαι Πηνελόπειαν, Ὀδυσσῆος παράκοιτιν.
αὐτὰρ ἐπὴν τόξου πειρήσεται ἠδὲ ἴδηται,
ἄλλην δή τιν' ἔπειτα Ἀχαιϊάδων εὐπέπλων 160
μνάσθω ἐέδνοισιν διζήμενος· ἡ δέ κ' ἔπειτα
γήμαιθ' ὅς κε πλεῖστα πόροι καὶ μόρσιμος ἔλθοι."

163–187 Antinous is angry with Leodes, and tells the goatherd to bring some lard, with which the suitors make the bow supple, but none of them can string it. Antinous and Eurymachus alone do not yet make the attempt.

Ὣς ἄρ' ἐφώνησεν καὶ ἀπὸ ἕο τόξον ἔθηκε,
κλίνας κολλητῇσιν ἐϋξέστῃς σανίδεσσιν,
αὐτοῦ δ' ὠκὺ βέλος καλῇ προσέκλινε κορώνῃ·   165
ἂψ δ' αὖτις κατ' ἄρ' ἕζετ' ἐπὶ θρόνου ἔνθεν ἀνέστη.
Ἀντίνοος δ' ἐνένιπεν ἔπος τ' ἔφατ' ἔκ τ' ὀνόμαζε·
" Λῃῶδες, ποῖόν σε ἔπος φύγεν ἕρκος ὀδόντων!
δεινόν τ' ἀργαλέον τε — νεμεσσῶμαι δέ τ' ἀκούων —
εἰ δὴ τοῦτό γε τόξον ἀριστῆας κεκαδήσει   170
θυμοῦ καὶ ψυχῆς, ἐπεὶ οὐ δύνασαι σὺ τανύσσαι.
οὐ γάρ τοι σέ γε τοῖον ἐγείνατο πότνια μήτηρ
οἷόν τε ῥυτῆρα βιοῦ τ' ἔμεναι καὶ ὀϊστῶν·
ἀλλ' ἄλλοι τανύουσι τάχα μνηστῆρες ἀγαυοί."
Ὣς φάτο, καί ῥ' ἐκέλευσε Μελάνθιον, αἰπόλον αἰγῶν·   175
" ἄγρει δή, πῦρ κῆον ἐνὶ μεγάροισι, Μελανθεῦ,
πὰρ δὲ τίθει δίφρον τε μέγαν καὶ κῶας ἐπ' αὐτοῦ,
ἐκ δὲ στέατος ἔνεικε μέγαν τροχὸν ἔνδον ἐόντος,
ὄφρα νέοι θάλποντες, ἐπιχρίοντες ἀλοιφῇ,
τόξου πειρώμεσθα καὶ ἐκτελέωμεν ἄεθλον."   180
Ὣς φάθ'· ὁ δ' αἶψ' ἀνέκαιε Μελάνθιος ἀκάματον πῦρ,
πὰρ δὲ φέρων δίφρον θῆκεν καὶ κῶας ἐπ' αὐτοῦ,
ἐκ δὲ στέατος ἔνεικε μέγαν τροχὸν ἔνδον ἐόντος·
τῷ ῥα νέοι θάλποντες ἐπειρῶντ'· οὐδ' ἐδύναντο
ἐντανύσαι, πολλὸν δὲ βίης ἐπιδευέες ἦσαν.   185
Ἀντίνοος δ' ἔτ' ἐπεῖχε καὶ Εὐρύμαχος θεοειδής,
ἀρχοὶ μνηστήρων· ἀρετῇ δ' ἔσαν ἔξοχ' ἄριστοι.

188-244 The faithful servants go out, followed by the beggar, who reveals himself as Odysseus by showing them his boar-scar. They must stop shedding tears of joy, and when the time comes Eumaeus is to give him the bow and Philoetius is to bar the outer doors of the courtyard.

Τὼ δ' ἐξ οἴκου βῆσαν ὁμαρτήσαντες ἅμ' ἄμφω
βουκόλος ἠδὲ συφορβὸς 'Οδυσσῆος θείοιο·
ἐκ δ' αὐτὸς μετὰ τοὺς δόμου ἤλυθε δῖος 'Οδυσσεύς. 190
ἀλλ' ὅτε δή ῥ' ἐκτὸς θυρέων ἔσαν ἠδὲ καὶ αὐλῆς,
φθεγξάμενός σφε ἔπεσσι προσηύδα μειλιχίοισι·
" βουκόλε καὶ σύ, συφορβέ, ἔπος τί κε μυθησαίμην,
ἦ αὐτὸς κεύθω; φάσθαι δέ με θυμὸς ἀνώγει.
ποῖοί κ' εἶτ' 'Οδυσῆϊ ἀμυνέμεν, εἴ ποθεν ἔλθοι 195
ὧδε μάλ' ἐξαπίνης καί τις θεὸς αὐτὸν ἐνείκαι;
ἤ κε μνηστήρεσσιν ἀμύνοιτ' ἦ 'Οδυσῆϊ;
εἴπαθ' ὅπως ὑμέας κραδίη θυμός τε κελεύει."
    Τὸν δ' αὖτε προσέειπε βοῶν ἐπιβουκόλος ἀνήρ·
" Ζεῦ πάτερ, αἲ γὰρ τοῦτο τελευτήσειας ἐέλδωρ, 200
ὡς ἔλθοι μὲν κεῖνος ἀνήρ, ἀγάγοι δέ ἑ δαίμων!
γνοίης χ' οἵη ἐμὴ δύναμις καὶ χεῖρες ἕπονται."
    Ὣς δ' αὔτως Εὔμαιος ἐπεύχετο πᾶσι θεοῖσι
νοστῆσαι 'Οδυσῆα πολύφρονα ὅνδε δόμονδε.
αὐτὰρ ἐπεὶ δὴ τῶν γε νόον νημερτέ' ἀνέγνω, 205
ἐξαῦτίς σφε ἔπεσσιν ἀμειβόμενος προσέειπεν·
"ἔνδον μὲν δὴ ὅδ' αὐτὸς ἐγώ· κακὰ πολλὰ μογήσας,
ἤλυθον εἰκοστῷ ἔτεϊ ἐς πατρίδα γαῖαν.
γιγνώσκω δ' ὡς σφῶϊν ἐελδομένοισιν ἱκάνω
οἴοισι δμώων· τῶν δ' ἄλλων οὔ τευ ἄκουσα 210
εὐξαμένου ἐμὲ αὖτις ὑπότροπον οἴκαδ' ἱκέσθαι.
σφῶϊν δ', ὡς ἔσεταί περ, ἀληθείην καταλέξω·
εἴ χ' ὑπ' ἐμοί γε θεὸς δαμάσῃ μνηστῆρας ἀγαυούς,
ἄξομαι ἀμφοτέροις ἀλόχους καὶ κτήματ' ὀπάσσω
οἰκία τ' ἐγγὺς ἐμεῖο τετυγμένα· καί μοι ἔπειτα 215

Τηλεμάχου ἑτάρω τε κασιγνήτω τε ἔσεσθον.
εἰ δ' ἄγε δὴ καὶ σῆμα ἀριφραδὲς ἄλλο τι δείξω,
ὄφρα μ' ἐῢ γνῶτον πιστωθῆτόν τ' ἐνὶ θυμῷ,
οὐλήν, τήν ποτέ με σῦς ἤλασε λευκῷ ὀδόντι
Παρνησόνδ' ἐλθόντα σὺν υἰάσιν Αὐτολύκοιο."   220
  "Ὣς εἰπὼν ῥάκεα μεγάλης ἀποέργαθεν οὐλῆς.
τὼ δ' ἐπεὶ εἰσιδέτην εὖ τ' ἐφράσσαντο ἕκαστα,
κλαῖον ἄρ' ἀμφ' Ὀδυσῆϊ δαΐφρονι χεῖρε βαλόντε,
καὶ κύνεον ἀγαπαζόμενοι κεφαλήν τε καὶ ὤμους·
ὣς δ' αὔτως Ὀδυσεὺς κεφαλὰς καὶ χεῖρας ἔκυσσε.   225
καί νύ κ' ὀδυρομένοισιν ἔδυ φάος ἠελίοιο,
εἰ μὴ Ὀδυσσεὺς αὐτὸς ἐρύκακε φώνησέν τε·
"παύεσθον κλαυθμοῖο γόοιό τε, μή τις ἴδηται
ἐξελθὼν μεγάροιο, ἀτὰρ εἴπῃσι καὶ εἴσω.
ἀλλὰ προμνηστῖνοι ἐσέλθετε, μηδ' ἄμα πάντες,   230
πρῶτος ἐγώ, μετὰ δ' ὔμμες. ἀτὰρ τόδε σῆμα τετύχθω·
ἄλλοι μὲν γὰρ πάντες, ὅσοι μνηστῆρες ἀγαυοί,
οὐκ ἐάσουσιν ἐμοὶ δόμεναι βιὸν ἠδὲ φαρέτρην·
ἀλλὰ σύ, δῖ' Εὔμαιε, φέρων ἀνὰ δώματα τόξον
ἐν χείρεσσιν ἐμοὶ θέμεναι, εἰπεῖν τε γυναιξὶ   235
κληῖσαι μεγάροιο θύρας πυκινῶς ἀραρυίας·
ἢν δέ τις ἢ στοναχῆς ἠὲ κτύπου ἔνδον ἀκούσῃ
ἀνδρῶν ἡμετέροισιν ἐν ἕρκεσι, μή τι θύραζε
προβλώσκειν, ἀλλ' αὐτοῦ ἀκὴν ἔμεναι παρὰ ἔργῳ.
σοὶ δέ, Φιλοίτιε δῖε, θύρας ἐπιτέλλομαι αὐλῆς   240
κληῖσαι κληῖδι, θοῶς δ' ἐπὶ δεσμὸν ἰῆλαι."
  "Ὣς εἰπὼν εἰσῆλθε δόμους εὖ ναιετάοντας·
ἕζετ' ἔπειτ' ἐπὶ δίφρον ἰών, ἔνθεν περ ἀνέστη.
ἐς δ' ἄρα καὶ τὼ δμῶε ἴτην θείου Ὀδυσῆος.

245-284 Eurymachus also is unable to string the bow and grieves at the disgrace. Antinous suggests that they should postpone the contest from that day, which is the festival of the archer-god Apollo, until the next day. The suitors begin drinking, and Odysseus requests to be allowed to try the bow.

Εὐρύμαχος δ' ἤδη τόξον μετὰ χερσὶν ἐνώμα, 245
θάλπων ἔνθα καὶ ἔνθα σέλᾳ πυρός· ἀλλά μιν οὐδ' ὧς
ἐντανύσαι δύνατο, μέγα δ' ἔστενε κυδάλιμον κῆρ.
ὀχθήσας δ' ἄρα εἶπεν ἔπος τ' ἔφατ' ἔκ τ' ὀνόμαζεν·
" ὦ πόποι, ἦ μοι ἄχος περί τ' αὐτοῦ καὶ περὶ πάντων·
οὔ τι γάμου τοσσοῦτον ὀδύρομαι, ἀχνύμενός περ — 250
εἰσὶ καὶ ἄλλαι πολλαὶ Ἀχαιΐδες, αἱ μὲν ἐν αὐτῇ
ἀμφιάλῳ Ἰθάκῃ, αἱ δ' ἄλλῃσιν πολίεσσιν —
ἀλλ' εἰ δὴ τοσσόνδε βίης ἐπιδευέες εἰμὲν
ἀντιθέου Ὀδυσῆος, ὅ τ' οὐ δυνάμεσθα τανύσσαι
τόξον· ἐλεγχείη δὲ καὶ ἐσσομένοισι πυθέσθαι." 255
Τὸν δ' αὖτ' Ἀντίνοος προσέφη, Εὐπείθεος υἱός·
" Εὐρύμαχ', οὐχ οὕτως ἔσται· νοέεις δὲ καὶ αὐτός.
νῦν μὲν γὰρ κατὰ δῆμον ἑορτὴ τοῖο θεοῖο
ἀγνή· τίς δέ κε τόξα τιταίνοιτ'; ἀλλὰ ἕκηλοι
κάτθετ'· ἀτὰρ πελέκεάς γε καὶ εἴ κ' εἰῶμεν ἅπαντας 260
ἑστάμεν — οὐ μὲν γάρ τιν' ἀναιρήσεσθαι ὀΐω
ἐλθόντ' ἐς μέγαρον Λαερτιάδεω Ὀδυσῆος.
ἀλλ' ἄγετ', οἰνοχόος μὲν ἐπαρξάσθω δεπάεσσιν,
ὄφρα σπείσαντες καταθείομεν ἀγκύλα τόξα·
ἠῶθεν δὲ κέλεσθε Μελάνθιον, αἰπόλον αἰγῶν, 265
αἶγας ἄγειν, αἳ πᾶσι μέγ' ἔξοχοι αἰπολίοισιν,
ὄφρ' ἐπὶ μηρία θέντες Ἀπόλλωνι κλυτοτόξῳ
τόξου πειρώμεσθα καὶ ἐκτελέωμεν ἄεθλον."
Ὣς ἔφατ' Ἀντίνοος· τοῖσιν δ' ἐπιήνδανε μῦθος.
τοῖσι δὲ κήρυκες μὲν ὕδωρ ἐπὶ χεῖρας ἔχευαν, 270
κοῦροι δὲ κρητῆρας ἐπεστέψαντο ποτοῖο,
νώμησαν δ' ἄρα πᾶσιν ἐπαρξάμενοι δεπάεσσιν.

οἱ δ' ἐπεὶ οὖν σπεῖσάν τ' ἔπιόν θ' ὅσον ἤθελε θυμός,
τοῖς δὲ δολοφρονέων μετέφη πολύμητις 'Οδυσσεύς·
" κέκλυτέ μευ, μνηστῆρες ἀγακλειτῆς βασιλείης·   275
ὄφρ' εἴπω τά με θυμὸς ἐνὶ στήθεσσι κελεύει·
Εὐρύμαχον δὲ μάλιστα καὶ 'Αντίνοον θεοειδέα
λίσσομ', ἐπεὶ καὶ τοῦτο ἔπος κατὰ μοῖραν ἔειπε,
νῦν μὲν παῦσαι τόξον, ἐπιτρέψαι δὲ θεοῖσιν·
ἠῶθεν δὲ θεὸς δώσει κράτος ᾧ κ' ἐθέλησιν.   280
ἀλλ' ἄγ' ἐμοὶ δότε τόξον ἐΰξοον, ὄφρα μεθ' ὑμῖν
χειρῶν καὶ σθένεος πειρήσομαι, ἤ μοι ἔτ' ἐστὶν
ἴς, οἵη πάρος ἔσκεν ἐνὶ γναμπτοῖσι μέλεσσιν,
ἦ ἤδη μοι ὄλεσσεν ἄλη τ' ἀκομιστίη τε."

*285–329 The suitors are angry at this request, and Antinous reminds Odysseus
of the fate of the centaur Eurytion, who also acted foolishly when drunk ; he warns
him of what will happen to him if he strings the bow. Penelope asks them to let
him try the bow, although she will never marry him, but Eurymachus points out
how shameful it will be if a beggar succeeds where they have failed.*

*Ὡς ἔφαθ'· οἱ δ' ἄρα πάντες ὑπερφιάλως νεμέσησαν,   285
δείσαντες μὴ τόξον ἐΰξοον ἐντανύσειεν.
'Αντίνοος δ' ἐνένιπεν ἔπος τ' ἔφατ' ἔκ τ' ὀνόμαζεν·
" ἆ δειλὲ ξείνων, ἔνι τοι φρένες οὐδ' ἠβαιαί·
οὐκ ἀγαπᾷς ὃ ἔκηλος ὑπερφιάλοισι μεθ' ἡμῖν
δαίνυσαι, οὐδέ τι δαιτὸς ἀμέρδεαι, αὐτὰρ ἀκούεις   290
μύθων ἡμετέρων καὶ ῥήσιος; οὐδέ τις ἄλλος
ἡμετέρων μύθων ξεῖνος καὶ πτωχὸς ἀκούει.
οἶνός σε τρώει μελιηδής, ὅς τε καὶ ἄλλους
βλάπτει, ὃς ἄν μιν χανδὸν ἕλῃ μηδ' αἴσιμα πίνῃ.
οἶνος καὶ Κένταυρον, ἀγακλυτὸν Εὐρυτίωνα,   295
ἄασ' ἐνὶ μεγάρῳ μεγαθύμου Πειριθόοιο,
ἐς Λαπίθας ἐλθόνθ'· ὁ δ' ἐπεὶ φρένας ἄασεν οἴνῳ,
μαινόμενος κάκ' ἔρεξε δόμον κάτα Πειριθόοιο·

ἥρωας δ' ἄχος εἷλε, διὲκ προθύρου δὲ θύραζε
ἕλκον ἀναΐξαντες, ἀπ' οὔατα νηλέϊ χαλκῷ   300
ῥῖνάς τ' ἀμήσαντες· ὁ δὲ φρεσὶν ἧσιν ἀασθεὶς
ἤϊεν ἣν ἄτην ὀχέων ἀεσίφρονι θυμῷ.
ἐξ οὗ Κενταύροισι καὶ ἀνδράσι νεῖκος ἐτύχθη,
οἷ δ' αὐτῷ πρώτῳ κακὸν εὕρετο οἰνοβαρείων.
ὣς καὶ σοὶ μέγα πῆμα πιφαύσκομαι, αἴ κε τὸ τόξον   305
ἐντανύσῃς· οὐ γάρ τευ ἐπητύος ἀντιβολήσεις
ἡμετέρῳ ἐνὶ δήμῳ, ἄφαρ δέ σε νηῒ μελαίνῃ
εἰς Ἔχετον βασιλῆα, βροτῶν δηλήμονα πάντων,
πέμψομεν· ἔνθεν δ' οὔ τι σαώσεαι· ἀλλὰ ἕκηλος
πῖνέ τε, μηδ' ἐρίδαινε μετ' ἀνδράσι κουροτέροισι."   310
    Τὸν δ' αὖτε προσέειπε περίφρων Πηνελόπεια·
" Ἀντίνο', οὐ μὲν καλὸν ἀτέμβειν οὐδὲ δίκαιον
ξείνους Τηλεμάχου, ὅς κεν τάδε δώμαθ' ἵκηται.
ἔλπεαι, αἴ χ' ὁ ξεῖνος Ὀδυσσῆος μέγα τόξον
ἐντανύσῃ χερσίν τε βίηφί τε ἧφι πιθήσας,   315
οἴκαδέ μ' ἄξεσθαι καὶ ἑὴν θήσεσθαι ἄκοιτιν;
οὐδ' αὐτός που τοῦτό γ' ἐνὶ στήθεσσιν ἔολπε·
μηδέ τις ὑμείων τοῦ γ' εἵνεκα θυμὸν ἀχεύων
ἐνθάδε δαινύσθω, ἐπεὶ οὐδὲ μὲν οὐδὲ ἔοικε."
    Τὴν δ' αὖτ' Εὐρύμαχος, Πολύβου πάϊς, ἀντίον ηὔδα·   320
" κούρη Ἰκαρίοιο, περίφρον Πηνελόπεια,
οὔ τί σε τόνδ' ἄξεσθαι ὀϊόμεθ', οὐδὲ ἔοικεν·
ἀλλ' αἰσχυνόμενοι φάτιν ἀνδρῶν ἠδὲ γυναικῶν,
μή ποτέ τις εἴπῃσι κακώτερος ἄλλος Ἀχαιῶν·
'ἦ πολὺ χείρονες ἄνδρες ἀμύμονος ἀνδρὸς ἄκοιτιν   325
μνῶνται, οὐδέ τι τόξον ἐΰξοον ἐντανύουσιν·
ἀλλ' ἄλλος τις πτωχὸς ἀνὴρ ἀλαλήμενος ἐλθὼν
ῥηϊδίως ἐτάνυσσε βιόν, διὰ δ' ἧκε σιδήρου.'
ὣς ἐρέουσ'· ἡμῖν δ' ἂν ἐλέγχεα ταῦτα γένοιτο."

330–358 Penelope reminds the suitors of their much more shameful conduct towards her in the past, and insists on letting the beggar try the bow. Telemachus declares that he alone has the right to dispose of the bow, even to the beggar if he so wishes, and sends his mother to her room, where Athena causes her to fall asleep.

Τὸν δ' αὖτε προσέειπε περίφρων Πηνελόπεια·   330
" Εὐρύμαχ', οὔ πως ἔστιν ἐϋκλείας κατὰ δῆμον
ἔμμεναι οἳ δὴ οἶκον ἀτιμάζοντες ἔδουσιν
ἀνδρὸς ἀριστῆος· τί δ' ἐλέγχεα ταῦτα τίθεσθε;
οὗτος δὲ ξεῖνος μάλα μὲν μέγας ἠδ' εὐπηγής,
πατρὸς δ' ἐξ ἀγαθοῦ γένος εὔχεται ἔμμεναι υἱός.   335
ἀλλ' ἄγε οἱ δότε τόξον ἐΰξοον, ὄφρα ἴδωμεν.
ὧδε γὰρ ἐξερέω, τὸ δὲ καὶ τετελεσμένον ἔσται·
εἴ κέ μιν ἐντανύσῃ, δώῃ δέ οἱ εὖχος Ἀπόλλων,
ἕσσω μιν χλαῖνάν τε χιτῶνά τε, εἵματα καλά,
δώσω δ' ὀξὺν ἄκοντα, κυνῶν ἀλκτῆρα καὶ ἀνδρῶν,   340
καὶ ξίφος ἄμφηκες· δώσω δ' ὑπὸ ποσσὶ πέδιλα,
πέμψω δ' ὅππῃ μιν κραδίη θυμός τε κελεύει."
Τὴν δ' αὖ Τηλέμαχος πεπνυμένος ἀντίον ηὔδα·
" μῆτερ ἐμή, τόξον μὲν Ἀχαιῶν οὔ τις ἐμεῖο
κρείσσων, ᾧ κ' ἐθέλω, δόμεναί τε καὶ ἀρνήσασθαι,   345
οὔθ' ὅσσοι κραναὴν Ἰθάκην κάτα κοιρανέουσιν,
οὔθ' ὅσσοι νήσοισι πρὸς Ἤλιδος ἱπποβότοιο·
τῶν οὔ τίς μ' ἀέκοντα βιήσεται αἴ κ' ἐθέλωμι
καὶ καθάπαξ ξείνῳ δόμεναι τάδε τόξα φέρεσθαι.
ἀλλ' εἰς οἶκον ἰοῦσα τὰ σ' αὐτῆς ἔργα κόμιζε,   350
ἱστόν τ' ἠλακάτην τε, καὶ ἀμφιπόλοισι κέλευε
ἔργον ἐποίχεσθαι· τόξον δ' ἄνδρεσσι μελήσει
πᾶσι, μάλιστα δ' ἐμοί· τοῦ γὰρ κράτος ἔστ' ἐνὶ οἴκῳ."
Ἡ μὲν θαμβήσασα πάλιν οἰκόνδε βεβήκει·
παιδὸς γὰρ μῦθον πεπνυμένον ἔνθετο θυμῷ.   355
ἐς δ' ὑπερῷ' ἀναβᾶσα σὺν ἀμφιπόλοισι γυναιξὶ

κλαῖεν ἔπειτ' Ὀδυσῆα, φίλον πόσιν, ὄφρα οἱ ὕπνον
ἡδὺν ἐπὶ βλεφάροισι βάλε γλαυκῶπις Ἀθήνη.

*359–387 Eumaeus puts down the bow through fear of the suitors, who laugh
when Telemachus rebukes him for disobedience and wishes that he had the strength
to drive them out. Odysseus takes the bow from Eumaeus and tells his old nurse
Eurycleia to bar the door of the women's quarters and keep the maidservants at
their work, whatever they hear in the hall.*

Αὐτὰρ ὁ τόξα λαβὼν φέρε καμπύλα δῖος ὑφορβός·
μνηστῆρες δ' ἄρα πάντες ὁμόκλεον ἐν μεγάροισιν·   360
ὧδε δέ τις εἴπεσκε νέων ὑπερηνορεόντων·
" πῇ δὴ καμπύλα τόξα φέρεις, ἀμέγαρτε συβῶτα,
πλαγκτέ; τάχ' αὖ σ' ἐφ' ὕεσσι κύνες ταχέες κατέδονται
οἶον ἀπ' ἀνθρώπων, οὓς ἔτρεφες, εἴ κεν Ἀπόλλων
ἡμῖν ἱλήκῃσι καὶ ἀθάνατοι θεοὶ ἄλλοι."   365
Ὣς φάσαν· αὐτὰρ ὁ θῆκε φέρων αὐτῇ ἐνὶ χώρῃ,
δείσας, οὕνεκα πολλοὶ ὁμόκλεον ἐν μεγάροισι.
Τηλέμαχος δ' ἑτέρωθεν ἀπειλήσας ἐγεγώνει·
" ἄττα, πρόσω φέρε τόξα· τάχ' οὐκ εὖ πᾶσι πιθήσεις·
μή σε καὶ ὁπλότερός περ ἐὼν ἀγρόνδε δίωμαι,   370
βάλλων χερμαδίοισι· βίηφι δὲ φέρτερός εἰμι.
αἲ γὰρ πάντων τόσσον, ὅσοι κατὰ δώματ' ἔασι,
μνηστήρων χερσίν τε βίηφί τε φέρτερος εἴην!
τῷ κε τάχα στυγερῶς τιν' ἐγὼ πέμψαιμι νέεσθαι
ἡμετέρου ἐξ οἴκου, ἐπεὶ κακὰ μηχανόωνται."   375
Ὣς ἔφαθ'· οἱ δ' ἄρα πάντες ἐπ' αὐτῷ ἡδὺ γέλασσαν
μνηστῆρες, καὶ δὴ μέθιεν χαλεποῖο χόλοιο
Τηλεμάχῳ· τὰ δὲ τόξα φέρων ἀνὰ δῶμα συβώτης
ἐν χείρεσσ' Ὀδυσῆϊ δαΐφρονι θῆκε παραστάς.
ἐκ δὲ καλεσσάμενος προσέφη τροφὸν Εὐρύκλειαν·   380
" Τηλέμαχος κέλεταί σε, περίφρων Εὐρύκλεια,
κλῆῖσαι μεγάροιο θύρας πυκινῶς ἀραρυίας·

ἢν δέ τις ἢ στοναχῆς ἠὲ κτύπου ἔνδον ἀκούσῃ
ἀνδρῶν ἡμετέροισιν ἐν ἔρκεσι, μή τι θύραζε
προβλώσκειν, ἀλλ᾽ αὐτοῦ ἀκὴν ἔμεναι παρὰ ἔργῳ." 385
Ὡς ἄρ᾽ ἐφώνησεν· τῇ δ᾽ ἄπτερος ἔπλετο μῦθος,
κλήϊσεν δὲ θύρας μεγάρων εὖ ναιεταόντων.

388–411 *Philoetius bars the outer door of the courtyard, and some of the suitors admire the way in which Odysseus handles the bow. Then without trouble he bends the bow and strings it, and makes the string ring out sweetly.*

Σιγῇ δ᾽ ἐξ οἴκοιο Φιλοίτιος ἇλτο θύραζε,
κλήϊσεν δ᾽ ἄρ᾽ ἔπειτα θύρας εὐερκέος αὐλῆς.
κεῖτο δ᾽ ὑπ᾽ αἰθούσῃ ὅπλον νεὸς ἀμφιελίσσης 390
βύβλινον, ᾧ ῥ᾽ ἐπέδησε θύρας, ἐς δ᾽ ἤϊεν αὐτός.
ἕζετ᾽ ἔπειτ᾽ ἐπὶ δίφρον ἰών, ἔνθεν περ ἀνέστη,
εἰσορόων Ὀδυσῆα. ὁ δ᾽ ἤδη τόξον ἐνώμα
πάντῃ ἀναστρωφῶν, πειρώμενος ἔνθα καὶ ἔνθα,
μὴ κέρα᾽ ἶπες ἔδοιεν ἀποιχομένοιο ἄνακτος. 395
ὧδε δέ τις εἴπεσκεν ἰδὼν ἐς πλησίον ἄλλον·
" ἦ τις θηητὴρ καὶ ἐπίκλοπος ἔπλετο τόξων.
ἦ ῥά νύ που τοιαῦτα καὶ αὐτῷ οἴκοθι κεῖται,
ἦ ὅ γ᾽ ἐφορμᾶται ποιησέμεν, ὡς ἐνὶ χερσὶ
νωμᾷ ἔνθα καὶ ἔνθα κακῶν ἔμπαιος ἀλήτης." 400
Ἄλλος δ᾽ αὖ εἴπεσκε νέων ὑπερηνορεόντων·
" αἲ γὰρ δὴ τοσσοῦτον ὀνήσιος ἀντιάσειεν
ὡς οὗτός ποτε τοῦτο δυνήσεται ἐντανύσασθαι!"
Ὡς ἄρ᾽ ἔφαν μνηστῆρες· ἀτὰρ πολύμητις Ὀδυσσεύς,
αὐτίκ᾽ ἐπεὶ μέγα τόξον ἐβάστασε καὶ ἴδε πάντῃ, 405
ὡς ὅτ᾽ ἀνὴρ φόρμιγγος ἐπιστάμενος καὶ ἀοιδῆς
ῥηϊδίως ἐτάνυσσε νέῳ περὶ κόλλοπι χορδήν,
ἅψας ἀμφοτέρωθεν ἐϋστρεφὲς ἔντερον οἰός,
ὣς ἄρ᾽ ἄτερ σπουδῆς τάνυσεν μέγα τόξον Ὀδυσσεύς.
δεξιτερῇ δ᾽ ἄρα χειρὶ λαβὼν πειρήσατο νευρῆς· 410
ἡ δ᾽ ὑπὸ καλὸν ἄεισε, χελιδόνι εἰκέλη αὐδήν.

412–434 The suitors turn pale with vexation, and Zeus sends a peal of thunder as a good omen. Odysseus then shoots an arrow straight through all the axe-sockets, and tells Telemachus that it is now time for 'supper' and other sport. Father and son stand side by side armed and ready for action.

Μνηστῆρσιν δ᾽ ἄρ᾽ ἄχος γένετο μέγα, πᾶσι δ᾽ ἄρα χρὼς
ἐτράπετο. Ζεὺς δὲ μεγάλ᾽ ἔκτυπε σήματα φαίνων·
γήθησέν τ᾽ ἄρ᾽ ἔπειτα πολύτλας δῖος Ὀδυσσεύς,
ὅττι ῥά οἱ τέρας ἧκε Κρόνου πάϊς ἀγκυλομήτεω.   415
εἵλετο δ᾽ ὠκὺν ὀϊστόν, ὅ οἱ παρέκειτο τραπέζῃ
γυμνός· τοὶ δ᾽ ἄλλοι κοίλης ἔντοσθε φαρέτρης
κείατο, τῶν τάχ᾽ ἔμελλον Ἀχαιοὶ πειρήσεσθαι.
τόν ῥ᾽ ἐπὶ πήχει ἑλὼν ἕλκεν νευρὴν γλυφίδας τε,
αὐτόθεν ἐκ δίφροιο καθήμενος, ἧκε δ᾽ ὀϊστὸν   420
ἄντα τιτυσκόμενος, πελέκεων δ᾽ οὐκ ἤμβροτε πάντων
πρώτης στειλειῆς, διὰ δ᾽ ἀμπερὲς ἦλθε θύραζε
ἰὸς χαλκοβαρής· ὁ δὲ Τηλέμαχον προσέειπε·
" Τηλέμαχ᾽, οὔ σ᾽ ὁ ξεῖνος ἐνὶ μεγάροισιν ἐλέγχει
ἥμενος, οὐδέ τι τοῦ σκοποῦ ἤμβροτον οὐδέ τι τόξον   425
δὴν ἔκαμον τανύων· ἔτι μοι μένος ἔμπεδόν ἐστιν,
οὐχ ὥς με μνηστῆρες ἀτιμάζοντες ὄνονται.
νῦν δ᾽ ὥρη καὶ δόρπον Ἀχαιοῖσιν τετυκέσθαι
ἐν φάει, αὐτὰρ ἔπειτα καὶ ἄλλως ἑψιάασθαι
μολπῇ καὶ φόρμιγγι. τὰ γάρ τ᾽ ἀναθήματα δαιτός."   430
Ἦ καὶ ἐπ᾽ ὀφρύσι νεῦσεν· ὁ δ᾽ ἀμφέθετο ξίφος ὀξὺ
Τηλέμαχος, φίλος υἱὸς Ὀδυσσῆος θείοιο,
ἀμφὶ δὲ χεῖρα φίλην βάλεν ἔγχεϊ, ἄγχι δ᾽ ἄρ᾽ αὐτοῦ
πὰρ θρόνον ἑστήκει κεκορυθμένος αἴθοπι χαλκῷ.

ANTIPHON

Introduction

ANTIPHON was born in Athens in about 480 B.C. and died in 411. He is the first of the Athenian orators whose works have been preserved, though only three actual speeches survive, all concerned with trials for murder, together with twelve model speeches in imaginary trials written for the instruction of his pupils, for he was a famous teacher of oratory who is said to have included Thucydides among his pupils. He was a 'logographos', i.e. a writer of speeches for a client to deliver on his own behalf in court, for at Athens each man had to speak for himself in a legal case. His speeches were austere and dignified in style and contained complex sentences which were at the same time clear and easy for the jury to understand.

Antiphon's politics were directed against the democratic party which had controlled affairs at Athens all through his life, and he was a powerful figure behind the scenes in the oligarchic party, whom he advised and for whom he wrote speeches to be delivered in the Assembly. In 411, after the defeat of the Athenian expedition in Sicily, the oligarchs at last managed to seize power, but only for a few months, for their policies failed and all but three of their leaders went into exile. Antiphon was one of the three who stood their ground and were tried for treason, when he made a speech on his own behalf which has not survived but which Thucydides (VIII, 68) describes as the best speech in defence of his life made by any man up to that time; he also

calls Antiphon second to none of the Athenians in excellence
of character. But he was found guilty of treason and was
handed over to the Eleven Police Commissioners for
execution, probably by being made to drink a poison called
hemlock, which was said to cause a painless death.

A trial for murder (δίκη φόνου) was normally held in the
open air, to avoid the pollution of blood-guilt, before the
court of the Areopagus (the 'Mars' hill' of Acts xvii. 22),
which consisted of ex-magistrates, and the prosecution was
always conducted by a kinsman of the victim, though both
he and the accused could recite a speech written for him by
a professional orator like Antiphon. The penalty for wilful
murder was death, but the accused could go into exile at
the end of the first day of the trial. Both parties and all
witnesses were bound by a solemn oath to speak the truth.

Other trials were heard before one of the courts
(δικαστήρια), where the jury-men (δικασταί) were chosen
by lot from among all the citzens and were paid three obols
a day (half a drachma; a drachma was a silver coin smaller
than a shilling but with a very much higher purchasing
power). The full panel of 6000 was divided into smaller
juries, sometimes as many as 501 (to avoid an equality of
votes) in an important case. A magistrate presided but did
not direct the jury or pass judgment, and the two principals
had to make a speech on their own behalf, again with the
help of a speech-writer if they wished. For offences like
theft, temple-robbing, kidnapping, and serious crimes short
of murder, called κακουργίαι, the prosecutor (always a
private citizen) could arrest the accused as a 'malefactor'
and hand him over to the Eleven, who might grant bail or
keep him in prison until the trial; such a process was called
ἀπαγωγὴ κακουργίας, summary arrest for 'malefaction', and

was used in the trial of the alleged murderer of Herodes. The evidence of witnesses, not under oath, was taken down at a preliminary hearing and kept sealed up until it was read at the trial, without cross-examination, when requested by the prosecutor and the accused during their own speeches. Each of them had a fixed time in which to address the jury, measured by a water-clock which was stopped during the reading of the evidence. After the speeches the jury voted; the penalty if they found the accused guilty was often fixed by law, but if it was not, each side suggested a penalty on which the jury voted again. The evidence of slaves was admitted, but only under torture, whch was sometimes applied to the same man by both sides. The presiding magistrate was one of the nine archons who were elected annually.

The facts in the case of the murder of Herodes were as follows. Herodes was an Athenian citizen who came to Mytilene in the island of Lesbos as a 'cleruch', or settler, after the revolt of Lesbos in 428 and its suppression in 427. One day in about 418 he took ship from Mytilene to Aenus in Thrace (on the northern shores of the Aegean) with some Thracian slaves, perhaps prisoners of war, whom he was intending to sell to their relatives. In the same open (undecked) ship was a young Mytilenean called Euxitheus, whose name is not mentioned in the speech, who was going to visit his father at Aenus. At Methymna on the north coast of Lesbos bad weather drove the ship into harbour, and the two men took shelter for the night in a neighbouring decked vessel, where they spent part of the night drinking wine together. Herodes went ashore and was never seen again, and Euxitheus was later arrested by Herodes' relatives and was accused of having murdered him because

(i) he was the last person to be in the company of the missing man, (ii) a slave confessed under torture that he had helped Euxitheus to commit the murder and dispose of the body in the sea, (iii) a letter was found in the decked ship which was said to have been written by Euxitheus to an Athenian called Lycinus living at Mytilene, stating that Euxitheus had successfully committed the murder. Since he was an alien living in a subject city, the trial of Euxitheus had to take place at Athens; he was accused, not as a murderer before the Areopagus, but as a 'malefactor' in one of the ordinary law-courts, and faced the danger of being tried again, this time for murder, by the Areopagus, if he was found not guilty at the first trial.

We do not know the result of this trial, but certainly today Euxitheus would be acquitted. The only real evidence against him was the testimony of the slave, perhaps a member of the crew of the decked ship, who first declared him innocent, then under torture accused him of murder with himself as an accomplice, and eventually was put to death protesting the innocence of them both. The prosecution had bought the slave from his owner before torturing him, and then illegally put him to death before the trial, ostensibly as being a self-confessed party to the murder, but according to Euxitheus in order to prevent him from telling the truth. The letter found in the ship seems to have been a clumsy forgery. The identity of the second man who was examined under torture, a freeman but a non-Greek, is doubtful because Euxitheus gives two accounts of him which are not easily reconciled; he may have been the servant of Euxitheus who accompanied him as far as Methymna and was then sent back to Mytilene to inform Herodes' family of his disappearance, or he may have been another member of the crew of the decked ship. Whoever he was, he continued to maintain the innocence of Euxitheus even under torture.

The circumstances of Herodes' death remain a mystery. A possible explanation is that he fell into the sea either from the decked ship or from the quay-side while returning drunk to his own vessel in the dark and was drowned. The Mediterreanean is almost tideless, but Methymna lies on a promontory and a current helped by a wind might have carried the body out of the harbour and into the open sea — as presumably happened if Euxitheus did kill Herodes and threw him into the sea from a rowing-boat, which is what he is alleged to have done. But he seems to have had no motive for the crime and there was no trustworthy evidence against him.

The Murder of Herodes

ΠΕΡΙ ΤΟΥ ΗΡΩΙΔΟΥ ΦΟΝΟΥ

In 1–19, not included in this book, the accused, whose name was Euxitheus, first makes the usual plea that the jury should excuse his inexperience and lack of oratorical skill, although his speech has in fact been written for him by Antiphon and learned by heart. He then complains of the illegality of the present trial, for a case of murder ought to be tried by the court of the Areopagus, whereas he has been arrested summarily as a 'malefactor' and has been kept in prison without bail and is now being tried by the ordinary jury-court without evidence being given on oath. He then proceeds as follows.

1–5 (20–24) The ship in which I was sailing to Aenus was storm-bound at Methymna, and Herodes and I moved across to a decked ship, where we spent much of the night drinking together. Herodes went ashore and disappeared, and next day I sent my servant to Mytilene to inform his relatives and then continued on my voyage.

1   Ἐγὼ δὲ τὸν μὲν πλοῦν ἐποιησάμην ἐκ τῆς Μυτιλή-
νης, ὦ ἄνδρες, ἐν τῷ πλοίῳ πλέων ᾧ Ἡρῴδης οὗτος, ὃν
φασὶν ὑπ' ἐμοῦ ἀποθανεῖν· ἐπλέομεν δὲ εἰς τὴν Αἶνον,
ἐγὼ μὲν ὡς τὸν πατέρα — ἐτύγχανε γὰρ ἐκεῖ ὢν τότε —,
ὁ δ' Ἡρῴδης ἀνδράποδα Θρᾳξὶν ἀνθρώποις ἀπολύσων.   5
συνέπλει δὲ τά τε ἀνδράποδα ἃ ἔδει αὐτὸν ἀπολῦσαι,
καὶ οἱ Θρᾷκες οἱ λυσόμενοι. τούτων δ' ὑμῖν τοὺς μάρτυρας παρέξομαι.

ΜΑΡΤΥΡΕΣ

2   Ἡ μὲν πρόφασις ἑκατέρῳ τοῦ πλοῦ αὕτη· ἐτύχομεν
δὲ χειμῶνί τινι χρησάμενοι, ὑφ' οὗ ἠναγκάσθημεν κατα-   10
σχεῖν εἰς τῆς Μηθυμναίας τι χωρίον, οὗ τὸ πλοῖον ὥρμει
τοῦτο εἰς ὃ μετεκβάντα φασὶν ἀποθανεῖν αὐτόν. καὶ

πρῶτον μὲν αὐτὰ ταῦτα σκοπεῖτε, εἴ μοι προνοίᾳ
μᾶλλον ἐγίγνετο ἢ τύχῃ. οὔτε γὰρ πείσας τὸν ἄνδρα
οὐδαμοῦ ἀπελέγχομαι σύμπλουν μοι γενέσθαι, ἀλλ᾿ 15
αὐτὸς καθ᾿ αὑτὸν τὸν πλοῦν πεποιημένος ἕνεκα πραγμά-
3 των ἰδίων· οὔτ᾿ αὖ ἐγὼ ἄνευ προφάσεως ἱκανῆς φαίνομαι τὸν πλοῦν ποιησάμενος εἰς τὴν Αἶνον, οὔτε κατασχόντες εἰς τὸ χωρίον τοῦτο ἀπὸ παρασκευῆς οὐδεμιᾶς,
ἀλλ᾿ ἀνάγκῃ χρησάμενοι· οὔτ᾿ αὖ ἐπειδὴ ὡρμισάμεθα, ἡ 20
μετέκβασις ἐγένετο εἰς τὸ ἕτερον πλοῖον οὐδενὶ μηχανήματι οὐδ᾿ ἀπάτῃ, ἀλλ᾿ ἀνάγκῃ καὶ τοῦτο ἐγίγνετο.. ἐν ᾧ
μὲν γὰρ ἐπλέομεν, ἀστέγαστον ἦν τὸ πλοῖον, εἰς ὃ δὲ
μετέβημεν, ἐστεγασμένον· τοῦ δὲ ὑετοῦ ἕνεκα ταῦτ᾿ ἦν.
τούτων δ᾿ ὑμῖν μάρτυρας παρέξομαι. 25

ΜΑΡΤΥΡΕΣ

4 Ἐπειδὴ δὲ μετεξέβημεν εἰς τὸ ἕτερον πλοῖον, ἐπίνομεν.
καὶ ὁ μέν ἐστι φανερὸς ἐκβὰς ἐκ τοῦ πλοίου καὶ οὐκ
εἰσβὰς πάλιν· ἐγὼ δὲ τὸ παράπαν οὐκ ἐξέβην ἐκ τοῦ
πλοίου τῆς νυκτὸς ἐκείνης. τῇ δ᾿ ὑστεραίᾳ, ἐπειδὴ ἀφανὴς ἦν ὁ ἀνήρ, ἐζητεῖτο οὐδέν τι μᾶλλον ὑπὸ τῶν ἄλλων 30
ἢ καὶ ὑπ᾿ ἐμοῦ· καὶ εἴ τῳ τῶν ἄλλων ἐδόκει δεινὸν εἶναι,
καὶ ἐμοὶ ὁμοίως. καὶ εἷς τε τὴν Μυτιλήνην ἐγὼ αἴτιος
5 ἢ πεμφθῆναι ἄγγελον, καὶ τῇ ἐμῇ γνώμῃ ἐπέμπετο. καὶ
ἄλλου οὐδενὸς ἐθέλοντος βαδίζειν, οὔτε τῶν ἀπὸ τοῦ
πλοίου οὔτε τῶν αὐτῷ τῷ Ἡρῴδῃ συμπλεόντων, ἐγὼ τὸν 35
ἀκόλουθον τὸν ἐμαυτοῦ πέμπειν ἕτοιμος ἦ· καίτοι οὐ
δήπου γε κατ᾿ ἐμαυτοῦ μηνυτὴν ἔπεμπον εἰδώς. ἐπειδὴ
δὲ ὁ ἀνὴρ οὔτε ἐν τῇ Μυτιλήνῃ ἐφαίνετο ζητούμενος
οὔτ᾿ ἄλλοθι οὐδαμοῦ, πλοῦς τε ἡμῖν ἐγίγνετο, καὶ τἆλλ᾿
ἀνήγετο πλοῖα ἅπαντα, ᾠχόμην κἀγὼ πλέων. τούτων δ᾿ 40
ὑμῖν τοὺς μάρτυρας παρασχήσομαι.

ΜΑΡΤΥΡΕΣ

6–11 (25–30) Herodes' relations later accused me of murdering him and throwing his body into the sea; but I can prove that I never left the ship all night, and no traces of human blood were found. So they examined two men under torture; the first one declared me innocent, the second one many days later falsely accused me of murder.

6 Τὰ μὲν γενόμενα ταῦτ᾽ ἐστίν· ἐκ δὲ τούτων ἤδη σκοπεῖτε τὰ εἰκότα. πρῶτον μὲν γὰρ πρὶν ἀνάγεσθαί με εἰς
τὴν Αἶνον, ὅτε ἦν ἀφανὴς ὁ ἀνήρ, οὐδεὶς ᾐτιάσατό με
ἀνθρώπων, ἤδη πεπυσμένων τούτων τὴν ἀγγελίαν· οὐ   45
γὰρ ἄν ποτε ᾠχόμην πλέων. ἀλλ᾽ εἰς μὲν τὸ παραχρῆμα
κρεῖσσον ἦν τὸ ἀληθὲς καὶ τὸ γεγενημένον τῆς τούτων
αἰτιάσεως, καὶ ἅμα ἐγὼ ἔτι ἐπεδήμουν· ἐπειδὴ δ᾽ ἐγώ τε
ᾠχόμην πλέων καὶ οὗτοι ἐξ ἐπιβουλῆς συνέθεσαν ταῦτα
καὶ ἐμηχανήσαντο κατ᾽ ἐμοῦ, τότε ᾐτιάσαντο.   50

7 Λέγουσι δὲ ὡς ἐν μὲν τῇ γῇ ἀπέθανεν ὁ ἀνήρ, κἀγὼ
λίθον αὐτῷ ἐνέβαλον εἰς τὴν κεφαλήν, ὃς οὐκ ἐξέβην τὸ
παράπαν ἐκ τοῦ πλοίου. καὶ τοῦτο μὲν ἀκριβῶς οὗτοι
ἴσασιν· ὅπως δ᾽ ἠφανίσθη ὁ ἀνήρ, οὐδενὶ λόγῳ εἰκότι
δύνανται ἀποφαίνειν. δῆλον γὰρ ὅτι ἐγγύς που τοῦ   55
λιμένος εἰκὸς ἦν τοῦτο γίγνεσθαι, τοῦτο μὲν μεθύοντος
τοῦ ἀνδρός, τοῦτο δὲ νύκτωρ ἐκβάντος ἐκ τοῦ πλοίου·
οὔτε γὰρ αὑτοῦ κρατεῖν ἴσως ἂν ἐδύνατο, οὔτε τῷ
ἀπάγοντι νύκτωρ μακρὰν ὁδὸν ἡ πρόφασις ἂν εἰκότως

8 ἐγίγνετο· ζητουμένου δὲ τοῦ ἀνδρὸς δύο ἡμέρας καὶ ἐν   60
τῷ λιμένι καὶ ἄπωθεν τοῦ λιμένος, οὔτε ὀπτὴρ οὐδεὶς
ἐφάνη οὔθ᾽ αἷμα οὔτ᾽ ἄλλο σημεῖον οὐδέν. κᾆτ᾽ ἐγὼ
συγχωρῶ τῷ τούτων λόγῳ, παρεχόμενος μὲν τοὺς
μάρτυρας ὡς οὐκ ἐξέβην ἐκ τοῦ πλοίου· εἰ δὲ καὶ ὡς
μάλιστα ἐξέβην ἐκ τοῦ πλοίου, οὐδενὶ τρόπῳ εἰκὸς ἦν   65
ἀφανισθέντα λαθεῖν τὸν ἄνθρωπον, εἴπερ γε μὴ πάνυ
πόρρω ἀπῆλθεν ἀπὸ τῆς θαλάσσης.

9 Ἀλλ' ὡς κατεποντώθη λέγουσιν. ἐν τίνι πλοίῳ;
δῆλον γὰρ ὅτι ἐξ αὐτοῦ τοῦ λιμένος ἦν τὸ πλοῖον. πῶς
ἂν οὖν οὐκ ἐξηυρέθη; καὶ μὴν εἰκός γε ἦν καὶ σημεῖόν 70
τι γενέσθαι ἐν τῷ πλοίῳ ἀνδρὸς τεθνεῶτος ἐντιθεμένου καὶ ἐκβαλλομένου νύκτωρ. νῦν δὲ ἐν μὲν ᾧ ἔπινε
πλοίῳ καὶ ἐξ οὗ ἐξέβαινεν, ἐν τούτῳ φασὶν εὑρεῖν σημεῖα, ἐν ᾧ αὐτοὶ μὴ ὁμολογοῦσιν ἀποθανεῖν τὸν ἄνδρα·
ἐν ᾧ δὲ κατεποντώθη, οὐχ ηὗρον οὔτ' αὐτὸ τὸ πλοῖον 75
οὔτε σημεῖον οὐδέν. τούτων δ' ὑμῖν τοὺς μάρτυρας
παρασχήσομαι.

ΜΑΡΤΥΡΕΣ

10 Ἐπειδὴ δὲ ἐγὼ μὲν φροῦδος ἦ πλέων εἰς τὴν Αἶνον,
τὸ δὲ πλοῖον ἧκεν εἰς τὴν Μυτιλήνην ἐν ᾧ ἐγὼ καὶ ὁ
Ἡρῴδης ἐπίνομεν, πρῶτον μὲν εἰσβάντες εἰς τὸ πλοῖον 80
ἠρεύνων, καὶ ἐπειδὴ τὸ αἷμα ηὗρον, ἐνταῦθα ἔφασαν
τεθνάναι τὸν ἄνδρα· ἐπειδὴ δὲ αὐτοῖς τοῦτο οὐκ ἐνεχώρει, ἀλλ' ἐφαίνετο τῶν προβάτων ὂν αἷμα, ἀποτραπόμενοι τούτου τοῦ λόγου συλλαβόντες ἐβασάνιζον τοὺς
11 ἀνθρώπους. καὶ ὃν μὲν τότε παραχρῆμα ἐβασάνισαν, 85
οὗτος μὲν οὐδὲν εἶπε περὶ ἐμοῦ φλαῦρον· ὃν δ' ἡμέραις
ὕστερον πολλαῖς ἐβασάνισαν, ἔχοντες παρὰ σφίσιν αὐτοῖς
τὸν πρόσθεν χρόνον, οὗτος ἦν ὁ πεισθεὶς ὑπὸ τούτων
καὶ καταψευσάμενος ἐμοῦ. παρέξομαι δὲ τούτων τοὺς 90
μάρτυρας.

ΜΑΡΤΥΡΕΣ

*12–16 (31–35) The second man denounced me because he wanted to escape from
the torture and receive freedom from slavery, but eventually he admitted that I was
innocent when he saw that he was doomed to die. The prosecution put to death their
own witness without giving me a chance to get the truth out of him.*

12   'Ως μὲν ὕστερον τοσούτῳ χρόνῳ ὁ ἀνὴρ ἐβασανίσθη,
μεμαρτύρηται ὑμῖν· προσέχετε δὲ τὸν νοῦν αὐτῇ τῇ βασάνῳ, οἷα γεγένηται. ὁ μὲν γὰρ δοῦλος, ᾧ ἴσως οὗτοι
τοῦτο μὲν ἐλευθερίαν ὑπέσχοντο, τοῦτο δ' ἐπὶ τούτοις
ἦν παύσασθαι κακούμενον αὐτόν, ἴσως ὑπ' ἀμφοῖν πει- 95
σθεὶς κατεψεύσατό μου, τὴν μὲν ἐλευθερίαν ἐλπίσας
οἴσεσθαι, τῆς δὲ βασάνου εἰς τὸ παραχρῆμα βουλόμενος
13   ἀπηλλάχθαι. οἶμαι δ' ὑμᾶς ἐπίστασθαι τοῦτο, ὅτι ἐφ' οἷς
ἂν τὸ πλεῖστον μέρος τῆς βασάνου, πρὸς τούτων εἰσὶν
οἱ βασανιζόμενοι λέγειν ὅσ' ἂν ἐκείνοις μέλλωσι χαριεῖ- 100
σθαι· ἐν τούτοις γὰρ αὐτοῖς ἐστιν ἡ ὠφέλεια, ἄλλως τε
κἂν μὴ παρόντες τυγχάνωσιν ὧν ἂν καταψεύδωνται. εἰ
μὲν γὰρ ἐγὼ ἐκέλευον αὐτὸν στρεβλοῦν ὡς οὐ τἀληθῆ
λέγοντα, ἴσως ἂν ἐν αὐτῷ τούτῳ ἀπετρέπετο μηδὲν κατ'
ἐμοῦ καταψεύδεσθαι, νῦν δὲ αὐτοὶ ἦσαν καὶ βασανισταὶ 105
καὶ ἐπιτιμηταὶ τῶν σφίσιν αὐτοῖς συμφερόντων.

14   Ἕως μὲν οὖν μετὰ χρηστῆς τῆς ἐλπίδος ἐγίγνωσκέ μου
καταψευσάμενος, τούτῳ διϊσχυρίζετο τῷ λόγῳ· ἐπειδὴ
δὲ ἐγίγνωσκεν ἀποθανούμενος, ἐνταῦθ' ἤδη τῇ ἀληθείᾳ
ἐχρῆτο, καὶ ἔλεγεν ὅτι πεισθείη ὑπὸ τούτων ἐμοῦ 110
15   καταψεύδεσθαι. διαπειραθέντα δ' αὐτὸν τὰ ψευδῆ λέγειν,
ὕστερον δὲ τἀληθῆ λέγοντα, οὐδέτερα ὠφέλησεν, ἀλλ'
ἀπέκτειναν ἄγοντες τὸν ἄνδρα, τὸν μηνυτήν, ᾧ πιστεύοντες ἐμὲ διώκουσι, τοὐναντίον ποιήσαντες ἢ οἱ ἄλλοι
ἄνθρωποι. οἱ μὲν γὰρ ἄλλοι τοῖς μηνυταῖς τοῖς μὲν 115
ἐλευθέροις χρήματα διδόασι, τοὺς δὲ δούλους ἐλευθε-
ροῦσιν· οὗτοι δὲ θάνατον τῷ μηνυτῇ τὴν δωρεὰν
ἀπέδοσαν, ἀπαγορευόντων τῶν φίλων τῶν ἐμῶν μὴ

ἐκ τοῦ πλοίου ἀποκτεῖναι τὸν ἄνδρα, καὶ αὐτὸς ἤδη
τεθνεῶτα συνανελεῖν μοι· ὁ δὲ τὸ παράπαν ἔφη οὐκ
ἐκβῆναί με ἐκ τοῦ πλοίου.

24–29 (44–48) I should have been insane to kill a man when so many people were close at hand; surely some traces of a struggle, or bloodstains, must have been found near by. Remember that the prosecution bought the slave and killed him when they had obtained his false evidence; they killed him without trial and ought themselves to be charged with murder.

24   Καίτοι τὸ εἰκὸς σύμμαχόν μοί ἐστιν. οὐ γὰρ δήπου 180
 οὕτω κακοδαίμων ἐγώ, ὥστε τὸ μὲν ἀποκτεῖναι τὸν
ἄνδρα προὐνοησάμην μόνος, ἵνα μοι μηδεὶς συνειδείη,
ἐν ᾧ μοι ὁ πᾶς κίνδυνος ἦν, ἤδη δὲ πεπραγμένου μοι
25   τοῦ ἔργου μάρτυρας καὶ συμβούλους ἐποιούμην. καὶ
ἀπέθανε μὲν ὁ ἀνὴρ οὑτωσὶ ἐγγὺς τῆς θαλάσσης καὶ 185
τῶν πλοίων, ὡς ὁ τούτων λόγος ἐστίν· ὑπὸ δὲ ἑνὸς
ἀνδρὸς ἀποθνήσκων οὔτε ἀνέκραγεν οὔτ᾽ αἴσθησιν οὐδεμίαν ἐποίησεν οὔτε τοῖς ἐν τῇ γῇ οὔτε τοῖς ἐν τῷ πλοίῳ;
καὶ μὴν πολλῷ ἐπὶ πλέον γεγωνεῖν ἔστι νύκτωρ ἢ μεθ᾽
ἡμέραν, ἐπ᾽ ἀκτῆς ἢ κατὰ πόλιν· καὶ μὴν ἔτι ἐγρηγο- 190
ρότων φασὶν ἐκβῆναι τὸν ἄνδρα ἐκ τοῦ πλοίου.

26   Ἔπειτα ἐν τῇ γῇ μὲν ἀποθανόντος, ἐντιθεμένου δὲ εἰς
τὸ πλοῖον, οὔτε ἐν τῇ γῇ σημεῖον οὐδὲ αἷμα ἐφάνη οὔτε
ἐν τῷ πλοίῳ, νύκτωρ μὲν ἀναιρεθέντος, νύκτωρ δ᾽·
ἐντιθεμένου εἰς τὸ πλοῖον. ἢ δοκεῖ ἂν ὑμῖν ἄνθρωπος 195
δύνασθαι ἐν τοιούτῳ πράγματι ὢν τά τ᾽ ἐν τῇ γῇ ὄντα
ἀναξύσαι καὶ τὰ ἐν τῷ πλοίῳ ἀποσπογγίσαι, ἃ οὐδὲ μεθ᾽
ἡμέραν ἄν τις οἷός τε ἐγένετο, ἔνδον ὢν αὐτοῦ καὶ
μὴ πεφοβημένος, τὸ παράπαν ἀφανίσαι; ταῦτα, ὦ
ἄνδρες, πῶς εἰκότα ἐστίν;   200

27   Ὁ δὲ δεῖ καὶ μάλιστα ἐνθυμεῖσθαι — καὶ μή μοι
ἄχθεσθε, ἂν ὑμᾶς πολλάκις ταὐτὰ διδάξω· μέγας γὰρ
ὁ κίνδυνός ἐστι, καθ᾽ ὅ τι δ᾽ ἂν ὑμεῖς ὀρθῶς γνῶτε, κατὰ

τοῦτο σῴζομαι, καθ' ὅ τι δ' ἂν ψευσθῆτε τἀληθοῦς,
κατὰ τοῦτο ἀπόλλυμαι — μὴ οὖν ἐξέληται τοῦτο ὑμῶν 205
μηδείς, ὅτι τὸν μηνυτὴν ἀκέκτειναν, καὶ διετείναντο
αὐτὸν μὴ εἰσελθεῖν εἰς ὑμᾶς, μηδ' ἐμοὶ ἐγγενέσθαι
28 παρόντι ἄξαι τὸν ἄνδρα καὶ βασανίσαι αὐτόν. καίτοι
πρὸς τούτων ἦν τοῦτο. νῦν δὲ πριάμενοι τὸν ἄνδρα,
ἰδίᾳ ἐπὶ σφῶν αὐτῶν ἀπέκτειναν, τὸν μηνυτήν, οὔτε 210
τῆς πόλεως ψηφισαμένης, οὔτε αὐτόχειρα ὄντα τοῦ
ἀνδρός. ὃν ἐχρῆν δεδεμένον αὐτοὺς φυλάσσειν, ἢ τοῖς
φίλοις τοῖς ἐμοῖς ἐξεγγυῆσαι, ἢ τοῖς ἄρχουσι τοῖς ὑμετέροις παραδοῦναι, καὶ ψῆφον περὶ αὐτοῦ γενέσθαι. νῦν
δὲ αὐτοὶ καταγνόντες τὸν θάνατον τοῦ ἀνδρὸς ἀπεκτεί- 215
νατε· ὃ οὐδὲ πόλει ἔξεστιν, ἄνευ Ἀθηναίων οὐδένα
θανάτῳ ζημιῶσαι. καὶ τῶν μὲν ἄλλων λόγων τῶν
ἐκείνου τουτουσὶ κριτὰς ἠξιώσατε γενέσθαι, τῶν δὲ
ἔργων αὐτοὶ δικασταὶ γίγνεσθε.

29   Καίτοι οὐδὲ οἱ τοὺς δεσπότας ἀποκτείναντες, ἐὰν 220
ἐπ' αὐτοφώρῳ ληφθῶσιν, οὐδ' οὗτοι ἀποθνήσκουσιν
ὑπ' αὐτῶν τῶν προσηκόντων, ἀλλὰ παραδιδόασιν αὐτοὺς
τῇ ἀρχῇ κατὰ νόμους ὑμετέρους πατρίους. εἴπερ γὰρ
καὶ μαρτυρεῖν ἔξεστι δούλῳ κατὰ τοῦ ἐλευθέρου τὸν
φόνον, καὶ τῷ δεσπότῃ, ἂν δοκῇ, ἐπεξελθεῖν ὑπὲρ τοῦ 225
δούλου, καὶ ἡ ψῆφος ἴσον δύναται τῷ δοῦλον ἀπο-
κτείναντι καὶ τῷ ἐλεύθερον, εἰκός τοι καὶ ψῆφον
γενέσθαι περὶ αὐτοῦ ἦν, καὶ μὴ ἄκριτον ἀποθανεῖν αὐτὸν
ὑφ' ὑμῶν. ὥστε πολλῷ ἂν ὑμεῖς δικαιότερον κρί-
νοισθε ἢ ἐγὼ νῦν φεύγω ὑφ' ὑμῶν ἀδίκως.   230

30–37 (49–56) The unaltered statement of the freeman in my favour is more valuable than the word of the slave who twice changed his story. The prosecution allege that they found a letter on the ship in which I told Lycinus that I had murdered Herodes, but this story does not agree with the statement that the slave made later under torture.

30 Σκοπεῖτε δή, ὦ ἄνδρες, καὶ ἐκ τοῖν λόγοιν τοῖν ἀνδροῖν ἑκατέροιν τοῖν βασανισθέντοιν τὸ δίκαιον καὶ τὸ εἰκός. ὁ μὲν γὰρ δοῦλος δύο λόγω ἔλεγε· τοτὲ μὲν ἔφη με εἰργάσθαι τὸ ἔργον, τοτὲ δὲ οὐκ ἔφη· ὁ δὲ ἐλεύθερος οὐδέπω νῦν εἴρηκε περὶ ἐμοῦ φλαῦρον οὐδέν, τῇ αὐτῇ 235

31 βασάνῳ βασανιζόμενος. τοῦτο μὲν γὰρ οὐκ ἦν αὐτῷ ἐλευθερίαν προτείναντας ὥσπερ τὸν ἕτερον πεῖσαι· τοῦτο δὲ μετὰ τοῦ ἀληθοῦς ἐβούλετο κινδυνεύων πάσχειν ὅ τι δέοι· ἐπεὶ τό γε συμφέρον καὶ οὗτος ἠπίστατο, ὅτι τότε παύσοιτο στρεβλούμενος, ὁπότε εἴποι τὰ τούτοις δο- 240 κοῦντα. ποτέρῳ οὖν εἰκός ἐστι πιστεῦσαι, τῷ διὰ τέλους τὸν αὐτὸν ἀεὶ λόγον λέγοντι, ἢ τῷ τοτὲ μὲν φάσκοντι τοτὲ δ' οὔ; ἀλλὰ καὶ ἄνευ βασάνου τοιαύτης οἱ τοὺς αὐτοὺς αἰεὶ περὶ τῶν αὐτῶν λόγους λέγοντες πιστότεροί εἰσι τῶν διαφερομένων σφίσιν αὐτοῖς. 245

32 Ἔπειτα δὲ καὶ ἐκ τῶν λόγων τῶν τοῦ ἀνθρώπου μερὶς ἑκατέροις ἴση ἂν εἴη, τούτοις μὲν τὸ φάσκειν, ἐμοὶ δὲ τὸ μὴ φάσκειν. καὶ μὲν δὴ τὰ ἐξ ἴσου γενόμενα τοῦ φεύγοντός ἐστι μᾶλλον ἢ τοῦ διώκοντος, εἴπερ γε καὶ τῶν ψήφων ὁ ἀριθμὸς ἐξ ἴσου γενόμενος τὸν 250 φεύγοντα μᾶλλον ὠφελεῖ ἢ τὸν διώκοντα.

33 Ἡ μὲν βάσανος, ὦ ἄνδρες, τοιαύτη ἐγένετο, ᾗ οὗτοι πιστεύοντες εὖ εἰδέναι φασὶν ὑπ' ἐμοῦ ἀποθανόντα τὸν ἄνδρα. καίτοι τὸ παράπαν ἔγωγ' ἂν εἴ τι συνῄδη ἐμαυτῷ καὶ εἴ τί μοι τοιοῦτον εἴργαστο, ἠφάνισ' ἂν τὼ 255 ἀνθρώπω, ὅτε ἐπ' ἐμοὶ ἦν τοῦτο μὲν εἰς τὴν Αἶνον ἀπάγειν ἅμα ἐμοί, τοῦτο δὲ εἰς τὴν ἤπειρον διαβιβάσαι,

καὶ μὴ ὑπολείπεσθαι μηνυτὰς κατ᾽ ἐμαυτοῦ τοὺς
34 συνειδότας. φασὶ δὲ γραμματείδιον εὑρεῖν ἐν τῷ πλοίῳ,
ὃ ἔπεμπον ἐγὼ Λυκίνῳ, ὡς ἀποκτείναιμι τὸν ἄνδρα. 260
καίτοι τί ἔδει με γραμματείδιον πέμπειν, αὐτοῦ συνει-
δότος τοῦ τὸ γραμματείδιον φέροντος; ὥστε τοῦτο μὲν
σαφέστερον αὐτὸς ἔμελλεν ἐρεῖν ὁ εἰργασμένος, τοῦτο
δὲ οὐδὲν ἔδει κρύπτειν αὐτόν· ἃ γὰρ μὴ οἷόν τε εἰδέναι
τὸν φέροντα, ταῦτ᾽ ἄν τις μάλιστα συγγράψας πέμψειεν. 265
35 Ἔπειτα δὲ ὅ τι μὲν μακρὸν εἴη πρᾶγμα, τοῦτο μὲν
ἄν τις ἀναγκασθείη γράψαι τῷ μὴ διαμνημονεύειν τὸν
ἀπαγγέλλοντα ὑπὸ πλήθους· τοῦτο δὲ βραχὺ ἦν ἀπαγγεῖλαι, ὅτι τέθνηκεν ὁ ἀνήρ. ἔπειτα ἐνθυμεῖσθε ὅτι
διάφορον ἦν τὸ γραμματείδιον τῷ βασανισθέντι, διά- 270
φορος δ᾽ ὁ ἄνθρωπος τῷ γραμματειδίῳ· ὁ μὲν γὰρ
βασανιζόμενος αὐτὸς ἔφη ἀποκτεῖναι, τὸ δὲ γραμματείδιον ἀνοιχθὲν ἐμὲ τὸν ἀποκτείναντα ἐμήνυε. καίτοι
36 ποτέρῳ χρὴ πιστεῦσαι; τὸ μὲν γὰρ πρῶτον οὐχ ηὗρον
ἐν τῷ πλοίῳ ζητοῦντες τὸ γραμματείδιον, ὕστερον δέ. 275
τότε μὲν γὰρ οὔπω οὕτως ἐμεμηχάνητο αὐτοῖς· ἐπειδὴ
δὲ ὁ ἄνθρωπος ὁ πρότερος βασανισθεὶς οὐδὲν ἔλεγε κατ᾽
ἐμοῦ, τότε εἰσβάλλουσιν εἰς τὸ πλοῖον τὸ γραμματείδιον,
37 ἵνα ταύτην ἔχοιεν ἐμοὶ τὴν αἰτίαν ἐπιφέρειν· ἐπειδὴ δὲ
ἀνεγνώσθη τὸ γραμματείδιον καὶ ὁ ὕστερος βασανιζόμε- 280
νος οὐ συνεφέρετο τῷ γραμματειδίῳ, οὐκέτι οἷόν τ᾽ ἦν
ἀφανίσαι τὰ ἀναγνωσθέντα. εἰ γὰρ ἡγήσαντο τὸν
ἄνδρα πείσειν ἀπὸ πρώτης καταψεύδεσθαί μου, οὐκ ἄν
ποτ᾽ ἐμηχανήσαντο τὰ ἐν τῷ γραμματειδίῳ. καί μοι
μάρτυρας τούτων κάλει. 285

ΜΑΡΤΥΡΕΣ

38–44 (57–63) I had no possible motive for wanting to kill Herodes, and Lycinus too had nothing to gain by his death. How could he have persuaded me to commit murder for him? He was actually in debt and was never a close friend of mine.

38   Τίνος γε δὴ ἕνεκα τὸν ἄνδρα ἀπέκτεινα; οὐδὲ γὰρ
ἔχθρα οὐδεμία ἦν ἐμοὶ κἀκείνῳ. λέγειν δὲ τολμῶσιν ὡς
ἐγὼ χάριτι τὸν ἄνδρα ἀπέκτεινα. καὶ τίς πώποτε χαριζόμενος ἑτέρῳ τοῦτο εἰργάσατο; οἶμαι μὲν γὰρ οὐδένα,
ἀλλὰ δεῖ μεγάλην τὴν ἔχθραν ὑπάρχειν τῷ τοῦτο μέλ- 290
λοντι ποιήσειν, καὶ τὴν πρόνοιαν ἐκ πολλῶν εἶναι φανερὰν ἐπιβουλευομένην. ἐμοὶ δὲ κἀκείνῳ οὐκ ἦν ἔχθρα
39   οὐδεμία. εἶεν, ἀλλὰ δείσας περὶ ἐμαυτοῦ μὴ αὐτὸς παρ'
ἐκείνου τοῦτο πάθοιμι; καὶ γὰρ ἂν τῶν τοιούτων ἕνεκά
τις ἀναγκασθείη τοῦτο ἐργάσασθαι. ἀλλ' οὐδέν μοι τοι- 295
οῦτον ὑπῆρκτο εἰς αὐτόν. ἀλλὰ χρήματα ἔμελλον λή-
40   ψεσθαι ἀποκτείνας αὐτόν; ἀλλ' οὐκ ἦν αὐτῷ. ἀλλὰ σοὶ
μᾶλλον ἐγὼ τὴν πρόφασιν ταύτην ἔχοιμ' ἂν εἰκότως
μετὰ τῆς ἀληθείας ἀναθεῖναι, ὅτι χρημάτων ἕνεκα ζητεῖς ἐμὲ ἀποκτεῖναι, μᾶλλον ἢ σὺ ἐμοὶ ἐκεῖνον· καὶ πολὺ 300
ἂν δικαιότερον ἁλοίης σὺ τοῦ φόνου ἐμὲ ἀποκτείνας
ὑπὸ τῶν ἐμοὶ προσηκόντων, ἢ ἐγὼ ὑπὸ σοῦ καὶ τῶν
ἐκείνου ἀναγκαίων. ἐγὼ μὲν γὰρ σοῦ φανερὰν τὴν πρόνοιαν εἰς ἐμὲ ἀποδείκνυμι, σὺ δ' ἐμὲ ἐν ἀφανεῖ λόγῳ
ζητεῖς ἀπολέσαι. 305
41   Ταῦτα μὲν ὑμῖν λέγω, ὡς αὐτῷ μοι πρόφασιν οὐδεμίαν εἶχε τἀποκτεῖναι τὸν ἄνδρα· δεῖ δέ με καὶ ὑπὲρ
Λυκίνου ἀπολογήσασθαι, ὡς ἔοικεν, ἀλλ' οὐχ ὑπὲρ αὐτοῦ μόνον, ὡς οὐδ' ἐκεῖνον εἰκότως αἰτιῶνται. λέγω τοίνυν ὑμῖν ὅτι ταὐτὰ ὑπῆρχεν αὐτῷ εἰς ἐκεῖνον ἅπερ ἐμοί· 310
οὔτε γὰρ χρήματα ἦν αὐτῷ ὁπόθεν ἂν ἔλαβεν ἀποκτείνας ἐκεῖνον, οὔτε κίνδυνος αὐτῷ ὑπῆρχεν οὐδεὶς ὅντινα
42   διέφευγεν ἀποθανόντος ἐκείνου. τεκμήριον δὲ μέγιστον
ὡς οὐκ ἐβούλετο αὐτὸν ἀπολέσαι· ἐξὸν γὰρ αὐτῷ ἐν

ἀγῶνι καὶ κινδύνῳ μεγάλῳ καταστήσαντι μετὰ τῶν νό- 315
μων τῶν ὑμετέρων ἀπολέσαι ἐκεῖνον, εἴπερ προωφείλετο
αὐτῷ κακόν, καὶ τό τε ἴδιον τὸ αὐτοῦ διαπράξασθαι καὶ
τῇ πόλει τῇ ὑμετέρᾳ χάριν καταθέσθαι, εἰ ἐπέδειξεν ἀδι-
κοῦντα ἐκεῖνον, οὐκ ἠξίωσεν, ἀλλ' οὐδ' ἦλθεν ἐπὶ τοῦ-
τον. καίτοι καλλίων γε ἦν ὁ κίνδυνος αὐτῷ. παρέξομαι 320
δὲ τούτων τοὺς μάρτυρας.

ΜΑΡΤΥΡΕΣ

43 Ἀλλὰ γὰρ ἐνταῦθα μὲν ἀφῆκεν αὐτόν· οὗ δὲ ἔδει
κινδυνεύειν αὐτὸν περί τε αὑτοῦ καὶ περὶ ἐμοῦ, ἐνταῦθα
δ' ἐπεβούλευεν, ἐν ᾧ γνωσθεὶς ἂν ἀπεστέρει μὲν ἐμὲ
τῆς πατρίδος, ἀπεστέρει δὲ αὐτὸν ἱερῶν καὶ ὁσίων καὶ 325
τῶν ἄλλων ἅπερ μέγιστα καὶ περὶ πλείστου ἐστὶν ἀνθρώποις. ἔπειτα δ' εἰ καὶ ὡς μάλιστα ἐβούλετο αὐτὸν ὁ
Λυκῖνος τεθνάναι — εἶμι γὰρ καὶ ἐπὶ τὸν τῶν κα-
τηγόρων λόγον —, οὗ αὐτὸς οὐκ ἠξίου αὐτόχειρ γενέσθαι, τοῦτο τὸ ἔργον ἐγώ ποτ' ἂν ἐπείσθην ἀντ' ἐκεί- 330
44 νου ποιῆσαι; πότερα ὡς ἐγὼ μὲν ἢ τῷ σώματι ἐπιτήδειος
διακινδυνεύειν, ἐκεῖνος δὲ χρήμασι τὸν ἐμὸν κίνδυνον
ἐκπρίασθαι; οὐ δῆτα· τῷ μὲν γὰρ οὐκ ἦν χρήματα, ἐμοὶ
δὲ ἦν· ἀλλ' αὐτὸ τοὐναντίον ἐκεῖνος τοῦτο θᾶσσον ἂν
ὑπ' ἐμοῦ ἐπείσθη κατά γε τὸ εἰκὸς ἢ ἐγὼ ὑπὸ τούτου, 335
ἐπεὶ ἐκεῖνός γ' ἑαυτὸν οὐδ' ὑπερήμερον γενόμενον ἑπτὰ
μνῶν δυνατὸς ἦν λύσασθαι, ἀλλ' οἱ φίλοι αὐτὸν ἐλύ-
σαντο. καὶ μὲν δὴ καὶ τῆς χρείας τῆς ἐμῆς καὶ τῆς Λυκίνου τοῦτο ὑμῖν μέγιστον τεκμήριόν ἐστιν, ὅτι οὐ σφό- 340
δρα ἐχρώμην ἐγὼ Λυκίνῳ φίλῳ, ὡς πάντα ποιῆσαι ἂν
τὰ ἐκείνῳ δοκοῦντα· οὐ γὰρ δήπου ἑπτὰ μὲν μνᾶς οὐκ
ἀπέτεισα ὑπὲρ αὐτοῦ δεδεμένου καὶ λυμαινομένου, κίνδυνον δὲ τοσοῦτον ἀράμενος ἄνδρα ἀπέκτεινα δι' ἐκεῖνον.

45-49 (64-68) I can no more say where the body of Herodes is than you can. When a man disappears, his associates are not necessarily guilty of his death. The friends of Ephialtes were not held liable when he was assassinated, and the real murderers did not give themselves away by trying to dispose of the body, as I am supposed to have done.

45 Ὡς μὲν οὖν οὐκ αὐτὸς αἴτιός εἰμι τοῦ πράγματος 345
οὐδὲ ἐκεῖνος, ἀποδέδεικται καθ' ὅσον ἐγὼ δύναμαι μάλιστα. τούτῳ δὲ χρῶνται πλείστῳ τῷ λόγῳ οἱ κατήγοροι, ὅτι ἀφανής ἐστιν ὁ ἀνήρ, καὶ ὑμεῖς ἴσως περὶ
τούτου αὐτοῦ ποθεῖτε ἀκοῦσαι. εἰ μὲν οὖν τοῦτο εἰκάζειν με δεῖ, ἐξ ἴσου τοῦτό ἐστι καὶ ὑμῖν καὶ ἐμοί· οὔτε 350
γὰρ ὑμεῖς αἴτιοι τοῦ ἔργου ἐστὲ οὔτε ἐγώ· εἰ δὲ δεῖ τοῖς
ἀληθέσι χρῆσθαι, τῶν εἰργασμένων τινὰ ἐρωτώντων·

46 ἐκείνου γὰρ ἄριστ' ἂν πύθοιντο. ἐμοὶ μὲν γὰρ τῷ μὴ
εἰργασμένῳ τοσοῦτον τὸ μακρότατον τῆς ἀποκρίσεώς
ἐστιν, ὅτι οὐκ εἴργασμαι· τῷ δὲ ποιήσαντι ῥᾳδία ἐστὶν 355
ἡ ἀπόδειξις, καὶ μὴ ἀποδείξαντι εὖ εἰκάσαι. οἱ μὲν γὰρ
πανουργοῦντες ἅμα τε πανουργοῦσι καὶ πρόφασιν εὑρί-
σκουσι τοῦ ἀδικήματος· τῷ δὲ μὴ εἰργασμένῳ χαλεπὸν
περὶ τῶν ἀφανῶν εἰκάζειν. οἶμαι δ' ἂν καὶ ὑμῶν ἕκαστον, εἴ τίς τινα ἔροιτο ὅ τι μὴ τύχοι εἰδώς, τοσοῦτον 360
ἂν εἰπεῖν, ὅτι οὐκ οἶδεν· εἰ δέ τις περαιτέρω τι κελεύοι

47 λέγειν, ἐν πολλῇ ἂν ἔχεσθαι ὑμᾶς ἀπορίᾳ δοκῶ. μὴ τοίνυν ἐμοὶ νείμητε τὸ ἄπορον τοῦτο, ἐν ᾧ μηδ' ἂν αὐτοὶ
εὐποροῖτε· μηδὲ ἐὰν εὖ εἰκάζω, ἐν τούτῳ μοι ἀξιοῦτε
τὴν ἀπόφευξιν εἶναι, ἀλλ' ἐξαρκείτω μοι ἐμαυτὸν ἀναί- 365
τιον ἀποδεῖξαι τοῦ πράγματος. ἐν τούτῳ οὖν ἀναίτιός
εἰμι, οὐκ ἐὰν ἐξεύρω ὅτῳ τρόπῳ ἀφανής ἐστιν ἢ ἀπόλωλεν ἀνήρ, ἀλλ' εἰ μὴ προσῆκε μοι μηδὲν ὥστ' ἀποκτεῖναι αὐτόν.

48 Ἤδη δ' ἔγωγε καὶ πρότερον ἀκοῇ ἐπίσταμαι 370
γεγονός, τοῦτο μὲν τοὺς ἀποθανόντας, τοῦτο δὲ τοὺς

ἀποκτείναντας οὐχ εὑρεθέντας· οὔκουν ἂν καλῶς
ἔχοι, εἰ τούτων δέοι τὰς αἰτίας ὑποσχεῖν τοὺς συγγενο-
μένους.   πολλοὶ δέ γ' ἤδη σχόντες ἑτέρων πραγμάτων
αἰτίας, πρὶν τὸ σαφὲς αὐτῶν γνωσθῆναι, προαπώλοντο.

49 αὐτίκα Ἐφιάλτην τὸν ὑμέτερον πολίτην οὐδέπω νῦν 375
ηὕρηνται οἱ ἀποκτείναντες· εἰ οὖν τις ἠξίου τοὺς συν-
όντας ἐκείνῳ εἰκάζειν οἵτινες ἦσαν οἱ ἀποκτείναντες
Ἐφιάλτην, εἰ δὲ μή, ἐνόχους εἶναι τῷ φόνῳ, οὐκ ἂν καλῶς εἶχε τοῖς συνοῦσιν.   ἔπειτα οἵ γε Ἐφιάλτην ἀποκτείναντες οὐκ ἐζήτησαν τὸν νεκρὸν ἀφανίσαι, οὐδ' ἐν 380
τούτῳ κινδυνεύειν μηνῦσαι τὸ πρᾶγμα, ὥσπερ οἵδε φασὶν ἐμὲ τῆς μὲν ἐπιβουλῆς οὐδένα κοινωνὸν ποιήσασθαι
τοῦ θανάτου, τῆς δ' ἀναιρέσεως.

50–54 (69–73) *The attempted murder of his master by a young slave would have
brought death upon the entire household, and all the Treasurers of Greece were put
to death on a false charge of embezzlement except one, who was saved just in time
by the discovery of the truth. I beseech you therefore not to be too hasty in finding me
guilty; perhaps time will one day reveal the murderer, for I am innocent.*

50   Τοῦτο δ' ἐντὸς οὐ πολλοῦ χρόνου παῖς ἐζήτησεν
οὐδὲ δώδεκα ἔτη γεγονὼς τὸν δεσπότην ἀποκτεῖ- 385
ναι·   καὶ εἰ μὴ φοβηθείς, ὡς ἀνεβόησεν, ἐγκατα-
λιπὼν τὴν μάχαιραν ἐν τῇ σφαγῇ ᾤχετο φεύγων,
ἀλλ' ἐτόλμησε μεῖναι, ἀπώλοντ' ἂν οἱ ἔνδον ὄντες
ἅπαντες.   οὐδεὶς γὰρ ἂν ᾤετο τὸν παῖδα τολμῆσαί ποτε
τοῦτο·   νῦν δὲ συλληφθεὶς αὐτὸς ὕστερον κατεῖπεν αὑ- 390
51 τοῦ.   τοῦτο δὲ περὶ χρημάτων αἰτίαν ποτὲ σχόντες οὐκ
οὖσαν, ὥσπερ ἐγὼ νῦν, οἱ Ἑλληνοταμίαι οἱ ὑμέτεροι,
ἐκεῖνοι μὲν ἅπαντες ἀπέθανον ὀργῇ μᾶλλον ἢ γνώμῃ,
πλὴν ἑνός, τὸ δὲ πρᾶγμα ὕστερον καταφανὲς ἐγένετο.
τοῦ δ' ἑνὸς τούτου — Σωσίαν ὄνομά φασιν αὐτῷ 395
εἶναι — κατέγνωστο μὲν ἤδη θάνατος, ἐτεθνήκει δὲ

οὔπω· καὶ ἐν τούτῳ ἐδηλώθη, τῷ τρόπῳ ἀπωλώλει
τὰ χρήματα, καὶ ὁ ἀνὴρ ἀπελύθη ὑπὸ τοῦ δήμου τοῦ
ὑμετέρου παραδεδομένος ἤδη τοῖς ἕνδεκα, οἱ δ' ἄλλοι
ἐτέθνασαν οὐδὲν αἴτιοι ὄντες.   400

52 Ταῦθ' ὑμῶν αὐτῶν ἐγὼ οἶμαι μεμνῆσθαι τοὺς πρεσβυτέρους, τοὺς δὲ νεωτέρους πυνθάνεσθαι ὥσπερ ἐμέ.
οὕτως ἀγαθόν ἐστι μετὰ τοῦ χρόνου βασανίζειν τὰ
πράγματα. καὶ τοῦτ' ἴσως ἂν φανερὸν γένοιτ' ἂν
ὕστερον, ὅπου καὶ ὅτῳ τρόπῳ τέθνηκεν ὁ ἄνθρωπος. 405
μὴ οὖν ὕστερον τοῦτο γνῶτε, ἀναίτιόν με ὄντα ἀπολέσαντες, ἀλλὰ πρότερόν γ' εὖ βουλεύσασθε, καὶ μὴ μετ'
ὀργῆς καὶ διαβολῆς, ὡς τούτων οὐκ ἂν γένοιντο ἕτεροι
53 πονηρότεροι σύμβουλοι. οὐ γὰρ ἔστιν ὅ τι ἂν ὀργιζόμενος
ἄνθρωπος εὖ γνοίη· αὐτὸ γὰρ ᾧ βουλεύεται, τὴν 410
γνώμην διαφθείρει τοῦ ἀνθρώπου. μέγα τοι ἡμέρα παρ'
ἡμέραν γιγνομένη γνώμην, ὦ ἄνδρες, ἐξ ὀργῆς μετα-
στῆσαι καὶ τὴν ἀλήθειαν εὑρεῖν τῶν γεγενημένων.

54 Εὖ δὲ ἴστε ὅτι ἐλεηθῆναι ὑφ' ὑμῶν ἄξιός εἰμι μᾶλλον ἢ
δίκην δοῦναι· δίκην μὲν γὰρ εἰκός ἐστι διδόναι τοὺς 415
ἀδικοῦντας, ἐλεεῖσθαι δὲ τοὺς ἀδίκως κινδυνεύοντας.
κρεῖσσον δὲ χρὴ γίγνεσθαι ἀεὶ τὸ ὑμέτερον δυνάμενον
ἐμὲ δικαίως σῴζειν, ἢ τὸ τῶν ἐχθρῶν βουλόμενον ἀδίκως
με ἀπολλύναι. ἐν μὲν γὰρ τῷ ἐπισχεῖν ἔστι καὶ τὰ
δεινὰ ταῦτα ποιῆσαι ἃ οὗτοι κελεύουσιν· ἐν δὲ τῷ 420
παραχρῆμα οὐκ ἔστιν ἀρχὴν ὀρθῶς βουλεύεσθαι.

In 74–84 the accused speaks on behalf of his father, who had been unwillingly involved in the revolt of Mytilene some years before, and asks the jury not to believe any slanders against him. He also says that, although murderers often bring shipwreck on their fellow-voyagers or ill-omened results at a sacrifice, his own innocence is attested by the fact that no such events have occurred in his case. He then comes to his peroration.

55–62 (85–92) I was illegally arrested and now a second trial perhaps awaits me if you acquit me. To condemn an innocent man to death is a terrible and irrevocable step, but an error on the side of clemency is never regretted.

55   "Οσα μὲν οὖν ἐκ τῶν κατηγορηθέντων μέμνημαι, ὦ
ἄνδρες, ἀπολελόγημαι· οἶμαι δὲ καὶ ὑμῶν αὐτῶν ἕνεκα
δεῖν ὑμᾶς μου ἀποψηφίσασθαι. ταὐτὰ γὰρ ἐμέ τε σῴζει,
καὶ ὑμῖν νόμιμα καὶ εὔορκα γίγνεται. κατὰ γὰρ τοὺς 425
νόμους ὠμόσατε δικάσειν· ἐγὼ δὲ καθ᾽ οὓς μὲν ἀπήχθην,
οὐκ ἔνοχός εἰμι τοῖς νόμοις, ὧν δ᾽ ἔχω τὴν αἰτίαν, ἀγών
μοι νόμιμος ὑπολείπεται. εἰ δὲ δύο ἐξ ἑνὸς ἀγῶνος γεγένησθον, οὐκ ἐγὼ αἴτιος, ἀλλ᾽ οἱ κατήγοροι. καίτοι οὐ
δήπου οἱ μὲν ἔχθιστοι οἱ ἐμοὶ δύο ἀγῶνας περὶ ἐμοῦ 430
πεποιήκασιν, ὑμεῖς δὲ οἱ τῶν δικαίων ἴσοι κριταὶ
56   προκαταγνώσεσθέ μου ἐν τῷδε τῷ ἀγῶνι τὸν φόνον. μὴ
ὑμεῖς γε, ὦ ἄνδρες· ἀλλὰ δότε τι καὶ τῷ χρόνῳ, μεθ᾽ οὗ
ὀρθότατα εὑρίσκουσιν οἱ τὴν ἀκρίβειαν ζητοῦντες τῶν
πραγμάτων. ἠξίουν μὲν γὰρ ἔγωγε περὶ τῶν τοιούτων, 435
ὦ ἄνδρες, εἶναι τὴν δίκην κατὰ τοὺς νόμους, κατὰ μέντοι
τὸ δίκαιον ὡς πλειστάκις ἐλέγχεσθαι. τοσούτῳ γὰρ
ἄμεινον ἂν ἐγιγνώσκετο· οἱ γὰρ πολλοὶ ἀγῶνες τῇ μὲν
ἀληθείᾳ σύμμαχοί εἰσι, τῇ δὲ διαβολῇ πολεμιώτατοι.

57   Φόνου γὰρ δίκη καὶ μὴ ὀρθῶς γνωσθεῖσα ἰσχυρότερον 440
τοῦ δικαίου καὶ τοῦ ἀληθοῦς ἐστιν· ἀνάγκη γάρ, ἐὰν
ὑμεῖς μου καταψηφίσησθε, καὶ μὴ ὄντα φονέα μηδ᾽
ἔνοχον τῷ ἔργῳ χρῆσθαι τῇ δίκῃ καὶ τῷ νόμῳ· καὶ
οὐδεὶς ἂν τολμήσειεν οὔτε τὴν δίκην τὴν δεδικασμένην
παραβαίνειν πιστεύσας αὐτῷ ὅτι οὐκ ἔνοχός ἐστιν, 445

οὔτε ξυνειδὼς αὑτῷ τοιοῦτον ἔργον εἰργασμένῳ μὴ οὐ
χρῆσθαι τῷ νόμῳ· ἀνάγκη δὲ τῆς τε δίκης νικᾶσθαι
παρὰ τὸ ἀληθές, αὐτοῦ τε τοῦ ἀληθοῦς, ἄλλως τε καὶ
58 ἐὰν μὴ ᾖ ὁ τιμωρήσων. αὐτῶν δὲ τούτων ἕνεκα οἵ τε
νόμοι καὶ αἱ διωμοσίαι καὶ τὰ τόμια καὶ αἱ προρρήσεις, 450
καὶ τἄλλ᾽ ὁπόσα γίγνεται τῶν δικῶν ἕνεκα τοῦ φόνου,
πολὺ διαφέροντά ἐστιν ἢ καὶ ἐπὶ τοῖς ἄλλοις, ὅτι καὶ
αὐτὰ τὰ πράγματα, περὶ ὧν οἱ κίνδυνοι, περὶ πλείστου
ἐστὶν ὀρθῶς γιγνώσκεσθαι· ὀρθῶς μὲν γὰρ γνωσθέντα
τιμωρία ἐστὶ τῷ ἀδικηθέντι, φονέα δὲ τὸν μὴ αἴτιον 455
ψηφισθῆναι ἁμαρτία καὶ ἀσέβειά ἐστιν εἴς τε τοὺς θεοὺς
καὶ εἰς τοὺς νόμους.

59 Καὶ οὐκ ἴσον ἐστὶ τόν τε διώκοντα μὴ ὀρθῶς αἰτιά-
σασθαι καὶ ὑμᾶς τοὺς δικαστὰς μὴ ὀρθῶς γνῶναι.
ἡ μὲν γὰρ τούτων αἰτίασις οὐκ ἔχει τέλος, ἀλλ᾽ ἐν ὑμῖν
ἐστι καὶ τῇ δίκῃ· ὅ τι δ᾽ ἂν ὑμεῖς ἐν αὐτῇ τῇ δίκῃ μὴ 460
ὀρθῶς γνῶτε, τοῦτο οὐκ ἔστιν ὅποι ἄν τις ἀνενεγκὼν
60 τὴν αἰτίαν ἀπολύσαιτο. πῶς ἂν οὖν ὀρθῶς δικάσαιτε
περὶ αὐτῶν; εἰ τούτους τε ἐάσετε τὸν νομιζόμενον ὅρκον διομοσαμένους κατηγορῆσαι, κἀμὲ περὶ αὐτοῦ τοῦ
πράγματος ἀπολογήσασθαι. πῶς δὲ ἐάσετε; ἐὰν νυνὶ 465
ἀποψηφίσησθέ μου. διαφεύγω γὰρ οὐδ᾽ οὕτω τὰς ὑμετέρας γνώμας, ἀλλ᾽ ὑμεῖς ἔσεσθε οἱ κἀκεῖ περὶ ἐμοῦ διαψηφιζόμενοι. καὶ φεισαμένοις μὲν ὑμῖν ἐμοῦ νῦν ἔξεστι
τότε χρῆσθαι ὅ τι ἂν βούλησθε, ἀπολέσασι δὲ οὐδὲ βου-
λεύσασθαι ἔτι περὶ ἐμοῦ ἐγχωρεῖ.   470

61 Καὶ μὴν εἰ δέοι ἁμαρτεῖν τι, τὸ ἀδίκως ἀπολῦσαι
ὁσιώτερον ἂν εἴη τοῦ μὴ δικαίως ἀπολέσαι· τὸ μὲν γὰρ
ἁμάρτημα μόνον ἐστί, τὸ δὲ ἕτερον καὶ ἀσέβημα. ἐν ᾧ
χρὴ πολλὴν πρόνοιαν ἔχειν, μέλλοντας ἀνήκεστον
ἔργον ἐργάζεσθαι. ἐν μὲν γὰρ ἀκεστῷ πράγματι καὶ 475
ὀργῇ χρησαμένους καὶ διαβολῇ πιθομένους ἔλασσόν

ἐστιν ἐξαμαρτεῖν· μεταγνοὺς γὰρ ἔτι ἂν ὀρθῶς βουλεύ-
σαιτο· ἐν δὲ τοῖς ἀνηκέστοις πλέον βλάβος τὸ μετανοεῖν
καὶ γνῶναι ἐξημαρτηκότας. ἤδη δέ τισιν ὑμῶν καὶ
μεταμέλησεν ἀπολωλεκόσι. καίτοι ὅπου ὑμῖν τοῖς 480
ἐξαπατηθεῖσι μετεμέλησεν, ἢ καὶ πάνυ τοι χρῆν τούς γε
ἐξαπατῶντας ἀπολωλέναι.

62   Ἔπειτα δὲ τὰ μὲν ἀκούσια τῶν ἁμαρτημάτων ἔχει
συγγνώμην, τὰ δὲ ἑκούσια οὐκ ἔχει. τὸ μὲν γὰρ ἀκούσιον
ἁμάρτημα, ὦ ἄνδρες, τῆς τύχης ἐστί, τὸ δὲ ἑκούσιον 485
τῆς γνώμης. ἑκούσιον δὲ πῶς ἂν εἴη μᾶλλον ἢ εἴ τις,
ὧν βουλὴν ποιοῖτο, ταῦτα παραχρῆμα ἐξεργάζοιτο;
καὶ μὴν τὴν ἴσην γε δύναμιν ἔχει, ὅστις τε ἂν τῇ χειρὶ
ἀποκτείνῃ ἀδίκως καὶ ὅστις τῇ ψήφῳ.

*63-66 (93-96) I put my trust in justice, and the soul that is conscious of its
innocence supports the body in time of trouble. If you acquit me now you till be able
to alter your decision at a second trial, but condemnation is final. Take time now
and make up your minds later on, when the prosecution is on oath, and I shall
not complain. Do your duty and you will acquit me.*

63   Εὖ δ' ἴστε ὅτι οὐκ ἄν ποτ' ἦλθον εἰς τὴν πόλιν, εἴ τι 490
ξυνῄδη ἐμαυτῷ τοιοῦτον· νῦν δὲ πιστεύων τῷ δικαίῳ,
οὗ πλέονος οὐδέν ἐστιν ἄξιον ἀνδρὶ συναγωνίζεσθαι,
μηδὲν αὐτῷ συνειδότι ἀνόσιον εἰργασμένῳ μηδ' εἰς
τοὺς θεοὺς ἠσεβηκότι· ἐν γὰρ τῷ τοιούτῳ ἤδη καὶ τὸ
σῶμα ἀπειρηκὸς ἡ ψυχὴ συνεξέσωσεν, ἐθέλουσα ταλαι- 495
πωρεῖν διὰ τὸ μὴ ξυνειδέναι ἑαυτῇ· τῷ δὲ ξυνειδότι τοῦτο
αὐτὸ πρῶτον πολέμιόν ἐστιν· ἔτι γὰρ καὶ τοῦ σώματος
ἰσχύοντος ἡ ψυχὴ προαπολείπει, ἡγουμένη τὴν τιμωρίαν
οἷ ἥκειν ταύτην τῶν ἀσεβημάτων· ἐγὼ δ' ἐμαυτῷ
τοιοῦτον οὐδὲν ξυνειδὼς ἥκω εἰς ὑμᾶς.   500

64   Τὸ δὲ τοὺς κατηγόρους διαβάλλειν οὐδέν ἐστι θαυμα-
στόν. τούτων γὰρ ἔργον τοῦτο, ὑμῶν δὲ τὸ μὴ πείθεσθαι

τὰ μὴ δίκαια. τοῦτο μὲν γὰρ ἐμοὶ πειθομένοις ὑμῖν
μεταμελῆσαι ἔστιν, καὶ τούτου φάρμακον τὸ αὖθις
κολάσαι, τοῦ δὲ τούτοις πειθομένους ἐξεργάσασθαι ἃ 505
βούλονται οὐχ ἔστιν ἴασις. οὐδὲ χρόνος πολὺς ὁ
διαφέρων, ἐν ᾧ ταῦτα νομίμως πράξεθ᾽ ἃ νῦν ὑμᾶς
παρανόμως πείθουσιν οἱ κατήγοροι ψηφίσασθαι. οὔ
τοι τῶν ἐπειγομένων ἐστὶ τὰ πράγματα, ἀλλὰ τῶν εὖ
βουλευομένων. νῦν μὲν οὖν γνωρισταὶ γίγνεσθε τῆς 510
δίκης, τότε δὲ δικασταί· νῦν μὲν δοξασταί, τότε δὲ κριταὶ
τῶν ἀληθῶν.

65 Ῥᾷστον δέ τοί ἐστιν ἀνδρὸς περὶ θανάτου φεύγοντος
τὰ ψευδῆ καταμαρτυρῆσαι. ἐὰν γὰρ τὸ παραχρῆμα
μόνον πείσωσιν ὥστε ἀποκτεῖναι, ἅμα τῷ σώματι καὶ 515
ἡ τιμωρία ἀπόλωλεν. οὔτε γὰρ οἱ φίλοι ἔτι θελήσουσιν
ὑπὲρ ἀπολωλότος τιμωρεῖν. ἐὰν δὲ καὶ βουληθῶσιν,
τί ἔσται πλέον τῷ γε ἀποθανόντι; νῦν μὲν οὖν ἀποψηφί-
66 σασθέ μου· ἐν δὲ τῇ τοῦ φόνου δίκῃ οὗτοί τε τὸν νομιζόμενον ὅρκον διομοσάμενοι ἐμοῦ κατηγορήσουσι, καὶ 520
ὑμεῖς περὶ ἐμοῦ κατὰ τοὺς κειμένους νόμους διαγνώσεσθε,
καὶ ἐμοὶ οὐδεὶς λόγος ἔσται ἔτι, ἐὰν τι πάσχω, ὡς παρανόμως ἀπωλόμην.

Ταῦτά τοι δέομαι ὑμῶν, οὔτε τὸ ὑμέτερον εὐσεβὲς
παρεὶς οὔτε ἐμαυτὸν ἀποστερῶν τὸ δίκαιον· ἐν δὲ τῷ 525
ὑμετέρῳ ὅρκῳ καὶ ἡ ἐμὴ σωτηρία ἔνεστι. πειθόμενοι
δὲ τούτων ὅτῳ βούλεσθε, ἀποψηφίσασθέ μου.

EURIPIDES

Introduction

THE origin of Tragedy (τραγῳδία, 'goat-singing') is uncertain; it may have arisen from rustic songs in Attica in competition for the prize of a goat or around a sacrificial goat. In about 534 B.C. Thespis gave a performance at a festival of Dionysus at Athens in which the lyric odes sung by a Chorus were interspersed with speeches in iambic verse delivered by an actor; and the fusion of this with lyric songs also in honour of Dionysus that were being developed in the Peloponnese led to the Athenian tragic drama of the fifth century, which was always based on some legendary story. These plays were produced at the Great or City Dionysia in the spring. The first of the three great tragedians, Aeschylus (525–456), who wrote in majestic poetry on themes of almost superhuman grandeur, added a second actor, reduced the part taken by the Chorus, and made real dialogue and dramatic action possible. Sophocles (496–406), the supreme artist in language and character drawing, introduced a third actor and stage scenery, and raised the number of the Chorus from 12 to 15.

The youngest of the three tragedians, Euripides (c. 480–406), the son of well-to-do parents, took no part in public affairs and lived quietly in Athens or Salamis, until he went to live at the court of Archelaus, king of Macedonia, where he spent the last two years of his life. He introduced to the stage romantic love between man and woman and represented his characters as real people with the virtues and vices of human beings; he paid particular attention to the psychology of women and gave his plots an exciting, sometimes almost melodramatic, turn; his treatment of the gods was original and often irreverent. In the dramatic competitions Aeschylus won first prize 13 times, Sophocles 18 times, and Euripides only 5 times; but by a quirk of fortune 19 of his 90 plays have survived (not all of the highest quality), compared with seven each of Aeschylus and Sophocles. Among his best plays are *Hippolytus*, describing the unwilling and tragic love of a woman for her stepson; *Medea*, the story of a wronged woman's terrible revenge; *Alcestis*, a loyal wife who died for her husband and was brought back from the grave; and *Bacchae*, the triumph of the god Dionysus over unbelievers.

The Theatre of Dionysus at Athens lies at the south-eastern foot of the Acropolis. The circular ὀρχήστρα, in which the Chorus sang and danced, was 66 feet in diameter; to the south-east was the stage, probably on the same level, about 66 feet long and 12 to 15 feet deep, with stage-buildings (σκηνή) two storeys high behind it; they were painted to represent a house or temple and had a door in the middle. To the north-west was the auditorium, dug out of the slope of the Acropolis and banked up in an irregular horseshoe shape, with wooden seats arranged in tiers and divided into blocks by radiating gangways; it could hold about 17,000 people. The present remains date from the fourth century B.C., when the theatre was rebuilt in stone. The most perfectly preserved Greek theatre, also of the fourth century, is at Epidaurus in the northern Peloponnese, where plays are again performed nowadays.

At the Great Dionysia three poets were chosen to compete out of a much larger number, and each exhibited four plays,

a 'trilogy' of tragedies, either all based on the same legend
or three unconnected plays, and a 'satyric' drama, which
was a grotesque and semi-comic version of a myth; only
one satyric play survives, Euripides' *Cyclops*. Three (sometimes five) comic poets also competed with one another.
The plays were produced at his own cost by a *chǫrēgus*, one
allotted to each contestant, and the judges who awarded the
prizes were drawn by lot. The three actors took all the
parts, both male and female, the 'protagonist' playing the
leading roles, and they wore masks, a head-dress, flowing
robes, and thick-soled boots coming half-way up the leg.
The Chorus of 15 (originally 12) players, under their leader
the *coryphaeus*, remained in the *orchēstra* all through the play
but became less important to the plot as the century proceeded, though they continued to sing odes of great poetic
beauty which had a connection with the theme of the
tragedy. In *Ion* the Chorus actually influences the develop-
ment of the plot. A tragedy began with a Prologue in iambic
verse, followed by the *parodos*, the first ode sung by the
Chorus; then came the *epeisodia*, scenes spoken by the actors,
separated by *stasima*, more choral odes; and the *exodos*
followed the last *stasimon*.

Euripides' *Ion* is described by one critic as 'one of the
most perfect and beautiful of the Greek tragedies', though
it is hardly a tragedy because it has a happy ending for
everyone; it might be called a romantic melodrama, in
which an unhappy mother tries to kill her long-lost and still
unrecognised son and the son tries to hand his mother over
to justice, but they recognise each other and are re-united
in the nick of time. It was perhaps written in about 418,
half-way through the poet's dramatic career and in the
middle of the Peloponnesian War (some authorities put it

later than this), and one of its objects was to provide a divine ancestry through Ion for the Ionian Greeks of Asia Minor, who were (wrongly) supposed to be descended from the Athenians of old. Hitherto the Ionians were said to be sprung from Xuthus, a foreigner from Phthia in Thessaly (then known as Achaea, but not the better-known Achaea in the northern Peloponnese). The first kings of Athens were said to be Cecrops I, Cranaus, Amphictyon, Erichthonius, Pandion, Erechtheus, Cecrops II. The daughter of Erechtheus, Creüsa, married Xuthus, who (in this play) was descended from Zeus through Aeolus and Hellen; Xuthus was the father of Dorus and Achaeus, and from this family come the names of the Aeolians, Dorians and Achaeans, three of the four main divisions of the Hellenic race (named after Hellen); Ion, now called the son of Creüsa by Apollo instead of by Xuthus, was ancestor of the Ionians, the fourth division of the Hellenes. Hermes in the Prologue outlines this version of the story, which was probably unknown to most of the audience, and has no basis in scientific ethnology.

Of the characters, Ion is an attractive youth in his late teens, a temple foundling who is proud to serve Apollo, impulsive and quick to take offence but friendly to strangers and eager to discover his real parentage. Creüsa is one of Euripides' best female characters. She was betrayed by Apollo as a girl, when she abandoned the new-born baby whom she longs to recover, and on being deceived by her old slave about the conduct of Xuthus she loses all self-control and is willing to murder her supposed stepson. Xuthus is a rather pathetic figure; he is an honest man of action, easily deceived by an oracle, and left alone at Delphi while his wife and her newly found son go home to Athens, though he will be allowed by them to believe that Ion is really his son. The old servant is a villain, absolutely loyal to Creüsa and the Erechtheid family but ready to egg her on with lies to commit murder and even to do it himself, whatever the cost. The Pythian priestess has been a loving foster-mother to Ion and by producing the cradle and its contents at the critical moment unwittingly brings about the final 'recognition', though she is, perhaps naturally, most anxious to maintain the sanctity of the shrine. The Chorus of Creüsa's attendants plays an unusual part in affecting the action of the play by telling Creüsa something that Xuthus has forbidden them to reveal on pain of death and by acquiescing in a statement by the old servant, which they know to be untrue, that Xuthus knows that Ion is his son by a slave-girl.

The character who really comes out worst in the play is one who never appears on the stage at all, though he is often mentioned — the god Phoebus Apollo. First he seduced an innocent girl and then abandoned her in the time of her greatest need. He allowed her to believe for nearly twenty years that she had lost her only son, and according to Hermes was quite content that she should never find him, though here his scheme went wrong. He gave a false oracle to Xuthus, or one so ambiguous that whatever happened he could maintain that he had foretold it—though that was a commonplace for the Delphic Oracle, to which Euripides was always hostile, partly no doubt because it had consistently favoured the Spartans in the Peloponnesian War. Finally Apollo was ashamed to appear in the last scene as a *deus ex machina* to round off the play but sent Athena instead. Yet in spite of all this Creüsa, though naturally bitter against him, remained loyal to the god, and Xuthus always and Ion nearly always spoke of him with reverence.

As a highly educated man Euripides could not credit the barbaric myths that were part of the religion of the masses. Yet though he criticised the wicked deeds of the gods and their lying oracles, as in this play, he did not really try to destroy Athenian religious beliefs, from which he wanted only the grosser elements to be removed. He was a poetic and speculative thinker rather than the iconoclast that some critics believe him to have been, and he surely would not have been allowed to go on competing with his plays at the religious festival of the Dionysia if his contemporaries had so regarded him.

THE IAMBIC METRE

Most of the spoken parts of a Greek tragedy were written in 'iambic trimeters' or 'iambic senarii', usually called 'iambics'. In its simplest form the line consisted of six metrical feet each consisting of an iambus ($\cup -$), like

$$\overset{\cup-}{Κρέου}- \mid \overset{\cup}{σα} \overset{-}{κἄκ}- \mid \overset{\cup-}{τίθη}- \mid \overset{\cup}{σιν} \parallel \overset{-}{ὡς} \mid \overset{\cup}{θανού}- \overset{-}{μενον}. (18)$$

The last syllable of the line can be either long or short.

But speeches consisting of lines all exactly alike in quantity would be very monotonous to hear, so for the sake of variety a spondee ($- -$) was allowed in the first, the third, and the fifth feet, like

$$\overset{-}{κἄμ}' \overset{-}{ὢν} \mid \overset{\cup-}{ἀδελ}- \mid \overset{-}{φὸς} \parallel \overset{-}{Φοῖ}- \mid \overset{\cup}{βος} \parallel \overset{-}{αἰ}- \mid \overset{- -}{τεῖται} \mid \overset{\cup\cup}{τάδε}. (28)$$

On the assumption that one long syllable is metrically equivalent to two short syllables, the long syllable of the iambus and the spondee can be 'resolved' into two short syllables, thus producing a tribrach ($\cup \cup \cup$), an anapaest

($\cup$ $\cup$ -), or a dactyl (- $\cup$ $\cup$). Tribrachs are allowed in any of the first four feet, dactyls in the first and third feet, and anapaests in the first foot only, except for proper names that could not otherwise appear in the line at all, for which an undivided anapaest can come in any foot except the last. Here are examples:

$$\overset{\cup}{\nu}\overset{-}{\acute{o}}\mu os \mid \overset{-}{\tau} \overset{-}{\iota}s \ \overset{\cup}{\check{e}}\sigma\text{-} \mid \overset{-}{\tau} \overset{\cup}{\iota\nu} \parallel \overset{\cup}{\check{o}}\overset{\cup}{\phi\epsilon}\text{-} \mid \overset{\cup}{\sigma}\overset{-}{\iota\nu} \parallel \overset{-}{\dot{\epsilon}}\nu \mid \overset{-}{\chi}\overset{-}{\rho}\nu\sigma\eta\text{-} \mid \overset{\cup}{\lambda}\overset{-}{\acute{a}}\tau ois. \quad (25)$$

$$\overset{-}{\Pi}\alpha\lambda\lambda\overset{\cup}{\acute{a}}\overset{\cup}{\delta}os \mid \overset{\cup}{\acute{v}}\pi' \overset{-}{\check{o}}\chi\text{-} \mid \overset{-}{\theta}\overset{-}{\dot{\omega}} \parallel \overset{-}{\tau}\hat{\eta}s \mid \overset{\cup}{'A}\overset{-}{\theta\eta}\text{-} \mid \nu\alpha\overset{-}{\iota}\omega\nu \mid \overset{\cup}{\chi}\overset{-}{\theta}ov\acute{o}s. \quad (12)$$

$$\overset{\cup}{\pi}\overset{\cup}{\rho}\overset{-}{o}\gamma\acute{o}\nu\omega\nu \mid \overset{\cup}{\nu}\acute{o}\overset{-}{\mu}ov \mid \overset{-}{\sigma}\overset{-}{\dot{\omega}}\zeta ov\text{-} \mid \overset{\cup}{\sigma}\overset{-}{a} \parallel \overset{\cup}{\tau}\acute{o}\nu \mid \overset{\cup}{\tau}\overset{-}{\epsilon} \gamma\eta\text{-} \mid \overset{\cup}{\gamma}\overset{-}{\epsilon}vo\hat{v}s. \quad (20)$$

Every line must have a 'caesura', a break between two words in the third or/and the fourth foot that binds together the two halves of the line and makes them into a rhythmic whole. In the examples given above the caesura is marked with a double line. Here is the complete scheme for iambics.

Another form of metre, which appears in 208–234, is the 'trochaic tetrameter'. This consists of seven trochees (- $\cup$) with the addition of a final syllable that can be either long or short, so that the line is similar to an iambic trimeter with the addition of — $\cup$ — at the beginning of the line. Spondees and 'resolved' feet are allowed in trochaics just as in iambics. The metres of the choric odes, none of which appears in this book except when Creüsa speaks two lines (486–487) in lyric verse, are too complicated to be explained briefly.

The scansion of iambics is comparatively easy. First count up the number of syllables in the line: if there are twelve, each foot must be an iambus or a spondee; if thirteen or fourteen, there are one or two 'resolved' feet. Here are some rules for the length of syllables.

(i) η, ω, diphthongs, contracted syllables, and vowels with a circumflex accent or an 'iota subscript' are always long.

(ii) ϵ and o are short, but form a long syllable when followed by ζ, ξ, ψ, sometimes by ρ in the next word, or by two consonants, either in the same word or in two separate words, with the following important exception:

(iii) A short vowel can either remain short or form a long syllable when followed by a 'mute' (β, δ, θ, κ, π, τ, ϕ, χ) and a 'liquid' (λ, μ, ν, ρ) in the same word, i.e. by pairs of words that can (generally) start a Greek word. Thus $\pi\alpha\tau\rho\acute{o}s$ can be scanned either $\overset{\cup}{\pi\alpha}|\overset{-}{\tau\rho\acute{o}s}$ or $\overset{-}{\pi\alpha\tau}|\overset{-}{\rho\acute{o}s}$.

(iv) Final α of the first declension singular is usually long when preceded by a vowel or ρ, and short when preceded by other consonants. Neuter plural α is short. Final ι and v are usually short.

IΩN
Ion

TA TOY ΔΡΑΜΑΤΟΣ ΠΡΟΣΩΠΑ
Characters of the Play

EPMHΣ	Hermes, messenger of the gods.
IΩN	Ion, a temple-servant at Delphi, really the son of Apollo and Creüsa.
KPEOYΣA	Creüsa, daughter of King Erechtheus of Athens and wife of Xuthus.
ΞOYΘOΣ	Xuthus, a Thessalian living at Athens, married to Creüsa.
ΠPEΣBYTHΣ	An old man, a slave in the family of Erechtheus.
ΘEPAΠΩN KPEOYΣHΣ	A servant of Creüsa.
ΠYΘIA HTOI ΠPOΦHTIΣ	The Pythia, prophetess of Apollo.

The scene is the front of the temple of Phoebus Apollo at Delphi in prehistoric times.
The play was first produced at the Great or City Dionysia at Athens in about 418 B.C. or a little later.

Ion

1–75 The Prologue. Hermes relates how his brother Apollo secretly loved Creüsa, daughter of Erechtheus, king of Athens, who had a baby son whom she left to die in a cave under the Acropolis. Hermes took the child to Delphi and left him in the temple, where he was found and brought up by the Pythian priestess to be a nameless temple-servant. Creüsa married Xuthus but they had no children, so they came to Delphi to consult the oracle. Apollo intends to give the boy, now almost grown up, to Xuthus as his own son, to be called Ion and to become the founder of the Ionian Greeks.

ΕΡΜΗΣ

Ἄτλας, ὁ νώτοις χαλκέοισιν οὐρανὸν
θεῶν παλαιὸν οἶκον ἐκτρίβων, θεῶν
μιᾶς ἔφυσε Μαῖαν, ἥ 'μ' ἐγείνατο
Ἑρμῆν μεγίστῳ Ζηνί, δαιμόνων λάτριν.
ἥκω δὲ Δελφῶν τήνδε γῆν, ἵν' ὀμφαλὸν   5
μέσον καθίζων Φοῖβος ὑμνῳδεῖ βροτοῖς
τά τ' ὄντα καὶ μέλλοντα θεσπίζων ἀεί.

ἔστιν γὰρ οὐκ ἄσημος Ἑλλήνων πόλις,
τῆς χρυσολόγχου Παλλάδος κεκλημένη,
οὗ παῖδ' Ἐρεχθέως Φοῖβος ἔζευξεν γάμοις   10
βίᾳ Κρέουσαν, ἔνθα προσβόρρους πέτρας
Παλλάδος ὑπ' ὄχθῳ τῆς Ἀθηναίων χθονὸς
Μακρὰς καλοῦσι γῆς ἄνακτες Ἀτθίδος.
ἀγνὼς δὲ πατρί — τῷ θεῷ γὰρ ἦν φίλον —
γαστρὸς διήνεγκ' ὄγκον. ὡς δ' ἦλθεν χρόνος,   15
τεκοῦσ' ἐν οἴκοις παῖδ' ἀπήνεγκεν βρέφος
ἐς ταὐτὸν ἄντρον οὗπερ ηὐνάσθη θεῷ
Κρέουσα, κἀκτίθησιν ὡς θανούμενον

κοίλης ἐν ἀντίπηγος εὐτρόχῳ κύκλῳ,
προγόνων νόμον σῴζουσα τοῦ τε γηγενοῦς   20
Ἐριχθονίου. κείνῳ γὰρ ἡ Διὸς κόρη
φρουρὼ παραζεύξασα φύλακε σώματος
δισσὼ δράκοντε, παρθένοις Ἀγλαυρίσι
δίδωσι σῴζειν· ὅθεν Ἐρεχθείδαις ἐκεῖ
νόμος τις ἔστιν ὄφεσιν ἐν χρυσηλάτοις   25
τρέφειν τέκν'. ἀλλ' ἦν εἶχε παρθένος χλιδὴν
τέκνῳ προσάψασ' ἔλιπεν ὡς θανουμένῳ.
κἄμ' ὧν ἀδελφὸς Φοῖβος αἰτεῖται τάδε·
" ὦ σύγγον', ἐλθὼν λαὸν εἰς αὐτόχθονα
κλεινῶν Ἀθηνῶν — οἶσθα γὰρ θεᾶς πόλιν —   30
λαβὼν βρέφος νεογνὸν ἐκ κοίλης πέτρας
αὐτῷ σὺν ἄγγει σπαργάνοισί θ' οἷς ἔχει
ἔνεγκε Δελφῶν τἀμὰ πρὸς χρηστήρια,
καὶ θὲς πρὸς αὐταῖς εἰσόδοις δόμων ἐμῶν.
τὰ δ' ἄλλ' — ἐμὸς γάρ ἐστιν, ὡς εἰδῇς, ὁ παῖς —   35
ἡμῖν μελήσει."
              Λοξίᾳ δ' ἐγὼ χάριν
πράσσων ἀδελφῷ πλεκτὸν ἐξάρας κύτος
ἤνεγκα, καὶ τὸν παῖδα κρηπίδων ἔπι
τίθημι ναοῦ τοῦδ', ἀναπτύξας κύτος
ἑλικτὸν ἀντίπηγος, ὡς ὁρῷθ' ὁ παῖς.   40
κυρεῖ δ' ἅμ' ἱππεύοντος ἡλίου κύκλῳ
προφῆτις ἐσβαίνουσα μαντεῖον θεοῦ·
ὄψιν δὲ προσβαλοῦσα παιδὶ νηπίῳ
ἐθαύμασ' εἴ τις Δελφίδων τλαίη κόρη
λαθραῖον ὠδῖν' ἐς θεοῦ ῥῖψαι δόμον,   45
ὑπέρ τε θυμέλας διορίσαι πρόθυμος ἦν·
οἴκτῳ δ' ἀφῆκεν ὠμότητα — καὶ θεὸς
συνεργὸς ἦν τῷ παιδὶ μὴ 'κπεσεῖν δόμων —
τρέφει δέ νιν λαβοῦσα. τὸν σπείραντα δὲ

οὐκ οἶδε Φοῖβον οὐδὲ μητέρ' ἧς ἔφυ,   50
ὁ παῖς τε τοὺς τεκόντας οὐκ ἐπίσταται.

νέος μὲν οὖν ὢν ἀμφὶ βωμίους τροφὰς
ἠλᾶτ' ἀθύρων· ὡς δ' ἀπηνδρώθη δέμας,
Δελφοί σφ' ἔθεντο χρυσοφ·'λακα τοῦ θεοῦ
ταμίαν τε πάντων πιστόν, ἐν δ' ἀνακτόροις   55
θεοῦ καταζῇ δεῦρ' ἀεὶ σεμνὸν βίον.
Κρέουσα δ' ἡ τεκοῦσα τὸν νεανίαν
Ξούθῳ γαμεῖται συμφορᾶς τοιᾶσδ' ὕπο·
ἦν ταῖς 'Αθήναις τοῖς τε Χαλκωδοντίδαις,
οἳ γῆν ἔχουσ' Εὐβοῖδα, πολέμιος κλύδων·
ὃν συμπονήσας καὶ συνεξελὼν δορὶ
γάμων Κρεούσης ἀξίωμ' ἐδέξατο,
οὐκ ἐγγενὴς ὤν, Αἰόλου δὲ τοῦ Διὸς
γεγὼς 'Αχαιός. χρόνια δὲ σπείρας λέχη
ἄτεκνός ἐστι, καὶ Κρέουσ'· ὧν οὕνεκα   65
ἥκουσι πρὸς μαντεῖ' 'Απόλλωνος τάδε
ἔρωτι παίδων. Λοξίας δὲ τὴν τύχην
ἐς τοῦτ' ἐλαύνει, κοὐ λέληθεν, ὡς δοκεῖ.
δώσει γὰρ εἰσελθόντι μαντεῖον τόδε
Ξούθῳ τὸν αὑτοῦ παῖδα, καὶ πεφυκέναι   70
κείνου σφε φήσει, μητρὸς ὡς ἐλθὼν δόμους
γνωσθῇ Κρεούσῃ, καὶ γάμοι τε Λοξίου
κρυπτοὶ γένωνται παῖς τ' ἔχῃ τὰ πρόσφορα.
"Ιωνα δ' αὐτόν, κτίστορ' 'Ασιάδος χθονός,
ὄνομα κεκλῆσθαι θήσεται καθ' 'Ελλάδα.   75

(*Ion, 76–257 Ion enters, greets the rising sun and Phoebus, and begins to sweep out the entrance to the temple. The Chorus of Athenian maidservants of Creüsa admire the decorations of the temple and are followed by Creüsa in tears, whom Ion addresses courteously.*)

76–179 (Ion, 258–361) Creüsa tells Ion of her parentage and the legends of her family, and how she married Xuthus but had no children by him, so that she has come to consult the oracle about her hopes of a child. Ion says that he is a foundling brought up in the temple as the servant of Apollo. Creüsa says that a friend of hers (really herself) was betrayed by Phoebus and left her child to die, a child who would be Ion's age if he had lived.

Ἰω. τίς δ' εἶ; πόθεν γῆς ἦλθες; ἐκ ποίας πάτρας
πέφυκας; ὄνομα τί σε καλεῖν ἡμᾶς χρεών;

Κρ. Κρέουσα μέν μοι τοὔνομ', ἐκ δ' Ἐρεχθέως
πέφυκα, πατρὶς γῆ δ' Ἀθηναίων πόλις.

Ἰω. ὦ κλεινὸν οἰκοῦσ' ἄστυ γενναίων τ' ἄπο   80
τραφεῖσα πατέρων, ὥς σε θαυμάζω, γύναι.

Κρ. τοσαῦτα κεὐτυχοῦμεν, ὦ ξέν', οὐ πέρα.

Ἰω. πρὸς θεῶν ἀληθῶς, ὡς μεμύθευται βροτοῖς . . .;

Κρ. τί χρῆμ' ἐρωτᾷς, ὦ ξέν'; ἐκμαθεῖν θέλω.

Ἰω. ἐκ γῆς πατρός σου πρόγονος ἔβλαστεν πατήρ;   85

Κρ. Ἐριχθόνιός γε· τὸ δὲ γένος μ' οὐκ ὠφελεῖ.

Ἰω. ἦ καί σφ' Ἀθάνα γῆθεν ἐξανείλετο;

Κρ. ἐς παρθένους γε χεῖρας, οὐ τεκοῦσά νιν.

Ἰω. δίδωσι δ', ὥσπερ ἐν γραφῇ νομίζεται . . .;

Κρ. Κέκροπός γε σῴζειν παισὶν οὐχ ὁρώμενον.   90

Ἰω. ἤκουσα λῦσαι παρθένους τεῦχος θεᾶς.

Κρ. τοιγὰρ θανοῦσαι σκόπελον ᾕμαξαν πέτρας.

Ἰω. εἶεν·
τί δαὶ τόδ'; ἆρ' ἀληθὲς ἢ μάτην λόγος . . .

Κρ. τί χρῆμ' ἐρωτᾷς; καὶ γὰρ οὐ κάμνω σχολῇ.

Ἰω. πατὴρ Ἐρεχθεὺς σὰς ἔθυσε συγγόνους;   95

Κρ. ἔτλη πρὸ γαίας σφάγια παρθένους κτανεῖν.

Ἰω. σὺ δ' ἐξεσώθης πῶς κασιγνήτων μόνη;

Κρ. βρέφος νεογνὸν μητρὸς ἦν ἐν ἀγκάλαις.

Ἰω. πατέρα δ' ἀληθῶς χάσμα σὸν κρύπτει χθονός;

Κρ. πληγαὶ τριαίνης ποντίου σφ' ἀπώλεσαν.   100

Ἰω. Μακραὶ δὲ χῶρός ἐστ' ἐκεῖ κεκλημένος;
Κρ. τί δ' ἱστορεῖς τόδ'; ὥς μ' ἀνέμνησάς τινος.
Ἰω. τιμᾷ σφε Πύθιος ἀστραπαί τε Πύθιαι.
Κρ. τιμᾷ; τί τιμᾷ; μήποτ' ὤφελόν σφ' ἰδεῖν.
Ἰω. τί δὲ στυγεῖς σὺ τοῦ θεοῦ τὰ φίλτατα;   105
Κρ. οὐδέν· ξύνοιδ' ἄντροισιν αἰσχύνην τινά.
Ἰω. πόσις δὲ τίς σ' ἔγημ' Ἀθηναίων, γύναι;
Κρ. οὐκ ἀστός, ἀλλ' ἐπακτὸς ἐξ ἄλλης χθονός.
Ἰω. τίς; εὐγενῆ νιν δεῖ πεφυκέναι τινά.
Κρ. Ξοῦθος, πεφυκὼς Αἰόλου Διός τ' ἄπο.   110
Ἰω. καὶ πῶς ξένος σ' ὢν ἔσχεν οὖσαν ἐγγενῆ;
Κρ. Εὔβοι' Ἀθήναις ἔστι τις γείτων πόλις . . .
Ἰω. ὅροις ὑγροῖσιν, ὡς λέγουσ', ὡρισμένη.
Κρ. ταύτην ἔπερσε Κεκροπίδαις κοινῷ δορί.
Ἰω. ἐπίκουρος ἐλθών; κᾆτα σὸν γαμεῖ λέχος;   115
Κρ. φερνάς γε πολέμου καὶ δορὸς λαβὼν γέρας.
Ἰω. σὺν ἀνδρὶ δ' ἥκεις ἢ μόνη χρηστήρια;
Κρ. σὺν ἀνδρί. σηκοὺς δ' ἐκστρέφει Τροφωνίου.
Ἰω. πότερα θεατὴς ἢ χάριν μαντευμάτων;
Κρ. κείνου τε Φοίβου θ' ἓν θέλων μαθεῖν ἔπος.   120
Ἰω. καρποῦ δ' ὕπερ γῆς ἥκετ', ἢ παίδων πέρι;
Κρ. ἄπαιδές ἐσμεν, χρόνι' ἔχοντ' εὐνήματα.
Ἰω. οὐδ' ἔτεκες οὐδὲν πώποτ', ἀλλ' ἄτεκνος εἶ;
Κρ. ὁ Φοῖβος οἶδε τὴν ἐμὴν ἀπαιδίαν.
Ἰω. ὦ τλῆμον, ὡς τἄλλ' εὐτυχοῦσ' οὐκ εὐτυχεῖς.   125
Κρ. σὺ δ' εἶ τίς; ὥς σου τὴν τεκοῦσαν ὤλβισα.
Ἰω. τοῦ θεοῦ καλοῦμαι δοῦλος εἰμί τ', ὦ γύναι.
Κρ. ἀνάθημα πόλεως, ἤ τινος πραθεὶς ὕπο;
Ἰω. οὐκ οἶδα πλὴν ἕν· Λοξίου κεκλήμεθα.
Κρ. ἡμεῖς σ' ἄρ' αὖθις, ὦ ξέν', ἀντοικτίρομεν.   130
Ἰω. ὡς μὴ εἰδόθ' ἥτις μ' ἔτεκεν ἐξ ὅτου τ' ἔφυν.
Κρ. ναοῖσι δ' οἰκεῖς τοισίδ' ἢ κατὰ στέγας;
Ἰω. ἅπαν θεοῦ μοι δῶμ', ἵν' ἂν λάβῃ μ' ὕπνος.

Κρ. παῖς δ' ὢν ἀφίκου ναὸν ἢ νεανίας;

Ιω. βρέφος λέγουσιν οἱ δοκοῦντες εἰδέναι.   135

Κρ. καὶ τίς γάλακτί σ' ἐξέθρεψε Δελφίδων;

Ιω. οὐπώποτ' ἔγνων μαστόν· ἢ δ' ἔθρεψέ με ...

Κρ. τίς, ὦ ταλαίπωρ'; ὡς νοσοῦσ' ηὗρον νόσους.

Ιω. Φοίβου προφῆτις, μητέρ' ὡς νομίζομεν.

Κρ. ἐς δ' ἄνδρ' ἀφίκου τίνα τροφὴν κεκτημένος;   140

Ιω. βωμοί μ' ἔφερβον οὑπιών τ' ἀεὶ ξένος.

Κρ. τάλαινά σ' ἡ τεκοῦσα· τίς ποτ' ἦν ἄρα;

Ιω. ἀδίκημά του γυναικὸς ἐγενόμην ἴσως.

Κρ. ἔχεις δὲ βίοτον· εὖ γὰρ ἤσκησαι πέπλοις.

Ιω. τοῖς τοῦ θεοῦ κοσμούμεθ', ᾧ δουλεύομεν.   145

Κρ. οὐδ' ᾖξας εἰς ἔρευναν ἐξευρεῖν γονάς;

Ιω. ἔχω γὰρ οὐδέν, ὦ γύναι, τεκμήριον.

Κρ. φεῦ·
πέπονθέ τις σῇ μητρὶ ταῦτ' ἄλλη γυνή.

Ιω. τίς; εἰ πόνου μοι ξυλλάβοι, χαίροιμεν ἄν.

Κρ. ἧς οὕνεκ' ἦλθον δεῦρο πρὶν πόσιν μολεῖν.   150

Ιω. ποῖόν τι χρήζουσ'; ὡς ὑπουργήσω, γύναι.

Κρ. μάντευμα κρυπτὸν δεομένη Φοίβου μαθεῖν.

Ιω. λέγοις ἄν· ἡμεῖς τἄλλα προξενήσομεν.

Κρ. ἄκουε δὴ τὸν μῦθον. — ἀλλ' αἰδούμεθα.

Ιω. οὔ τἄρα πράξεις οὐδέν· ἀργὸς ἡ θεός.   155

Κρ. Φοίβῳ μιγῆναί φησί τις φίλων ἐμῶν.

Ιω. Φοίβῳ γυνὴ γεγῶσα; μὴ λέγ', ὦ ξένη.

Κρ. καὶ παῖδά γ' ἔτεκε τῷ θεῷ λάθρα πατρός.

Ιω. οὐκ ἔστιν· ἀνδρὸς ἀδικίαν αἰσχύνεται.

Κρ. οὔ φησιν αὐτή, καὶ πέπονθεν ἄθλια.   160

Ιω. τί χρῆμα δράσασ', εἰ θεῷ συνεζύγη;

Κρ. τὸν παῖδ' ὃν ἔτεκεν ἐξέθηκε δωμάτων.

Ιω. ὁ δ' ἐκτεθεὶς παῖς ποῦ 'στιν; εἰσορᾷ φάος;

Κρ. οὐκ οἶδεν οὐδείς. ταῦτα καὶ μαντεύομαι.

Ιω. εἰ δ' οὐκέτ' ἔστι, τίνι τρόπῳ διεφθάρη;   165
Κρ. θήρας σφε τὸν δύστηνον ἐλπίζει κτανεῖν.
Ιω. ποίῳ τόδ' ἔγνω χρωμένη τεκμηρίῳ;
Κρ. ἐλθοῦσ' ἵν' αὐτὸν ἐξέθηκ' οὐχ ηὗρ' ἔτι.
Ιω. ἦν δὲ σταλαγμὸς ἐν στίβῳ τις αἵματος;
Κρ. οὔ φησι. καίτοι πόλλ' ἐπεστράφη πέδον.   170
Ιω. χρόνος δὲ τίς τῷ παιδὶ διαπεπραγμένῳ;
Κρ. σοὶ ταὐτὸν ἥβης, εἴπερ ἦν, εἶχ' ἂν μέτρον.
Ιω. οὔκουν ἔτ' ἄλλον γ' ὕστερον τίκτει γόνον;
Κρ. ἀδικεῖ νιν ὁ θεός· οὐ τεκοῦσα δ' ἀθλία.
Ιω. τί δ', εἰ λάθρα νιν Φοῖβος ἐκτρέφει λαβών;   175
Κρ. τὰ κοινὰ χαίρων οὐ δίκαια δρᾷ μόνος.
Ιω. οἴμοι· προσῳδὸς ἡ τύχη τὠμῷ πάθει.
Κρ. καί σ', ὦ ξέν', οἶμαι μητέρ' ἀθλίαν ποθεῖν.
Ιω. ἆ, μή γ' ἐπ' οἰκτόν μ' ἔξαγ' οὗ 'λελήσμεθα.

(*Ion, 362–400. Ion advises Creüsa not to accuse the god of such wickedness in his own
temple. She reproaches Apollo for not answering her questions about his own sort.*)

*180–207 (Ion, 401–428) Enter Xuthus, who has been told by the oracle of
Trophonius that neither he nor Creüsa will return home childless. He speaks a few
words to Ion and enters the temple to consult Apollo's oracle. Creüsa is doubtful of
the result and leaves the stage.*

ΞΟΥΘΟΣ

    πρῶτον μὲν ὁ θεὸς τῶν ἐμῶν προσφθεγμάτων   180
    λαβὼν ἀπαρχὰς χαιρέτω, σύ τ', ὦ γύναι.
    μῶν χρόνιος ἐλθών σ' ἐξέπληξ' ὀρρωδίᾳ;
Κρ. οὐδέν γ'· ἀφίκου δ' ἐς μέριμναν. ἀλλά μοι
    λέξον, τί θέσπισμ' ἐκ Τροφωνίου φέρεις,
    παίδων ὅπως νῷν σπέρμα συγκραθήσεται;   185
Ξο. οὐκ ἠξίωσε τοῦ θεοῦ προλαμβάνειν
    μαντεύμαθ'· ἐν δ' οὖν εἶπεν· οὐκ ἄπαιδά με
    πρὸς οἶκον ἥξειν οὐδέ σ' ἐκ χρηστηρίων.
Κρ. ὦ πότνια Φοίβου μῆτερ, εἰ γὰρ αἰσίως

ἔλθοιμεν, ἅ τε νῶν συμβόλαια πρόσθεν ἦν   190
ἐς παῖδα τὸν σόν, μεταπέσοι βελτίονα.
Ξο. ἔσται τάδ'· ἀλλὰ τίς προφητεύει θεοῦ;
Ιω. ἡμεῖς τά γ' ἔξω, τῶν ἔσω δ' ἄλλοις μέλει,
οἳ πλησίον θάσσουσι τρίποδος, ὦ ξένε,
Δελφῶν ἀριστῆς, οὓς ἐκλήρωσεν πάλος.   195
Ξο. καλῶς· ἔχω δὴ πάνθ' ὅσων ἐχρήζομεν.
στείχοιμ' ἂν εἴσω· καὶ γάρ, ὡς ἐγὼ κλύω,
χρηστήριον πέπτωκε τοῖς ἐπήλυσι
κοινὸν πρὸ ναοῦ· βούλομαι δ' ἐν ἡμέρᾳ
τῆδ' — αἰσία γάρ — θεοῦ λαβεῖν μαντεύματα.   200
σὺ δ' ἀμφὶ βωμούς, ὦ γύναι, δαφνηφόρους
λαβοῦσα κλῶνας, εὐτέκνους εὔχου θεοῖς
χρησμούς μ' ἐνεγκεῖν ἐξ Ἀπόλλωνος δόμων.
Κρ. ἔσται τάδ', ἔσται. Λοξίας δ' ἐὰν θέλῃ
νῦν ἀλλὰ τὰς πρὶν ἀναλαβεῖν ἁμαρτίας,   205
ἅπας μὲν οὐ γένοιτ' ἂν εἰς ἡμᾶς φίλος,
ὅσον δὲ χρήζει — θεὸς γάρ ἐστι — δέξομαι.

(*Ion, 429–516 Ion wonders what the stranger lady means and ventures to criticise Apollo and other gods for their treatment of mortal women. The Chorus sing an ode to their native Athens and pray that their mistress may be blessed with children.*)

208–234 (*Ion, 517–542*) *Trochaic tetrameters. Xuthus re-enters and greeting Ion as his son tries to embrace him. Ion replies coldly and even threatens Xuthus with violence, until he is told that the oracle of Apollo has declared that the first person that Xuthus meets on leaving the temple is his own son and that Ion is this person; but Xuthus cannot understand who the mother can be.*

Ξο. ὦ τέκνον, χαῖρ'· ἡ γὰρ ἀρχὴ τοῦ λόγου πρέπουσά μοι.
Ιω. χαίρομεν· σὺ δ' εὖ φρόνει γε, καὶ δύ' ὄντ' εὖ πράξομεν.
Ξο. δὸς χερὸς φίλημά μοι σῆς σώματός τ' ἀμφιπτυχάς.   210
Ιω. εὖ φρονεῖς μέν; ἤ σ' ἔμηνε θεοῦ τις, ὦ ξένε, βλάβη;
Ξο. σωφρονῶ· τὰ φίλταθ' εὑρὼν οὐ φυγεῖν ἐφίεμαι.
Ιω. παῦε, μὴ ψαύσας τὰ τοῦ θεοῦ στέμματα ῥήξῃς χερί.

Ξο. ἅψομαι· κοὐ ῥυσιάζω, τἀμὰ δ' εὑρίσκω φίλα.

Ιω. οὐκ ἀπαλλάξῃ, πρὶν εἴσω τόξα πλευμόνων λαβεῖν;   215

Ξο. ὡς τί δὴ φεύγεις με, σαυτοῦ γνωρίσας τὰ φίλτατα;

Ιω. οὐ φιλῶ φρενοῦν ἀμούσους καὶ μεμηνότας ξένους.

Ξο. κτεῖνε καὶ πίμπρη· πατρὸς γάρ, ἢν κτάνῃς, ἔσῃ φονεύς.

Ιω. ποῦ δέ μοι πατὴρ σύ; ταῦτ' οὖν οὐ γέλως κλύειν ἐμοί;

Ξο. οὔ· τρέχων ὁ μῦθος ἄν σοι τἀμὰ σημήνειεν ἄν.   220

Ιω. καὶ τί μοι λέξεις;   Ξο. πατὴρ σός εἰμι καὶ σὺ παῖς
ἐμός.

Ιω. τίς λέγει τάδ';   Ξο. ὅς σ' ἔθρεψεν ὄντα Λοξίας
ἐμόν.

Ιω. μαρτυρεῖς σαυτῷ.   Ξο. τὰ τοῦ θεοῦ γ' ἐκμαθὼν
χρηστήρια.

Ιω. ἐσφάλης αἴνιγμ' ἀκούσας.   Ξο. οὐκ ἄρ' ὀρθ' ἀκούομεν.

Ιω. ὁ δὲ λόγος τίς ἐστι Φοίβου;   Ξο. τὸν συναντήσαντά
μοι . . .   225

Ιω. τίνα συνάντησιν;   Ξο. δόμων τῶνδ' ἐξιόντι τοῦ
θεοῦ

Ιω. συμφορᾶς τίνος κυρῆσαι;   Ξο. παῖδ' ἐμὸν πεφυκέναι.

Ιω. σὸν γεγῶτ', ἢ δῶρον ἄλλως;   Ξο. δῶρον, ὄντα δ'
ἐξ ἐμοῦ.

Ιω. πρῶτα δῆτ' ἐμοὶ ξυνάπτεις πόδα σόν;   Ξο. οὐκ
ἄλλῳ, τέκνον.

Ιω. ἡ τύχη πόθεν ποθ' ἥκει;   Ξο. δύο μίαν θαυμάζομεν. 230

Ιω. ἐκ τίνος δέ σοι πέφυκα μητρός;   Ξο. οὐκ ἔχω
φράσαι.

Ιω. οὐδὲ Φοῖβος εἶπε;   Ξο. τερφθεὶς τοῦτο, κεῖν' οὐκ
ἠρόμην.

Ιω. γῆς ἄρ' ἐκπέφυκα μητρός.   Ξο. οὐ πέδον τίκτει
τέκνα.

Ιω. πῶς ἂν οὖν εἴην σός;   Ξο. οὐκ οἶδ', ἀναφέρω δ' ἐς
τὸν θεόν.

(Ion, 553–949 Ion embraces his supposed father but is doubtful of the reception that he will get as a stranger in Athens if Xuthus is determined to take him there. Xuthus is going to hold a birth-sacrifice for him at a public banquet, and gives him the name of Ion, threatening the Chorus with death if they tell the news to Creüsa before the right time has come for her to learn about her stepson. Xuthus and Ion leave the stage, and the Chorus sing an ode of sympathy for Creüsa, who now enters with her old servant, and at once tell her the forbidden news. The old man suspects a plot to oust Creüsa from her home and falsely declares that Ion is a son of Xuthus by a slave-girl and that Xuthus wants to make him king of Athens on the authority of the oracle. He says that Creüsa must kill Ion, with his assistance. Creüsa bewails her lot and remembers the son that she bore to Apollo.)

235–325 (Ion, 950–991, 994–1034, 1036–1038) Creüsa tells the old man about her son's birth and he urges her to avenge herself by burning Apollo's temple or by killing her husband or at least his son. She hesitates and then thinks of the two drops of Gorgon's blood that she inherited from Erichthonius, one for healing disease, the other a deadly poison; the old servant must drop the poisonous one into Ion's cup at the feast.

Πρ. ὁ παῖς δὲ ποῦ 'στιν; ἵνα σὺ μηκέτ' ἦς ἄπαις.   235
Κρ. τέθνηκεν, ὦ γεραιέ, θηρσὶν ἐκτεθείς.
Πρ. τέθνηκ'; Ἀπόλλων δ' ὁ κακὸς οὐδὲν ἤρκεσεν;
Κρ. οὐκ ἤρκεσ'· Ἅιδου δ' ἐν δόμοις παιδεύεται.
Πρ. τίς γάρ νιν ἐξέθηκεν; οὐ γὰρ δὴ σύ γε.
Κρ. ἡμεῖς, ἐν ὄρφνῃ σπαργανώσαντες πέπλοις.   240
Πρ. οὐδὲ ξυνῄδει σοί τις ἔκθεσιν τέκνου;
Κρ. αἱ ξυμφοραί γε καὶ τὸ λανθάνειν μόνον.
Πρ. καὶ πῶς ἐν ἄντρῳ παῖδα σὸν λιπεῖν ἔτλης;
Κρ. πῶς δ'; οἰκτρὰ πολλὰ στόματος ἐκβαλοῦσ' ἔπη.
Πρ. φεῦ·
     τλήμων σὺ τόλμης, ὁ δὲ θεὸς μᾶλλον σέθεν.   245
Κρ. εἰ παῖδά γ' εἶδες χεῖρας ἐκτείνοντά μοι.
Πρ. μαστὸν διώκοντ' ἢ πρὸς ἀγκάλαις πεσεῖν;
Κρ. ἐνταῦθ', ἵν' οὐκ ὢν ἄδικ' ἔπασχεν ἐξ ἐμοῦ.
Πρ. σοὶ δ' ἐς τί δόξ' ἐσῆλθεν ἐκβαλεῖν τέκνον;

Κρ. ὡς τὸν θεὸν σῴζοντα τόν γ' αὐτοῦ γόνον.   250

Πρ. οἴμοι, δόμων σῶν ὄλβος ὡς χειμάζεται.

Κρ. τί κρᾶτα κρύψας, ὦ γέρον, δακρυρροεῖς;

Πρ. σὲ καὶ πατέρα σὸν δυστυχοῦντας εἰσορῶ.

Κρ. τὰ θνητὰ τοιαῦτ'· οὐδὲν ἐν ταὐτῷ μένει.

Πρ. μή νυν ἔτ' οἴκτων, θύγατερ, ἀντεχώμεθα.   255

Κρ. τί γάρ με χρὴ δρᾶν; ἀπορία τὸ δυστυχεῖν.

Πρ. τὸν πρῶτον ἀδικήσαντά σ' ἀποτίνου θεόν.

Κρ. καὶ πῶς τὰ κρείσσω θνητὸς οὖσ' ὑπερδράμω;

Πρ. πίμπρη τὰ σεμνὰ Λοξίου χρηστήρια.

Κρ. δέδοικα· καὶ νῦν πημάτων ἄδην ἔχω.   260

Πρ. τὰ δυνατά νυν τόλμησον, ἄνδρα σὸν κτανεῖν.

Κρ. αἰδούμεθ' εὐνὰς τὰς τόθ' ἡνίκ' ἐσθλὸς ἦν.

Πρ. σὺ δ' ἀλλὰ παῖδα τὸν ἐπὶ σοὶ πεφηνότα.

Κρ. πῶς; εἰ γὰρ εἴη δυνατόν· ὡς θέλοιμί γ' ἄν.

Πρ. ξιφηφόρους σοὺς ὁπλίσασ' ὀπάονας.   265

Κρ. στείχοιμ' ἄν· ἀλλὰ ποῦ γενήσεται τόδε;

Πρ. ἱεραῖσιν ἐν σκηναῖσιν, οὗ θοινᾷ φίλους.

Κρ. ἐπίσημον ὁ φόνος, καὶ τὸ δοῦλον ἀσθενές.

Πρ. ὤμοι, κακίζῃ· φέρε, σὺ νῦν βούλευέ τι.

Κρ. καὶ μὴν ἔχω γε δόλια καὶ δραστήρια.   270

Πρ. ἀμφοῖν ἂν εἴην τοῦνδ' ὑπηρέτης ἐγώ.

Κρ. ἄκουε τοίνυν· οἶσθα γηγενῆ μάχην;

Πρ. οἶδ', ἣν Φλέγρᾳ Γίγαντες ἔστησαν θεοῖς.

Κρ. ἐνταῦθα Γοργόν' ἔτεκε Γῆ, δεινὸν τέρας.

Πρ. ἦ παισὶν αὐτῆς σύμμαχον, θεῶν πόνον;   275

Κρ. ναί· καί νιν ἔκτειν' ἡ Διὸς Παλλὰς θεά.

Πρ. ἆρ' οὗτός ἐσθ' ὁ μῦθος ὃν κλύω πάλαι;

Κρ. ταύτης Ἀθάναν δέρος ἐπὶ στέρνοις ἔχειν.

Πρ. ἣν αἰγίδ' ὀνομάζουσι, Παλλάδος στολήν;

Κρ. τόδ' ἔσχεν ὄνομα θεῶν ὅτ' ᾖξεν ἐς δόρυ.   280

Πρ. τί δῆτα, θύγατερ, τοῦτο σοῖς ἐχθροῖς βλάβος;

Κρ. Ἐριχθόνιον οἶσθ', ἦ — ; τί δ' οὐ μέλλεις, γέρον;

Πρ. ὃν πρῶτον ὑμῶν πρόγονον ἐξανῆκε γῆ;

Κρ. τούτῳ δίδωσι Παλλὰς ὄντι νεογόνῳ ...

Πρ. τί χρῆμα; μέλλον γάρ τι προσφέρεις ἔπος. 285

Κρ. δισσοὺς σταλαγμοὺς αἵματος Γοργοῦς ἄπο.

Πρ. ἰσχὺν ἔχοντας τίνα πρὸς ἀνθρώπου φύσιν;

Κρ. τὸν μὲν θανάσιμον, τὸν δ' ἀκεσφόρον νόσων.

Πρ. ἐν τῷ καθάψασ' ἀμφὶ παιδὶ σώματος;

Κρ. χρυσοῖσι δεσμοῖς· ὁ δὲ δίδωσ' ἐμῷ πατρί. 290

Πρ. κείνου δὲ κατθανόντος ἐς σὲ ἀφίκετο;

Κρ. ναί· κἀπὶ καρπῷ γ' αὖτ' ἐγὼ χερὸς φέρω.

Πρ. πῶς οὖν κέκρανται δίπτυχον δῶρον θεᾶς;

Κρ. κοίλης μὲν ὅστις φλεβὸς ἀπέσταζεν φόνῳ ...

Πρ. τί τῷδε χρῆσθαι; δύνασιν ἐκφέρει τίνα; 295

Κρ. νόσους ἀπείργει καὶ τροφὰς ἔχει βίου.

Πρ. ὁ δεύτερος δ' ἀριθμὸς ὢν λέγεις τί δρᾷ;

Κρ. κτείνει, δρακόντων ἰὸς ὢν τῶν Γοργόνος.

Πρ. ἐς ἓν δὲ κραθέντ' αὐτὸν ἢ χωρὶς φορεῖς;

Κρ. χωρίς· κακῷ γὰρ ἐσθλὸν οὐ συμμείγνυται. 300

Πρ. ὦ φιλτάτη παῖ, πάντ' ἔχεις ὅσων σε δεῖ.

Κρ. τούτῳ θανεῖται παῖς· σὺ δ' ὁ κτείνων ἔσῃ.

Πρ. ποῦ καὶ τί δράσας; σὸν λέγειν, τολμᾶν δ' ἐμόν.

Κρ. ἐν ταῖς Ἀθήναις, δῶμ' ὅταν τοὐμὸν μόλῃ.

Πρ. οὐκ εὖ τόδ' εἶπας· καὶ σὺ γὰρ τοὐμὸν ψέγεις. 305

Κρ. πῶς; ἆρ' ὑπείδου τοῦθ' ὃ κἄμ' ἐσέρχεται;

Πρ. σὺ παῖδα δόξεις διολέσαι, κεἰ μὴ κτενεῖς.

Κρ. ὀρθῶς· φθονεῖν γάρ φασι μητρυιὰς τέκνοις.

Πρ. αὐτοῦ νυν αὐτὸν κτεῖν', ἵν' ἀρνήσῃ φόνους.

Κρ. προλάζυμαι γοῦν τῷ χρόνῳ τῆς ἡδονῆς. 310

Πρ. καὶ σόν γε λήσεις πόσιν ἅ σε σπεύδει λαθεῖν.

Κρ. οἶσθ' οὖν ὃ δρᾶσον; χειρὸς ἐξ ἐμῆς λαβὼν
χρύσωμ' Ἀθάνας τόδε, παλαιὸν ὄργανον,
ἐλθὼν ἵν' ἡμῖν βουθυτεῖ λάθρα πόσις,

δείπνων ὅταν λήγωσι καὶ σπονδὰς θεοῖς   315
μέλλωσι λείβειν, ἐν πέπλοις ἔχων τόδε
κάθες βαλὼν ἐς πῶμα τῷ νεανίᾳ
τῷ τῶν ἐμῶν μέλλοντι δεσπόζειν δόμων.
κἄνπερ διέλθῃ λαιμόν, οὔποθ' ἵξεται
κλεινὰς Ἀθήνας, κατθανὼν δ' αὐτοῦ μενεῖ.   320

(*Ion, 1039–1176 The Chorus prays that their mistress's scheme may be successful. Another servant of Creüsa now enters and says that Xuthus told Ion to prepare the festal tent for the banquet while he himself went up the mountain to make the birth-sacrifice there. The tent was made ready and the visitors started to feast.*)

321–370 (Ion, 1177–1226) The servant goes on to tell how the old slave called for larger goblets when the libations to the gods began. He gave Ion a full cup into which he had dropped the poison, but before Ion could drink it another slave uttered an ill-omened word and so Ion poured out his wine on to the ground and told all the other guests to do the same. A flock of doves flew in and drank the spilt wine, and the bird that tasted Ion's fell dead in agony. Ion compelled the old man to confess the whole plot and an emergency court of law condemned Creüsa to be flung down from a rock; everyone went off to find her.

ΘΕΡΑΠΩΝ

ἐπεὶ δ' ἐς αὐλοὺς ἧκον ἐς κρατῆρά τε
κοινόν, γέρων ἔλεξ'. "ἀφαρπάζειν χρεὼν
οἰνηρὰ τεύχη σμικρά, μεγάλα δ' ἐσφέρειν,
ὡς θᾶσσον ἔλθωσ' οἵδ' ἐς ἡδονὰς φρενῶν."
ἦν δὴ φερόντων μόχθος ἀργυρηλάτους   325
χρυσέας τε φιάλας· ὁ δὲ λαβὼν ἐξαίρετον,
ὡς τῷ νέῳ δὴ δεσπότῃ χάριν φέρων,
ἔδωκε πλῆρες τεῦχος, εἰς οἶνον βαλὼν
ὅ φασι δοῦναι φάρμακον δραστήριον
δέσποιναν, ὡς παῖς ὁ νέος ἐκλίποι φάος·   330
κοὐδεὶς τάδ' ᾔδειν. ἐν χεροῖν ἔχοντι δὲ
σπονδὰς μετ' ἄλλων παιδὶ τῷ πεφηνότι

βλασφημίαν τις οἰκετῶν ἐφθέγξατο·
ὁ δ', ὡς ἐν ἱερῷ μάντεσίν τ' ἐσθλοῖς τραφείς,
οἰωνὸν ἔθετο, κἀκέλευσ' ἄλλον νέον   335
κρατῆρα πληροῦν· τὰς δὲ πρὶν σπονδὰς θεοῦ
δίδωσι γαίᾳ, πᾶσί τ' ἐκσπένδειν λέγει.
σιγὴ δ' ὑπῆλθεν. ἐκ δ' ἐπίμπλαμεν δρόσου
κρατῆρας ἱεροὺς Βυβλίνου τε πώματος.
κἂν τῷδε μόχθῳ πτηνὸς ἐσπίπτει στέγην   340
κῶμος πελειῶν — Λοξίου γὰρ ἐν δόμοις
ἄτρεστα ναίουσ' — ὡς δ' ἀπέσπεισαν μέθυ,
ἐς αὐτὸ χείλη πώματος κεχρημέναι
καθῆκαν, εἷλκον δ' εὐπτέρους ἐς αὐχένας.
καὶ ταῖς μὲν ἄλλαις ἄνοσος ἦν λοιβὴ θεοῦ·   345
ἣ δ' ἕζετ' ἔνθ' ὁ καινὸς ἔσπεισεν γόνος,
ποτοῦ τ' ἐγεύσατ', εὐθὺς εὔπτερον δέμας
ἔσεισε κἀβάκχευσεν, ἐκ δ' ἔκλαγξ' ὄπα
ἀξύνετον αἰάζουσ'· ἐθάμβησεν δὲ πᾶς
θοινατόρων ὅμιλος ὄρνιθος πόνους.   350
θνῄσκει δ' ἀπασπαίρουσα, φοινικοσκελεῖς
χηλὰς παρεῖσα. γυμνὰ δ' ἐκ πέπλων μέλη
ὑπὲρ τραπέζης ἦχ' ὁ μαντευτὸς γόνος,
βοᾷ δέ· "τίς μ' ἔμελλεν ἀνθρώπων κτενεῖν;
σήμαινε, πρέσβυ· σὴ γὰρ ἡ προθυμία,   355
καὶ πῶμα χειρὸς σῆς ἐδεξάμην πάρα."
εὐθὺς δ' ἐρευνᾷ γραῖαν ὠλένην λαβών,
ἐπ' αὐτοφώρῳ πρέσβυν ὡς ἔχονθ' ἕλοι.
ὤφθη δὲ καὶ κατεῖπ' ἀναγκασθεὶς μόγις
τόλμας Κρεούσης πώματός τε μηχανάς.   360
θεῖ δ' εὐθὺς ἔξω συλλαβὼν θοινάτορας
ὁ πυθόχρηστος Λοξίου νεανίας,
κἂν κοιράνοισι Πυθικοῖς σταθεὶς λέγει·
" ὦ γαῖα σεμνή, τῆς Ἐρεχθέως ὕπο,

ξένης γυναικός, φαρμάκοισι θνήσκομεν." 365
Δελφῶν δ' ἄνακτες ὥρισαν πετρορριφῆ
θανεῖν ἐμὴν δέσποιναν οὐ ψήφῳ μιᾷ,
τὸν ἱερὸν ὡς κτείνουσαν ἔν τ' ἀνακτόροις
φόνον τιθεῖσαν. πᾶσα δὲ ζητεῖ πόλις
τὴν ἀθλίως σπεύσασαν ἀθλίαν ὁδόν. 370

(*Ion, 1227–1319* The Chorus bewail their own and their mistress's future fate. Creüsa enters and on their advice takes refuge at the altar, where Ion, entering, finds her. He tells his attendants to seize the would-be murderess, although she is in sanctuary, but Creüsa defends her conduct and refuses to leave the altar.)

371–489 (*Ion, 1320–1367, 1369–1444*) Enter the Pythian priestess, who warns Ion not to commit sacrilege in the temple. Before leaving the stage she gives him the cradle in which she found him in infancy, containing relics that may help him to find his mother. Creüsa recognises the cradle and embraces her son, who thinks she is mad to leave the altar, but she describes the pattern that she once wove into the clothes left in the cradle, the necklace of golden serpents that she put round his neck to protect him, and the olive-wreath, still miraculously fresh, which she placed on his head. Ion at last acknowledges her as his mother, and they embrace one another with great joy.

ΠΡΟΦΗΤΙΣ

ἐπίσχες, ὦ παῖ· τρίποδα γὰρ χρηστήριον
λιποῦσα θριγκοῦ τοῦδ' ὑπερβάλλω πόδα
Φοίβου προφῆτις, τρίποδος ἀρχαῖον νόμον
σῴζουσα, πασῶν Δελφίδων ἐξαίρετος.
Ιω. χαῖρ', ὦ φίλη μοι μῆτερ, οὐ τεκοῦσά περ. 375
Πρ. ἀλλ' οὖν λεγώμεθ'· ἡ φάτις δ' οὔ μοι πικρά.
Ιω. ἤκουσας ὥς μ' ἔκτεινεν ἥδε μηχαναῖς;
Πρ. ἤκουσα· καὶ σὺ δ' ὠμὸς ὢν ἁμαρτάνεις.
Ιω. οὐ χρή με τοὺς κτείνοντας ἀνταπολλύναι;
Πρ. προγονοῖς δάμαρτες δυσμενεῖς ἀεί ποτε. 380
Ιω. ἡμεῖς δὲ μητρυιαῖς γε πάσχοντες κακῶς.

Πρ. μὴ ταῦτα· λείπων ἱερὰ καὶ στείχων πάτραν . . .
Ιω. τί δή με δρᾶσαι νουθετούμενον χρεών;
Πρ. καθαρὸς Ἀθήνας ἔλθ' ὑπ' οἰωνῶν καλῶν.
Ιω. καθαρὸς ἅπας τοι πολεμίους ὃς ἂν κτάνῃ.   385
Πρ. μὴ σύ γε· παρ' ἡμῶν δ' ἔκλαβ' οὓς ἔχω λόγους.
Ιω. λέγοις ἄν· εὔνους δ' οὖσ' ἐρεῖς ὅσ' ἂν λέγῃς.
Πρ. ὁρᾷς τόδ' ἄγγος χερὸς ὑπ' ἀγκάλαις ἐμαῖς;
Ιω. ὁρῶ παλαιὰν ἀντίπηγ' ἐν στέμμασιν.
Πρ. ἐν τῇδέ σ' ἔλαβον νεόγονον βρέφος ποτέ.   390
Ιω. τί φής; ὁ μῦθος εἰσενήνεκται νέος.
Πρ. σιγῇ γὰρ εἶχον αὐτά· νῦν δὲ δείκνυμεν.
Ιω. πῶς οὖν ἔκρυπτες τόδε λαβοῦσ' ἡμᾶς πάλαι;
Πρ. ὁ θεός σ' ἐβούλετ' ἐν δόμοις ἔχειν λάτριν.
Ιω. νῦν δ' οὐχὶ χρῄζει; τῷ τόδε γνῶναί με χρή;   395
Πρ. πατέρα κατειπὼν τῆσδέ σ' ἐκπέμπει χθονός.
Ιω. σὺ δ' ἐκ κελευσμῶν ἢ πόθεν σῴζεις τάδε;
Πρ. ἐνθύμιόν μοι τότε τίθησι Λοξίας . . .
Ιω. τί χρῆμα δρᾶσαι; λέγε, πέραινε σοὺς λόγους.
Πρ. σῶσαι τόδ' εὕρημ' ἐς τὸν ὄντα νῦν χρόνον.   400
Ιω. ἔχει δέ μοι τί κέρδος . . . ἢ τίνα βλάβην;
Πρ. ἐνθάδε κέκρυπται σπάργαν' οἷς ἐνῆσθα σύ.
Ιω. μητρὸς τάδ' ἡμῖν ἐκφέρεις ζητήματα;
Πρ. ἐπεί γ' ὁ δαίμων βούλεται· πάροιθε δ' οὔ.
Ιω. ὦ μακαρίων μοι φασμάτων ἥδ' ἡμέρα.   405
Πρ. λαβών νυν αὐτὰ τὴν τεκοῦσαν ἐκπόνει.
Ιω. πᾶσάν γ' ἐπελθὼν Ἀσιάδ' Εὐρώπης θ' ὅρους.
Πρ. γνώσῃ τάδ' αὐτός. τοῦ θεοῦ δ' ἕκατί σε
ἔθρεψά τ', ὦ παῖ, καὶ τάδ' ἀποδίδωμί σοι,
ἃ κεῖνος ἀκέλευστόν μ' ἐβουλήθη λαβεῖν   410
σῶσαί θ'· ὅτου δ' ἐβούλεθ' οὕνεκ', οὐκ ἔχω,
ᾔδει δὲ θνητῶν οὔτις ἀνθρώπων τάδε
ἔχοντας ἡμᾶς, οὐδ' ἵν' ἦν κεκρυμμένα.

καὶ χαῖρ'· ἴσον γάρ σ' ὡς τεκοῦσ' ἀσπάζομαι.

Ιω. φεῦ φεῦ· κατ' ὄσσων ὡς ὑγρὸν βάλλω δάκρυ,   415
ἐκεῖσε τὸν νοῦν δούς, ὅθ' ἡ τεκοῦσά με
κρυφαῖα νυμφευθεῖσ' ἀπημπόλα λάθρα
καὶ μαστὸν οὐχ ὑπέσχεν· ἀλλ' ἀνώνυμος
ἐν θεοῦ μελάθροις εἶχον οἰκέτην βίον.
τὰ τοῦ θεοῦ μὲν χρηστά, τοῦ δὲ δαίμονος   420
βαρέα· χρόνον γὰρ ὅν με χρῆν ἐν ἀγκάλαις
μητρὸς τρυφῆσαι καί τι τερφθῆναι βίου,
ἀπεστερήθην φιλτάτης μητρὸς τροφῆς.
τλήμων δὲ χἠ τεκοῦσά μ'· ὡς ταὐτὸν πάθος
πέπονθε, παιδὸς ἀπολέσασα χαρμονάς.   425
   καὶ νῦν λαβὼν τήνδ' ἀντίπηγ' οἴσω θεῷ
ἀνάθημ', ἵν' εὕρω μηδὲν ὧν οὐ βούλομαι.
εἰ γάρ με δούλη τυγχάνει τεκοῦσά τις,
εὑρεῖν κάκιον μητέρ' ἢ σιγῶντ' ἐᾶν.
ὦ Φοῖβε, ναοῖς ἀνατίθημι τήνδε σοῖς . . .   430
   καίτοι τί πάσχω; τοῦ θεοῦ προθυμίᾳ
πολεμῶ, τὰ μητρὸς σύμβολ' ὃς σέσωκέ μοι.
ἀνοικτέον τάδ' ἐστὶ καὶ τολμητέον·
τὰ γὰρ πεπρωμέν' οὐχ ὑπερβαίην ποτ' ἄν.
ὦ στέμμαθ' ἱερά, τί ποτέ μοι κεκεύθατε,   435
καὶ σύνδεθ', οἷσι τἄμ' ἐφρουρήθη φίλα;
   ἰδοὺ περίπτυγμ' ἀντίπηγος εὐκύκλου
ὡς οὐ γεγήρακ' ἔκ τινος θεηλάτου,
εὑρώς τ' ἄπεστι πλεγμάτων· ὁ δ' ἐν μέσῳ
χρόνος πολύς δὴ τοῖσδε θησαυρίσμασιν.   440

Κρ. τί δῆτα φάσμα τῶν ἀνελπίστων ὁρῶ;
Ιω. σίγα σύ· πολλὰ καὶ πάροιθεν οἶσθά μοι . . .
Κρ. οὐκ ἐν σιωπῇ τἀμά· μή με νουθέτει.
ὁρῶ γὰρ ἄγγος οὗ 'ξέθηκ' ἐγώ ποτε . . .
σέ γ', ὦ τέκνον μοι, βρέφος ἔτ' ὄντα νήπιον,   445

λείψω δὲ βωμὸν τόνδε, κεἰ θανεῖν με χρή.

Ιω. λάζυσθε τήνδε· θεομανὴς γὰρ ἥλατο
βωμοῦ λιποῦσα ξόανα· δεῖτε δ' ὠλένας.

Κρ. σφάζοντες οὐ λήγοιτ' ἄν· ὡς ἀνθέξομαι
καὶ τῆσδε καὶ σοῦ τῶν τε σῶν κεκρυμμένων.   450

Ιω. τάδ' οὐχὶ δεινά; ῥυσιάζομαι δόλῳ.

Κρ. οὔκ, ἀλλὰ σοῖς φίλοισιν εὑρίσκῃ φίλος.

Ιω. ἐγὼ φίλος σός; κᾆτά μ' ἔκτεινες λάθρα;

Κρ. παῖς γ', εἰ τόδ' ἐστὶ τοῖς τεκοῦσι φίλτατον.

Ιω. παῦσαι πλέκουσα. — λήψομαί σ' ἐγὼ καλῶς.   455

Κρ. ἐς τοῦθ' ἱκοίμην, τοῦδε τοξεύω, τέκνον.

Ιω. κενὸν τόδ' ἄγγος ἢ στέγει πλήρωμά τι;

Κρ. σά γ' ἔνδυθ', οἷσί σ' ἐξέθηκ' ἐγώ ποτε.

Ιω. καὶ τοὔνομ' αὐτῶν ἐξερεῖς πρὶν εἰσιδεῖν;

Κρ. κἂν μὴ φράσω γε, κατθανεῖν ὑφίσταμαι.   460

Ιω. λέγ'· ὡς ἔχει τι δεινὸν ἥ γε τόλμα σου.

Κρ. σκέψασθ' ὃ παῖς ποτ' οὖσ' ὕφασμ' ὕφην' ἐγώ.

Ιω. ποῖόν τι; πολλὰ παρθένων ὑφάσματα.

Κρ. οὐ τέλεον, οἷον δ' ἐκδίδαγμα κερκίδος.

Ιω. μορφὴν ἔχον τίν'; ὥς με μὴ ταύτῃ λάβῃς.   465

Κρ. Γοργὼ μὲν ἐν μέσοισιν ἠτρίοις πέπλων.

Ιω. ὦ Ζεῦ, τίς ἡμᾶς ἐκκυνηγετεῖ πότμος;

Κρ. κεκρασπέδωται δ' ὄφεσιν αἰγίδος τρόπον.

Ιω. ἰδού·
τόδ' ἔσθ' ὕφασμα· θέσφαθ' ὡς εὑρίσκομεν.

Κρ. ὦ χρόνιον ἱστῶν παρθένευμα τῶν ἐμῶν.   470

Ιω. ἔστιν τι πρὸς τῷδ', ἢ μόνῳ τῷδ' εὐτυχεῖς;

Κρ. δράκοντες· ἀρχαῖόν τι παγχρύσῳ γένυι
δώρημ' Ἀθάνας, ᾗ τέκν' ἐντρέφειν λέγει,
Ἐριχθονίου γε τοῦ πάλαι μιμήματα.

Ιω. τί δρᾶν, τί χρῆσθαι, φράζε μοι, χρυσώματι;   475

Κρ. δέραια παιδὶ νεογόνῳ φέρειν, τέκνον.

Ιω. ἔνεισιν οἶδε· τὸ δὲ τρίτον ποθῶ μαθεῖν.

Κρ. στέφανον ἐλαίας ἀμφέθηκά σοι τότε,
    ἣν πρῶτ' Ἀθάνα σκόπελον εἰσηνέγκατο,
    ὅς, εἴπερ ἔστιν, οὔποτ' ἐκλείπει χλόην,   480
    θάλλει δ', ἐλαίας ἐξ ἀκηράτου γεγώς.

Ιω. ὦ φιλτάτη μοι μῆτερ, ἄσμενός σ' ἰδὼν
    πρὸς ἀσμένας πέπτωκα σὰς παρηίδας.

Κρ. ὦ τέκνον, ὦ φῶς μητρὶ κρεῖσσον ἡλίου —
    συγγνώσεται γὰρ ὁ θεός — ἐν χεροῖν σ' ἔχω,   485
    ἄελπτον εὕρημ', ὃν κατὰ γᾶς ἐνέρων
    χθόνιον μετὰ Περσεφόνας τ' ἐδόκουν ναίειν.

Ιω. ἀλλ', ὦ φίλη μοι μῆτερ, ἐν χεροῖν σέθεν
    ὁ κατθανών τε κοὐ θανὼν φαντάζομαι.

(*Ion, 1445-1622* Creüsa tells Ion that his father is Apollo, *who has given him to Xuthus to inherit the name and house of a mortal man. Ion is not quite convinced of this, until Athena appears as a* dea ex machina, *i.e. a deity suspended in a kind of crane in the air above the stage, and says that she has come from Apollo to tell Ion that he is truly Apollo's son. He is to go to Athens and become king, and from him will spring the Ionian Greeks. Xuthus and Creüsa will have two sons, Dorus and Achaeus, ancestors of the Dorians and Achaeans, but Xuthus must continue to think that he is Ion's father. Thus all ends happily.*)

THUCYDIDES

Introduction

THUCYDIDES, the son of Olorus, an Athenian, was born in about 460 B.C. and died in about 400. His family had connections with Thrace (on the northern shores of the Aegean), where it obtained wealth from gold-mines, and he is said to have been a pupil of the orator Antiphon. He tells us himself that he began to collect materials for his history at the outbreak of the Peloponnesian War in 431 and suffered from the great Plague that attacked Athens in 430; that he was elected one of the ten generals in 424, but, because he failed to relieve Amphipolis in the campaign against the great Spartan general Brasidas, he was exiled in that year and remained in exile for twenty years, with the result that he was able to visit the Peloponnese and observe the affairs of both sides in the war. He returned from exile to Athens in 404 and may have spent the last years of his life in Thrace. His history ends suddenly, unfinished, while describing the events of 411, and his tomb, perhaps a cenotaph, was in a suburb of Athens next to the tombs of Miltiades and Cimon, a famous father and son of an earlier generation of Athenians, to whom Thucydides' family was related.

The Peloponnesian War between Athens and Sparta (Lacedaemon) broke out in 431, was interrupted for a brief period in 421, and ended with the total defeat of Athens in 404. It was a struggle between the democratic sea-power of Ionian Athens and her allies on the one side and the oligarchic land-power of Dorian Sparta and her Peloponnesian allies on the other. The Athenians had made the Confederacy of Delos, which was a combination of Aegean islands and some Greek cities of Asia Minor formed under the leadership of Athens in 478 to resist Persian aggression, into an Athenian maritime empire which roused the hostility of Sparta and together with its threat to the commercial prosperity of Corinth led to the outbreak of war. The last straw was the Theban attack on Plataea, an old ally of Athens, before war was officially declared. For the first ten years the Spartans (Lacedaemonians) merely invaded Attica nearly every summer and ravaged the countryside, while the Athenians generally refused to risk a land battle and relied on maritime operations, during which they secured a base on Spartan soil at Pylos in 425. The Spartan Brasidas won some victories in Thrace, including the capture of Amphipolis (which caused the exile of Thucydides), but his death and that of the Athenian war-monger Cleon allowed the Peace of Nicias to be made in 421.

This peace did not last long and fighting soon broke out again, largely inspired by the Athenian aristocrat Alcibiades, who in 415 persuaded his fellow-citizens to send a great expedition against Syracuse, a colony of Corinth and the leading city of Sicily. After a successful start the expedition ended in complete disaster in 413, but Athens continued the struggle until Sparta made an alliance with Persia, and in spite of Athenian victories at sea their defeat at the naval battle of Aegospotami in 405 forced the Athenians to accept Spartan terms in the following year when the war at last came to an end.

Thucydides is the first critical and scientific historian,

and one of the greatest of any age. His account of ordinary events is straightforward, clear, vivid, and strictly accurate, for he took much trouble to verify the facts; but when he describes events of great historical importance, or inserts the speeches which he puts into the mouths of the principal characters (not verbatim reports of what they actually said, but conveying in the historian's words the gist of the speakers' arguments) his style becomes elaborate, complex, and so closely-packed that strict syntax is sometimes abandoned and the meaning requires careful working out. As befits one who was himself a commander in the field, his accounts of naval and military operations are factual and easily understood. He is generally unbiased in his judgments on individuals, though once or twice his personal feelings seem to show through his impartiality, as in his account of the demagogue Cleon who did Athens great damage and was perhaps mainly responsible for Thucydides' exile after Amphipolis. He himself calls his history a κτῆμα ἐς αἰεί, 'a possession for ever'. Among the most famous passages in his history are the Funeral Speech of Pericles (the great Athenian statesman whom he greatly admired) and the account of the Plague at Athens, both in Book II, and the Sicilian Expedition in Books VI and VII. The extracts from Books II and III which are included in this book, describing in detail the siege of Plataea, are strikingly dramatic and give an excellent idea of Thucydides' narrative power; a short (and easy) selection from the speeches is included.

The Siege of Plataea

In 446 B.C. the Thirty Years Peace was made between Athens and Sparta, together with their allies on each side. Athens had with her the Confederacy of Delos (mentioned in the Introduction), Plataea in Boeotia, and a few cities and islands in the west of Greece; Sparta had the whole of the Peloponnese (except Argos and Achaea), Corinth, Megara, Boeotia (except Plataea) in northern Greece, and the remaining cities and islands in the west of Greece. Athens had great financial resources and a large and well-trained fleet; Sparta was pre-eminent on land and had at first only the Corinthian navy, which was inferior to that of Athens.

The Spartans' and Corinthians' fear and jealousy of Athens made war inevitable, but three separate incidents led up to it. They were: (i) party strife in 433 at Epidamnus, a colony of Corcyra, itself a colony of Corinth, in consequence of which Athens agreed to help Corcyra against Corinth; (ii) the revolt in 432 of Potidaea (in the peninsula of Chalcidice in the northern Aegean) an ally of Athens but a colony of Corinth, during which Athens besieged the town and defeated the Corinthians, who urged the Spartans to declare war on Athens; and (iii) the Megarian Decree, also in 432, whereby the Athenians excluded Megara from all the markets of the Athenian empire, thus threatening with ruin an important member of the Peloponnesian League. The League therefore decided to make war on

Athens, but nearly a year was taken up with trivial demands on both sides, and the first blow was actually struck by the Theban attack on her neighbour and old enemy Plataea (both in Boeotia) without warning in 431, while the Thirty Years Peace was still in being.

1 (Thuc. II, 2, 1–4) Early April 431 B.C. An advance party of 300 Thebans are brought into Plataea at night by some Plataean traitors and call upon the citizens to abandon their alliance with Athens and return to the ancient Boeotian confederacy.

1   Τέσσαρα μὲν γὰρ καὶ δέκα ἔτη ἐνέμειναν αἱ τριακοντούτεις σπονδαὶ αἳ ἐγένοντο μετὰ Εὐβοίας ἅλωσιν· τῷ δὲ πέμπτῳ καὶ δεκάτῳ ἔτει μετὰ τὴν ἐν Ποτειδαίᾳ μάχην μηνὶ ἕκτῳ καὶ ἅμα ἦρι ἀρχομένῳ Θηβαίων ἄνδρες ὀλίγῳ πλείους τριακοσίων (ἡγοῦντο 5 δὲ αὐτῶν βοιωταρχοῦντες Πυθάγγελός τε ὁ Φυλείδου καὶ Διέμπορος ὁ Ὀνητορίδου) ἐσῆλθον περὶ πρῶτον ὕπνον ξὺν ὅπλοις ἐς Πλάταιαν τῆς Βοιωτίας οὖσαν
2 Ἀθηναίων ξυμμαχίδα. ἐπηγάγοντο δὲ καὶ ἀνέῳξαν τὰς πύλας Πλαταιῶν ἄνδρες, Ναυκλείδης τε καὶ οἱ μετ' 10 αὐτοῦ, βουλόμενοι ἰδίας ἕνεκα δυνάμεως ἄνδρας τε τῶν πολιτῶν τοὺς σφίσιν ὑπεναντίους διαφθεῖραι καὶ τὴν
3 πόλιν Θηβαίοις προσποιῆσαι. ἔπραξαν δὲ ταῦτα δι' Εὐρυμάχου τοῦ Λεοντιάδου ἀνδρὸς Θηβαίων δυνατω-τάτου. προϊδόντες γὰρ οἱ Θηβαῖοι ὅτι ἔσοιτο ὁ 15 πόλεμος, ἐβούλοντο τὴν Πλάταιαν αἰεὶ σφίσι διάφορον οὖσαν ἔτι ἐν εἰρήνῃ τε καὶ τοῦ πολέμου μήπω φανεροῦ καθεστῶτος προκαταλαβεῖν. ᾗ καὶ ῥᾷον ἔλαθον
4 ἐσελθόντες, φυλακῆς οὐ προκαθεστηκυίας. θέμενοι δὲ ἐς τὴν ἀγορὰν τὰ ὅπλα τοῖς μὲν ἐπαγαγομένοις οὐκ 20 ἐπείθοντο ὥστ' εὐθὺς ἔργου ἔχεσθαι καὶ ἰέναι ἐς τὰς οἰκίας τῶν ἐχθρῶν, γνώμην δὲ ἐποιοῦντο κηρύγμασί τε

χρήσασθαι ἐπιτηδείοις καὶ ἐς ξύμβασιν μᾶλλον καὶ
φιλίαν τὴν πόλιν ἀγαγεῖν (καὶ ἀνεῖπεν ὁ κῆρυξ, εἴ τις
βούλεται κατὰ τὰ πάτρια τῶν πάντων Βοιωτῶν ξυμ- 25
μαχεῖν, τίθεσθαι παρ' αὐτοὺς τὰ ὅπλα), νομίζοντες
σφίσι ῥᾳδίως τούτῳ τῷ τρόπῳ προσχωρήσειν τὴν πόλιν.

2 (II, 3) *The Plataeans at first agree to discuss terms, but on realising the small
numbers of the Thebans they secretly collect a force and attack them while it is still
dark.*

1   Οἱ δὲ Πλαταιῆς, ὡς ᾔσθοντο ἔνδον τε ὄντας τοὺς
Θηβαίους καὶ ἐξαπιναίως κατειλημμένην τὴν πόλιν,
καταδείσαντες καὶ νομίσαντες πολλῷ πλείους ἐσελη- 30
λυθέναι (οὐ γὰρ ἑώρων ἐν τῇ νυκτί), πρὸς ξύμβασιν
ἐχώρησαν καὶ τοὺς λόγους δεξάμενοι ἡσύχαζον, ἄλλως
τε καὶ ἐπειδὴ ἐς οὐδένα οὐδὲν ἐνεωτέριζον. πράσσοντες
2 δέ πως ταῦτα κατενόησαν οὐ πολλοὺς τοὺς Θηβαίους
ὄντας καὶ ἐνόμισαν ἐπιθέμενοι ῥᾳδίως κρατήσειν· τῷ 35
γὰρ πλήθει τῶν Πλαταιῶν οὐ βουλομένῳ ἦν τῶν
Ἀθηναίων ἀφίστασθαι. ἐδόκει οὖν ἐπιχειρητέα εἶναι
3 καὶ ξυνελέγοντο διορύσσοντες τοὺς κοινοὺς τοίχους
παρ' ἀλλήλους, ὅπως μὴ διὰ τῶν ὁδῶν φανεροὶ ὦσιν
ἰόντες, ἁμάξας τε ἄνευ τῶν ὑποζυγίων ἐς τὰς 40
ὁδοὺς καθίστασαν, ἵν' ἀντὶ τείχους ᾖ, καὶ τἆλλα
ἐξήρτυον ᾗ ἕκαστον ἐφαίνετο πρὸς τὰ παρόντα ξύμ-
4 φορον ἔσεσθαι. ἐπεὶ δὲ ὡς ἐκ τῶν δυνατῶν ἑτοῖμα
ἦν, φυλάξαντες ἔτι νύκτα καὶ αὐτὸ τὸ περίορθρον ἐχώρουν ἐκ τῶν οἰκιῶν ἐπ' αὐτούς, ὅπως μὴ κατὰ φῶς 45
θαρσαλεωτέροις οὖσι προσφέρωνται καὶ σφίσιν ἐκ τοῦ
ἴσου γίγνωνται, ἀλλ' ἐν νυκτὶ φοβερώτεροι ὄντες
ἥσσους ὦσι τῆς σφετέρας ἐμπειρίας τῆς κατὰ τὴν
πόλιν. προσέβαλόν τε εὐθὺς καὶ ἐς χεῖρας ᾖσαν κατὰ
τάχος.   50

3 (II, 4) After a short resistance the Thebans turn and flee, but only a few manage to escape from the city; most of them are trapped in a building near the wall, and they and the other survivors surrender unconditionally.

1 Οἱ δ' ὡς ἔγνωσαν ἠπατημένοι, ξυνεστρέφοντό τε ἐν
σφίσιν αὐτοῖς καὶ τὰς προσβολὰς ᾗ προσπίπτοιεν

2 ἀπεωθοῦντο. καὶ δὶς μὲν ἢ τρὶς ἀπεκρούσαντο, ἔπειτα
πολλῷ θορύβῳ αὐτῶν τε προσβαλόντων καὶ τῶν
γυναικῶν καὶ τῶν οἰκετῶν ἅμα ἀπὸ τῶν οἰκιῶν κραυγῇ 55
τε καὶ ὀλολυγῇ χρωμένων λίθοις τε καὶ κεράμῳ βαλλόντων, καὶ ὑετοῦ ἅμα διὰ νυκτὸς πολλοῦ ἐπιγενομένου,
ἐφοβήθησαν καὶ τραπόμενοι ἔφυγον διὰ τῆς πόλεως,
ἄπειροι μὲν ὄντες οἱ πλείους ἐν σκότῳ καὶ πηλῷ τῶν
διόδων ᾗ χρὴ σωθῆναι (καὶ γὰρ τελευτῶντος τοῦ μηνὸς 60
τὰ γιγνόμενα ἦν), ἐμπείρους δὲ ἔχοντες τοὺς διώκοντας,

3 ὥστε διεφθείροντο οἱ πολλοί. τῶν δὲ Πλαταιῶν τις τὰς
πύλας ᾗ ἐσῆλθον καὶ αἵπερ ἦσαν ἀνεῳγμέναι μόναι,
ἔκλῃσε στυρακίῳ ἀκοντίου ἀντὶ βαλάνου χρησάμενος ἐς
τὸν μοχλόν, ὥστε μηδὲ ταύτῃ ἔτι ἔξοδον εἶναι. 65

4 διωκόμενοί τε κατὰ τὴν πόλιν οἱ μέν τινες αὐτῶν ἐπὶ
τὸ τεῖχος ἀναβάντες ἔρριψαν ἐς τὸ ἔξω σφᾶς αὐτοὺς καὶ
διεφθάρησαν οἱ πλείους, οἱ δὲ κατὰ πύλας ἐρήμους
γυναικὸς δούσης πέλεκυν λαθόντες καὶ διακόψαντες τὸν
μοχλὸν ἐξῆλθον οὐ πολλοί (αἴσθησις γὰρ ταχεῖα ἐπεγέ- 70
νετο), ἄλλοι δὲ ἄλλῃ τῆς πόλεως σποράδην ἀπώλλυντο.

5 τὸ δὲ πλεῖστον καὶ ὅσον μάλιστα ἦν ξυνεστραμμένον
ἐσπίπτουσιν ἐς οἴκημα μέγα, ὃ ἦν τοῦ τείχους καὶ αἱ
θύραι ἀνεῳγμέναι ἔτυχον αὐτοῦ, οἰόμενοι πύλας τὰς

6 θύρας τοῦ οἰκήματος εἶναι καὶ ἄντικρυς δίοδον ἐς τὸ 75
ἔξω. ὁρῶντες δὲ αὐτοὺς οἱ Πλαταιῆς ἀπειλημμένους
ἐβουλεύοντο εἴτε κατακαύσωσιν ὥσπερ ἔχουσιν, ἐμπρή-

7 σαντες τὸ οἴκημα, εἴτε τι ἄλλο χρήσωνται. τέλος δὲ
οὗτοί τε καὶ ὅσοι ἄλλοι τῶν Θηβαίων περιῆσαν κατὰ

τὴν πόλιν πλανώμενοι ξυνέβησαν τοῖς Πλαταιεῦσι παρα- 80
δοῦναι τὸ ὅπλα καὶ σφᾶς αὐτοὺς χρήσασθαι ὅ τι ἂν
8 βούλωνται. οἱ μὲν δὴ ἐν τῇ Πλαταίᾳ οὕτως ἐπεπράγεσαν.

4 (II, 5) The main Theban force arrives too late to rescue their comrades and
decides to withdraw, claiming afterwards that the Plataeans agreed to spare their
prisoners' lives if they did retire; but the Plataeans deny this and put all the
Theban prisoners to death.

1   Οἱ δὲ ἄλλοι Θηβαῖοι οὓς ἔδει ἔτι τῆς νυκτὸς παραγενέσθαι πανστρατιᾷ, εἴ τι ἄρα μὴ προχωροίη τοῖς 85
ἐσεληλυθόσι, τῆς ἀγγελίας ἅμα καθ' ὁδὸν αὐτοῖς
2 ῥηθείσης περὶ τῶν γεγενημένων ἐπεβοήθουν. ἀπέχει
δὲ ἡ Πλάταια τῶν Θηβῶν σταδίους ἑβδομήκοντα, καὶ
τὸ ὕδωρ τὸ γενόμενον τῆς νυκτὸς ἐποίησε βραδύτερον
αὐτοὺς ἐλθεῖν· ὁ γὰρ Ἀσωπὸς ποταμὸς ἐρρύη μέγας 90
3 καὶ οὐ ῥᾳδίως διαβατὸς ἦν. πορευόμενοί τε ἐν ὑετῷ
καὶ τὸν ποταμὸν μόλις διαβάντες ὕστερον παρεγένοντο,
ἤδη τῶν ἀνδρῶν τῶν μὲν διεφθαρμένων, τῶν δὲ ζώντων
4 ἐχομένων. ὡς δ' ᾔσθοντο οἱ Θηβαῖοι τὸ γεγενημένον,
ἐπεβούλευον τοῖς ἔξω τῆς πόλεως τῶν Πλαταιῶν (ἦσαν 95
γὰρ καὶ ἄνθρωποι κατὰ τοὺς ἀγροὺς καὶ κατασκευή,
οἷα ἀπροσδοκήτου κακοῦ ἐν εἰρήνῃ γενομένου)· ἐβούλοντο γὰρ σφίσιν εἴ τινα λάβοιεν ὑπάρχειν ἀντὶ τῶν
5 ἔνδον, ἢν ἄρα τύχωσί τινες ἐζωγρημένοι. καὶ οἱ μὲν
ταῦτα διενοοῦντο· οἱ δὲ Πλαταιῆς, ἔτι διαβουλευομένων 100
αὐτῶν ὑποτοπήσαντες τοιοῦτόν τι ἔσεσθαι καὶ δείσαντες περὶ τοῖς ἔξω κήρυκα ἐξέπεμψαν παρὰ τοὺς
Θηβαίους, λέγοντες ὅτι οὔτε τὰ πεποιημένα ὁσίως
δράσειαν ἐν σπονδαῖς σφῶν πειραθέντες καταλαβεῖν
τὴν πόλιν, τά τε ἔξω ἔλεγον αὐτοῖς μὴ ἀδικεῖν. εἰ δὲ 105
μή, καὶ αὐτοὶ ἔφασαν αὐτῶν τοὺς ἄνδρας ἀποκτενεῖν

οὓς ἔχουσι ζῶντας· ἀναχωρησάντων δὲ πάλιν ἐκ τῆς γῆς
6 ἀποδώσειν. Θηβαῖοι μὲν ταῦτα λέγουσι καὶ ἐπομόσαι
φασὶν αὐτούς· Πλαταιῆς δ' οὐχ ὁμολογοῦσι τοὺς
ἄνδρας εὐθὺς ὑποσχέσθαι ἀποδώσειν, ἀλλὰ λόγων 110
πρῶτον γενομένων ἤν τι ξυμβαίνωσι, καὶ ἐπομόσαι οὔ
7 φασιν. ἐκ δ' οὖν τῆς γῆς ἀνεχώρησαν οἱ Θηβαῖοι οὐδὲν
ἀδικήσαντες· οἱ δὲ Πλαταιῆς, ἐπειδὴ τὰ ἐκ τῆς χώρας
κατὰ τάχος ἐσεκομίσαντο, ἀπέκτειναν τοὺς ἄνδρας
εὐθύς. ἦσαν δὲ ὀγδοήκοντα καὶ ἑκατὸν οἱ ληφθέντες, 115
καὶ Εὐρύμαχος εἷς αὐτῶν ἦν, πρὸς ὃν ἔπραξαν οἱ
προδιδόντες.

5 (II, 6) On first hearing the news the Athenians arrest any Boeotians who are
in Athens and tell the Plataeans not to harm their prisoners, but the message arrives
too late to save them. They then provision and reinforce Plataea and take away all
the non-combatants to Athens.

1 Τοῦτο δὲ ποιήσαντες ἔς τε τὰς Ἀθήνας ἄγγελον
ἔπεμπον καὶ τοὺς νεκροὺς ὑποσπόνδους ἀπέδοσαν τοῖς
Θηβαίοις, τά τ' ἐν τῇ πόλει καθίσταντο πρὸς τὰ παρόντα 120
2 ᾗ ἐδόκει αὐτοῖς. τοῖς δ' Ἀθηναίοις ἠγγέλθη εὐθὺς τὰ περὶ
τῶν Πλαταιῶν γεγενημένα, καὶ Βοιωτῶν τε παραχρῆμα
ξυνέλαβον ὅσοι ἦσαν ἐν τῇ Ἀττικῇ καὶ ἐς τὴν Πλάταιαν
ἔπεμψαν κήρυκα, κελεύοντες μηδὲν νεώτερον ποιεῖν
περὶ τῶν ἀνδρῶν οὓς ἔχουσι Θηβαίων, πρὶν ἄν τι καὶ 125
αὐτοὶ βουλεύσωσι περὶ αὐτῶν· οὐ γὰρ ἠγγέλθη αὐτοῖς
3 ὅτι τεθνηκότες εἶεν. ἅμα γὰρ τῇ ἐσόδῳ γιγνομένῃ
τῶν Θηβαίων ὁ πρῶτος ἄγγελος ἐξῄει, ὁ δὲ δεύτερος
ἄρτι νενικημένων τε καὶ ξυνειλημμένων· καὶ τῶν
ὕστερον οὐδὲν ᾔδεσαν. οὕτω δὴ οὐκ εἰδότες οἱ Ἀθηναῖοι 130
ἐπέστελλον· ὁ δὲ κῆρυξ ἀφικόμενος ηὗρε τοὺς ἄνδρας
4 διεφθαρμένους. καὶ μετὰ ταῦτα οἱ Ἀθηναῖοι στρατεύ-
σαντες ἐς Πλάταιαν σῖτόν τε ἐσήγαγον καί φρουροὺς

ἐγκατέλιπον, τῶν τε ἀνθρώπων τοὺς ἀχρειοτάτους ξὺν
γυναιξὶ καὶ παισὶν ἐξεκόμισαν.   140.

(*In II, 7–70 Thucydides describes the outbreak of the Peloponnesian War in
June 431, the invasion of Attica by King Archidamus of Sparta to ravage the
countryside, the withdrawal of the Athenians from the country into the city, and the
terrible Plague that the overcrowding caused in 430; Pericles, the great leader of
the Athenians, died as a result of the plague in 429. Potidaea fell in 430 after a
long siege, and in the summer of 429 the attack on Plataea began.*)

6 (*II, 71*) Summer 429. After an interval of two years King Archidamus of Sparta
leads a Peloponnesian army to attack Plataea. The Plataeans remind him that his
predecessor Pausanias declared their city independent for ever because of the courage
shown by their fathers at the Battle of Plataea against the Persians (479). They
request him to abide by the oaths then made and withdraw from their country.

1   Τοῦ δ' ἐπιγιγνομένου θέρους οἱ Πελοποννήσιοι καὶ
οἱ ξύμμαχοι ἐς μὲν τὴν Ἀττικὴν οὐκ ἐσέβαλον, ἐστρά-
τευσαν δ' ἐπὶ Πλάταιαν· ἡγεῖτο δὲ Ἀρχίδαμος ὁ
Ζευξιδάμου Λακεδαιμονίων βασιλεύς. καὶ καθίσας τὸν
στρατὸν ἔμελλε δῃώσειν τὴν γῆν· οἱ δὲ Πλαταιῆς 145
εὐθὺς πρέσβεις πέμψαντες πρὸς αὐτὸν ἔλεγον τοιάδε·

2   "Ἀρχίδαμε καὶ Λακεδαιμόνιοι, οὐ δίκαια ποιεῖτε οὐδ'
ἄξια οὔτε ὑμῶν οὔτε πατέρων ὧν ἐστε ἐς γῆν τὴν
Πλαταιῶν στρατεύοντες. Παυσανίας γὰρ ὁ Κλεομβρότου
Λακεδαιμόνιος ἐλευθερώσας τὴν Ἑλλάδα ἀπὸ τῶν Μήδων 150
μετὰ Ἑλλήνων τῶν ἐθελησάντων ξυνάρασθαι τὸν κίνδυνον τῆς μάχης ἣ παρ' ἡμῖν ἐγένετο, θύσας ἐν τῇ
Πλαταιῶν ἀγορᾷ Διὶ ἐλευθερίῳ καὶ ξυγκαλέσας πάντας
τοὺς ξυμμάχους ἀπεδίδου Πλαταιεῦσι γῆν καὶ πόλιν τὴν
σφετέραν ἔχοντας αὐτονόμους οἰκεῖν, στρατεῦσαί τε 155
μηδένα ποτὲ ἀδίκως ἐπ' αὐτοὺς μηδ' ἐπὶ δουλείᾳ· εἰ δὲ

3   μή, ἀμύνειν τοὺς παρόντας ξυμμάχους κατὰ δύναμιν. τάδε
μὲν ἡμῖν πατέρες οἱ ὑμέτεροι ἔδοσαν ἀρετῆς ἕνεκα καὶ

προθυμίας τῆς ἐν ἐκείνοις τοῖς κινδύνοις γενομένης,
ὑμεῖς δὲ τἀναντία δρᾶτε· μετὰ γὰρ Θηβαίων τῶν ἡμῖν 160
4 ἐχθίστων ἐπὶ δουλείᾳ τῇ ἡμετέρᾳ ἥκετε. μάρτυρας
δὲ θεοὺς τούς τε ὁρκίους τότε γενομένους ποιούμενοι
καὶ τοὺς ὑμετέρους πατρῴους καὶ ἡμετέρους ἐγχωρίους
λέγομεν ὑμῖν τὴν γῆν τὴν Πλαταιίδα μὴ ἀδικεῖν μηδὲ
παραβαίνειν τοὺς ὅρκους, ἐᾶν δὲ οἰκεῖν αὐτονόμους 165
καθάπερ Παυσανίας ἐδικαίωσεν."

7 (II, 72) *Archidamus replies that the Plataeans must either help the rest of
Greece to throw off the domination of Athens or at any rate remain neutral.
The Plataeans said that they must consult the Athenians, and Archidamus suggests
that they should evacuate their city and entrust it to the care of the Lacedaemonians
until the end of the war.*

1 Τοσαῦτα εἰπόντων Πλαταιῶν Ἀρχίδαμος ὑπολαβὼν
εἶπε· "Δίκαια λέγετε, ὦ ἄνδρες Πλαταιῆς, ἢν ποιῆτε
ὅμοια τοῖς λόγοις. καθάπερ γὰρ Παυσανίας ὑμῖν
παρέδωκεν, αὐτοί τε αὐτονομεῖσθε καὶ τοὺς ἄλλους 170
ξυνελευθεροῦτε, ὅσοι μετασχόντες τῶν τότε κινδύνων
ὑμῖν τε ξυνώμοσαν καί εἰσι νῦν ὑπ' Ἀθηναίοις, παρασκευή τε τοσήδε καὶ πόλεμος γεγένηται αὐτῶν ἕνεκα καὶ
τῶν ἄλλων ἐλευθερώσεως. ἧς μάλιστα μὲν μετασχόντες
καὶ αὐτοὶ ἐμμείνατε τοῖς ὅρκοις· εἰ δὲ μή, ἅπερ 175
καὶ τὸ πρότερον ἤδη προυκαλεσάμεθα, ἡσυχίαν ἄγετε
νεμόμενοι τὰ ὑμέτερα αὐτῶν, καὶ ἔστε μηδὲ μεθ' ἑτέρων,
δέχεσθε δὲ ἀμφοτέρους φίλους, ἐπὶ πολέμῳ δὲ μηδ'
ἑτέρους. καὶ τάδε ἡμῖν ἀρκέσει." ὁ μὲν Ἀρχίδαμος
2 τοσαῦτα εἶπεν· οἱ δὲ Πλαταιῶν πρέσβεις ἀκούσαντες 180
ταῦτα ἐσῆλθον ἐς τὴν πόλιν καὶ τῷ πλήθει τὰ ῥηθέντα
κοινώσαντες ἀπεκρίναντο αὐτῷ ὅτι ἀδύνατα σφίσιν
εἴη ποιεῖν ἃ προκαλεῖται ἄνευ Ἀθηναίων· παῖδες
γὰρ σφῶν καὶ γυναῖκες παρ' ἐκείνοις εἶεν· δεδιέναι
δὲ καὶ περὶ τῇ πάσῃ πόλει μὴ ἐκείνων ἀποχωρη-

σάντων Ἀθηναῖοι ἐλθόντες σφίσιν οὐκ ἐπιτρέπωσιν, 185
ἢ Θηβαῖοι, ὡς ἔνορκοι ὄντες κατὰ τὸ ἀμφοτέρους
δέχεσθαι, αὖθις σφῶν τὴν πόλιν πειράσωσι καταλαβεῖν.

3 ὁ δὲ θαρσύνων αὐτοὺς πρὸς ταῦτα ἔφη, "Ὑμεῖς δὲ
πόλιν μὲν καὶ οἰκίας ἡμῖν παράδοτε τοῖς Λακεδαι-
μονίοις καὶ γῆς ὅρους ἀποδείξατε καὶ δένδρα ἀριθμῷ 190
τὰ ὑμέτερα καὶ ἄλλο εἴ τι δυνατὸν ἐς ἀριθμὸν ἐλθεῖν·
αὐτοὶ δὲ μεταχωρήσατε ὅποι βούλεσθε ἕως ἂν ὁ πόλεμος
ᾖ. ἐπειδὰν δὲ παρέλθῃ, ἀποδώσομεν ὑμῖν ἃ ἂν
παραλάβωμεν. μέχρι δὲ τοῦδε ἕξομεν παρακαταθήκην,
ἐργαζόμενοι καὶ φορὰν φέροντες ἣ ἂν ὑμῖν μέλλῃ ἱκανὴ 195
ἔσεσθαι."

8 (II, 73) *The Plataeans reply that they will follow the advice of the Athenians.*
Archidamus gives them a truce during which they send word to the Athenians, who
promise them all possible aid if they will remain loyal.

1   Οἱ δ' ἀκούσαντες ἐσῆλθον αὖθις ἐς τὴν πόλιν, καὶ
βουλευσάμενοι μετὰ τοῦ πλήθους ἔλεξαν ὅτι βούλονται
ἃ προκαλεῖται Ἀθηναίοις κοινῶσαι πρῶτον, καὶ ἢν
πείθωσιν αὐτούς, ποιεῖν ταῦτα· μέχρι δὲ τούτου 200
σπείσασθαι σφίσιν ἐκέλευον καὶ τὴν γῆν μὴ δῃοῦν. ὁ
δὲ ἡμέρας τε ἐσπείσατο ἐν αἷς εἰκὸς ἦν κομισθῆναι καὶ
2 τὴν γῆν οὐκ ἔτεμνεν. ἐλθόντες δὲ οἱ Πλαταιῆς πρέσβεις
ὡς τοὺς Ἀθηναίους καὶ βουλευσάμενοι μετ' αὐτῶν
πάλιν ἦλθον ἀπαγγέλλοντες τοῖς ἐν τῇ πόλει τοιάδε· 205
3 " Οὔτ' ἐν τῷ πρὸ τοῦ χρόνῳ, ὦ ἄνδρες Πλαταιῆς, ἀφ'
οὗ ξύμμαχοι ἐγενόμεθα, Ἀθηναῖοί φασιν ἐν οὐδενὶ
ὑμᾶς προέσθαι ἀδικουμένους οὔτε νῦν περιόψεσθαι,
βοηθήσειν δὲ κατὰ δύναμιν. ἐπισκήπτουσί τε ὑμῖν πρὸς
τῶν ὅρκων οὓς οἱ πατέρες ὤμοσαν μηδὲν νεωτερίζειν 210
περὶ τὴν ξυμμαχίαν."

9 *(II, 74) The Plataeans reject the proposals of Archidamus, who calls upon the gods of the country to witness that the Spartans are not the aggressors in this war.*

1   Τοιαῦτα τῶν πρέσβεων ἀπαγγειλάντων οἱ Πλαταιῆς
ἐβουλεύσαντο Ἀθηναίους μὴ προδιδόναι, ἀλλ᾽ ἀνέχεσθαι
καὶ γῆν τεμνομένην, εἰ δεῖ, ὁρῶντας καὶ ἄλλο πάσχοντας
ὅ τι ἂν ξυμβαίνῃ· ἐξελθεῖν τε μηδένα ἔτι, ἀλλ᾽ ἀπὸ τοῦ 215
τείχους ἀποκρίνασθαι ὅτι ἀδύνατα σφίσι ποιεῖν ἐστιν

2 ἃ Λακεδαιμόνιοι προκαλοῦνται. ὡς δὲ ἀπεκρίναντο,
ἐντεῦθεν δὴ πρῶτον μὲν ἐς ἐπιμαρτυρίαν καὶ θεῶν καὶ
ἡρώων τῶν ἐγχωρίων Ἀρχίδαμος βασιλεὺς κατέστη,

3 λέγων ὧδε. " Θεοὶ ὅσοι γῆν τὴν Πλαταιίδα ἔχετε καὶ 220
ἥρωες, ξυνίστορες ἔστε ὅτι οὔτε τὴν ἀρχὴν ἀδίκως,
ἐκλιπόντων δὲ τῶνδε πρότερον τὸ ξυνώμοτον, ἐπὶ γῆν
τήνδε ἤλθομεν, ἐν ᾗ οἱ πατέρες ἡμῶν εὐξάμενοι ὑμῖν
Μήδων ἐκράτησαν καὶ παρέσχετε αὐτὴν εὐμενῆ ἐναγωνίσασθαι τοῖς Ἕλλησιν, οὔτε νῦν, ἤν τι ποιῶμεν, 225
ἀδικήσομεν· προκαλεσάμενοι γὰρ πολλὰ καὶ εἰκότα οὐ
τυγχάνομεν. ξυγγνώμονες δὲ ἔστε τῆς μὲν ἀδικίας
κολάζεσθαι τοῖς ὑπάρχουσι προτέροις, τῆς δὲ τιμωρίας
τυγχάνειν τοῖς ἐπιφέρουσι νομίμως."

10 *(II, 75) The Peloponnesians build a stockade round the city and raise a huge mound against the wall. The defenders increase the height of the wall opposite this with a framework of wood strengthened by bricks, and draw away earth from the bottom of the mound where it touches the wall.*

1   Τοσαῦτα ἐπιθειάσας καθίστη ἐς πόλεμον τὸν στρα- 230
τόν, καὶ πρῶτον μὲν περιεσταύρωσεν αὐτοὺς τοῖς
δένδρεσιν ἃ ἔκοψαν, τοῦ μηδένα ἔτι ἐξιέναι, ἔπειτα χῶμα
ἔχουν πρὸς τὴν πόλιν, ἐλπίζοντες ταχίστην τὴν αἵρεσιν
ἔσεσθαι αὐτῶν στρατεύματος τοσούτου ἐργαζομένου.

2 ξύλα μὲν οὖν τέμνοντες ἐκ τοῦ Κιθαιρῶνος παρῳκο- 235

δόμουν ἑκατέρωθεν, φορμηδὸν ἀντὶ τοίχων τιθέντες,
ὅπως μὴ διαχέοιτο ἐπὶ πολὺ τὸ χῶμα· ἐφόρουν δὲ ὕλην
ἐς αὐτὸ καὶ λίθους καὶ γῆν καὶ εἴ τι ἄλλο ἀνύτειν μέλλοι
3 ἐπιβαλλόμενον. ἡμέρας δὲ ἔχουν ἑπτακαίδεκα καὶ
νύκτας ξυνεχῶς διῃρημένοι κατ' ἀναπαύλας ὥστε τοὺς 240
μὲν φέρειν, τοὺς δὲ ὕπνον τε καὶ σῖτον αἱρεῖσθαι· Λακεδαιμονίων τε οἱ ξεναγοὶ ἑκάστης πόλεως ξυνεφεστῶτες
4 ἠνάγκαζον ἐς τὸ ἔργον. οἱ δὲ Πλαταιῆς ὁρῶντες τὸ χῶμα
αἱρόμενον, ξύλινον τεῖχος ξυνθέντες καὶ ἐπιστήσαντες
τῷ ἑαυτῶν τείχει ᾗ προσεχοῦτο, ἐσῳκοδόμουν ἐς αὐτὸ 245
5 πλίνθους ἐκ τῶν ἐγγὺς οἰκιῶν καθαιροῦντες. ξύνδεσμος
δ' ἦν αὐτοῖς τὰ ξύλα, τοῦ μὴ ὑψηλὸν γιγνόμενον ἀσθενὲς
εἶναι τὸ οἰκοδόμημα· καὶ προκαλύμματα εἶχε δέρσεις
καὶ διφθέρας ὥστε τοὺς ἐργαζομένους καὶ τὰ ξύλα
μήτε πυρφόροις ὀϊστοῖς βάλλεσθαι ἐν ἀσφαλεῖ τε εἶναι. 250
ᾖρετο δὲ τὸ ὕψος τοῦ τείχους μέγα καὶ τὸ χῶμα οὐ
σχολαίτερον ἀντανῄει αὐτῷ. καὶ οἱ Πλαταιῆς τοιόνδε
τι ἐπινοοῦσι· διελόντες τοῦ τείχους ᾗ προσέπιπτε τὸ
χῶμα ἐσεφόρουν τὴν γῆν.

11 (II, 76) The attackers counter this by using clay packed in reed baskets, whereupon the Plataeans dig a mine under the mound to draw away more earth, and build a crescent-shaped wall inside their old wall. They pull up the enemy battering-rams with nooses or break off the heads of the rams by dropping weights onto them.

1 Οἱ δὲ Πελοποννήσιοι αἰσθόμενοι ἐν ταρσοῖς καλάμου 255
πηλὸν ἐνίλλοντες ἐσέβαλλον ἐς τὸ διῃρημένον, ὅπως μὴ
2 διαχεόμενον ὥσπερ ἡ γῆ φοροῖτο. οἱ δὲ ταύτῃ ἀπο-
κληόμενοι τοῦτο μὲν ἐπέσχον, ὑπόνομον δ' ἐκ τῆς
πόλεως ὀρύξαντες καὶ ξυντεκμηράμενοι ὑπὸ τὸ χῶμα
ὑφεῖλκον αὖθις παρὰ σφᾶς τὸν χοῦν· καὶ ἐλάνθανον ἐπὶ 260
πολὺ τοὺς ἔξω, ὥστ' ἐπιβάλλοντας ἧσσον ἀνύτειν ὑπαγο-

μένου αὐτοῖς κάτωθεν τοῦ χώματος καὶ ἱζάνοντος αἰεὶ
3 ἐπὶ τὸ κενούμενον. δεδιότες δὲ μὴ οὐδ' οὕτω δύνωνται
ὀλίγοι πρὸς πολλοὺς ἀντέχειν, προσεπεξηῦρον τόδε· τὸ
μὲν μέγα οἰκοδόμημα ἐπαύσαντο ἐργαζόμενοι τὸ κατὰ 265
τὸ χῶμα, ἔνθεν δὲ καὶ ἔνθεν αὐτοῦ ἀρξάμενοι ἀπὸ τοῦ
βραχέος τείχους ἐκ τοῦ ἐντὸς μηνοειδὲς ἐς τὴν πόλιν προσῳκοδόμουν, ὅπως εἰ τὸ μέγα τεῖχος ἁλίσκοιτο, τοῦτ'
ἀντέχοι, καὶ δέοι τοὺς ἐναντίους αὖθις πρὸς αὐτὸ χοῦν,
καὶ προχωροῦντας ἔσω διπλάσιόν τε πόνον ἔχειν καὶ ἐν 270
4 ἀμφιβόλῳ μᾶλλον γίγνεσθαι. ἅμα δὲ τῇ χώσει καὶ
μηχανὰς προσῆγον τῇ πόλει οἱ Πελοποννήσιοι, μίαν
μέν, ἣ τοῦ μεγάλου οἰκοδομήματος κατὰ τὸ χῶμα
προσαχθεῖσα ἐπὶ μέγα τε κατέσεισε καὶ τοὺς Πλαταιᾶς
ἐφόβησεν, ἄλλας δὲ ἄλλῃ τοῦ τείχους, ἃς βρόχους τε 275
περιβάλλοντες ἀνεῖλκον οἱ Πλαταιῆς, καὶ δοκοὺς
μεγάλας ἀρτήσαντες ἁλύσεσι μακραῖς σιδηραῖς ἀπὸ τῆς
τομῆς ἑκατέρωθεν ἀπὸ κεραιῶν δύο ἐπικεκλιμένων καὶ
ὑπερτεινουσῶν ὑπὲρ τοῦ τείχους ἀνελκύσαντες ἐγκαρσίας,
ὁπότε προσπεσεῖσθαί πῃ μέλλοι ἡ μηχανή, ἀφίεσαν 280
τὴν δοκὸν χαλαραῖς ταῖς ἁλύσεσι καὶ οὐ διὰ χειρὸς
ἔχοντες· ἡ δὲ ῥύμη ἐμπίπτουσα ἀπεκαύλιζε τὸ προέχον
τῆς ἐμβολῆς.

*12 (II, 77) The Peloponnesians make a last attempt to take Plataea by piling
up brushwood against the wall and setting fire to it. The tremendous conflagration
nearly overwhelms the defenders, but a thunder-shower puts out the fire and saves
them.*

1   Μετὰ δὲ τοῦτο οἱ Πελοποννήσιοι, ὡς αἵ τε μηχαναὶ
οὐδὲν ὠφέλουν καὶ τῷ χώματι τὸ ἀντιτείχισμα ἐγίγνετο, 285
νομίσαντες ἄπορον εἶναι ὑπὸ τῶν παρόντων δεινῶν
ἑλεῖν τὴν πόλιν πρὸς τὴν περιτείχισιν παρεσκευάζοντο.
2 πρότερον δὲ πυρὶ ἔδοξεν αὐτοῖς πειρᾶσαι εἰ δύναιντο

πνεύματος γενομένου ἐπιφλέξαι τὴν πόλιν οὖσαν οὐ
μεγάλην· πᾶσαν γὰρ δὴ ἰδέαν ἐπενόουν, εἴ πως σφίσιν 290
3 ἄνευ δαπάνης καὶ πολιορκίας προσαχθείη. φοροῦντες
δὲ ὕλης φακέλους παρέβαλλον ἀπὸ τοῦ χώματος ἐς τὸ
μεταξὺ πρῶτον τοῦ τείχους καὶ τῆς προσχώσεως, ταχὺ
δὲ πλήρους γενομένου διὰ πολυχειρίαν ἐπιπαρένησαν καὶ
τῆς ἄλλης πόλεως ὅσον ἐδύναντο ἀπὸ τοῦ μετεώρου 295
πλεῖστον ἐπισχεῖν, ἐμβαλόντες δὲ πῦρ ξὺν θείῳ καὶ
4 πίσσῃ ἧψαν τὴν ὕλην. καὶ ἐγένετο φλὸξ τοσαύτη ὅσην
οὐδείς πω ἔς γε ἐκεῖνον τὸν χρόνον χειροποίητον εἶδεν·
ἤδη γὰρ ἐν ὄρεσιν ὕλη τριφθεῖσα ὑπ᾽ ἀνέμων πρὸς
αὑτὴν ἀπὸ ταὐτομάτου πῦρ καὶ φλόγα ἀνῆκε. τοῦτο 300
5 δὲ μέγα τι ἦν καὶ τοὺς Πλαταιᾶς τἆλλα διαφυγόντας
ἐλαχίστου ἐδέησε διαφθεῖραι· ἐντὸς γὰρ πολλοῦ τῆς
πόλεως οὐκ ἦν πελάσαι, πνεῦμά τε εἰ ἐπεγένετο αὐτῇ
ἐπίφορον, ὅπερ καὶ ἤλπιζον οἱ ἐναντίοι, οὐκ ἂν διέφυγον.
νῦν δὲ καὶ τόδε λέγεται ξυμβῆναι, ὕδωρ πολὺ καὶ βροντὰς 305
γενομένας σβέσαι τὴν φλόγα καὶ οὕτω παυθῆναι τὸν
κίνδυνον.

*13 (II, 78) Mid-September 429. The Peloponnesians build a wall all round the
city, leave a small force to garrison the wall, and withdraw their main army.
400 Plataeans, 80 Athenians, and 110 women-slaves to prepare food remain in
the city to withstand the siege.*

1   Οἱ δὲ Πελοποννήσιοι ἐπειδὴ καὶ τούτου διήμαρτον,
μέρος μέν τι καταλιπόντες τοῦ στρατοπέδου, τὸ δὲ
πλέον ἀφέντες, περιετείχιζον τὴν πόλιν κύκλῳ, διελόμενοι 310
κατὰ πόλεις τὸ χωρίον· τάφρος δὲ ἐντός τε ἦν καὶ
2 ἔξωθεν ἐξ ἧς ἐπλινθεύσαντο. καὶ ἐπειδὴ πᾶν ἐξείργαστο
περὶ ἀρκτούρου ἐπιτολάς, καταλιπόντες φύλακας τοῦ
ἡμίσεος τείχους (τὸ δὲ ἥμισυ Βοιωτοὶ ἐφύλασσον)
ἀνεχώρησαν τῷ στρατῷ καὶ διελύθησαν κατὰ πόλεις. 315

3 Πλαταιῆς δὲ παῖδας μὲν καὶ γυναῖκας καὶ τοὺς πρεσ-
βυτάτους τε καὶ πλῆθος τὸ ἄχρηστον τῶν ἀνθρώπων
πρότερον ἐκκεκομισμένοι ἦσαν ἐς τὰς Ἀθήνας, αὐτοὶ
δ' ἐπολιορκοῦντο ἐγκαταλελειμμένοι τετρακόσιοι, Ἀθηναίων δὲ ὀγδοήκοντα, γυναῖκες δὲ δέκα καὶ ἑκατὸν 320
4 σιτοποιοί. τοσοῦτοι ἦσαν οἱ ξύμπαντες ὅτε ἐς τὴν πολι-
ορκίαν καθίσταντο, καὶ ἄλλος οὐδεὶς ἦν ἐν τῷ τείχει
οὔτε δοῦλος οὔτε ἐλεύθερος. τοιαύτη μὲν ἡ Πλαταιῶν
πολιορκία κατεσκευάσθη.

(*In II, 79–III, 20 Thucydides describes naval operations in the Gulf of Corinth
during the late summer of 429, in which the Athenian Phormio won a brilliant
victory over a Peloponnesian fleet. In 429 Archidamus invaded Attica again and
had just withdrawn when news arrived that Mytilene and most of the island of
Lesbos had revolted from the Athenians, who immediately blockaded Mytilene.*)

*14 (III, 20) Winter 428. Hard-pressed by shortage of food the defenders decide
to try to escape from Plataea, but only 220 eventuallly make the attempt. They
count the layers of bricks in the besiegers' wall and make ladders long enough to
reach the top of it.*

1   Τοῦ δ' αὐτοῦ χειμῶνος οἱ Πλαταιῆς (ἔτι γὰρ ἐπολι- 325
ορκοῦντο ὑπὸ τῶν Πελοποννησίων καὶ Βοιωτῶν) ἐπειδὴ
τῷ τε σίτῳ ἐπιλείποντι ἐπιέζοντο καὶ ἀπὸ τῶν Ἀθηνῶν
οὐδεμία ἐλπὶς ἦν τιμωρίας οὐδὲ ἄλλη σωτηρία ἐφαίνετο,
ἐπιβουλεύουσιν αὐτοί τε καὶ Ἀθηναίων οἱ ξυμπολιορκού-
μενοι πρῶτον μὲν πάντες ἐξελθεῖν καὶ ὑπερβῆναι τὰ τείχη 330
τῶν πολεμίων, ἢν δύνωνται βιάσασθαι, ἐσηγησαμένων
τὴν πεῖραν αὐτοῖς Θεαινέτου τε τοῦ Τολμίδου ἀνδρὸς
μάντεως καὶ Εὐπομπίδου τοῦ Δαϊμάχου, ὃς καὶ
2 ἐστρατήγει· ἔπειτα οἱ μὲν ἡμίσεις ἀπώκνησάν πως τὸν
κίνδυνον μέγαν ἡγησάμενοι, ἐς δὲ ἄνδρας διακοσίους καὶ 335
εἴκοσι μάλιστα ἐνέμειναν τῇ ἐξόδῳ ἐθελονταὶ τρόπῳ
3 τοιῷδε. κλίμακας ἐποιήσαντο ἴσας τῷ τείχει τῶν

πολεμίων· ξυνεμετρήσαντο δὲ ταῖς ἐπιβολαῖς τῶν
πλίνθων, ᾗ ἔτυχε πρὸς σφᾶς οὐκ ἐξαληλιμμένον τὸ τεῖχος
αὐτῶν. ἠριθμοῦντο δὲ πολλοὶ ἅμα τὰς ἐπιβολάς, καὶ 340
ἔμελλον οἱ μέν τινες ἁμαρτήσεσθαι οἱ δὲ πλείους τεύξεσ-
θαι τοῦ ἀληθοῦς λογισμοῦ, ἄλλως τε καὶ πολλάκις
ἀριθμοῦντες καὶ ἅμα οὐ πολὺ ἀπέχοντες, ἀλλὰ ῥᾳδίως
4 καθορωμένου ἐς ὃ ἐβούλοντο τοῦ τείχους. τὴν μὲν οὖν
ξυμμέτρησιν τῶν κλιμάκων οὕτως ἔλαβον, ἐκ τοῦ πάχους 345
τῆς πλίνθου εἰκάσαντες τὸ μέτρον.

*15 (III, 21) There are two encircling walls sixteen feet apart, containing quarters
for the sentries in between, roofed over to make a continuous wall with battlements
on both sides. At every tenth battlement there is a tower with a passage through the
middle, in which the sentries shelter during bad weather.*

1 Τὸ δὲ τεῖχος ἦν τῶν Πελοποννησίων τοιόνδε τῇ
οἰκοδομήσει. εἶχε μὲν δύο τοὺς περιβόλους, πρός τε
Πλαταιῶν καὶ εἴ τις ἔξωθεν ἀπ᾽ Ἀθηνῶν ἐπίοι, διεῖχον
δὲ οἱ περίβολοι ἑκκαίδεκα πόδας μάλιστα ἀπ᾽ ἀλλήλων. 350
2 τὸ οὖν μεταξὺ τοῦτο, οἱ ἑκκαίδεκα πόδες, τοῖς φύλαξιν
οἰκήματα διανενεμημένα ᾠκοδόμητο, καὶ ἦν ξυνεχῆ
ὥστε ἓν φαίνεσθαι τεῖχος παχὺ ἐπάλξεις ἔχον ἀμφοτέ-
3 ρωθεν. διὰ δέκα δὲ ἐπάλξεων πύργοι ἦσαν μεγάλοι καὶ
ἰσοπλατεῖς τῷ τείχει, διήκοντες ἔς τε τὸ ἔσω μέτωπον 355
αὐτοῦ καὶ οἱ αὐτοὶ καὶ τὸ ἔξω, ὥστε πάροδον μὴ εἶναι
4 παρὰ πύργον, ἀλλὰ δι᾽ αὐτῶν μέσων διῇσαν. τὰς οὖν
νύκτας, ὁπότε χειμὼν εἴη νοτερός, τὰς μὲν ἐπάλξεις
ἀπέλειπον, ἐκ δὲ τῶν πύργων ὄντων δι᾽ ὀλίγου καὶ
ἄνωθεν στεγανῶν τὴν φυλακὴν ἐποιοῦντο. τὸ μὲν οὖν 360
τεῖχος ᾧ περιεφρουροῦντο οἱ Πλαταιῆς τοιοῦτον ἦν.

16 (III, 22) On a stormy night the escapers leave Plataea, climb the wall and send six men to seize each of two adjoining towers. At the alarm the blockading garrison rushes to the wall, but the Plataeans in the city make a diversion and raise fire-signals to confuse the signals that are being made to Thebes.

1 Οἱ δ', ἐπειδὴ παρεσκεύαστο αὐτοῖς, τηρήσαντες
νύκτα χειμέριον ὕδατι καὶ ἀνέμῳ καὶ ἅμ' ἀσέληνον
ἐξῇσαν· ἡγοῦντο δὲ οἵπερ καὶ τῆς πείρας αἴτιοι ἦσαν.
καὶ πρῶτον μὲν τὴν τάφρον διέβησαν ἣ περιεῖχεν αὐτούς, 365
ἔπειτα προσέμειξαν τῷ τείχει τῶν πολεμίων λαθόντες
τοὺς φύλακας, ἀνὰ τὸ σκοτεινὸν μὲν οὐ προϊδόντων
αὐτῶν, ψόφῳ δὲ τῷ ἐκ τοῦ προσιέναι αὐτοὺς ἀντιπα-
2 ταγοῦντος τοῦ ἀνέμου οὐ κατακουσάντων· ἅμα δὲ καὶ
διέχοντες πολὺ ἦσαν, ὅπως τὰ ὅπλα μὴ κρουόμενα πρὸς 370
ἄλληλα αἴσθησιν παρέχοι. ἦσαν δὲ εὐσταλεῖς τε τῇ
ὁπλίσει καὶ τὸν ἀριστερὸν μόνον πόδα ὑποδεδεμένοι
3 ἀσφαλείας ἕνεκα τῆς πρὸς τὸν πηλόν. κατὰ οὖν
μεταπύργιον προσέμισγον πρὸς τὰς ἐπάλξεις, εἰδότες
ὅτι ἐρῆμοί εἰσι, πρῶτον μὲν οἱ τὰς κλίμακας φέροντες, 375
καὶ προσέθεσαν· ἔπειτα ψιλοὶ δώδεκα ξὺν ξιφιδίῳ καὶ
θώρακι ἀνέβαινον, ὧν ἡγεῖτο Ἀμμέας ὁ Κοροίβου καὶ
πρῶτος ἀνέβη· μετὰ δὲ αὐτὸν οἱ ἑπόμενοι ἐξ ἐφ' ἑκάτερον
τῶν πύργων ἀνέβαινον. ἔπειτα ψιλοὶ ἄλλοι μετὰ τούτους 380
ξὺν δορατίοις ἐχώρουν, οἷς ἕτεροι κατόπιν τὰς ἀσπίδας
ἔφερον, ὅπως ἐκεῖνοι ῥᾷον προσβαίνοιεν, καὶ ἔμελλον
4 δώσειν ὁπότε πρὸς τοῖς πολεμίοις εἶεν. ὡς δὲ ἄνω
πλείους ἐγένοντο, ᾔσθοντο οἱ ἐκ τῶν πύργων φύλακες·
κατέβαλε γάρ τις τῶν Πλαταιῶν ἀντιλαμβανόμενος 385
ἀπὸ τῶν ἐπάλξεων κεραμίδα, ἣ πεσοῦσα δοῦπον
5 ἐποίησεν. καὶ αὐτίκα βοὴ ἦν, τὸ δὲ στρατόπεδον ἐπὶ
τὸ τεῖχος ὥρμησεν· οὐ γὰρ ᾔδει ὅ τι ἦν τὸ δεινὸν
σκοτεινῆς νυκτὸς καὶ χειμῶνος ὄντος, καὶ ἅμα οἱ ἐν τῇ
πόλει τῶν Πλαταιῶν ὑπολελειμμένοι ἐξελθόντες προσ- 390

ἔβαλον τῷ τείχει τῶν Πελοποννησίων ἐκ τοὔμπαλιν
ἢ οἱ ἄνδρες αὐτῶν ὑπερέβαινον, ὅπως ἥκιστα πρὸς

6 αὐτοὺς τὸν νοῦν ἔχοιεν. ἐθορυβοῦντο μὲν οὖν κατὰ χώραν
μένοντες, βοηθεῖν δὲ οὐδεὶς ἐτόλμα ἐκ τῆς ἑαυτῶν
φυλακῆς, ἀλλ' ἐν ἀπόρῳ ἦσαν εἰκάσαι τὸ γιγνόμενον. 395

7 καὶ οἱ τριακόσιοι αὐτῶν, οἷς ἐτέτακτο παραβοηθεῖν εἴ
τι δέοι, ἐχώρουν ἔξω τοῦ τείχους πρὸς τὴν βοήν.

8 φρυκτοί τε ἤροντο ἐς τὰς Θήβας πολέμιοι· παρανῖσχον
δὲ καὶ οἱ ἐκ τῆς πόλεως Πλαταιῆς ἀπὸ τοῦ τείχους
φρυκτοὺς πολλοὺς πρότερον παρεσκευασμένους ἐς αὐτὸ 400
τοῦτο, ὅπως ἀσαφῆ τὰ σημεῖα τῆς φρυκτωρίας τοῖς
πολεμίοις ᾖ καὶ μὴ βοηθοῖεν, ἄλλο τι νομίσαντες τὸ
γιγνόμενον εἶναι ἢ τὸ ὄν, πρὶν σφῶν οἱ ἄνδρες οἱ
ἐξιόντες διαφύγοιεν καὶ τοῦ ἀσφαλοῦς ἀντιλάβοιντο.

*17 (III, 23) The leading Plataeans climb to the top of the two towers and keep
the enemy away while their comrades cross the wall. The main party then covers the
descent of the first body and nearly all get across the half-frozen outer ditch.*

1 Οἱ δ' ὑπερβαίνοντες τῶν Πλαταιῶν ἐν τούτῳ, ὡς 405
οἱ πρῶτοι αὐτῶν ἀνεβεβήκεσαν καὶ τοῦ πύργου ἑκατέ-
ρου τοὺς φύλακας διαφθείραντες ἐκεκρατήκεσαν, τάς
τε διόδους τῶν πύργων ἐνστάντες αὐτοὶ ἐφύλασσον
μηδένα δι' αὐτῶν ἐπιβοηθεῖν, καὶ κλίμακας προσθέντες
ἀπὸ τοῦ τείχους τοῖς πύργοις καὶ ἐπαναβιβάσαντες 410
ἄνδρας πλείους, οἱ μὲν ἀπὸ τῶν πύργων τοὺς ἐπιβοη-
θοῦντας καὶ κάτωθεν καὶ ἄνωθεν εἶργον βάλλοντες, οἱ
δ' ἐν τούτῳ οἱ πλείους πολλὰς προσθέντες κλίμακας ἅμα
καὶ τὰς ἐπάλξεις ἀπώσαντες διὰ τοῦ μεταπυργίου

2 ὑπερέβαινον. ὁ δὲ διακομιζόμενος αἰεὶ ἵστατο ἐπὶ τοῦ 415
χείλους τῆς τάφρου καὶ ἐντεῦθεν ἐτόξευόν τε καὶ ἠκόντιζον, εἴ τις παραβοηθῶν παρὰ τὸ τεῖχος κωλυτὴς γίγ-

3 νοιτο τῆς διαβάσεως. ἐπεὶ δὲ πάντες διεπεπεραίωντο,
οἱ ἀπὸ τῶν πύργων χαλεπῶς οἱ τελευταῖοι καταβαίνοντες ἐχώρουν ἐπὶ τὴν τάφρον, καὶ ἐν τούτῳ οἱ 420
4 τριακόσιοι αὐτοῖς ἐπεφέροντο λαμπάδας ἔχοντες. οἱ
μὲν οὖν Πλαταιῆς ἐκείνους ἑώρων μᾶλλον ἐκ τοῦ
σκότους ἑστῶτες ἐπὶ τοῦ χείλους τῆς τάφρου, καὶ
ἐτόξευόν τε καὶ ἐσηκόντιζον ἐς τὰ γυμνά, αὐτοὶ δὲ ἐν
τῷ ἀφανεῖ ὄντες ἧσσον διὰ τὰς λαμπάδας καθεωρῶντο, 425
ὥστε φθάνουσι τῶν Πλαταιῶν καὶ οἱ ὕστατοι διαβάντες
5 τὴν τάφρον, χαλεπῶς δὲ καὶ βιαίως· κρύσταλλός τε
γὰρ ἐπεπήγει οὐ βέβαιος ἐν αὐτῇ ὥστ' ἐπελθεῖν, ἀλλ'
οἷος ἀπηλιώτου ὑδατώδης μᾶλλον, καὶ ἡ νὺξ τοιούτῳ
ἀνέμῳ ὑπονειφομένη πολὺ τὸ ὕδωρ ἐν αὐτῇ ἐπεποιήκει, 430
ὃ μόλις ὑπερέχοντες ἐπεραιώθησαν. ἐγένετο δὲ καὶ ἡ
διάφευξις αὐτοῖς μᾶλλον διὰ τοῦ χειμῶνος τὸ μέγεθος.

18 (III, 24) The escapers first move northwards towards Thebes, then turn south-east, reach the mountains, and get safely to Athens, 212 men in all, while their pursuers at once go south-east to the Oak's Heads pass and so miss them. The Plataeans in the city at first believe that all have been captured but soon learn the truth.

1 Ὁρμήσαντες δὲ ἀπὸ τῆς τάφρου οἱ Πλαταιῆς
ἐχώρουν ἀθρόοι τὴν ἐς Θήβας φέρουσαν ὁδόν, ἐν δεξιᾷ
ἔχοντες τὸ τοῦ Ἀνδροκράτους ἡρῷον, νομίζοντες ἥκιστ' 435
ἂν σφᾶς ταύτην αὐτοὺς ὑποτοπῆσαι τραπέσθαι τὴν ἐς
τοὺς πολεμίους· καὶ ἅμα ἑώρων τοὺς Πελοποννησίους
τὴν πρὸς Κιθαιρῶνα καὶ Δρυὸς κεφαλὰς τὴν ἐπ'
2 Ἀθηνῶν φέρουσαν μετὰ λαμπάδων διώκοντας. καὶ
ἐπὶ μὲν ἓξ ἢ ἑπτὰ σταδίους οἱ Πλαταιῆς τὴν ἐπὶ τῶν 440
Θηβῶν ἐχώρησαν, ἔπειθ' ὑποστρέψαντες ἦσαν τὴν πρὸς
τὸ ὄρος φέρουσαν ὁδὸν ἐς Ἐρύθρας καὶ Ὑσιάς, καὶ
λαβόμενοι τῶν ὀρῶν διαφεύγουσιν ἐς τὰς Ἀθήνας,

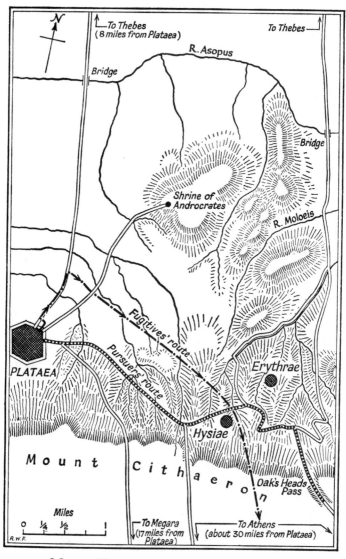

Map to illustrate the escape from Plataea

ἄνδρες δώδεκα καὶ διακόσιοι ἀπὸ πλειόνων· εἰσὶ γάρ
τινες αὐτῶν οἳ ἀπετράποντο ἐς τὴν πόλιν πρὶν ὑπερ- 445
βαίνειν, εἷς δ' ἐπὶ τῇ ἔξω τάφρῳ τοξότης ἐλήφθη.

3 οἱ μὲν οὖν Πελοποννήσιοι κατὰ χώραν ἐγένοντο τῆς
βοηθείας παυσάμενοι· οἱ δ' ἐκ τῆς πόλεως Πλαταιῆς
τῶν μὲν γεγενημένων εἰδότες οὐδέν, τῶν δὲ ἀποτραπο-
μένων σφίσιν ἀπαγγειλάντων ὡς οὐδεὶς περίεστι, 450
κήρυκα ἐκπέμψαντες, ἐπεὶ ἡμέρα ἐγένετο, ἐσπένδοντο
ἀναίρεσιν τοῖς νεκροῖς, μαθόντες δὲ τὸ ἀληθὲς ἐπαύσαντο. οἱ μὲν δὴ τῶν Πλαταιῶν ἄνδρες οὕτως ὑπερ-
βάντες ἐσώθησαν.

(*In III, 25–51 Thucydides describes how in the summer of 427 the democrats in
Mytilene insisted on surrendering the city to the blockading Athenians. At the first
meeting of the Assembly the Athenians decided to kill all the Mytilenians without
exception, but they met again next day and in spite of opposition from the demagogue
Cleon they rescinded the decree and sent a trireme that arrived just in time to prevent
the slaughter, though the most guilty were killed and the territory of Lesbos was
divided up amongst Athenian settlers.*)

*19 (III, 52) Summer 427. The Plataeans can no longer hold out through lack
of food, but as the Spartan commander has been ordered not to take the city by storm
he invites them to submit to the decision of five Spartan commissioners. They
surrender, and on being asked by the commissioners whether they have helped Sparta
at all in the war they ask to be allowed to plead their cause through two spokesmen.*

1   Ὑπὸ δὲ τοὺς αὐτοὺς χρόνους τοῦ θέρους τούτου καὶ 455
οἱ Πλαταιῆς οὐκέτι ἔχοντες σῖτον οὐδὲ δυνάμενοι πολιορκεῖσθαι ξυνέβησαν τοῖς Πελοποννησίοις τοιῷδε
2 τρόπῳ.   προσέβαλλον αὐτῶν τῷ τείχει, οἱ δὲ οὐκ
ἐδύναντο ἀμύνεσθαι. γνοὺς δὲ ὁ Λακεδαιμόνιος ἄρχων
τὴν ἀσθένειαν αὐτῶν βίᾳ μὲν οὐκ ἐβούλετο ἑλεῖν (εἰρη- 460
μένον γὰρ ἦν αὐτῷ ἐκ Λακεδαίμονος, ὅπως, εἰ σπονδαὶ
γίγνοιντό ποτε πρὸς Ἀθηναίους καὶ ξυγχωροῖεν ὅσα

πολέμῳ χωρία ἔχουσιν ἑκάτεροι ἀποδίδοσθαι, μὴ
ἀνάδοτος εἴη ἡ Πλάταια ὡς αὐτῶν ἑκόντων προσχωρησάντων), προσπέμπει δὲ αὐτοῖς κήρυκα λέγοντα, εἰ 465
βούλονται παραδοῦναι τὴν πόλιν ἑκόντες τοῖς Λακε-
δαιμονίοις καὶ δικασταῖς ἐκείνοις χρήσασθαι, τούς τε
3 ἀδίκους κολάσειν, παρὰ δίκην δὲ οὐδένα. τοσαῦτα μὲν
ὁ κῆρυξ εἶπεν· οἱ δέ (ἦσαν γὰρ ἤδη ἐν τῷ ἀσθενεστάτῳ)
παρέδοσαν τὴν πόλιν. καὶ τοὺς Πλαταιᾶς ἔτρεφον οἱ 470
Πελοποννήσιοι ἡμέρας τινάς, ἐν ὅσῳ οἱ ἐκ τῆς Λακε-
4 δαίμονος δικασταὶ πέντε ἄνδρες ἀφίκοντο. ἐλθόντων
δὲ αὐτῶν κατηγορία μὲν οὐδεμία προυτέθη, ἠρώτων
δὲ αὐτοὺς ἐπικαλεσάμενοι τοσοῦτον μόνον, εἴ τι Λακεδαιμονίους καὶ τοὺς ξυμμάχους ἐν τῷ πολέμῳ τῷ 475
5 καθεστῶτι ἀγαθὸν εἰργασμένοι εἰσίν. οἱ δ' ἔλεγον
αἰτησάμενοι μακρότερα εἰπεῖν καὶ προτάξαντες σφῶν
αὐτῶν Ἀστύμαχόν τε τὸν Ἀσωπολάου καὶ Λάκωνα τὸν
Αἰειμνήστου πρόξενον ὄντα Λακεδαιμονίων· καὶ ἐπελθόντες ἔλεγον τοιάδε.   480

(*In III, 53–58, 3 Thucydides reports the speech of the Plataeans.* "*We helped you
you both in the Persian War and against the revolt of the Helots, and we joined the
Athenians, whom we cannot now desert, because you refused us aid against the
Thebans, a people who joined the Persian invaders against their fellow-Greeks.
Will you now destroy Plataea, whose deeds are commemorated on the tripod dedicated
at Delphi, just to please the Thebans? Do not slay your benefactors who surrendered
voluntarily to you.*")

20 (III, 58, 4–5) "Look at the tombs of your fathers who were slain by the Persians and whom we honour every year. Pausanias buried them in a friendly land, but if you give our country to Thebes you will make it the property of their murderers and will destroy the temples of the gods to whom they prayed before defeating the Persians."

1   " Ἀποβλέψατε γὰρ ἐς πατέρων τῶν ὑμετέρων θήκας,
οὓς ἀποθανόντας ὑπὸ Μήδων καὶ ταφέντας ἐν τῇ
ἡμετέρᾳ ἐτιμῶμεν κατὰ ἔτος ἕκαστον δημοσίᾳ ἐσ-
θήμασί τε καὶ τοῖς ἄλλοις νομίμοις, ὅσα τε ἡ γῆ ἡμῶν
ἀνεδίδου ὡραῖα, πάντων ἀπαρχὰς ἐπιφέροντες, εὖνοι 485
μὲν ἐκ φιλίας χώρας, ξύμμαχοι δὲ ὁμαίχμοις ποτὲ
γενομένοις. ὧν ὑμεῖς τοὐναντίον ἂν δράσαιτε μὴ ὀρθῶς

2 γνόντες. σκέψασθέ τε· Παυσανίας μὲν γὰρ ἔθαπτεν
αὐτοὺς νομίζων ἐν γῇ τε φιλίᾳ τιθέναι καὶ παρ' ἀνδράσι
τοιούτοις· ὑμεῖς δὲ εἰ κτενεῖτε ἡμᾶς καὶ χώραν τὴν 490
Πλαταιίδα Θηβαΐδα ποιήσετε, τί ἄλλο ἢ ἐν πολεμίᾳ τε
καὶ παρὰ τοῖς αὐθένταις πατέρας τοὺς ὑμετέρους καὶ
ξυγγενεῖς ἀτίμους γερῶν ὧν νῦν ἴσχουσι καταλείψετε;
πρὸς δὲ καὶ γῆν ἐν ᾗ ἠλευθερώθησαν οἱ Ἕλληνες
δουλώσετε, ἱερά τε θεῶν οἷς εὐξάμενοι Μήδων ἐκρά- 495
τησαν ἐρημοῦτε καὶ θυσίας τὰς πατρίους τῶν ἐσσα-
μένων καὶ κτισάντων ἀφαιρήσεσθε."

21 (III, 59, 2–4) "*We appeal to you in the name of the gods by whom your fathers swore and beg that we should not be handed over to our bitterest foes.* . *We surrendered to you, whom we trusted, not to the Thebans, and we ask you to save us, who were the most patriotic of the Greeks, and are now your suppliants.*"

1　" Ἡμεῖς τε, ὡς πρέπον ἡμῖν καὶ ὡς ἡ χρεία προάγει,
αἰτούμεθα ὑμᾶς, θεοὺς τοὺς ὁμοβωμίους καὶ κοινοὺς
τῶν Ἑλλήνων ἐπιβοώμενοι, πεῖσαι τάδε, προφερόμενοι 500
θ' ὅρκους οὓς οἱ πατέρες ὑμῶν ὤμοσαν ἱκέται γιγνόμεθα
ὑμῶν τῶν πατρῴων τάφων καὶ ἐπικαλούμεθα τοὺς
κεκμηκότας μὴ γενέσθαι ὑπὸ Θηβαίοις μηδὲ τοῖς
ἐχθίστοις φίλτατοι ὄντες παραδοθῆναι. ἡμέρας τε
ἀναμιμνήσκομεν ἐκείνης ᾗ τὰ λαμπρότατα μετ' αὐτῶν 505
πράξαντες νῦν ἐν τῇδε τὰ δεινότατα κινδυνεύομεν
2　παθεῖν. ὅπερ δὲ ἀναγκαῖόν τε καὶ χαλεπώτατον τοῖς
ὧδε ἔχουσι λόγου τελευτᾶν, διότι καὶ τοῦ βίου ὁ κίνδυνος ἐγγὺς μετ' αὐτοῦ, παυόμενοι λέγομεν ἤδη ὅτι
οὐ Θηβαίοις παρέδομεν τὴν πόλιν (εἱλόμεθα γὰρ ἂν 510
πρό γε τούτου τῷ αἰσχίστῳ ὀλέθρῳ λιμῷ τελευτῆσαι),
ὑμῖν δὲ πιστεύσαντες προσήλθομεν (καὶ δίκαιον, εἰ μὴ
πείθομεν, ἐς τὰ αὐτὰ καταστήσαντας τὸν ξυντυχόντα
3　κίνδυνον ἐᾶσαι ἡμᾶς αὐτοὺς ἑλέσθαι), ἐπισκήπτομέν τε
ἅμα μὴ Πλαταιῆς ὄντες οἱ προθυμότατοι περὶ τοὺς 515
Ἕλληνας γενόμενοι Θηβαίοις τοῖς ἡμῖν ἐχθίστοις ἐκ
τῶν ὑμετέρων χειρῶν καὶ τῆς ὑμετέρας πίστεως, ἱκέται
ὄντες, ὦ Λακεδαιμόνιοι, παραδοθῆναι, γενέσθαι δὲ
σωτῆρας ἡμῶν καὶ μὴ τοὺς ἄλλους Ἕλληνας ἐλευθε-
ροῦντας ἡμᾶς διολέσαι."　　　　　　　　　　　520

(*In III, 60–67 the Thebans demand the right to reply.* "*The Plataeans alone of all the Boeotians refused to accept our leadership. We joined the Persians under compulsion, but afterwards we resisted the encroachments of Athens. We entered Plataea invited by its leading citizens, but their opponents slew our people in violation of their agreement. Ignore these appeals to the past and vindicate the law of the Greeks which they have outraged.*"

22 (III, 68) The Spartan commissioners decide that the Spartans are released from their obligations to the treaty of Pausanias, and again ask the Plataeans whether they have given any help to the Spartans in the war. Those who say 'no' are at once killed, 200 Plataeans and 25 Athenians. The Spartans give Plataea to some Megarians and 'loyal' Plataeans for a year and then destroy it, building near the site a temple of Hera and an inn for her worshippers; they confiscate the Plataean territory and lease it out to Theban settlers on a ten-year lease.

1   Τοιαῦτα δὲ οἱ Θηβαῖοι εἶπον. οἱ δὲ Λακεδαιμόνιοι
δικασταὶ νομίζοντες τὸ ἐπερώτημα σφίσιν ὀρθῶς ἕξειν,
εἴ τι ἐν τῷ πολέμῳ ὑπ' αὐτῶν ἀγαθὸν πεπόνθασι, διότι
τόν τε ἄλλον χρόνον ἠξίουν δῆθεν αὐτοὺς κατὰ τὰς
παλαιὰς Παυσανίου μετὰ τὸν Μῆδον σπονδὰς ἡσυχάζειν 525
καὶ ὅτε ὕστερον ἃ πρὸ τοῦ περιτειχίζεσθαι προείχοντο
αὐτοῖς, κοινοὺς εἶναι κατ' ἐκεῖνα, οὐκ ἐδέξαντο, ἡγούμενοι τῇ ἑαυτῶν δικαίᾳ βουλήσει ἔκσπονδοι ἤδη ὑπ'
αὐτῶν κακῶς πεπονθέναι, αὖθις τὸ αὐτὸ ἕνα ἕκαστον 530
παραγαγόντες καὶ ἐρωτῶντες, εἴ τι Λακεδαιμονίους
καὶ τοὺς ξυμμάχους ἀγαθὸν ἐν τῷ πολέμῳ δεδρακότες
εἰσίν, ὁπότε μὴ φαῖεν, ἀπάγοντες ἀπέκτεινον καὶ
2   ἐξαίρετον ἐποιήσαντο οὐδένα. διέφθειραν δὲ Πλαταιῶν
μὲν αὐτῶν οὐκ ἐλάσσους διακοσίων, Ἀθηναίων δὲ 535
πέντε καὶ εἴκοσιν, οἳ ξυνεπολιορκοῦντο· γυναῖκας δὲ
3   ἠνδραπόδισαν. τὴν δὲ πόλιν ἐνιαυτὸν μέν τινα Μεγαρέων
ἀνδράσι κατὰ στάσιν ἐκπεπτωκόσι καὶ ὅσοι τὰ σφέτερα
φρονοῦντες Πλαταιῶν περιῆσαν ἔδοσαν ἐνοικεῖν· ὕστερον δὲ καθελόντες αὐτὴν ἐς ἔδαφος πᾶσαν ἐκ τῶν 540
θεμελίων ᾠκοδόμησαν πρὸς τῷ Ἡραίῳ καταγώγιον
διακοσίων ποδῶν πανταχῇ κύκλῳ οἰκήματα ἔχον
κάτωθεν καὶ ἄνωθεν, καὶ ὀροφαῖς καὶ θυρώμασι τοῖς
τῶν Πλαταιῶν ἐχρήσαντο, καὶ τοῖς ἄλλοις ἃ ἦν ἐν τῷ
τείχει ἔπιπλα, χαλκὸς καὶ σίδηρος, κλίνας κατασκευά- 545
σαντες ἀνέθεσαν τῇ Ἥρᾳ, καὶ νεὼν ἑκατόμπεδον λίθινον

ῳκοδόμησαν αὐτῇ. τὴν δὲ γῆν δημοσιώσαντες ἀπεμίσ-
4 θωσαν ἐπὶ δέκα ἔτη, καὶ ἐνέμοντο Θηβαῖοι. σχεδὸν δέ
τι καὶ τὸ ξύμπαν περὶ Πλαταιῶν οἱ Λακεδαιμόνιοι
οὕτως ἀποτετραμμένοι ἐγένοντο Θηβαίων ἕνεκα, νομί- 550
ζοντες ἐς τὸν πόλεμον αὐτοὺς ἄρτι τότε καθιστάμενον
5 ὠφελίμους εἶναι. καὶ τὰ μὲν κατὰ Πλάταιαν ἔτει τρίτῳ
καὶ ἐνενηκοστῷ ἐπειδὴ Ἀθηναίων ξύμμαχοι ἐγένοντο
οὕτως ἐτελεύτησεν.

Notes

ALL Homeric forms of words are given in the Vocabulary, indicated by 'H', and peculiarities of Homeric syntax are explained in the Notes. There is therefore no separate section dealing with Homeric grammar and syntax.

l. 1. τῇ, the emphatic and demonstrative use of the article, which is nearly always a pronoun in Homer; in this line it looks forward to κούρῃ and Πηνελοπείῃ; it is also a dative of advantage, almost equivalent to a possessive genitive; 'Athene suggested to her heart, even to the heart of . . . , that she should set up (θέμεν) . . .', lit. 'put in the heart to her, even to . . .'. θῆκε, the absence of the augment is common in Homer. We must remember that at this time only Telemachus and the old nurse Eurycleia knew that Odysseus had come home; Penelope still thought that the stranger was really a beggar.

l. 2. For the 'hiatus' (absence of elision) between κούρῃ and 'Ικαρίοιο, see page 9.

l. 3. πολιὸν σίδηρον, 'the grey iron', referring to the twelve axes set up in a row in the hall, through which the suitors had to shoot an arrow, if they could first string the great bow of Odysseus, to decide which one should marry Penelope, who was now presumed to be a widow. The question of what Homer meant by this competition is discussed on pages 141-2. This is one of the few mentions of iron in Homer; it was just beginning to come into use at the end of the Bronze Age.

l. 4. ἄεθλια . . . ἀρχήν, in apposition to τόξον and σίδηρον. '(to be) the weapons for the contest and the beginning of . . .'. For the scansion of φόνου ἀρχήν, see page 9.

l. 5. προσβήσετο, 'she went up'. Penelope's bedroom was in the upper storey of the house, the other rooms on the ground floor. οἷο is the genitive of ὅς, ἥ, ὅν, the Homeric third person possessive pronoun (not the same word as the relative pronoun, whose neuter is ὅ, not ὅν, and whose genitive is οὗ or ὅου, not οἷο). δόμοιο is 'room', not 'house'.

l. 6. παχείῃ, 'strong', not perhaps a suitable epithet for a lady's hand;

it may simply be one of the Homeric 'formulaic' epithets mentioned on page 4 and here used without regard for its aptness (see also the note on l. 80), though even queens in Homeric times worked hard with their hands. The κληΐς is described in the note on l. 46.

l. 7. Notice the absence of a conjunction between καλήν and χαλκείην, and that the α of καλήν is long in Homer though short in later poets.

l. 8. βῆ ἴμεναι = ἔβη ἰέναι, 'she proceeded to go', an infinitive of purpose. The suffix -δε is added to θάλαμον to indicate motion towards, and ἔσχατον agrees with θάλαμον, 'to her chamber in the innermost part of the house'.

l. 9. οἱ is the dative of ἕ and in Homer is the same as αὐτῇ; here it is used like τῇ in l. 1 and must be taken with ἄνακτος, 'of her lord'. For the 'digammas' in this line, see page 10.

l. 13. τά = ἅ, the relative pronoun, and οἱ = αὐτῷ, i.e. Odysseus. Λακεδαίμονι τυχήσας, 'having met him in Lacedaemon'.

l. 15. τώ, the demonstrative use of the article, as in l. 1, here nominative dual; ξυμβλήτην and ἀλλήλοιϊν are also dual: 'these two met one another'. This line is unusual in containing six spondees and no dactyl at all.

l. 16. οἴκῳ ἐν = ἐν οἴκῳ.

l. 17. μετὰ χρεῖος, 'to recover (lit. 'after') a debt'. τό = ὅ, and οἱ = αὐτῷ again.

l. 18. ἄειραν, 'lifted', a word still used for the activities of sheep-stealers.

l. 19. τριηκόσια agrees with μῆλα. ἠδὲ νομῆας, 'and their shepherds too', who were also carried off by the robbers, presumably to be sold as slaves.

l. 20. τῶν ἔνεκα, 'to get them back', lit. 'for their sake'. ἐξεσίην . . . ἦλθεν, 'went on a mission, a long journey'; both nouns are 'internal' accusatives, used in an adverbial sense after an intransitive verb.

l. 21. παιδνὸς ἐών, concessive, 'though he was only a boy'. πρὸ . . . ἧκε = προῆκε; the division of a compound word into two parts by an intervening word (as in English 'what man soever' = 'whatsoever man') is called 'tmesis' ('cutting') in the later stages of the Greek language, but in Homer's time it was not so much that the compound word was divided as that the position of the preposition that helped to make up the compound word was not yet decided; it is therefore not strictly correct to call this process tmesis in Homer.

l. 22. αὔθ' = αὔθι, 'there'. Supply ἦλθε as the verb in this sentence. αἵ οἱ (= αὐτῷ) ὄλοντο, 'which he had lost', lit. 'which were lost to him', dative of disadvantage. We should make δώδεκα θηλείαι the object with ἵππους, 'searching for twelve brood mares'.

l. 23. ὑπὸ δέ, supply ἦσαν, 'and with them (lit. 'beneath') were . . .'. Mules are the offspring of mares mated with asses, and are the hardest workers of all beasts of burden.

l. 24. αἵ . . . γένοντο, 'and these indeed later were (the cause of) death and doom for him'.

l. 25. υἱὸν ἀφίκετο. πρός, to govern υἱόν, is omitted with this verb of motion. This line is unusual metrically because it begins with an iambus (∪ –) instead of a spondee (– –).

l. 26. φῶθ' Ἡρακλῆα, 'the (mighty) man, Heracles'. μεγάλων ἔργων are either 'monstrous deeds', like the slaying of Iphitus on this occasion, or 'mighty toils', the Twelve Labours of Heracles; or perhaps generally, 'great adventures'. For the quantity of Ἡρακλῆα, see page 10.

l. 27. μιν, Iphitus. ξεῖνον ἐόντα, concessive, as in l. 21, 'though he was his guest'. ᾧ is 'his', as in l. 5. Iphitus rightly suspected Heracles of having stolen his mares and came to Tiryns to recover them, whereupon Heracles first entertained and then murdered him, adding transgression of the laws of hospitality to his theft; hence σχέτλιος, 'cruel man that he was'. For the 'hiatus' in this line, see page 9.

l. 29. τὴν ἥν, demonstrative and relative pronouns: 'the one indeed that he set before him'. πέφνε καὶ αὐτόν, 'he killed the man himself too', as well as stealing his mares.

l. 31. τὰς ἐρέων, 'while enquiring for them', i.e. the mares. We now return to the history of the bow.

l. 32. τό, the article is here used as a relative pronoun, and πρίν is an adverb, 'previously'. ὁ παιδὶ κάλλιπε, 'he left it to his son', Iphitus, who is referred to as τῷ, 'to him', in l. 34.

l. 33 has a spondee instead of a dactyl in the fifth foot.

l. 35. ἀρχήν, in apposition to ξίφος καὶ ἔγχος, 'as the beginning of . . .', as in l. 4. οὐδὲ . . . ἀλλήλων, 'but they did not get to know one another at the table (of hospitality)', i.e. in the home of either of them.

l. 36. πρίν is an adverb again, 'previously'.

l. 37 is almost identical with l. 14.

l. 38. τό . . . ᾑρεῖτο (from αἱρέω), 'never took it with him on board . . .', i.e. on piratical raids before the Trojan War.

l. 40. αὐτοῦ is further explained by ἐνὶ μεγάροισι, 'it lay there in his halls as a memorial of . . .'.

l. 41. The subject of φόρει is Odysseus: 'he used to carry it in his own country, when hunting'. φόρει is the imperfect with augment omitted, not the present, φορεῖ.

l. 42. ἡ ... γυναικῶν, 'but when she, the noble lady', lit. 'noble of (i.e. among) women'; this is the 'attributive' use of the pronoun in Homer, which sometimes, when placed immediately before a noun, is almost equivalent to the Attic definite article. τόν in this line is demonstrative: 'to the chamber, that one', i.e. 'to that treasure-chamber', whose contents are described in ll. 9–12. The accusative expresses motion towards, without a preposition.

l. 43. προσεβήσετο here means 'set foot upon'. τόν = ὅν, the relative pronoun.

l. 44. This is another line with a fifth-foot spondee. ἐπὶ στάθμην ἴθυνεν, 'set it straight to the carpenter's line', a wooden ruler or perhaps a chalked piece of string.

l. 45. ἐν ... ἄρσε forms one word, ἔναρσε (from ἐναραρίσκω); see the note on l. 21.

l. 46. αὐτίκ' ἄρ' ἡ, this begins the main sentence of which the 'when'-clause starts at ὅτε in l. 42: 'straightway then she ...', ἡ being the demonstrative pronoun again. ἱμάντα κορώνης, the process of bolting and locking the double doors (θύραι) seems to have been as follows. The doors opened inwards and had two bolts, one in each leaf, fitted on the inside and each sliding into a socket in the other leaf; these bolts could be 'shot' or 'unshot' from the inside in the ordinary way. Near each bolt was a small hole in the door, through which a leather strap (ἱμάς) ran to the outside, attached to the bolt in such a way that a person who shut the door on the outside could pull the strap towards him and thus shoot the bolt. He would then tie the end of the strap to the hook or handle (κορώνη) with which he had shut the door. To open the door from the outside he first untied the strap, then inserted through the 'keyhole' a pointed metal key (κληΐς) with a carved handle of wood or ivory, the point of which fitted into a small hole in the bolt, or hooked on to a projecting piece of metal, and thus shot back the bolt. The process had to be repeated for the bolt in the other leaf of the door. Some care was needed to get the key into the hole in the bolt, which was invisible from the outside; hence ἄντα τιτυσκομένη, 'aiming straight at it'. The town gates of Plataea were barred in much the same way, but the bar was fastened with an iron pin and could be unfastened, from the inside only, with a special 'key' that fitted into the head of the pin (see the note on Thucydides II, 3).

l. 47. ἐν ... ἧκε = ἐνῆκε, as explained in the note on l. 21. ὀχῆας, plural because there was a bolt in each leaf of the door. For θύρεων, see page 10.

l. 48. τὰ δέ, 'and they', referring to the θύρετρα in l. 49, but it may be clearer to take καλὰ θύρετρα here and call them 'they' in l. 49. Presumably they 'roared' because the treasure-chamber was not often opened during Odysseus' absence and the hinges were rusty, as well as the bolts. τόσα is 'so loudly', adverbial accusative.

l. 50. πληγέντα κλήϊδι, 'when struck by the key', a strange expression for 'when opened by means of the key'. οἱ = αὐτῇ, 'to her'.

l. 51. ἡ ... βῆ, 'she stepped on to the lofty floor' of the treasure-chamber, which was upstairs; or perhaps 'she approached the lofty shelf' or 'platform', on which the treasure-chests stood.

l. 52. ἐν δ' ἄρα τῇσι, 'and in them', or we might say 'in which'. ἄρα meaning 'then' or 'indeed' can hardly be translated here, like ῥα in l. 58. The clothes were 'fragrant' because they were kept in cedar-wood chests or were treated with some perfume to keep moths away.

l. 53. ἔνθεν, 'then', or 'from there', referring to the 'lofty platform'.

l. 54. αὐτῷ γηρυτῷ, 'case and all', lit. 'with the case itself'. ὅς ... φαεινός, 'which enclosed it, all shining'; οἱ is dative, governed by περικεῖτο.

l. 55. ἑζομένη κατ' = καθεζομένη; prepositions of two syllables sometimes stand after the noun that they govern, or in Homer, as here, after the verb with which they are compounded. φίλοις, when used with parts of the body means 'one's own': 'placing it upon her knees'. In l. 56 ἐκ ... ἥρεε = ἐξῄρει, the imperfect of ἐξαιρέω. For the quantity of μάλᾱ, see page 10.

l. 58. βῆ ἔμεναι, as in l. 8. For ῥα see the note on ἄρα in l. 52. μετά, 'to find', lit. 'after'.

ll. 59–60 are almost the same as ll. 11–12.

l. 61. ἅμα is a preposition governing τῇ: 'and with her'. ἀμφίπολοι is here feminine.

l. 62. ἀέθλια τοῖο ἄνακτος, 'the war-gear of their master'; τοῖο (=τοῦ) is here almost equivalent to the Attic article, instead of having its usual (Homeric) demonstrative sense; or it may mean 'of their famous master', as in l. 258.

l. 63. ἡ ... γυναικῶν, see the note on the similar phrase in l. 42.

l. 64. παρὰ ... ποιήτου, 'beside the pillar of the well-built roof', perhaps one of the central pillars that supported the roof.

l. 65. ἄντα . . . σχομένη, 'holding in front of . . .'. This line has a fifth foot spondee.

l. 66. οἱ is governed by παρέστη, 'stood beside her'.

l. 68. οἱ . . . πινέμεν, 'who have been eager to drink and eat away this house'.

l. 70. ἀνδρὸς ἀποιχομένου, genitive absolute, 'when its master has been away for a long time'. οὐδὲ . . . ἐδύνασθε, 'and you could not find any other pretext', lit. 'make any other excuse for your story'. She might have continued with 'any other pretext for your presence than your desire to marry me', but says instead, 'but desiring to marry me and make me the wife (of one of you)'.

l. 73. φαίνετ᾽ = φαίνεται; a diphthong is sometimes elided in Homer: 'this is the prize that is set before you', lit. 'this prize appears', i.e. herself, to be the prize of the victorious suitor.

l. 74. θήσω, 'I shall bring forward'. This is another line with a fifth-foot spondee.

l. 75. ὅς κε would be ὅστις ἄν in Attic Greek: 'whoever most easily strings the bow . . .'. When not in use a bow is 'unstrung', i.e. the string is loosened so that the bow is not kept taut, but before it is used again it must be 'strung', a process requiring some skill and strength for a large bow and involving bending it and at the same time slipping the string over one end so that the bow is taut and ready for use. A description of the great bow of Odysseus and the method of stringing it is given on pages 140–1.

l. 76. πελέκεων, the last two syllables are pronounced as one by what is called 'synizesis': 'through all twelve axes', called the 'grey iron' in l. 3; the test is discussed on pages 141–2.

l. 77. ἅμα and ἑσποίμην both govern the dative: 'I should follow him', or 'go with him'. We might expect the future indicative instead of κεν with the optative in a conditional clause that starts with 'whoever strings . . .' in l. 75.

l. 78. κουρίδιον . . . βιότοιο, 'my bridal home, which is most beautiful and full of all (the necessities of) life'.

l. 79. τοῦ is relative: 'which I think I shall . . . (even) though (only) in a dream'.

l. 80. δῖον, 'goodly' or 'noble', the same epithet as that applied to Odysseus and Penelope, which when used of the swineherd may be regarded as one of the Homeric 'formulaic' epithets mentioned in the note on l. 6 which are not always apt.

l. 83. ἄλλοθι, 'in another part of the hall', but near enough to recognize his master's bow.

l. 84. ἐκ . . . ὀνόμαζε = ἐξονόμαζε; see the note on l. 21.

l. 85. ἐφημέρια φρονέοντες, 'you who have thoughts only for the things of the present day'.

l. 86. There are several adjectives and verbs in the dual number in this and the following lines. δειλώ, τί . . . ὀρίνετον; 'wretched pair, why do you . . . and disturb the heart of the lady . . . ?' γυναικί is the (possessive) dative of disadvantage, like τῇ in l. 1, and ᾗ in l. 87.

l. 87. It is not possible to translate τε when it is used to give a 'generalising' sense to a relative pronoun or to ὡς or δέ; it is thus used in Attic Greek in ὥστε, ἐφ' ᾧτε, and οἷός τε. Here we must say 'her heart lies in grief for another reason (ἄλλως) also', lit. 'to whom the heart . . .'. Antinous unfairly rebukes the rustics for giving their mistress a further cause of grief.

l. 89. δαίνυσθε and κλαίετον are imperative, one plural, the other dual.

l. 90. κατ' . . . λιπόντε = καταλιπόντε.

l. 91. ἄεθλον, in apposition to τόξα, '(to be) a terrible contest for . . .'.

l. 92. ῥηιδίως ἐντανύεσθαι, future infinitive: 'will easily be strung'.

l. 93. μέτα = μέτεστι, 'no man is present . . . such as Odysseus was'.

l. 95. πάϊς is scanned as two syllables by what is called 'diaeresis', and δέ here is an example of Homeric 'parataxis', i.e. there are two main verbs connected by 'and' instead of a dependent verb and a main verb; 'and I was still a young child' really means 'although I was still a young child'.

l. 96. τῷ is another (possessive) dative of advantage and refers to Antinous: 'but his heart . . . hoped that he would . . .'; the subject of the two infinitives, being different from the subject of the main verb, would normally be expressed in the accusative.

l. 98. ἦ τοι . . . ἔμελλε, 'indeed he was to be the first to taste the arrow shot from . . .'.

l. 99. τότε, 'recently', when he taunted the disguised Odysseus and threw a bone at him (not in this book).

l. 100. ἐπὶ . . . ὄρνυε = ἐπόρνυε.

l. 101. ἱερὴ ἲς Τηλεμάχοιο, 'the mighty prince Telemachus', lit. 'the sacred might of . . .'.

l. 102. ὢ πόποι, here an exclamation of surprise, like 'good heavens!' We see from l. 105 that Telemachus laughed at Antinous' words, or at the prospect of his father's coming revenge, and he now excuses himself for having apparently laughed foolishly on hearing of his mother's intention to marry one of the suitors; 'good heavens, Zeus has indeed deprived me of my wits', lit. 'has made me witless'.

l. 103. μοι, probably with μήτηρ, as in l. 1, 'my dear mother', not with φησί. περ is here used to strengthen the adjective πινυτή, 'wise as she is', not with its more common concessive meaning.

l. 104 is almost the same as l. 77, and l. 106 = l. 73.

l. 107. The antecedent of οἵη is γυνή, which must be taken first in apposition to ἄεθλον: 'this prize . . . , even a lady such as (or 'like whom') there is no one in the land of Achaea or in sacred Pylos . . .'; the genitive cases in these lines are locative.

l. 109. ἠπείροιο μελαίνης, 'on the dark mainland', which had darker and more fertile soil.

l. 110. καὶ δ' . . . ἴστε, 'and indeed (δέ) you know this yourselves'. χρή here takes an accusative and a genitive: 'what need have I of (i.e. to speak of) my mother's praises?'

l. 111. ἄγε, 'come now'; the singular is used as an interjection though Telemachus is addressing several people. μὴ . . . ἴδωμεν, 'do not drag out (the affair) with . . . , and do not refrain any longer from the stringing . . . , that we may see (the result)'.

l. 113. καὶ . . . πειρησαίμην, 'and indeed I myself would (i.e. should like to) make trial of . . .'. This is another line with a fifth-foot spondee.

l. 114. εἴ κεν with the subjunctive is equivalent to the Attic ἐάν, which is here followed in the main clause by κε (= ἄν) with the optative in a 'mixed' conditional sentence; 'if I string it, my lady mother would not cause me sorrow by leaving this house', lit. 'would not leave . . . to me sorrowing', dative of disadvantage.

l. 116. ὅτε . . . οἷός τε, 'since I should be left behind, now able to . . .'. ἀέθλια . . . ἀνελέσθαι has been taken to mean 'to win the splendid prizes', 'to take up the noble weapons', or 'to undertake the splendid contest'; perhaps the first is the most likely.

l. 118. ἦ, 'he spoke', imperfect of ἠμί. ὤμοιϊν is genitive dual. θέτο, 'put off'. The οε of φοινικόεσσαν is pronounced as one long syllable (by 'synizesis'), so that the fifth foot is a spondee.

l. 119. ὀρθὸς ἀναΐξας, 'springing up to his full height', lit. 'straight'. ἀπὸ . . . θέτο = ἀπόθετο, in which ἀπό governs ὤμων: 'he took off his baldric from . . .'. In l. 118 the simple verb θέτο is used, with ἀπό as an ordinary preposition. A baldric was a sword-belt which went across the body and over the right shoulder.

l. 120. πελέκεας is scanned ∪ ∪ –, like πελέκεων in l. 76. διὰ ... ὀρύξας = διορύξας, 'digging one long trench for them all'; the floor of the hall was made of earth beaten down hard.

l. 121. ἐπὶ στάθμην ἴθυνεν, see the note on l. 44; it was necessary to make the trench, or rather the earth dug out of it, exactly straight and of equal height all along, so that there should be a straight line for an arrow to be shot through the axe-heads.

l. 122. ἀμφί, an adverb, 'round about'. τάφος ... ἰδόντας, 'amazement seized them all as they saw it'.

l. 123. ὡς ... στῆσε, an indirect question, 'how well he placed them in order', because 'he had never seen it done before'; but it seems likely that Penelope or even Odysseus had told him how to do it and he may even have done the preliminary work on this laborious task before the suitors assembled. The problem of the trench and how the axe-heads were arranged is discussed on pages 142–3.

l. 124. ἰών, present participle where we might expect 'having gone'. The imperfect πειρήτιζε means 'began to make trial of'. This line has another fifth-foot spondee.

l. 125. ἐπιελπόμενος τὸ θυμῷ, 'though he hoped indeed in his heart (to do) it', followed by an infinitive which explains τό, '(that is,) to string the bow ...', lit. 'stretch the string'.

l. 128. κε ἐτάνυσσε, 'he would have strung it, straining at it ... for the fourth time'; τέταρτον is adverbial accusative. Instead of an εἰ-clause in l. 129 we have 'but Odysseus made a sign of dissent and restrained him, though he was eager (to try it)'. Even today Greeks signify refusal by nodding their heads upwards (ἀνανεύειν) and agreement by nodding downwards (κατανεύειν).

l. 130 is the same as l. 101.

l. 131. ἦ μὴν ... ἀπαμύνασθαι, 'indeed I shall be a coward ... even in the future (ἔπειτα), or else I am too young and do not yet trust my hands to defend myself against a man'.

l. 133. πρότερος, 'unprovoked', lit. 'first'.

l. 134. οἵ ... ἐστε, 'you who are superior in strength to me'; ἐμεῖο is genitive of comparison.

l. 135. πειρήσεσθε, aorist imperative. ἐκτελέωμεν is an exhortation: 'let us finish the contest'.

l. 136. ἀπὸ ἕο (=οὗ, from ἕ); 'away from himself'.

l. 137. κλίνας σανίδεσσιν, 'leaning it against the . . . planks', that formed the double doors.

l. 138. αὐτοῦ, 'there'. βελος is the arrow and κορώνη (probably) the hooked tip at one end of the bow, over which the string was hitched when the bow was bent and strung; the arrow was therefore the same length as the unstrung bow, which was much shorter than the famous six-foot 'long bow' of the English archers; the older 'short bow' was a less effective weapon when made of wood, but the 'composite' bow, like this bow of Odysseus (see pages 140–1), was as powerful as the long bow. It is possible that the κορώνη is the door-handle here, as in l. 46, but if this is so, since Telemachus was standing inside the door, there must have been a handle on the inside as well as the usual outside handle described in the note on l. 46.

l. 139. κατ' . . . ἕζετ' =καθέζετο.

l. 141. ἐπιδέξια, adverbial neuter plural accusative: 'rise up in order from left to right', beginning with the man sitting just to the left of the κρητήρ, the bowl in which the wine and water were mixed; he then handed the bowl to the man on his right, and so on; nowadays we regard it as unlucky to pass the port after dinner 'widdershins', i.e. counter-clockwise, as the Greeks used to do. Wine in Greece and Rome was seldom drunk 'neat', but usually mixed with water.

l. 142. ἀρξάμενοι . . . οἰνοχοεύει, 'beginning from the place where he (the cup-bearer) pours out the wine'; τε is the 'generalising' particle mentioned in the note on l. 87.

l. 144. πρῶτος ἀνίστατο, 'was the first to stand up'.

l. 145. ὅ, the relative pronoun: 'who was their soothsayer'. παρά is 'beside'.

l. 146. μυχοίτατος, 'at the far end of the hall', lit. 'innermost'. ἀτασθαλίαι . . . ἔσαν, 'to him alone their reckless follies were hateful'.

l. 148. ὅς . . . λάβε, 'he indeed then was the first to take . . .'.

l. 149 is the same as l. 124.

l. 150. οὐδέ, 'but did not . . .'. πρίν is an adverb, and χεῖρας an internal accusative of respect; lit. 'he grew weary in his hands', i.e. 'his . . . hands grew weary as he tried to bend the bow'. Notice the absence of a conjunction between the two adjectives, as in l. 7, and the contrast between Leodes' 'unworn and delicate' hands and Penelope's 'strong' hand in l. 6 (but see the note there on Homer's 'formulaic' adjectives).

l. 151. μετά may govern μνηστῆρσιν, 'among the suitors', or it may combine with ἔειπε to form one word (see the note on l. 21); the meaning the same in either case.

l. 152. οὐ τανύω, 'I cannot bend it'. λαβέτω is aorist imperative: 'let another indeed take it'.

l. 153. Leodes probably means only that failure to bend the bow will cause bitter disappointment to the suitors and even suicide to some, but to Homer's hearers and readers he is foretelling the vengeance of Odysseus; on the Attic stage this double meaning is called 'dramatic irony'.

l. 154. θυμοῦ καὶ ψυχῆς, 'of spirit and life', genitives of separation. ἦ here is 'indeed', but ἤ in l. 155 is 'than': 'indeed it is much better (for us) to die than that living on (this agrees with ἡμᾶς understood) we should fail to obtain (the prize) for the sake of which (τε is the 'generalising' particle again, as in l. 87) we always assemble here, expecting it every day'; the object of ἁμαρτεῖν is ἀέθλου understood, here meaning marriage with Penelope.

l. 157. νῦν τις καί, 'even now some (of you) hope'; notice the elision of -αι in ἔλπετ', as in l. 73.

l. 159. πειρήσεται = πειράσηται, aorist subjunctive, like ἴδηται, after ἐπήν, which = ἐπεὶ ἄν. Supply some word like 'the result' as the object of ἴδηται.

l. 160. This is another line with a fifth-foot spondee.

l. 161. μνάσθω . . . διζήμενος, 'let him woo . . . desiring (to marry her)'. ἡ δέ κ' . . . ἔλθοι, 'and Penelope would (almost = 'will') marry whoever brings most (gifts) and comes appointed by fate'. In Homer κε (as in l. 162) is used with the optative in an indefinite relative clause in historic sequence (in this sentence historic because the main verb is optative), whereas in Attic Greek the subjunctive is used with ἄν in primary sequence, the optative without ἄν in historic sequence.

ll. 163–166 are almost the same as ll. 137–139, and l. 167 is the same as l. 84.

l. 168. ποῖον . . . ὀδόντων, 'what a word has escaped you, even the barrier of your teeth'; σε . . . ἕρκος is an example of what is called the 'whole and part' construction.

l. 169. The two adjectives agree with ἔπος in l. 168, which must be repeated here: 'a hard and grievous word'. For δέ τε see the note on l. 87; here it is translated simply as 'and'.

l. 172. οἷόν τε . . . ὀιστῶν, 'strong enough to be able to draw a bow and (shoot) arrows', lit. 'such as to be able to be a drawer of a bow . . .'.

l. 174. τανύουσι, future, as in l. 92.

l. 175. The treacherous goatherd Melanthius had twice grossly insulted the supposed beggar (not in this book), and had supported the suitors against Penelope and Telemachus.

l. 177. πὰρ . . . τίθει = παρατίθει, imperative: 'place beside it'.

l. 178. ἐκ . . . ἔνεικε = ἐξένεικε, Homeric aorist imperative of ἐκφέρω. στέατος, which depends on τροχόν, is scanned as two syllables (– ⏑) by 'synizesis'. ἔνδον ἐόντος, 'that is in (the kitchen)'.

l. 178. ὄφρα . . . πειρώμεσθα (= πειρώμεθα), 'that we young men, warming it (and) greasing it with fat, may make trial of the bow'; the melted fat would make the bow more supple and easy to bend. ll. 182–184 are nearly the same as ll. 177–178, except that the two imperatives are now third person aorist indicative. τῷ in l. 184 is 'with it', or 'with which'.

l. 185. πολλὸν . . . ἦσαν, 'they were greatly (adverbial accusative) lacking in strength'.

l. 186. ἐπεῖχε, 'held back' from the attempt, intransitive, and singular to agree with the nearest subject, though referring also to Eurymachus. In ll. 245 ff. Eurymachus fails in the test and Antinous puts off his attempt until the next day, which never came for him.

l. 187. ἀρετῇ, 'in strength', or 'in valour', but not in courtesy or chivalry, though Homer calls Eurymachus 'goodly' in l. 186, which may be one of the 'formulaic' epithets mentioned in the note on l. 6, not at all applicable to any of the suitors; the swineherd is similarly called noble', in l. 80, perhaps with more justice.

l. 188. τώ, demonstrative nominative dual, looking forward to the two nouns in the next line: 'so those two . . . , both walking together, the oxherd and . . .'; ὁμαρτήσαντες is aorist with present meaning, and l. 189 has a fifth-foot spondee.

l. 190. ἐκ . . . ἤλυθε = ἐξήλυθε. δόμου is genitive of separation, and μετὰ τούς is 'after them'. This is only the second mention of Odysseus' presence in the hall in this book; he has been sitting quietly listening to what is going on, though he gave his son a warning look in l. 129.

l. 191. αὐλῆς, the open courtyard in front of the great hall, μέγαρον, surrounded by an outside wall, ἕρκος, whose doors admitted visitors into is the αὐλή, from which other doors opened into the hall.

l. 192. φθεγξάμενος, another aorist with present meaning. σφε, 'them', the object of προσηύδα.

l. 193. τί, not interrogative, but indefinite with the accent thrown back from κε: 'should I utter a word or am I to conceal it?' κεύθω is a subjunctive in a 'deliberative' question, and l. 193 has a fifth-foot spondee.

l. 195. εἶτε, optative of εἰμί: 'what kind of men would you be for helping Odysseus (the infinitive is 'epexegetic' or explanatory), if he were to come like this, quite suddenly, from somewhere, and if some god were to bring him?'

l. 197. ἤ κε ... ἤ, 'would you help ... or ...?'

l. 198. εἴπαθ' ὅπως, 'tell me, just as your ...'. ὑμέας (= ὑμᾶς) is pronounced as two long syllables, by 'synizesis'.

l. 199. In ἀνήρ the a is long, though short in Attic Greek.

l. 200. αἲ γάρ with the optative is a wish: 'O that you would fulfil this desire, that that man should come (back) ...'.

l. 202. γνοίης κε, the main clause of a conditional sentence of which the εἰ-clause is not expressed: 'you would then know (i.e. if my wish were granted) what my strength (is) and (how) my hands follow (my wishes)'.

l. 203. ὡς αὔτως = ὡσαύτως. ἐπεύχετο is followed by an accusative and infinitive: 'prayed ... that Odysseus should return ...'. In l. 204 the suffix-δε, denoting motion towards, is attached to the possessive pronoun as well as to the noun: 'to his home'.

l. 205. νημερτέα, accusative, used predicatively with νόον; 'when he knew their intentions for certain'.

l. 207. ἔνδον ... ἐγώ, 'here I (am) myself, at home'.

l. 208. There are several metrical irregularities in this line, which are explained on page 10.

l. 209. ὡς ... δμώων, 'that I have come welcomed by you two alone of the servants', lit. 'to you desiring (it)'; this use of the dative of advantage occurs in Thucydides 2, 2 (in this book), τῷ πλήθει οὐ βουλομένῳ ἦν ἀφίστασθαι, 'the people were not willing to break away'.

l. 210. τῶν ἄλλων ... ἱκέσθαι, 'I have not heard any (τευ = τινος) of the others praying that I should return ...'.

l. 212. ὡς ἔσεταί περ, 'just as it shall come to pass', lit. 'shall be'.

l. 213. εἴ κε = ἐάν. ὑπ' ἐμοί, 'under my power'.

l. 214. ἀμφοτέροις ἀλόχους, 'I shall provide a wife for each of you'.

l. 215. ἐγγὺς ἐμεῖο τετυγμένα, 'built near mine', lit. 'near me'.

l. 216. ἔσεσθον, future dual, 'you shall be the comrades ...'.

l. 217. εἰ δ' ἄγε δή, 'but come now', a strengthened form of ἄγε; for the singular, see the note on l. 111.

l. 218. γνῶτον, πιστωθῆτον, second person dual aorist subjunctive: 'that you may know me well'.

l. 219. οὐλήν, in apposition to σῆμα, 'even the scar which the boar dealt me'. με is the direct object of ἤλασε (from ἐλαύνω), and τήν, the relative pronoun, is internal (cognate) accusative, lit. 'which he struck me'.

l. 221. μεγάλης ... οὐλῆς, 'he drew back ... from the long scar'. For the quantity of ῥάκεα, in which the final -α is lengthened before μ in μεγάλης, see page 10.

l. 222. One verb is dual, the other plural: 'when those two (τὼ) looked at it and noted well every detail'. In l. 223 χεῖρε βαλόντε are also dual: 'throwing their arms round . . .'.

l. 224. κύνεον ἀγαπαζόμενοι, 'kept on kissing his face and hands lovingly' lit. 'loving (him)'; the imperfect shows repeated action, while the aorist ἔκυσσε perhaps means that Odysseus kissed them once only. ὤμους usually means 'shoulders'.

l. 226. καί νύ κ' . . . φάος, 'and indeed the light . . . would have gone down while they were still weeping', lit. 'to them weeping'. They were of course weeping for joy.

l. 228. παυέσθον, dual imperative, with a genitive of separation: cease from . . .'.

l. 229. μεγάροιο, governed by the ἐξ of ἐξέλθων. ἀτάρ is 'and' rather than 'but', and εἴπῃσι is still part of the purpose clause introduced by μή, 'and then report it also within'.

l. 230. ἐσέλθετε is imperative, addressed to the two servants, but as it is followed by μηδ' ἅμα πάντες and then by ἐγώ, it is better translated as 'let us go in . . . , not all together, but first I, then you'; μετά is an adverb.

l. 231. τόδε σῆμα τετύχθω, 'let this arrangement be made between us', lit. 'let this sign be arranged'; no actual sign is mentioned, but Odysseus means that when the suitors refuse to give him the bow Eumaeus is to hand it to him and give the women their orders.

l. 232. ὅσοι, supply εἰσί, lit. 'as many as are . . .', but we should say 'the others, all the proud suitors, . . .'. The object of ἐάσουσιν in l. 233 is 'anyone'; the first two vowels of ἐάσουσιν are scanned as one long syllable, by 'synizesis'.

l. 234. ἀνὰ δώματα, 'through the hall'.

l. 235. ἐμοί, (possessive) dative of advantage: 'in my hands'. θεμέναι and εἰπεῖν are infinitives used as second person plural imperatives, and εἰπεῖν with the dative here means 'order'.

l. 236. κληῖσαι . . . ἀραρυίας, 'to shut the well-fitted doors of the hall', to prevent the suitors from escaping. μεγάροιο may perhaps refer to the women's chamber, in which they must now shut themselves up; in any case they are to leave the great hall.

l. 237. ἤν τις, 'if any of them'. ἀκούσῃ governs the genitives στοναχῆς and κτύπου, upon which ἀνδρῶν depends. ἔνδον may go with ἀκούσῃ, 'in their own quarters', or may look forward to ἡμετέροισιν ἐν ἔρκεσιν, 'the sound of men inside, within our walls', which enclosed the whole palace.

l. 239. The infinitives are again imperative, this time third person plural: 'let them not go out of the doors at all (τι), but stay (lit. 'be') there in silence at their work', of spinning.

l. 241. κληῖδι, 'with a bolt', not with the sort of key described in the note on l. 46. ἐπὶ . . . ἰῆλαι = ἐπιῆλαι, 'to put a fastening on it as well'; in ll. 390–391 Philoetius uses 'a rope of byblus' from a ship to make the door of the courtyard quite safe against help coming to the suitors from outside.

l. 244. ἐς . . . ἴτην = ἐσίτην, dual imperfect of ἔσειμι: 'the two servants . . . also went in'.

l. 245. The main narrative is now resumed after the digression in ll. 188–244. ἤδη is 'by this time'; all the suitors except Eurymachus and Antinous have now tried to string the bow.

l. 246. οὐδ ὧς, 'not even so'.

l. 247. μέγα, used adverbially, 'loudly', or 'deeply'. καρπάλιμον κῆρ, 'in his noble heart', an internal accusative of respect; for the unsuitable 'formulaic' epithet see the note on l. 6.

l. 249. ἦ μοι ἄχος (ἐστὶ) περί τ' αὐτοῦ, 'indeed I am vexed both for my-self . . .'.

l. 250. οὔ τι τοσσοῦτον, adverbial accusative: 'not so much for . . .', with a genitive. περ is concessive, like καίπερ, with a participle: 'though I am angry'.

l. 251. καί, 'also'. αἱ μὲν . . . αἱ δέ, 'some in . . . , others in . . .'.

l. 253. Repeat ὀδύρομαι (from l. 250) before εἰ, which is the usual con-junction after verbs of surprise and annoyance, instead of ὅτι; 'but I am grieved because we are so inferior in strength to . . .'; ἐπιδευέες has first a genitive of respect, βίης, showing in what they were inferior, and then a genitive of comparison, Ὀδυσῆος, showing to whom they were inferior.

l. 254. ὅ τε, accusative of respect, with the 'generalising' τε, as in l. 87: 'in that we cannot', lit. 'with regard to the fact that we cannot . . .'.

l. 255. Supply ἔσται with ἐλεγχείη: 'it will be a disgrace even for those still to be (born) to hear of it'.

l. 257. οὐχ . . . αὐτός, 'it shall not be so, and you yourself also know it'.

l. 258. Supply ἐστί as the verb: 'today (νῦν) it is the sacred festival of the (archer) god', i.e. Apollo, mentioned by name in l. 267, whose feast was by 'dramatic irony' (see the note on l. 153) a suitable day for Odysseus' slaughter of the suitors with his bow. τοῖο θεοῖο, the article in Homer sometimes implies distinction: 'the famous god'. Antinous makes an excuse for putting off his attempt to string the bow, which in fact he will never have the chance of doing, though one might think that the festival of the archer god was a very suitable day for such an attempt, in spite of his saying in l. 259 'who would want to bend the bow (today)?' ἔκηλοι κάτθετε (aorist imperative of κατατίθημι), 'quietly put it aside'.

l. 260. καὶ εἴ κε, this conditional clause has no main sentence: 'even if we let all the axes stand (where they are) . . .'; he then breaks off, leaving unsaid something like 'what does it matter?' and goes on 'for I do not think that anyone will come . . . and take them away'. ἑστάμεν = ἑστάναι, perfect infinitive of ἕστημι.

l. 262. The last two syllables of Λαερτιάδεω are scanned as one long syllable, by 'synizesis'; so also the last two syllables of πελέκεας in l. 260.

l. 263. ἐπαρξάσθω, aorist imperative: 'let the wine-bearer pour the first drops into the cups', which were emptied out as a 'libation' (offering) to the gods before the real drinking began.

l. 264. καταθείομεν = καταθῶμεν, aorist subjunctive of κατατίθημι.

l. 266. Supply εἰσί with αἴ, but we put the superlative adjective in the main clause: 'to bring the very (μέγα) best goats that there are in . . .'.

l. 267. ἐπὶ . . . θέντες = ἐπιθέντες, 'after offering the thigh-pieces'; it was customary to offer to the gods only the thigh-pieces, wrapped in two folds of fat.

l. 270. τοῖσι . . . ἐπὶ χεῖρας, 'on to their hands', (possessive) dative of advantage.

l. 272. πᾶσιν, with νώμησαν, and δεπάεσσιν with ἐπαρξάμενοι, as in l. 263.

l. 273. ὅσον . . . θυμός, 'to their hearts' content', lit. 'as much as their hearts wished'.

l. 274. δέ here shows the main verb after a temporal clause; it is called δέ 'in apodosis'; there are two slightly different examples in Antiphon, 23 and 43.

l. 276. τά, a relative pronoun: 'what my heart bids me do'.

l. 277. The -εα of θεοείδεα is scanned as one long syllable, by 'synizesis'.

l. 278. λίσσομ' = λίσσομαι, with the diphthong elided, as in l. 73. ἐπεὶ ... ἔειπε, 'since he has indeed (καί) spoken these words aright', lit. 'according to fate'.

l. 279. The infinitives depend on λίσσομαι: 'to put a stop to the archery (lit. 'the bow') and entrust (the result) to the gods'.

l. 280. δώσει ... ἐθέλῃσιν, 'will give the victory to whomever he wishes'.

l. 281. ὄφρα ... ἄλη τ', 'that in your presence I may make trial (aorist subjunctive) of my hands ... (to see) whether I still have the strength such as was formerly in my ..., or whether my wanderings ... have now destroyed it'; ἤ ... ἤ = πότερον ... ἤ in a double indirect question.

l. 288. δειλὲ ξείνων, 'wretched stranger', lit. 'of strangers'. ἔνι = ἔνεισι; 'there is no sense in you, not even the smallest'. This line, like l. 284, has a fifth-foot spondee.

l. 289. ὅ, accusative of respect: 'are you not satisfied that (lit. 'with regard to the fact that') you are feasting at your ease among us honourable men?'

l. 291. ἡμετέρων μύθων, governed by ἀκούεις.

l. 293. ὅς τε ... πίνῃ, 'which harms others too, anyone who (lit. 'whoever') takes it greedily and does not drink in moderation'; for ὅς τε see the note on l. 87. αἴσιμα is adverbial accusative, and μηδείς the normal negative in an indefinite clause.

l. 295. καί, 'also'. The Centaurs in Homer are a fierce race of men living on Mount Pelion in Thessaly. In the *Iliad* he calls them 'wild shaggy beasts', and here (l. 303) they are contrasted with 'men', though references to their being half-man and half-horses are not earlier than Pindar in the fifth century B.C.; the legend no doubt arose from their skill in horsemanship. At the wedding-feast of Pirithous, king of the Lapithae, and Hippodamia, the centaur Eurytion got drunk and tried to abduct the bride, which led to the famous fight between the Lapiths and the Centaurs.

l. 298. δόμον, governed by κάτα, which when it follows the word it governs is accentuated on the first instead of on the second syllable: 'in the house'.

l. 299. ἥρωας, i.e. the Lapiths: 'wrath seized the heroes'.

l. 300. ἕλκον, 'they dragged away', ἀπ' ... ἀμήσαντες = ἀπαμήσαντες.

l. 302. ἤιεν ... ὀχέων, 'he went about, carrying (the burden of) his (ἥν) folly'. In l. 301, 'infatuated in his heart', seems to mean that his senses were permanently deranged as the result of the treatment he received from the Lapiths, though in the preceding lines the same verb is used of the infatuation caused by wine.

l. 303. ἐξ οὗ, 'from that time'. νεῖκος ἐτύχθη, 'enmity was caused between ...'.

l. 304. οἱ αὐτῷ = ἑαυτῷ, 'he brought evil upon himself first (by) being ...'.

l. 305. ὣς καί, 'so too'. αἴ κε = ἐάν. τό is here used almost like the Attic definite article, or it may mean 'the famous ...'; see the notes on ll. 42 and 258.

l. 306. τευ ἐπητύος, 'any kindness', or 'kindness from anyone', governed by ἀντιβολήσεις.

l. 308. King Echetus, the typical ogre-king of mythology, is mentioned only twice by Homer.

l. 309. οὔ τι σαώσεαι, the future middle of σῴζω: 'you will never come back safe'.

l. 310. τε connects the two verbs: 'drink at your ease and do not ...'.

l. 312. Supply ἐστί as the verb: 'it is not right or just to ...'.

l. 313. ὅς κεν ... ἵκηται, 'any who (lit. 'whoever', as in l. 294) come to ...'. τάδε δώματα is accusative of goal of motion without a reposition.

l. 314. ἔλπεαι ... ἄκοιτιν, 'do you expect that if (αἴ κε = ἐάν) the stranger bends ..., he will take me to his home and make me his wife?' πιθήσας, 'trusting in'; -φι can be added to all declensions, singular and plural, in the genitive and dative cases. The subject of ἄξεσθαι is αὐτόν understood.

l. 318. μηδέ ... ἔοικε, 'let none of you feast here sad at heart because of that (τοῦ), since that would never, never be right', lit. 'is right'. θυμόν is an internal accusative (of respect), and οὐδὲ μὲν οὐδέ is a strong negative. There is 'dramatic irony' in the fact that Penelope is defending the supposed beggar while regarding marriage with him as quite impossible.

l. 320. τήν, governed by ηὔδα, with ἀντίον used adverbially: 'spoke to her in reply'. πάϊς, two syllables, as in l. 95.

l. 322. οὔ τι . . . ὀϊόμεθα, 'we certainly do not think that this man . . .'. οὐδὲ ἔοικε, as in l. 318: 'nor would it be right (for us to think so)'.

l. 323. αἰσχυνόμενοι, we should expect a main verb, parallel with ὀϊόμεθα: 'but we feel shame at the talk . . . , (fearing) that someone among the Achaeans, a more worthless man, will say'; he pretends to be afraid of the gossip of uncharitable people.

l. 325. ἤ . . . μνῶνται, 'indeed men who are far too inferior are wooing . . .'.

l. 326. οὐδὲ . . . ἐντανύουσιν, 'and they cannot string . . . at all'; τι is adverbial accusative.

l. 327. ἄλλος . . . ἀλαλήμενος, 'someone else, a wandering beggar'.

l. 328. διὰ . . . ἧκε = διῆκε.

l. 329. ἡμῖν . . . γένοιτο, 'this would be a disgrace to us', though he does not think that the whole behaviour of the suitors towards Penelope is at all disgraceful, in spite of her plain speaking in the lines that follow.

l. 331. ἔστιν = ἔξεστιν, an impersonal verb followed by an accusative and infinitive: 'it is not possible that (men) should be renowned among the people when they (lit. 'who') dishonour and eat up the house . . .'.

l. 333. ἐλέγχεα refers to Eurymachus' fear of what people may say about the suitors' being defeated by the beggar: 'why do you reckon this (to be) a disgrace?' Like the Pharisees, they were straining at a gnat and swallowing a camel.

l. 334. μάλα μέγας (ἐστί), 'is very tall'. This line has a fifth-foot spondee.

l. 335. γένος, accusative of respect: 'he declares that he is by birth (γένος) a son (sprung) from a noble father'. In XIX, ll. 170 ff. the beggar told Penelope that he was Aethon, son of Deucalion and grandson of Minos, king of Crete, so that as far as birth was concerned he was not unworthy to marry her, despite her disclaimer in l. 319; he also told a maidservant in XIX, ll. 71 ff. that he had been rich but had come down in the world by the will of Zeus. It seems cruel that he did not at once make himself known to his faithful wife after twenty years' absence, but perhaps he thought that in her joy she might not be able to keep the secret from the suitors until he had had his revenge upon them.

l. 336. οἱ = αὐτῷ; so also in l. 338. ὄφρα ἴδωμεν, 'so that we may see (the result)'.

l. 337. τὸ . . . ἔσται, 'and it shall surely (καί) be accomplished'.

l. 339. ἔσσω (from ἕννυμι) takes two accusatives: 'I shall clothe him in . . .', with εἵματα καλά, 'fair raiment', in apposition to χλαῖνάν τε χιτῶνά τε.

l. 340. ἀλκτῆρα, 'to protect him against . . .', lit. 'the driver off of . . .'.

l. 341. ὑπὸ ποσσί, 'for (lit. 'under') his feet'.

l. 342. ὅππῃ, 'wherever', with the indicative, which would be subjunctive with ἄν in Attic Greek in an indefinite clause.

l. 344. τόξον is the object of δόμεναί τε καὶ ἀρνήσασθαι, but we can keep its emphatic position by saying 'as for the bow, no one . . . has greater authority (lit. 'is more powerful') than I to give it or (lit. 'and') refuse it to whomever I wish'. l. 345 has a fifth-foot spondee.

l. 346. οὔθ' ὅσσοι . . . πρός, 'neither of those who (lit. 'as many as') rule in . . . nor in the islands (local dative) in the direction of . . .'; κάτα, with the accent on the first syllable, governs the words that precede it, as in l. 298, and the neighbouring islands are Dulichium, Same, and Zacynthus. Notice this meaning of πρός with a genitive.

l. 348. τῶν . . . φέρεσθαι, 'none of them shall compel me against my will (not to do it), even if (αἴ κε καί) I want to give it to the stranger once (and for all) to take away', as a present; hence the middle voice, φέρεσθαι, which is an 'epexegetic' or explanatory infinitive.

l. 350. εἰς οἶκον, 'to your room', not her private bedchamber upstairs, to which she goes in l. 356, but to the women's quarters where the spinning and other tasks were done. τὰ σὰ αὐτῆς ἔργα κόμιζε, 'look after your own tasks'; αὐτῆς agrees with the possessive genitive σου, which is understood in the possessive pronoun σά.

l. 351. κέλευε here governs the dative.

l. 352. τόξον . . . ἔστ', 'the bow shall be the concern of all the men but especially of me, for mine is the authority . . .'; the demonstrative pronoun τοῦ is equivalent to ἐμοῦ.

l. 354. ἡ μὲν θαμβήσασα, 'so she in amazement', at her son's unexpected display of authority; she went first to the women's quarters and then upstairs to her own room, ὑπερῷα.

l. 355. παιδὸς . . . θυμῷ, 'she kept in her heart her son's wise words', like Mary when she was rebuked by Christ as a boy in St. Luke II, 19 and 51.

l. 357. κλαῖεν, perhaps because her son's behaviour or appearance reminded her more than ever of her absent husband. ὄφρα is 'until' and οἱ (= αὐτῇ) is a (possessive) dative of advantage with βλεφάροισιν 'upon her eyelids'. From XXII, l. 429 it seems that Athena caused Penelope to go to sleep unusually early so that she should not see the events that were to take place in the hall.

l. 359. ὁ . . . δῖος ὑφορβός, 'he, the goodly swineherd'; the adjective, for which see the note on l. 80, contrasts strangely with ἀμέγαρτε and πλαγκτέ, which 'one of the haughty young men' calls him in ll. 362 and 363.

l. 363. ταχ' . . . ἰλήσκῃσι, 'soon indeed will the swift hounds which you (yourself) bred devour you among the swine, alone (and away) from men, if Apollo is gracious to us'.

l. 366. ὁ . . . χώρῃ, 'he, bearing the bow, put it down in that very place', instead of taking it to Odysseus, as was arranged in ll. 234–235.

l. 367. δείσας, οὕνεκα, 'being afraid because'; veritus is similarly used in Latin with a present meaning, and ἀπειλήσας in l. 368, another aorist participle, can be translated 'threateningly'.

l. 369. ἄττα, a friendly form of address from a younger to an older man, though Telemachus is angry with Eumaeus for endangering his father's plan by not carrying out his orders exactly. τάχα . . . πιθήσεις 'you will soon see that you cannot obey everyone', lit. 'you will soon not obey all well', i.e. he must obey Telemachus alone.

l. 370. μὴ . . . δίωμαι depends on some verb of precaution, like φυλάσσου, understood: 'take care that, though I am indeed (περ ἐών) younger than you, I do not chase you . . .'.

l. 372. αἰ γάρ with the optative generally expresses a wish for the future, but is here used in a wish for the present: 'I wish I were as superior in . . . to all the suitors (genitive of comparison) who (lit. 'as many as') are in the house (as I am superior to you)'.

l. 374. τῷ . . . νέεσθαι, 'in that case (i.e. if I were stronger than they; τῷ is the demonstrative use of the article) I should soon send some of them away to depart miserably . . .'; νέεσθαι is an infinitive of purpose.

l. 376. ἡδύ, adverbial accusative: 'laughed merrily at him'; it was to be the last time that they ever laughed. Catullus and Horace imitate this phrase in dulce ridentem, which when applied to a girl means 'laughing sweetly'.

l. 377. μέθιεν (=μεθίεσαν) . . . χόλοιο, 'ceased from their bitter anger against . . .'.

l. 379. 'Οδυσῆϊ, (possessive) dative of advantage: 'put it into the hands of Odysseus'.

l. 380. ἐκ . . . καλεσσάμενος = ἐκκαλεσσάμενος. This line and the next have fifth-foot spondees.

ll. 382–385 are the same as ll. 236–239.

l. 386. τῇ . . . μῦθος, 'his words stayed wingless within her', lit. 'were wingless to her', which perhaps means that they stayed in her mind without flying away, so that she did not forget to carry out his orders, or that she obeyed without making any reply, words being regarded as passing on wings from one person to another.

l. 390. ὑπ' αἰθούσῃ, 'in the colonnade', here a verandah built against the outer wall of the courtyard, facing the doors of the great hall. ὅπλον βύβλινον, 'a rope of byblus', made from Egyptian papyrus and imported from Egypt; it was also used for making paper, hence the word 'Bible'. νεός = νεώς, 'ship'. In l. 391 ἐς . . . ἤϊεν = ἐσῄει.

l. 393 is the same as l. 243.

l. 394. πειρώμενος ἔνθα καὶ, ἔνθα, 'testing it this way and that'.

l. 395. μὴ . . . ἄνακτος, 'for fear that worms might have eaten away the horn while its owner was away', genitive absolute. Insects called scolytidae feed on horn; for a description of the bow, see pages 140–1. The optative or subjunctive with verbs of fearing usually refer to the future (here 'would eat'), but in this context the optative must refer to the past but not so definitely as the aorist indicative, 'had eaten'.

l. 396. ἰδὼν . . . ἄλλον, 'looking at another, next to him'.

l. 397. ἦ . . . ἔπλετο, 'surely he must be an expert (lit. 'he was an admirer') and skilled in . . .'.

l. 398. ἤ ῥα . . . ἀλήτης, 'either, I think (που), he too has such a bow lying at home, or he is eager to make one, so (skilfully) does he . . . , this vagabond practised in evil'.

l. 402. αἲ γὰρ . . . δυνήσεται, 'I hope this man will obtain success just as much as he shall ever be able to string this bow', lit. 'may he obtain as much success (partitive genitive) as this man shall be able . . .', which he thinks will be no success at all, for he is sure that the beggar will fail in his attempt.

l. 405. αὐτίκ' ἐπεὶ . . . πάντῃ, 'as soon as Odysseus . . . inspected it on every side'. The name Ὀδυσσεύς occurs twice in this sentence, once near the beginning and again at the end.

l. 406. ὡς ὅτε, 'as when a man . . .'; this and the next two lines contain the simile of a lyre-player. ἐπιστάμενος is followed by objective genitives, 'skilled in the lyre . . .'.

l. 407. ἐτάνυσσε, the so-called 'gnomic' aorist, i.e. the description in the aorist indicative of something that habitually takes place, to be translated by a present tense in English: 'stretches a (new) string round a new peg, after fastening at both ends the well-twisted sheep-gut'; in the simile both the string and the peg have to be replaced.

l. 408. οἰός, from ὄϊς.

l. 409. ὣς . . . σπουδῆς, 'just so, without effort'. The method employed by Odysseus is described on page 141.

l. 411. ὑπὸ . . . ἄεισε = ὑπάεισε: 'and it sang sweetly at his touch (ὑπό), in sound like (the voice of) a swallow'; καλόν is adverbial accusative, and αὐδήν is accusative of respect, 'similar in sound'. The figure of speech by which Homer says that the sound was 'like a swallow' instead of 'like the voice of a swallow' is called 'brachylogy' or 'comparatio compendiaria', i.e. abbreviated comparison, and is common in all languages.

l. 412. ἄχος γένετο, 'grief fell upon . . .', because the beggar had succeeded where they had failed. πᾶσι is (possessive) dative of disadvantage: 'the colour of all was changed', i.e. they turned pale, though some may have flushed with shame or anger.

l. 413. μέγαλα, adverbial accusative: 'thundered loudly, showing signs (of approval)'.

l. 415. ὅττι . . . πάϊς, 'because the son . . . had sent him (οἱ) a portent'. πάϊς is scanned as two syllables, and the -εω of ἀγκυλομήτεω as one syllable.

l. 416. ὅ . . . γυμνός, 'which lay beside him on the table, ready for use', lit. 'naked'; this was perhaps the arrow mentioned in ll. 138, 148, and 165.

l. 417. τοί = οἱ, the definite article, but τῶν in l. 418 is a relative pronoun: 'which the Achaeans were soon about to experience', lit. 'make trial of', but not in the same way that they had been making trial of the bow. κείατο = κεῖντο, i.e. ἔκειντο. This line (418) has a fifth-foot spondee.

l. 419. τόν . . . γλυφίδας τε, 'taking it (and setting it) on the bridge (of the bow), he drew back the string and the arrow-notches'; πήχει is the metal cylinder half-way up the bow which the archer gripped with his left hand, and γλυφίδας are the notches at the end of the arrow (perhaps two, crossing each other at right angles), in which the string was placed when the archer drew it back; or possibly grooves round the end of the shaft to give him a firm grip.

l. 420. αὐτόθεν . . . καθήμενος, 'from that very place, from his chair, as he sat'; the axe-heads must have been level with his eyes if he could shoot straight through their sockets from a sitting position, so they must have been raised some feet above ground-level; see pages 141–2.

l. 421. ἄντα . . . ἰός, 'taking straight aim, he shot the arrow and did not miss the opening of the socket (lit. 'did not miss the first socket') of any of the axes (the last two syllables of πελέκεων are scanned as one long syllable), and the . . . arrow went straight through (and) out (at the other end)'. διὰ . . . ἀμπερές = διαμπερές, and θύραζε is simply 'out', not 'out of the door', which is its usual meaning.

l. 424. οὐ . . . ἥμενος, 'the stranger who sits in your hall does not disgrace you'.

l. 425. τι, adverbial accusative (twice): 'nor did I miss the mark at all nor become at all weary with bending the bow for a long time'.

l. 426. μοι μένος, 'my strength', (possessive) dative of advantage, like μήτηρ μοι in l. 102.

l. 427. οὐχ . . . ὄνονται, 'not (feeble), as the suitors say insultingly, dishonouring me'.

l. 428. νῦν . . . ἐψιάασθαι, 'now it is time indeed (καί) to make supper ready . . . in the daylight, and then to enjoy ourselves in other ways too, with . . .'; supper, by which Odysseus means the slaughter of the suitors (a grim example of 'dramatic irony') is to be taken early, not after sunset, as was usual; with the same irony μολπῇ may refer to the dance of death, and φόρμιγγι to the twanging of the bowstring, not of the lyre.

l. 430. τὰ . . . δαιτός, 'for these things are the ornaments of the feast'; for this use of τε, see the note on l. 87.

l. 431. ἤ, from ἡμί. ἐπ' . . . νεῦσεν = ἐπένευσεν. ἀμφέθετο, in l. 119 Telemachus had taken off his sword.

l. 432 has a fifth-foot spondee.

l. 433. ἀμφὶ . . . βάλεν = ἀμφίβαλεν, which takes an accusative and a dative: 'placed his hand around (i.e. 'grasped') his spear'; for φίλην meaning 'his', see the note on l. 55. αὐτοῦ is Odysseus.

l. 434. πὰρ θρόνον, 'beside his high seat'; the supposed beggar had an ordinary chair, δίφρος (l. 420).

THE BOW OF ODYSSEUS, AND THE AXE-HEADS

The great bow of Odysseus, which was given to him by his friend Iphitus, was most probably what is now called a 'composite' bow, made of a core of wood reinforced on the inner side with strips of horn and on the outer side (i.e. away from the archer as he holds the bow) with sinews, all glued tightly together and fitted in the middle with a metal bridge or grip, called πῆχυς in l. 419. When not in use the bow was of course unstrung, and as it was more powerful than the ordinary wooden bow it required both strength and experience to bend and string it. The archer had to sit or squat on the ground and brace the bow under the left knee and over the right thigh, as Heracles is shown doing in the accompanying illustration of a fifth-century coin of Thebes, in which the typical backward curve at each tip of the bow can also be seen. This was the weapon of the Scythian archers and, in vase-paintings, of Amazons and other foreigners, and of some heroes, especially Heracles and Paris of Troy. Penelope's suitors could not string Odysseus' bow because they were unfamiliar with this type of weapon and stood up when trying to do it, whereas Odysseus sat both to string and shoot it, for it was usual to shoot with the composite bow from a sitting or crouching position. Probably Telemachus knew how to set about it and sat down while attempting to string the bow, which he nearly succeeded in doing until he was stopped by a warning look from his father in ll. 128–129. The composite bow is still used today, but it is now longer than Odysseus' bow was, so that the modern archer stands up to shoot it, though even now he sometimes sits down to string it, using exactly the same method as the one just described and illustrated on the coin of Thebes. The bowstring was made of twisted thongs of leather or horse-hair, and would of course have perished after twenty years' disuse, so Penelope must have told Telemachus to provide a new one when she decided to hold the contest. This bow was quite unlike the yew 'long bow' of the Middle Ages, which was nearly six feet long and was fired from a standing position; the wooden 'short bow' that preceded it was a much inferior weapon, but the 'composite' bow of Odysseus was perhaps nearly as powerful as the famous English 'long bow'.

The problem of the axes has not yet been completely solved. In a previous book of the *Odyssey* (XIX, ll. 572–575) Penelope says, 'I shall arrange a contest (with) the axes that Odysseus used to set up in a row in his hall, like props for the keel of a ship, twelve in all, and standing a long way off he used to shoot an arrow through them all'; and in this book we have (ll. 120–122) 'he set up the axes, after digging a long trench for them all, and made them straight to a carpenter's line, and stamped down the earth round about'; and later (ll. 419–425) 'he drew the string in that very place, from the chair as he sat, and taking straight aim he shot the arrow and did not miss the opening of the socket (lit. 'did not miss the first socket', πρώτης στειλειῆς) of any of the axes, but the bronze-weighted arrow went straight through and out (at the other end)'.

There must therefore have been an opening in the iron axe-heads themselves through which the arrow could pass. The word στελειόν, which Homer uses in *Od.* V, l. 236, means the wooden handle of the Homeric double-axe, and it seems very likely that the rare word στειλειή which appears in l. 422 (quoted above) means the hole between the two blades that was used as the socket for the wooden handle. If this is so, the axe-heads were arranged in a line, a little distance apart, so that the sockets formed a straight tunnel through which the competitor had to shoot an arrow.

The arrangement of the axe-heads is also uncertain. It must have been a laborious task for Telemachus to dig a long trench in the hard-packed earth floor of the hall and set up the axes, especially as we are told that he had never done it before; but we may wonder whether he had not really made the preparations before, under Penelope's, or even Odysseus', instructions. He could hardly have placed the axe-heads *in* the trench, because they would not have projected far enough above ground-level. Probably he dug the trench in order to get loose earth which he piled up beside the trench and then placed the axe-heads in the heaped-up soil some feet above the floor-level, because the line of sockets had to be raised high enough to be at eye-level for Odysseus to aim through them when sitting down. The mention of his doing it when standing, στάς, in the first passage quoted above, may mean only that he 'took up a position a long way off', for he could not have shot through the axes when standing unless they were raised to head height, which seems impossible. The line of axe-heads when set up as in the accompanying sketch would look something like the wooden props on which the keel of a ship rested when the vessel was being built. (The description of Odysseus' bow is taken mainly from F. H. Stubbings's article on 'Arms and Armour' in *A Companion to Homer*, pp. 518–520, and the explanation of the contest of the axe-heads from W. B. Stanford's note on *Od.* XIX, ll. 572 ff., with the illustration from p. 535 of *A Companion to Homer*, where F. H. Stubbings deals with the same problem.)

Heracles stringing a composite bow:
from a fifth-century coin of Thebes

The arrangement of the axe-heads, as suggested
by F. H. Stubbings

ANTIPHON, *THE MURDER OF HERODES*

1

ἐν τῷ πλοίῳ ᾧ, 'in the (same) ship as . . .'. φασιν ἀποθανεῖν, 'they (i.e. the prosecution) say was murdered'; ἀποθνῄσκειν is regularly used as the passive of ἀποκτείνειν. ὡς, 'to visit'. ἀνδράποδα . . . ἀπολύσων, a purpose clause after a verb of motion; 'to release some slaves to (certain) Thracians'. Herodes had perhaps bought some prisoners of war as slaves and was now selling them back (at a profit) to their relatives in Thrace. It is not clear why the men 'who were going to ransom' (notice this meaning of the middle voice of λύω) the slaves could not have paid the money at Mytilene and saved Herodes the double voyage. Presumably the sale was cancelled by the murder and the whole party had to return to Mytilene and negotiate again with Herodes' heirs. ἃ ἔδει αὐτὸν ἀπολῦσαι, 'whom he was to (lit. 'had to') release'. The word ΜΑΡΤΥΡΕΣ that occurs here and at intervals in the rest of the speech means that the evidence of witnesses was read out in court at these points, but no cross-examination of them was allowed. During the giving of the evidence the water-clock (κλεψύδρα), that worked on the same principle as an old-fashioned egg-timer, except that water was used instead of sand, was stopped so that the total time allowed for the speech should not be reduced.

2

αὕτη, supply ἦν: 'these were the reasons that each of us had for (making) the . . .'. ἐτύχομεν . . . χρησάμενοι, 'we happened to meet (lit. 'use') a storm'. ὑφ' οὗ, the dative of the instrument is much more common with inanimate things than the genitive of the agent with ὑπό. Supply χώρας with the adjective Μηθυμναίας, 'in the territory of Methymna', on the north-west coast of Lesbos; it remained independent when the rest of the island was taken over by Athens, because it alone had not joined in the revolt of Lesbos in 428; see page 33. τοῦτο, we should omit this and just say 'the ship'; οὗ is an adverb, 'where'. αὐτόν, Herodes; the reason for the move from one ship to the other is given in the next section. αὐτὰ ταῦτα is the object of σκοπεῖτε, but we should make it the subject of ἐγίγνετο: 'consider whether these circumstances themselves happened by chance rather than by design', though Antiphon puts it round the other way and makes Euxitheus say 'by design rather than by chance'. We should make ἀπελέγχομαι an impersonal verb and say 'it has nowhere been proved that I persuaded the man to be my fellow voyager, but that I made the voyage independently (αὐτὸς καθ' αὑτόν)', lit. 'I am not proved having made . . .'; αὑτόν, the third person reflexive, is sometimes used to mean ἐμαυτόν, 'myself', as here. There seems to be no reason for the change of tense in the two participles, πείσας and πεποιημένος, except perhaps to avoid having ποιησάμενος here and again with φαίνομαι in 3. ἕνεκα is generally placed after the genitive case that it governs; the phrase means 'on private business'.

3

οὔτ' . . . ποιησάμενος, 'and it is clear that I did not make . . .'. Supply φαινόμεθα with κατασχόντες and χρησάμενοι, but say 'and that we did not put in . . . as the result of (ἀπό) any previous arrangement but by force of (lit. 'using') necessity'. The aorist ἐγένετο is 'took place', but the imperfect ἐγίγνετο means something like 'this too (καί) then had to follow'. Notice three pairs of double negatives in these two sections, which in Greek intensify one another, instead of cancelling; thus οὔτ' . . . οὐδενὶ μηχανήματι means 'nor . . . by any plot'. The antecedent of ᾧ is πλοῖον, which must be taken before ἐν ᾧ and repeated before εἰς ὃ δέ, 'but the ship into which . . .'. τοῦτ' ἦν, 'all this took place', i.e. the change from one ship to another. The move to the decked ship was only temporary, to shelter from the rain (9–10); the slaves had to stay in the open vessel.

4

ἐπίνομεν, 'we began to drink'. ὁ μὲν . . . ἐκβάς, 'it is clear that Herodes left . . .'. τὸ παράπαν, accusative of respect, though παράπαν is really an adverb which is always used with τό, 'at all'. τῆς νυκτὸς ἐκείνης, 'during that night', genitive of time within which. οὐδέν τι, another accusative of respect, lit. 'in no way at all more by the others than by me also', i.e. 'by me also just as much as by the others'. So too, εἴ τῳ (=τινι) . . . ὁμοίως is lit. 'if it seemed to anyone . . . equally also to me', i.e. 'if anyone thought it was a serious matter, so too did I'. καὶ εἷς . . . ἐπέμπετο, 'and not only (τε) was I responsible for a messenger's being sent . . . but also (καί) it was on my suggestion that he was sent'; the meaning of the imperfect here is probably 'it was decided that he should be sent', after some discussion (see the note on ἔπεμπον in Thucydides, 5, 1).

5

ἄλλου οὐδενὸς ἐθέλοντος, genitive absolute, 'when nobody else was willing', followed by two partitive genitives, 'either of those who were on board (lit. 'from the ship', i.e. the other passengers and the crew) or of those who were sailing with ...', presumably the Thracians who were ransoming the slaves. οὐ δήπου ... εἰδώς, 'surely I was not deliberately (lit. 'knowing') offering to send (another meaning of the imperfect) an informer against myself'. ἐφαίνετο here means 'did not appear (or 'could not be found') when searched for'. πλοῦς ... ἐγίγνετο, 'good sailing weather began for us'. ᾠχόμην κἀγὼ (=καὶ ἐγὼ) πλέων, 'I too went off on my journey', to Aenus, without his servant, the possible identity of whom is discussed in the note on 10. The combination of τὰ ἄλλα into τἄλλα and καὶ ἐγώ into κἀγώ is called 'crasis' ('mixing').

6

τὰ γενόμενα ταῦτ' ἐστίν, 'this is what (actually) happened', or 'these are the facts of the case'. ἐκ τούτων τὰ εἰκότα, 'the probable results of these events'. πρὶν ἀνάγεσθαί με, 'before I put out to sea'; despite the negative οὐδείς, πρίν does not here mean 'until', so that the infinitive is used. οὐδεὶς ἀνθρώπων, partitive genitive, 'nobody at all', but πεπυσμένων τούτων is genitive absolute, 'although my accusers (lit. 'these men'); he perhaps points to them in court) had heard ...'. οὐ γὰρ ἄν, 'for otherwise I should never have ...'; the εἰ-clause ('if they had accused me') is omitted. εἰς τὸ παραχρῆμα, 'for the moment'; the article makes the adverb into a noun. τὸ ἀληθὲς καὶ τὸ γεγενημένον, 'the true facts of the case', lit. 'the truth and the thing that had happened', an example of the figure of speech called 'hendiadys' ('one by means of two'), whereby two words connected by 'and' are used instead of a compound phrase, e.g. 'nice and warm' really means 'nicely warm'. κρεῖσσον ... αἰτιάσεως, 'was more powerful than any accusation (genitive of comparison) made by these men'. ἐπεδήμουν, 'I was still in Lesbos', before sailing on to Aenus. ἐξ ἐπιβουλῆς, 'in accordance with their plot'. κατ' ἐμοῦ, 'against me'.

7

ὡς . . . εἰς τὴν κεφαλήν, 'that . . . and that I hit him on the head with a stone', lit. 'threw a stone to him at his head'. ὃς οὐκ ἐξέβην, concessive, 'though I did not . . .'. τοῦτο, i.e. that I never left the ship. ὅπως is 'how' in an indirect question. οὐδενὶ λόγῳ εἰκότι, 'by no reasonable explanation'. δῆλον . . . γίγνεσθαι, '(it is) plain that it is likely that this (crime) was committed . . .'. τοῦτο μὲν . . . τοῦτο δέ, 'because on the one hand (lit. 'with regard to this', accusative of respect) the man was drunk, and on the other hand he had left . . .', causal genitive absolute. οὔτε ἂν ἐδύνατο, a conditional sentence with the εἰ-clause omitted: 'he would not have been able to control himself (if he had tried to walk very far)'. οὔτε . . . ἐγίγνετο, 'nor would there reasonably have been any excuse for a man who was taking him a long way away . . .'; the imperfect indicative is used with ἄν to denote continuous action in the past, while the aorist is used for a single action. μάκραν ὁδόν, accusative of extent of space.

8

δύο ἡμέρας, accusative of duration of time. καὶ . . . καί, 'both . . . and'. αἷμα, we shall see in 9–10 that bloodstains from sacrificed sheep were found in the decked ship after it returned to Mytilene, but it is strange that neither vessel was (apparently) thoroughly searched at Methymna as soon as Herodes disappeared. παρεχόμενος, concessive, 'though I can produce witnesses to prove that . . .'; he refers to the evidence of the freeman, mentioned in 23. εἰ . . . πλοίου, 'even if I did leave the ship as much as you please', i.e. however true it may be that I did leave it. εἰκὸς . . . ἄνθρωπον, 'it was in no way likely that the man remained undiscovered (λαθεῖν) after he disappeared'.

9

The subject of λέγουσιν is 'the prosecution', and ἐστί must be supplied with δῆλον. ἦν here means 'came'. πῶς . . . ἐξευρέθη, 'how could it not have been identified?'; the suggestion was that Euxitheus induced Herodes to go on board another vessel, perhaps a rowing-boat, murdered him there, rowed out into the harbour, and threw the body overboard. καὶ σημεῖόν . . . γενέσθαι, 'that at least (καί) some clue should have been found'. τεθνεῶτος, the contracted form of τεθνηκότος, in a genitive

absolute clause, 'when a dead man was being put on board . . .'.
ἐν ᾧ . . . ἐν τούτῳ . . . ἐν ᾧ, the antecedent is put inside the relative clause:
'they say that they have found clues in the ship in which he was drinking . . . (which is the very ship) in which they themselves admit that the man was not killed', lit. 'in which ship he was drinking . . . in this they say that . . .'. μή is placed before instead of after ὁμολογοῦσιν for emphasis, and is used instead of the normal οὐ in indirect statement for the same reason (μή is the usual negative with verbs of promising, hoping, and swearing). The antecedent of the third ἐν ᾧ is αὐτὸ τὸ πλοῖον.

10

φροῦδος ἦ πλέων, 'I went off on my voyage', lit. 'I was gone, sailing'. The subject of ἠρεύνων is 'the prosecution'. There were no police to enquire into cases of suspected murder; all the investigation had to be done by the relatives or friends of the victim, and legal proceedings were also taken by them. ἐνταῦθα . . . τεθνάναι, 'they said that the man had been killed there'. αὐτοῖς . . . ἐνεχώρει, 'this (theory) did not turn out well for them', because 'it was proved to be the blood of the (sacrificed) sheep', presumably on the evidence of those who had been present at the sacrifice; there was of course no scientific method at that time of distinguishing between human and animal blood. ἀποτραπόμενοι . . . λόγου, 'abandoning (lit. 'having turned away from') this suggestion'. τοὺς ἀνθρώπους, 'the (two) men'; this is the first mention of the two witnesses whose evidence was so important and contradictory. From 30 we know that one of them was a freeman and the other a slave, and since both were examined under torture the freeman cannot have been a Greek, for free Greeks were not subjected to torture. One of the many horrible features of slavery in Greece and Rome was that the evidence of slaves was accepted only after torture, a process that was not likely to produce the truth, as Euxitheus (or Antiphon) remarks in 13. We know from 23 that the freeman had been with Euxitheus all through the voyage, which seems to imply that he accompanied him from Mytilene to Methymna and then on to Aenus, though from 33 it appears that he did not go on to Aenus but left the ship at Methymna; it is possible that he was Euxitheus' (free) servant, who was sent back to Mytilene in 3 to report Herodes' disappearance to his family; he was perhaps seized by them and examined under torture, but refused to incriminate Euxitheus. The slave may have been a member of the crew of the decked ship in which Herodes and Euxitheus were drinking during the night; he was perhaps arrested by Herodes' relations when the open ship returned to Mytilene. But we know nothing for certain about either of these men; the last sentence of this section suggests that they were both arrested and tortured together, so perhaps they were both members of the crew of the decked ship, though this theory does not agree with the statement made by Euxitheus in 23 and contradicted by him in 33, that the freeman accompanied him throughout his voyage.

11

The antecedent of ὄν, both here and in the next sentence, is the οὗτος that follows. οὐδὲν φλαῦρον, 'nothing compromising', i.e. nothing to connect Euxitheus with the murder. ἡμέραις ὕστερον πολλαῖς, 'many days later'. ἔχοντες . . . χρόνον, 'keeping him under their own control during the intervening time', lit. 'the former time'; the article makes an adverb into an adjective. ἦν ὁ πεισθείς, 'was the man who was persuaded'.

12

μεμαρτύρηται ὑμῖν should be taken first; 'evidence has been given to you (to show) how long afterwards . . .', lit. 'that afterwards by so long a time'. Antiphon several times uses μέν in a new sentence without the οὖν, γάρ, or δή that usually accompanies it; see also 2 and 6. προσέχετε . . . γεγένηται, 'pay attention to the nature of the examination itself', lit. 'to the examination itself, of what sort it has been'. τοῦτο μέν . . . τοῦτο δέ, 'on the one hand . . . on the other', as in 7. ἐπὶ τούτοις . . . αὐτόν, 'it was in their power to give him release from his ill-treatment', lit. 'that he should cease (from) being treated badly'; the relative clause ᾧ . . . ὑπέσχοντο is not continued in the τοῦτο δέ sentence, which interrupts the main sentence ὁ δοῦλος . . . ἴσως . . . κατεψεύσατό μου. ὑπ' ἀμφοῖν, 'by both considerations', which are explained in the next two lines; we should expect the dative of the instrument instead of ὑπό with a genitive; see also ὑφ' οὗ in 2. βασάνου is genitive of separation after ἀπηλλάχθαι. εἰς τὸ παραχρῆμα, 'immediately', lit. 'for the immediate (moment)'; the article makes the adverb into an adjective, like τὸν πρόσθεν χρόνον in 11, where παραχρῆμα occurs as an adverb without the article.

13

ἐφ' οἷς, the antecedent is τούτων: 'that those who are being examined under torture are biased in favour of (εἰσὶ πρός) those under whose control (ἐφ' οἷς) the greatest part of the torture (is), so that they say (lit. 'to say') anything with which (lit. 'whatever') they are likely to gratify them'; both ἄν-clauses are indefinite, of which ᾗ, the verb of μέρος, is understood. ἐν τούτοις αὐτοῖς ἐστιν, 'rests with these men alone'. κἂν = καὶ ἐάν, and the antecedent of ὧν is ἐκεῖνοι understood: 'especially (ἄλλως τε καί) if those against whom they are telling lies happen not to be present'. When both parties to a trial were present to examine a slave under torture, the wretched man was almost literally between two fires, but the authorities never seem to have realised how valueless was evidence procured in this way. Antiphon here argues against obtaining evidence from slaves by torture, but in another speech he says that a slave's word cannot be believed except under torture. εἰ ... καταψεύδεσθαι, 'if I had been ordering (the torturers) to put him on the rack again for not ..., perhaps he would have been dissuaded by this very action (lit. 'turned away in this itself') from telling lies ...'; an imperfect indicative with ἄν is used for a continuous action in past time, as in 7. The Greeks preferred to say 'I ordered (someone) to rack him' instead of 'I ordered him to be racked'. μηδέν is the usual redundant (i.e. unnecessary) negative used with the infinitive after a verb of preventing. καὶ ... συμφερόντων, 'both torturers and assessors of what concerned their own interests', lit. 'of the things expedient to themselves'.

14

καταψευσάμενος depends on ἐγίγνωσκε: 'as long as he realised that he had been telling lies against me with good hope (of gaining his freedom), he persisted in his (false) statement'; so also ἀποθανούμενος is 'that he would be killed', a participle being used instead of an infinitive after a verb of perception. ἐχρῆτο, 'he had recourse to'. πεισθείη is optative in indirect speech after ὅτι; the indicative ἐπείσθη could have been used.

15

οὐδέτερα, 'neither course', neuter plural, as the accent shows. The two courses are described in the two participles, which agree with αὐτόν:

'when he tried . . . and afterwards when he spoke . . . , neither course helped him'. For ἄγοντες, like ἀπάγοντες in 19, we might expect the aorist participle: 'they took away and killed the man, the informer, on whose evidence they rely to prosecute me', lit. 'trusting in whom they prosecute me'; in the language of the law courts διώκειν means 'to prosecute' and φεύγειν 'to be prosecuted'. τὸ ἐνάντιον ἢ . . . ἄνθρωποι, 'doing the exact opposite of what (lit. 'than') other men (do)'. τὴν δωρεάν is sarcastic: 'presented the informer with death as a gift', instead of giving him liberty. We shall see in 28 that the prosecution purchased this slave (possibly from the owner of the ship in which he may have been a member of the crew), but even so they were not legally permitted to put him to death without a trial. ἀπαγορευόντων . . . ἐμῶν, concessive genitive absolute, 'although my friends ordered (them) not to kill . . .'; μή with a verb of forbidding is 'redundant', like μή with a verb of preventing in 13. πρὶν ἔλθοιμι, 'until I came back', optative because it refers to the future and is therefore indefinite in a negative πρίν clause.

16

δῆλον (ἐστὶν) . . . λόγων, 'it is clear that they had no need of his life (lit. 'body') but only of his evidence'. ζῶν and ἰών are equivalent to εἰ-clauses: 'if he had been alive and had been tortured by me in the same way (lit. 'going through the same torture'), he would have denounced the plot of the prosecution', lit. would have been becoming a denouncer of . . .'. τὸν ἔλεγχον . . . ἀπολλυμένου, 'he took away my (chance of) proving the truth through the loss of his life', lit. 'through his body itself which was perishing'. τοῖς λόγοις . . . ἀπόλλυμαι, 'I am being ruined by the statements falsely made by him as if (ὡς) they were true'. κάλει, imperative, addressed to the clerk of the court; μοι is the so-called 'ethic' dative, which gives the view-point of the person interested in the action; here μοι κάλει means 'please call'.

17

ἐχρῆν . . . ἐμέ, 'they ought to have proved me guilty . . . by producing the informer himself here (in court)'. αὐτῷ . . . ἀγωνίσματι, 'to have used this very action (or 'this man himself') as the basis of their case (lit. 'plea'), producing the slave openly'. κελεύοντας (ἐμέ) has βασανίζειν depending on it, but μὴ ἀποκτεῖναι depends on ἐχρῆν αὐτούς. φέρε was originally the imperative of φέρω, but it came to be used as an interjection with a verb of any person or number, like ἄγε, to mean 'come now' or 'well then'. ποτέρῳ τῶν λόγων, 'which of his two statements'. The first πότερα that follows is an adverb introducing a double question, with ἤ as the second part of the question, '(will they use) the one which he told first or . . .', and the second πότερα is an adjective, 'which of the two (stories) is true, (the one) when he said . . .', ᾧ is 'relative attraction' for τῷ λόγῳ ὅν. ὅτ' = ὅτε. οὐκ ἔφη, 'said that I had not (done so)'.

18

ἐκ τοῦ εἰκότος, 'by the test of probability', lit. 'from what is likely'. φαίνονται, supply ὄντες, 'are obviously more true'. ἐπ' ὠφελείᾳ τῇ ἑαυτοῦ, 'for his own benefit'. διὰ τὸ . . . ψεύδεσθαι, 'because of his lying'. κατειπών is equivalent to an εἰ-clause; 'he thought (ἡγήσατο) that if he spoke the truth he would be saved by it'. τῆς ἀληθείας . . . οὐδείς, 'he had no one to support the truth (of his second statement)'. ᾧπερ . . . λόγων, 'I whom the truth of . . . defended', lit. 'to whom the truth . . . was an ally'. ἦσαν οἱ ἀφανιοῦντες . . . καταστῆναι: 'there were (people) who were ready to set apart his first, false, statement, so that it could never be restored to the truth'; ἀφανίζειν really means 'to suppress' or 'get rid of', as in the next sentence, but the prosecution did not want to suppress the false statement but only the man who made it.

19

καθ' ὧν . . . τις, 'against whom anyone lays information'; τις becomes plural in τοὺς μηνύοντας. We should omit οὗτοι in English. The tense of ἀπάγοντες, present instead of aorist, like ἄγοντες in 15, is strange, especially with ζητοῦντες in the same sentence; we must say 'these men, who themselves took away the slave and were enquiring into . . .'. εἰ . . . ἤθελον . . . ἔλεγχον, 'if I had . . . or were unwilling . . . or were evading any other enquiry, they would be treating these facts themselves (as) very strong (evidence) in the case'; notice the change of tenses from aorist to imperfect in this conditional sentence. We can supply ἄν with ἦν, though it is sometimes omitted with a past tense of εἰμί, as here: 'this would be their strongest evidence against me'. νῦν δέ, 'but as it is'. ὁπότε is causal, 'since', and προκαλουμένων . . . ἐμῶν is genitive absolute:

'since, when my friends challenged (them to an enquiry), they evaded (the challenge)'. ἐμοὶ ... τεκμήρια, 'these same (facts) ought to be evidence for me against them'. ὡς ... ᾐτιῶντο, the English order would be 'that the charge which they were bringing against me was not true', lit. 'that they were bringing the charge, of which they accused me, not true'.

20

ἔτι καὶ ... ἄνδρα, 'moreover they say this also, that ... that he helped me kill the man'; ἄνθρωπος contrasted with ἀνήρ means 'the fellow', i.e. the slave. φημὶ ... οὐ, instead of the usual οὔ φημι, occurs also in 23, perhaps for emphasis in both places. The present infinitive λέγειν represents the imperfect indicative of direct speech: 'I declare that he was not saying this'. We are not told how Euxitheus got information of what the slave said under torture, apart from the evidence given in court during the prosecution's speech; Herodes' relatives would of course have tried to suppress his dying statement, mentioned in 22, that Euxitheus was really innocent. The two ὅτι-clauses depend on λέγειν, with aorist optatives representing the aorist indicatives of direct speech: '(but I declare that he said) that he conducted Herodes and me ... and that when Herodes had been killed by me he helped me to pick him up, put him ... and threw him into the sea'. τὸ πλοῖον, presumably a rowing-boat (previously mentioned in the evidence already given, hence the definite article) which the slave said that he and Euxitheus rowed out to sea to dispose of the corpse further from land.

21

πρὶν ... ἀναβῆναι, 'before being placed on (lit. 'before he went up to') the wheel', to which the victim was bound while being tortured. μέχρι ... ἀνάγκης, 'right up to the final compulsion', when he could endure the pain no longer. The imperfects that follow mean 'he maintained (lit. 'was using') the truth and continued to clear me of ...'. For τῇ ἀνάγκῃ χρώμενος we should say 'compelled by necessity', and ἤδη with the imperfect means 'only then did he begin to ...'.

22

ἐπαύσατο βασανιζόμενος, 'the torture was over', lit. 'he stopped being tortured'. οὐκέτι ... οὐδέν, another double negative; 'no longer ... any

of these things'. τὸ τελευταῖον, adverbial accusative, 'in the end'. ὡς
ἀδίκως ἀπολλυμένους, lit. 'as being killed unjustly', i.e. 'saying that we
were both being killed unjustly'; he realised that his false accusation
must cause the death of Euxitheus. οὐ χάριτι . . . κατεψεύσατο, 'not to do
me a favour — how could he, when he had falsely accused me?' ὑπὸ
τοῦ ἀληθοῦς, another instance of ὑπό with the genitive instead of a dative
of the instrument, like χειμῶνι . . . ὑφ' οὗ in 2. βεβαιῶν . . . εἰρημένους,
'confirming the truth of his first statement', lit. 'confirming his first
words as being spoken true'. If the unfortunate slave really did say, both
before and after his examination under torture, that Euxitheus was
innocent, and incriminated him only when on the rack, his hostile
evidence was obviously worthless. A witness could hardly be expected
to speak the truth if he knew that it would involve more torture and
probably death — but that was part of the legal system at Athens. It is
not clear why the prosecution killed the slave, unless they were afraid
that he would stick to the two statements that cleared Euxitheus, in
spite of the torture. The freeman withstood the torture and refused to
give false evidence, but he was not entirely at the mercy of the prosecution, who could not go too far in examining a freeman, so that his life
at least was safe.

23

ὁ ἕτερος, the freeman, on whose identity see the last note on 10. συνεφέρετο
. . . διαφέρετο, 'confirmed . . . contradicted', both with the dative. In this
section the slave is again called τὸν ἄνθρωπον and Herodes τὸν ἄνδρα,
though elsewhere the slave is also ὁ ἀνήρ; when the two are contrasted,
it is better to call them 'the slave' and 'Herodes', to avoid confusion.
διὰ τέλους με ἀπέλυε, 'continued to declare me innocent to the very end'.
τούτοις δέ, this is an example of δέ 'in apodosis', which is sometimes used
in the main clause of a conditional sentence or of a temporal sentence
(as in Homer, Odyssey XXI, l. 274, in this book) or in a sentence in which
the relative clause comes before the main clause, as here and in 43,
ἐνταῦθα δέ; it is omitted in English, but here we might say 'but as for the
slave's statements made on the wheel, which he made from
necessity . . . , these he contradicted'. ὁ μέν is the slave, ὁ δέ the freeman.
ἐκβάντα με . . . αὐτός, an example of an accusative in indirect statement
depending on ἔφη, followed by a nominative when the subject of the
infinitive is the same as the subject of ἔφη: 'he said that I . . . killed

Herodes and that he himself helped me to pick him up when he was already dead'. τὸ παράπαν (see the note on 4) goes with ἐκβῆναι. For the order of words in ἔφη οὐκ, see the note on 20.

24

τὸ εἰκός . . . ἐστιν, 'probability supports me', lit. 'is an ally to me'. κακοδαίμων means originally 'having an evil genius', then 'unfortunate', and here 'crazy'; the verb is ἦ (or ἦν) understood. τὸ ἀποκτεῖναι, the article makes the infinitive into a noun, 'the murder of Herodes', but it could here have been omitted and the prolative infinitive used: 'so crazy as to plan to murder Herodes by myself (μόνος)'. The antecedent of ᾧ is taken from the purpose clause ἵνα . . . συνειδείη, but we must say 'for in this (i.e. the possibility that someone might share his guilty secret) was my whole danger'. πεπραγμένου τοῦ ἔργου is probably genitive absolute, with μοι dative of the agent, 'when the deed had been done by me', or it might depend on μάρτυρας καὶ συμβούλους, 'witnesses and partners in the deed . . .'. ἐποιούμην is still in the ὥστε clause; the imperfect middle means 'I proceeded to get for myself'.

25

ὡς . . . λόγος ἐστίν, 'according to the story of the prosecution'. ἀποθνήσκων, used again as the passive of ἀποκτείνειν: 'though he was being murderously attacked by (only) one man'. οὔτ' αἴσθησιν οὐδεμίαν ἐποίησεν, 'nor attracted any attention by calling out to . . .', lit. 'nor made any perception either to those on shore . . .'; but Euxitheus does not mention that he might have been struck unconscious or dead by the first blow. πολλῷ, dative of measure of difference; 'it is possible (ἔστιν = ἔξεστιν) to make oneself heard (lit. 'to shout') over a far greater (distance) . . .', lit. 'greater by far'. ἐγρηγορότων, genitive absolute, with τῶν ἄλλων understood: 'while (the others) on board were still awake'.

26

The four participles in this sentence in the genitive case are concessive and agree with Ἡρώδου understood, which depends on σημεῖον and αἷμα: 'though Herodes was murdered . . . and was being placed . . . , no sign or bloodstain was to be seen (ἐφάνη), even though he was picked up ... and was being placed ...'; the present participles indicate that the action took longer than the action of the aorist participles. In the δοκεῖ sentence ἄν goes with δύνασθαι: 'do you think that a man who was in such a situation would have been able to smooth out the traces (τὰ ὄντα, perhaps agreeing with σημεῖα understood) on land ...'; it might have been possible to smooth out (lit. 'scrape up') signs of a struggle on the quay-side or in the sand, but modern murder trials have shown that it would have been almost impossible to wash bloodstains completely out of timber, if Herodes had been murdered on board ship. ἃ οὐδὲ ... ἀφανίσαι, 'traces which a man (τις) would not have been able ... even in the daytime (and if he were) in full control of himself ...'. μή is used with πεφοβημένος because the participles are equivalent to a conditional clause. ὦ ἄνδρες, 'members of the jury'.

27

The antecedent of ὅ is τοῦτο in μὴ οὖν ... μηδείς, but the long parenthesis that intervenes makes the speaker forget how he started, so that he makes a fresh start with μὴ οὖν; we must say '(there is one thing) which you must indeed (καί) consider above all (μάλιστα) ... ; let no one therefore remove from your minds (lit. 'from you') this fact, that ...'. ἄν = ἐάν, and διδάξω is aorist subjunctive; 'if I tell you the same thing ...'. καθ' ὅτι ... κατὰ τοῦτο, lit. 'and according to whatever you rightly decide, according to this I am saved', i.e. 'and my safety depends on how far you come to the right decision'. Similarly with ψευσθῆτε ... ἀπόλλυμαι, 'my ruin depends on how far you are defrauded of the truth'. διετείναντο ... ὑμᾶς, 'they exerted themselves so that he should not appear before you'. ἐγγενέσθαι is an impersonal verb, also depending on διετείναντο: 'and so that it should be impossible for me on my return (lit. 'being present', i.e. at Mytilene) to take ...'; ἄξαι is another form of the aorist infinitive of ἄγω.

28

πρὸς τούτων ἦν τοῦτο, 'it was to their advantage (to let me do) this', but only if the slave maintained under the second examination by torture that his evidence against Euxitheus was true, which he was hardly likely to do even if it was in fact true. νῦν δέ, 'but as it was'. ἐπὶ σφῶν αὐτῶν (= ἑαυτῶν), 'on their own responsibility'. τὸν μηνυτήν, 'although he was their own informer (against me)'. The participles that follow are again concessive, the first being genitive absolute: 'although the city did not decree it nor was he the murderer . . .'; ὄντα agrees with μηνυτήν. ὅν, a relative pronoun at the beginning of a sentence (a 'connecting' relative) is not nearly so common in Greek or English as in Latin: 'they ought to have kept him in confinement (lit. 'bound')'. ἐξεγγυῆσαι, 'to hand over on bail', means that the prosecution would hand over the slave to the friends of Euxitheus, who would deposit a sum of money with them which would be forfeited if they failed to produce the slave at the trial. τοῖς . . . ὑμετέροις, 'to your magistrates here' at Athens, where the trial was taking place because Herodes was a citizen of Athens and Euxitheus a citizen of Mytilene, a subject-city of Athens. ψῆφον . . . γενέσθαι depends on ἐχρῆν, which first governed αὐτούς; we might say 'until the decision of the court could be made about him', lit. 'a vote ought to have been made . . .'. αὐτοί, addressed to the prosecution, not to the jury; 'on your own responsibility'. ὃ . . . ζημιῶσαι, 'it is not permitted even to an allied city to do this, that is, to execute anyone without the (consent of the) Athenians'; inscriptions show that allied cities in the Confederacy of Delos, which became the Athenian maritime empire, had to transfer cases involving the death-penalty to Athens for trial; the rule applied even to the murder of slaves, although they were the absolute property of their owners, but a slave would normally have no relative to prosecute his murderer. τουτουσί, an emphatic form of τούτους. κριτάς and δικασταί seem here to be the same thing, though normally a δικαστής was an official member of the jury in a court of law and a κριτής was an unofficial, self-appointed judge of any question (except that it was the official name for the judges of plays at a dramatic festival): 'you thought it right that these (jurors) should be judges of . . . , but you yourselves passed judgment (lit. 'became judges') on his deeds'. The reason given by the prosecution for killing the slave was no doubt that he was a self-confessed accomplice in the murder.

29

οὐδὲ . . . προσηκόντων, the first οὐδέ is 'not even' and the second emphasises the negative by repeating it: 'not even those who have killed their masters . . . , not even those slaves are put to death by the relatives (τῶν προσηκόντων) of the victim themselves'. The subject of παραδιδόασιν is οἱ προσήκοντες, and τῇ ἀρχῇ is 'to the authorities'. εἴπερ ... φόνου, 'if a slave is in fact (καί) allowed to give evidence in a charge of murder against a (lit. 'the') free man', though only under torture. τῷ δεσπότῃ also depends on ἔξεστιν, and ἄν = ἐάν; 'to take proceedings (ἐπεξελθεῖν), if he thinks fit (lit. 'if it seems good'), on behalf of a slave (against his murderer)'. καὶ ... τῷ ἐλευθέρον, 'and if the verdict (of the court) is equally effective against the man who has killed a slave and against the man who has killed a free man'. εἰκὸς ... ἦν, this is the main sentence after three εἰ-clauses: 'it was surely reasonable that there should also have been a trial (lit. 'a vote') about this slave's death (lit. 'about him') and that he should not have been ...'. ὑμεῖς, Euxitheus is still addressing the prosecution, but with ὦ ἄνδρες in 30 he turns again to the jury: 'you would be standing trial with far greater justice (πολλῷ is dative of measure of difference, lit. 'by far') than I am now being prosecuted...'; φεύγειν is regarded as the passive of διώκειν, 'to prosecute', and is followed by ὑπό and a genitive.

30

σκοπεῖτε, imperative. Notice the eight words in the dual number beginning with τοῖν: 'consider also from the two statements of the two men ... (the claims of) justice and probability', i.e. consider which statement is supported by justice and probability. λόγω, accusative dual. τοτὲ μὲν ... τοτὲ δέ, 'at one time ..., at another ...'. βασανιζόμενος, 'though he was examined ...'.

31

τοῦτο μὲν ... τοῦτο δέ, 'on the one hand ... on the other', as in 7 and 12. οὐκ ἦν = οὐκ ἐξῆν, an impersonal verb: 'it was not possible (that they should) persuade him, like the other one, by offering him ...'; προτείναντας agrees with αὐτούς understood, the subject of the accusative and infinitive clause after (ἐξ)ῆν, which might have been followed by the dative, the case normally governed by ἔξεστιν; see also τὸν φέροντα in 34. μετὰ τοῦ ἀληθοῦς, 'with truth on his side'; in 22 we had ὑπὸ τοῦ ἀληθοῦς; in both places the dative might have been used. ὅτι δέοι, indefinite; 'whatever he had (to suffer)'. ἐπεὶ ... δοκοῦντα, 'for he too knew what was advantageous (to him), that he would stop ... just as soon as (lit. 'then whenever') he said what the prosecution wanted', lit. 'the things that seemed good to these men'. ποτέρῳ ... τοτὲ δ' οὔ, 'which of the two is it reasonable for you to believe, the one who ... or the one who at one time made a statement (φάσκοντι) and at another time denied it?' καὶ ἀνεῦ, 'even without ...'. τῶν διαφερομένων σφίσιν αὐτοῖς (= ἑαυτοῖς), 'than those who contradict themselves', genitive of comparison.

32

ἔπειτα δὲ καί, 'and then too'. ἐκ τῶν ... μὴ φάσκειν, 'some of the statements of the slave are favourable (lit. 'would be equal') to both sides; his affirmation (of my guilt) is favourable to the prosecution, his (later) denial supports me'; τὸ μὴ φάσκειν is the infinitive of οὐ φάσκω, 'I deny', made into a noun by the article. In καὶ μὲν δή, 'and indeed', μέν is used instead of μήν. τὰ ἐξ ἴσου ... διώκοντος, 'this equal result (lit. 'the things that happen from equality') is (in favour) of the accused rather than of the prosecutor'; so also ὁ ἀριθμὸς ... γενόμενος is 'an equal number of votes (on each side)'. Panels of jurymen at Athens consisted of a round number plus one, e.g. 501 in an important case, and if owing to the absence of a juror the votes turned out to be equal the verdict was acquittal. ἐπεί γε καί, 'since indeed'. For this meaning of φεύγειν and διώκειν, see the last note on 29.

33

ἡ μὲν ... ἐγένετο, 'such was the (result of the) examination under torture'. μὲν here has no δέ to balance it but is followed by καίτοι instead. ἀποθανόντα, a participle is used instead of an infinitive after the verb of perception εἰδέναι: 'the prosecution say that they know well that Herodes was killed ...'. ἂν ... ἄν, the first ἄν is not to be translated; it prepares the hearer for the second ἄν with the main verb ἠφάνισα: 'if I had been conscious in my own mind (ἐμαυτῷ) of any guilt at all (τὸ παράπαν) and if any such deed had been committed by me (dative of the agent), I should have got rid of both men'. τί is not the accented interrogative pronoun but the indefinite pronoun with the accent thrown back from the 'enclitic' μοι that follows. ὅτε ἐπ' ἐμοὶ ἦν, 'when it was in my power ...'. τοῦτο μὲν ... τοῦτο δέ here means 'either ... or ...'; see the note on 7 for a different meaning. ἅμα, a preposition, 'with me'; this statement supports the theory that the freeman was a servant of Euxitheus, but it does not agree with Euxitheus' previous statement in 23 that the man 'was sailing in the same ship as he was and was with him continually', which implies that he went on with him from Methymna to Aenus, whereas in this section he says clearly that the freeman did not accompany him to Aenus. It is possible that Euxitheus was distorting the facts in 23 and telling the truth here, but it is hard to see how he could have taken the slave with him to Aenus or sent him to Asia Minor unless he had at once purchased him from his owner (who may have been the captain of the decked ship), before the prosecution could do so. 'The mainland' means Asia Minor. ὑπολείπεσθαι, middle, depending on ἐπ' ἐμοὶ ἦν, but we might say 'instead of leaving men who knew the facts to inform against me', lit. 'and not leave . . .'.

34

φασὶ . . . εὑρεῖν, 'the prosecution say that they found . . .'. ὃ . . . ἄνδρα, 'which I was going to send to Lycinus (saying) that I had killed Herodes'; ἀποκτείναιμι is aorist optative in indirect statement giving the contents of the note; the aorist indicative could have been used. Nothing is known about this Lycinus, who was said by the prosecution to have persuaded Euxitheus to kill Herodes. αὐτοῦ . . . φέροντος, genitive absolute, 'when the man who carried . . . was himself my accomplice (lit. 'being aware (of it)'; presumably it was alleged that the slave was to take the note to Lycinus, but it is hard to see how this man could be expected to leave his owner and go off on an errand for Euxitheus. τοῦτο μὲν . . . τοῦτο δέ, as in 7 and 33 but here meaning 'not only was the man who did the deed likely to tell the story more clearly himself, but also there was no need to conceal the message from him', by writing it in the letter, which in any case he probably could not read. ἃ μή is 'generic', i.e. 'such things as', ταῦτ' ἄν . . . πέμψειεν must be taken first, and ἐστί is to be understood with οἷόν τε: 'a man would generally (μάλιστα) send a message in writing (lit. 'having written it') which it is not expedient (lit. 'possible') for the bearer to know'; τὸν φέροντα would normally be dative after οἷόν τε (ἐστί), but see the note on προτείναντας in 31.

35

ὅτι . . . τοῦτο, the order of clauses is again reversed, as in the preceding sentence, and μέν is repeated: 'a man would be compelled to write down any long message (lit. 'whatever was a long affair'), so that because of its length the messenger should not have to remember it'. τῷ with the infinitive is another way of expressing purpose, and ὑπό is again used instead of a dative of the instrument. ἀπαγγεῖλαι, 'epexegetic' or explanatory infinitive: 'short (enough) to give verbally': the message could merely be 'the man is dead'. ἐνθυμεῖσθε, imperative, followed by ὅτι instead of the usual accusative and infinitive after verbs of thinking. διάφορον . . . τῷ βασανισθέντι, 'contradicted the slave who was tortured', who is called ὁ ἄνθρωπος in the next clause. ἔφη, in 20; but the slave did not say that he had murdered Herodes 'by himself', αὐτός, but had helped in the murder; and Euxitheus in that section declared that the man did not even say this but merely admitted having helped to dispose of the body, both statements, according to Euxitheus, being false and wrung out of him by torture. ἀνοιχθὲν . . . ἐμήνυε, 'when opened, declared that I was the murderer'.

36

ποτέρῳ, 'which of the two statements', i.e. the slave's own statement under torture, or the evidence of the letter. Notice that both incriminated Euxitheus equally, but his point is that such contradictory evidence was obviously manufactured and worthless. Supply ὑμᾶς (or ἡμᾶς) as the object of χρή. τὸ πρῶτον is adverbial accusative, with the same meaning as the adverb πρῶτον. ἐμεμηχάνητο αὐτοῖς, impersonal passive with dative of the agent: 'this scheme had not yet been devised by them'. ὁ πρότερος, the freeman. εἰσβάλλουσιν is historic present, and ἐπιφέρειν is infinitive of purpose after ἔχοιεν: 'that they might have this charge to bring against me'. It certainly seems that the note was a forgery.

37

οὐκέτι . . . ἀναγνωσθέντα, 'it was no longer possible to suppress the message that had been read in the letter', which said that Euxitheus had killed Herodes by himself, whereas the slave said that he had assisted him to do so. εἰ ἡγήσαντο . . . γραμματειδίῳ, 'if they had thought that they would (be able to) persuade . . . , they would never have invented the (message contained in) the note'. ἀπὸ πρώτης, like our 'from the first'; πρώτης agrees with ἀρχῆς, 'beginning', understood. μοι κάλει, 'please call', ethic dative, as in 16 (note).

38

τίνος ἕνεκα, 'for what reason', lit. 'for the sake of what'. ἐμοὶ καὶ ἐκείνῳ, 'between him and me'. χάριτι, 'as a favour', to Lycinus; so also χαριζόμενος ἑτέρῳ, 'doing a favour to another'. δεῖ ... μέλλοντι, 'the enmity (towards his victim) must be very great for a man who is intending ...'. τὴν πρόνοιαν ... ἐπιβουλευομένην, 'it must be clear from many (indications) that the design is being planned', lit. 'must be clear being planned'.

39

δείσας, this sentence has no main verb; we must supply something like 'did I commit the crime' and go on with δείσας, 'because I was afraid (lit. 'fearing for myself') that I should suffer this treatment at his hands', i.e. be killed by him. ἄν ... ἀναγκασθείη, 'anyone might be compelled ... for such a motive'; this is the main part of a conditional sentence with the εἰ-clause not expressed, or contained in τῶν τοιούτων ἕνεκα, which is equivalent to 'if he had such a motive'. ὑπῆρκτο, from ὑπάρχω: 'I had no such (feelings) towards him', lit. 'no such thing had been to me ...'. ἀποκτείνας αὐτόν, 'by killing him', or 'if I killed him'. οὐκ ἦν αὐτῷ, 'he had none'; perhaps Herodes had told Euxitheus that he had not brought much money with him because he was going to get the price of the slaves when he sold them at Aenus.

40

σοί, Euxitheus now addresses the chief prosecutor alone. μᾶλλον, with εἰκότως: 'I could more reasonably and with truth assign this motive to you, that you ...'; ἔχω often means 'I am able', and μετά with the genitive is again used instead of the simple dative. μᾶλλον ... ἐκεῖνον, a compressed clause with two verbs omitted: 'rather than that you (should accuse) me (of murdering) him'. πολὺ ... προσηκόντων, 'you might much more justly be convicted (from ἀλίσκομαι) of murder by my relatives for having killed me'; he means 'for trying to kill me by this charge of murder'. ἐγὼ ... ἀποδείκνυμι, 'I can show clear proof of your scheme against me', lit. 'I am showing clear(ly) your scheme'. ἐν ἀφανεῖ λόγῳ, 'by a statement that cannot be proved'. In fact the prosecution would obtain no financial advantage by securing Euxitheus' condemnation, so that the money-motive suggested here (χρημάτων ἕνεκα) for bringing him to trial was groundless.

41

ὑμῖν, Euxitheus turns to the jury again. τἀποκτεῖναι = τὸ ἀποκτεῖναι; this is the subject of εἶχε, lit. 'that killing the man had no motive for me myself', i.e. 'that I personally had no motive for killing . . .'. καὶ ὑπὲρ Λυκίνου, 'on behalf of Lycinus as well'. αὐτοῦ here = ἐμαυτοῦ, as in 2; for ἀλλ' . . . μόνον we should say 'and not on behalf of myself alone', instead of 'but . . .'. ὡς . . . αἰτιῶνται, 'to prove that they are not accusing him either with any justice'. ταὐτὰ . . . ἐμοί, 'the same (arguments) held good for him with regard to Herodes as (they did) for me'. χρήματα is the object of ἔλαβεν in the relative clause, though it is misplaced and put in the main clause: 'Lycinus had no chance of getting money by killing Herodes', lit. 'there was not to him whence he would have got money'; Euxitheus said in 39 that Herodes had brought no money with him on the voyage. οὔτε . . . διέφευγεν, 'and there was no danger threatening him (αὐτῷ ὑπῆρχεν) which he hoped to escape'; notice this meaning of the imperfect διέφευγεν.

42

Supply ἐστί with τεκμήριον: 'here is the greatest proof that . . .'. ἔξον, neuter participle of ἔξεστι and accusative absolute, which is used with impersonal verbs instead of the genitive absolute, lit. 'it being possible', here used with a concessive sense, 'though it was possible for Lycinus to put (καταστήσαντι) Herodes on trial and (place him) in great danger and with the help of your laws to . . .'. εἴπερ . . . κακόν, 'if a grudge was previously owed to him'; such a grudge would have had to be concerned with a crime committed by Herodes against Lycinus in the past. διαπράξασθαι and καταθέσθαι depend on ἔξον; 'to obtain his own private revenge and to win favour with . . .'. εἰ . . . ἐκεῖνον, 'if he proved Herodes to be a criminal'. οὐκ ἠξίωσεν, 'he did not wish to do so'. ἀλλ' οὐδ' ἦλθεν, 'and he did not even take legal proceedings against him'. καίτοι . . . αὐτῷ: it is thought that some words are missing from the text here, e.g. 'and yet the danger (of losing his case) was more honourable for him (than the danger of getting me to murder Herodes)'; if he failed to get a verdict against Herodes and also failed to get a certain number of the jury's votes he would have had to pay a fine to the court. We know nothing whatever about the relations between Lycinus and Herodes, so that the references to Lycinus in this part of the speech are by no means clear.

43

ἀλλὰ γάρ is often used to introduce and refute a real or pretended argument that may be put forward by the other side: 'but, you will say, on this count (ἐνταῦθα) he let Herodes alone, whereas (δέ) in the matter in which (οὗ) he was bound to endanger both himself . . ., in that point (ἐνταῦθα δέ) he plotted against Herodes'; the δέ after ἐνταῦθα is another example of δέ 'in apodosis', which is explained in the note on τούτοις δέ in 23. It would be better to begin a new sentence at ἐν ᾧ: 'if he had been discovered doing this (lit. 'in which being discovered') he would have deprived me of my country', i.e. he would have caused me to be sent into exile; the imperfect indicative with ἄν is used again to express a continuous action in the past instead of the aorist of a single action, though here there is hardly any difference between the two: lit. 'would have been depriving'. ἱερῶν καὶ ὁσίων, 'of all divine and human rights'; in this context ἱερά means things sacred to the gods, ὅσια things permitted to men. περὶ πλείστου, 'most precious'; περί is often used to denote value. εἰ . . . τεθνάναι, 'even if Lycinus was as eager as possible for Herodes to be killed'. εἶμι . . . λόγον, 'I shall actually accept the argument . . .', lit. 'I shall even go towards . . .'. οὗ . . . τοῦτο, the τοῦτο clause must be taken first: 'should I ever have been persuaded to do on his behalf this deed of which he himself refused (οὐκ ἠξίου) to be the perpetrator?'

44

πότερα introduces a single question (not the usual double question) here, with ἦν understood before ὡς: 'was it that I was physically (σώματι) fitted to . . . and that he was financially able to pay for the danger that I ran?'; we must supply ἐπιτηδεῖος ἦν, understood from the previous clause, with ἐκεῖνος. τῷ . . . οὐκ ἦν, 'for he had no money'; τῷ is the demonstrative use of the article, very common in Homer and found in Attic Greek in οἱ μέν . . . οἱ δέ, 'some . . . others', and in ὁ δέ at the beginning of a sentence, 'and he'. αὐτὸ τοὐναντίον, adverbial accusative, 'on the exact contrary'. τοῦτο is governed by ποιεῖν, understood, depending on ἐπείσθη.

ἑαυτὸν ... λύσασθαι, 'he could not even obtain his own release when imprisoned for arrears of debt of seven minae', lit. 'having become liable to arrest for non-payment of . . .'; Lycinus had to stay in prison until his friends paid his debt and procured his release (hence the middle voice, twice used here; in 1 λύεσθαι meant 'to ransom', or 'to purchase the freedom of'). A mina was a sum of money, 100 drachmas, worth about £4 in silver but with a very much higher purchasing power at that time. For καὶ μὲν δή see the note on the same words in 32; the καὶ ... καί that follow mean 'both ... and'. τῆς χρείας ... Λυκίνου, 'the (business) relationship between me and Lycinus'. ὅτι ... δοκοῦντα, 'that I was not on such good terms of friendship with Lycinus (lit. 'I did not use Lycinus very much a friend') that (ὡς = ὥστε) I should do everything that he wanted', lit. 'everything that seemed good to him'. οὐ γὰρ δήπου is sarcastic and negatives both parts of this sentence: 'for surely I did not refuse to pay (οὐκ ἀπέτεισα) . . . for him when he was suffering hardships in prison (lit. 'when bound and ill-treated') and then run so great a risk and kill a man on account of him', or 'to please him'.

45

ὡς ... δύναμαι, 'it has been proved to the best of my ability that I . . .'. τούτῳ ... ὅτι, 'rely mostly on this argument, that. . .'. περὶ τούτου αὐτοῦ, 'about this very point', i.e. Euxitheus' own explanation of the disappearance of Herodes, about which of course he declared that he knew nothing. ἐξ ἴσου ... ἐμοί, 'it is equally (possible) for you (to make a guess) as it is for me', or in the modern idiom, 'your guess is as good as mine'. τοῖς ἀληθέσι χρῆσθαι, 'to get at the truth'. ἐρωτώντων is imperative, 'let them (i.e. the prosecution) ask one of those who did the deed; they would learn it best from him'; but nobody knew who the murderers were, if Euxitheus himself was innocent.

46

ἐμοὶ ... ὅτι, 'the most that can be said in reply by me (lit. 'the greatest of the reply for me') who did not do the deed is only this (τοσοῦτον), that . . .'; μή is 'generic', i.e. 'the sort of person who did not . . .', which can hardly be brought out in translation, and τῆς ἀποκρίσεως is a partitive genitive. ἡ ἀπόδειξις, 'a full revelation of the facts'. μὴ ... εἰκάσαι, 'if he has not revealed them (lit. 'for him not having revealed') it is easy (ῥᾴδιόν ἐστι understood) for him to make a good guess', by accusing someone else of the crime that he has himself committed. ἅμα τε ... καί, lit. 'at the same time ... and ...', i.e. 'as soon as criminals have committed a crime they also invent an explanation of it', which will divert suspicion from themselves. χαλεπόν, supply ἐστι. περὶ τῶν ἀφανῶν, 'about unknown circumstances'. οἶμαι ἂν ... ἄν, as in 35, the first ἄν is not to be translated but prepares the hearer for the second one, which goes with εἰπεῖν in the indirect statement: 'I think that each one of you also ... would say only this (τοσοῦτον)'. εἴ τίς τινα, the accent of τινα is thrown back on to τις, which is of course not interrogative: 'if anyone were to ask him (lit. 'anyone') what he did not happen to know'; μὴ τύχοι is indefinite, and optative because it depends on the optative ἔροιτο. ἐν πολλῇ ... δοκῶ, 'I think you would be involved in a serious difficulty'.

47

μὴ ... τοῦτο, 'do not bring this difficulty upon me'. μηδέ, in the relative clause is 'generic' again, but we must say 'in which not even you yourselves would come off well', i.e. find it easy to give the right answer. μηδὲ ... εἶναι, 'do not demand (ἀξιοῦτε) that my acquittal should depend on this point, if I can make a good guess (about the murderer)'. ἐξαρκείτω μοι, imperative: 'let it be enough for me ...'. ἐν τούτῳ, 'in this respect', which is explained in the conditional clauses that follow, 'not if I discover in what way ..., but if I had no motive at all for killing him', lit. 'if it did not concern me at all so as to kill him'; but we might say 'my innocence depends on this point, not on my discovering ... but on my having no motive ...'. ἀνήρ = ὁ ἀνήρ.

48

ἤδη ... εὑρεθέντας, 'I know by hearsay that it has also already happened previously that sometimes (τοῦτο μέν) the murdered men and sometimes (τοῦτο δέ) their murderers have not been found'; γεγονός and εὑρεθέντας depend on the verb of perception ἐπίσταμαι, and τοῦτο μὲν ... τοῦτο δέ have appeared in 31, 33, and 34 with slightly different meanings. ἂν καλῶς ἔχοι = ἂν καλὸν εἴη: 'it would not be fair if those who had been in the company (of men who had disappeared) had to bear the blame for their murder', lit. 'of them'. ὑποσχεῖν and σχόντες come from ὑπέχω and ἔχω. ἑτέρων πραγμάτων, 'for other people's deeds'. τὸ σαφὲς αὐτῶν, 'the truth about them'.

49

αὐτίκα here means 'for example'. Ephialtes, 'your fellow-citizen', a democratic statesman and friend of Pericles, was murdered by an unknown hand in 461 because he was trying to reduce the powers of the Areopagus. εἰ ... εἶχε, 'if anyone had required those who had been in his company to guess who ... and if they failed to do so (εἰ δὲ μή) to be held liable for his murder, it would not have been fair . . .'. κινδυνεύειν depends on some verb understood from ἐζήτησαν; 'nor (did they venture) to run the risk of revealing (their part in) the deed by doing so (ἐν τούτῳ)'. ἐμὲ ... ἀναιρέσεως, 'that I made no one my accomplice in planning the death of Herodes, but (did so) in disposing of the body'.

50

τοῦτο δέ, 'again', lit. 'with regard to this', accusative of respect; so also in the sentence that begins after the next full stop. ἔντος ... χρόνου, 'quite recently', lit. 'within a not long time'. δέκα ... γεγονώς, like the Latin natus, 'not even twelve years old'. εἰ μὴ ... φεύγων, 'if, when his master cried out, he had not been afraid and had not gone off in flight . . .'. ἀπώλοντ' ἂν ... ἅπαντες, 'all the slaves (in the house) would have been put to death', the usual fate both in Greece and Rome when their master was murdered by someone unknown. ἂν ᾤετο, 'would have thought'. νῦν δὲ συλληφθείς, 'but as it was he was arrested and . . .'.

51

τοῦτο δὲ ... ὥσπερ ἐγὼ νῦν, 'again, your Hellenotamiae once faced a charge of embezzlement (lit. 'about money') which was groundless (lit. 'non-existent'), as I am now (facing this charge)'. Nothing is known about this incident; the 'Treasurers of Greece' were the commissioners who collected and administered the contributions of money made by the allied states in the Confederacy of Delos, which were originally intended to be used in a war against Persia but which Athens eventually diverted for her own purposes when she became head of the Confederacy, as though it were an Athenian empire. ὀργῇ ... γνώμῃ, 'through anger

rather than right judgment'. τὸ πρᾶγμα, 'the true facts of the case'.
τοῦ ἑνός . . . κατέγνωστο, 'sentence of death had been passed against this
one'; there are four verbs in the pluperfect tense in this section. ἐν
τούτῳ . . . τὰ χρήματα, 'meanwhile it was revealed how (τῷ = τίνι, lit·
'in what way') the money had been lost'. ὑπὸ τοῦ δήμου τοῦ ὑμετέρου, 'by
your democratic Assembly'; the accusation must have been brought
before the Ἐκκλησία, the Assembly of the whole Athenian people; 'The
Eleven' were the Commissioners of Police, one of whose duties was to
execute prisoners condemned to death. οὐδέν, 'in no way', adverbial
accusative.

52

ὑμῶν αὐτῶν, depending on πρεσβυτέρους, 'the older men among you'.
For the present tense πυνθάνεσθαι, we should say 'have heard of it'.
μετὰ τοῦ χρόνου, 'with the help of time'. ταῦτ' ἴσως . . . ὅτῳ τρόπῳ, 'this
question may perhaps be answered (lit. 'become clear'), where and
how (ὅτῳ is from ὅστις) . . .'; or we might say 'the place and manner
of Herodes' death may perhaps be revealed'. μὴ οὖν . . . ἀπολέσαντες,
'do not discover when it is too late (ὕστερον) that you have put me to
death though I am innocent'. πρότερον εὖ βουλεύσασθε, 'come to the right
decision while there is still time'. ὡς . . . σύμβουλοι, 'for there could not
be any (lit. 'other') worse counsellors than these', i.e. than anger and
prejudice (genitive of comparison).

53

οὐ γὰρ . . . γνοίη, 'for it is impossible for an angry man to make a correct
decision', lit. 'there is not (anything) with regard to which an angry man
would decide well'. The subject of διαφθείρει is ὀργή, understood from
ὀργιζόμενος, and τὴν γνώμην is in apposition to αὐτό, though we might take
τὴν γνώμην first: 'anger destroys a man's judgment, the very faculty
(αὐτό) with which he makes a decision'. μέγα is neuter, though ἡμέρα . . .
γιγνομένη is feminine: 'day succeeding day is a great thing for turning
aside . . .'; the two infinitives are explanatory ('epexegetic') after μέγα.

54

ἴστε, imperative of οἶδα. δίκην δοῦναι, 'to be punished', lit. 'to pay the
penalty'. εἰκός ἐστι . . . ἀδικοῦντας, 'it is right for the guilty to . . .'. τὸ

δυνάμενον and τὸ βουλόμενον are used as nouns, with ὑμέτερον agreeing with one and τῶν ἐχθρῶν depending on the other: 'your ability to . . . ought always to be more powerful than the desire of my enemies to . . .' ἐν τῷ . . . ποιῆσαι, 'by delaying it is still possible for you to do those terrible things . . .', i.e. condemn me to death; ἔστι = ἔξεστι, twice in this sentence. The article with παραχρῆμα makes the adverb into a noun: 'by immediate action it is impossible to deliberate fairly at all'; ἀρχήν is used adverbially, lit. 'in the beginning'.

55

ὅσα . . . ἀπολελόγημαι, 'I have defended myself against all the charges that I can remember', lit. 'as many things as I remember from what has been charged against (me)'; Euxitheus is perhaps asking for sympathy from the jury because he is not a professional orator and has had to learn by heart this long speech written for him by Antiphon. The five words between ὑμῶν and ἀποψηφίσασθαι were suggested by a modern editor to fill what was obviously a gap in the text. καὶ ὑμῶν αὐτῶν ἕνεκα, 'for your own sakes too'. σῴζει and γίγνεται almost have a future sense; 'this same verdict will both save my life and will be in accordance with the law and with your oath'. καθ' οὕς, the antecedent is τοῖς νόμοις: 'I am not liable to prosecution under the laws according to which I was arrested, but a legal trial is still left for me (for the crime) of which I am accused'. This refers to the complaint of Euxitheus in the first part of his speech (omitted in this book) that he had not been charged with murder on a δίκη φόνου before the court of the Areopagus, but as a malefactor, κακοῦργος, before an ordinary jury-court, so that even if he was acquitted in the lower court he would still be liable to be charged with murder before the Areopagus. γεγενέσθων, third person dual of the perfect of γίγνομαι: 'if two trials have been made out of one'. αἴτιος here is 'responsible', not 'guilty'. οὐ δήπου negatives both parts of the sentence; we might make the μέν sentence concessive and say 'surely it cannot be that although my bitterest enemies have instituted two trials against me, you who are impartial judges . . . will prematurely find me guilty of murder . . .'.

56

μή, supply τοῦτο ποιήσητε. δότε . . . πραγμάτων, 'give a chance (τι) to time also, with the help of which those who try to find the exact truth

of events find it with most certainty'. ἠξίουν, 'I could wish'; ἄν is sometimes omitted with an imperfect indicative when someone wishes that
something were now happening which is not happening: 'I could wish
that in such cases the trial should be held (εἶναι τὴν δίκην) according to
law, but that the truth should be established (ἐλέγχεσθαι, used imperson-
ally) as often as possible according to justice'. τοσούτῳ . . . ἐγιγνώσκετο,
'for the case would then be much better understood', lit. 'by so much
the better', dative of measure of difference. οἱ πολλοὶ ἀγῶνες, 'repeated
trials (of the same case)'.

57

φόνου . . . ἐστιν, 'the verdict in a trial for murder, even if not correctly
given, carries greater weight (lit. 'is a more powerful thing') than
justice . . .'. ὄντα agrees with ἐμέ understood, which depends on ἀνάγκη
(ἐστί): 'though I am not a murderer nor liable for the crime (ἔργῳ),
I must submit (χρῆσθαι) to . . .'. πιστεύσας . . . ἐστιν, 'though he believed
in his own mind (lit. 'having trusted himself') that he was . . .'. οὔτε
ξυνειδὼς . . . χρῆσθαι, 'nor, if he were conscious of having committed
(lit. 'being aware with himself having done') such a crime, would he
dare to refuse to submit to . . .'; μὴ οὐ is the 'redundant' (unnecessary)
double negative often used with infinitives when the main verb is itself
negative, lit. 'nobody would dare not to use the law'; μή alone would
have the same meaning. νικᾶσθαι, here followed by a genitive of comparison: '(a man) must give way to a verdict contrary to the true facts,
as well as (τε) to the true facts themselves, especially if there is no one to
support his cause', e.g. if a man had no relatives or friends to assist him
with his defence, or perhaps to avenge him after his death, as in 65.

58

αὐτῶν τούτων ἕνεκα, 'for these very reasons'. προρρήσεις, 'proclamations'
made by the prosecutor in a trial for murder, telling the accused to keep
away from all temples and public places until the trial was over. τἀλλ' . . .
φόνου, 'everything else that takes place in connection with trials for
murder'. πολὺ . . . ἄλλοις, 'are very different from (what happens) at
other trials'; διαφέρειν, 'to be different from', usually takes a genitive of
comparison instead of ἤ. ὅτι καὶ . . . γιγνώσκεσθαι, 'because it is of
the greatest importance (περὶ πλείστου ἐστίν) that the facts themselves,

with which danger (to life is concerned), should be rightly understood'. The subject of ἐστί is πράγματα understood: 'facts rightly understood mean vengeance for the injured man', i.e. for the victim of murder; and we must supply τό before φονέα ... ψηφισθῆναι: 'but for an innocent person to be condemned as a murderer is ...'. εἰς, 'against'.

59

ἴσον ... καί, 'the same ... as', like idem ... ac in Latin: 'it is not the same thing for the prosecutor ... as it is for you jurymen to pass a wrong verdict'. τούτων, the prosecution. οὐκ ἔχει ... δίκῃ, 'has no lasting effect, but (the result) depends on you and on the trial'. τοῦτο, accusative of respect, lit. 'with regard to this': 'whatever wrong verdict you give ... in this (τοῦτο) there is no (higher court) to which you (lit. 'anyone') could refer and relieve yourselves of (responsibility for) the error'; a verdict of guilty would mean Euxitheus' immediate execution, though an acquittal would still leave him open to a charge of murder before the Areopagus; no doubt the prosecution would be unlikely to accuse him again if he was acquitted in the lower court by a large majority.

60

τὸν νομιζόμενον ... κατηγορῆσαι, 'to bring their case (against me only) after they have taken the customary oath'; ὅρκον is a 'cognate' accusative, used after an intransitive verb when the noun repeats the meaning contained in the verb, like 'to swear an oath' or 'to run a race'. Euxitheus is referring to the solemn oath taken by both parties and their witnesses at a trial for murder (δίκη φόνου) heard before the Areopagus, as opposed to the less solemn affidavit (διωμοσία) made by plaintiff and defendant at other trials, where witnesses were not on oath; it was under this latter procedure that he was now being tried as a κακοῦργος (malefactor). περὶ ... πράγματος, 'on the actual charge', without having to deal with matters that did not concern the alleged crime itself. οὐδ' οὕτω, 'not even so'. τὰς ὑμετέρας γνώμας, 'your judgment'. ὑμεῖς ... διαψηφιζόμενοι, 'it will be you who give the verdict in the other court too', lit. 'there too', i.e. in the trial for murder before the Areopagus that might follow if he was acquitted by the present jury. In fact the juries would not be the same, even in part, because the Areopagites were all ex-magistrates, whereas the jury in the ordinary courts were ordinary citizens. Euxitheus however calls them all ὑμεῖς, 'you Athenians', as being natives of the city, whatever their position, while he was an alien from Lesbos; this was perhaps flattery, or a pretended ignorance of Athenian legal procedure. ἔξεστι and ἐγχωρεῖ are both impersonal: 'if you spare me now it is possible for you in the future (τότε) to treat me in whatever way you wish, but if you put me to death (ἀπολέσασι) it is not open to you even to discuss my case (any more)'.

61

εἰ δέοι ... ἀπολέσαι, 'if (you) had to make a mistake, to acquit me unjustly would be a more righteous act than to put me to death contrary to justice'. τὸ μὲν ... ἀσέβημα, 'the one thing is merely a mistake, but the other is also a sin'. ἐν ᾧ, 'in this case'. Supply ὑμᾶς as the object of χρή. ἐν ἀκέστῳ ... ἐξαμαρτεῖν, 'in a matter that can be remedied it is less serious (for men) to make a mistake either (καί) through giving way to anger or (καί) through believing a false accusation'; the two participles agree with ἄνδρας understood in an accusative and infinitive clause depending on ἔλασσόν ἐστιν. μεταγνούς, 'if a man changed his mind', singular, though we have the plural in the previous sentence and in the one that follows. ἐν τοῖς ... ἐξημαρτηκότας, 'in matters where a decision is irrevocable it is a greater injury (for men) to ... and realise that they have made a mistake'; the verb is ἐστί understood, whose subject is τὸ μετανοεῖν καὶ γνῶναι, with ἄνδρας again understood as the subject of the infinitives, lit. 'the (fact that men) change their minds ... (is) a greater injury ...'. ἤδη ... ἀπολωλεκόσι (dative plural of the perfect participle of ἀπόλλυμι), 'before now (ἤδη) some of you have in fact (καί) repented after condemning men to death'; this refers to the two debates in the Athenian Assembly in 427 (ten or twelve years before the time of this speech), when the people first of all voted to kill all the men and enslave all the women and children of Mytilene (the native city of Euxitheus) because it had revolted in the previous year; next day the Athenians repented of this decision and sent another ship to Lesbos which arrived just in time to stop the massacre. Herodes' father was probably one of the Athenian settlers ('cleruchs') to whom land near Mytilene was allotted, and Euxitheus' father was one of the citizens of Mytilene who took part in the revolt. ὅπου ... ἀπολωλέναι, 'when you who were misled repented, most certainly (ἦ καὶ πάνυ τοι) those who were misleading you ought to have been put to death'; χρῆν = ἐχρῆν; the demagogue Cleon was one of the principal speakers in favour of the massacre of the people of Mytilene.

62

τῶν ἁμαρτημάτων, partitive genitive depending on ἑκούσια, 'involuntary mistakes can be excused (ἔχει συγγνώμην)'. τῆς τύχης . . . γνώμης, 'is (a matter) of chance . . . of choice'. ἑκούσιον . . . ποιοῖτο, 'how could there be a more voluntary (act) than when (lit. 'if') a man immediately performs a deed (ταῦτα) of which he has formed the plan?'; ποιοῖτο is indefinite, in historic sequence depending on the optative εἴη. Nowadays a crime committed on the spur of the moment is considered less serious than one planned long in advance, but the contrast here is merely between an involuntary and a voluntary act. τὴν ἴσην . . . ψήφῳ, 'it has the same effect when a man (lit. 'whoever') puts to death . . . as (καί) with his judicial vote'.

63

οὐκ ἂν ἦλθον, 'I should not have come'; he could have fled to Thrace or Asia Minor. εἰ . . . τοιοῦτον, 'if I had been conscious in my own mind (of having committed) such a crime'. νῦν δὲ πιστεύων, this participle has no main verb because the sentence is interrupted by the long parenthesis from ἐν γὰρ τῷ τοιούτῳ down to τῶν ἀσεβημάτων, after which Euxitheus resumes with ἐγὼ δ' ἐμαυτῷ; we should take πιστεύων as though it were the main verb: 'but as it is I put my trust in justice'. οὗ, genitive of comparison: 'than which there is nothing more valuable (πλέονος ἄξιον) to aid a man when he is conscious in his own mind (αὑτῷ) that he has done nothing (μηδέν is 'generic') . . .'. ἐν τῷ τοιούτῳ . . . ἑαυτῇ, 'at such a time even when the body is weary the spirit has often (ἤδη) come to its aid . . . because it has no guilty knowledge in itself', lit. 'on account of the fact that it is not aware in itself (that it is guilty)'; so also in the next sentence τῷ ξυνειδότι . . . ἐστιν, 'for the man who has a guilty conscience this very fact (i.e. the knowledge of his guilt) is his greatest enemy', lit. 'the first hostile thing'. In this section ξυνοῖδα is spelled with ξυν- three times and with συν- once; ξυν- is the old Attic form, which is always used by Thucydides, frequently by Homer and Euripides (often to lengthen a preceding short syllable), and sometimes by Antiphon. This verb with a reflexive pronoun in the dative case does not necessarily mean *guilty knowledge*, as here. ἔτι καὶ ... ἰσχύοντος, 'moreover, when the body is still strong'. ἡγουμένη ... ταύτην, 'thinking that this is the punishment that has come upon it for ...'; οἷ is the dative of the indirect reflexive pronoun ἕ, which is seldom used in Attic Greek but is common in Homer; the plural σφᾶς, σφῶν, σφίσι, is normal in Attic Greek. τοιοῦτον οὐδὲν ξυνειδώς, 'with no such guilty knowledge'.

64

τὸ ... διαβάλλειν, 'the fact that my prosecutors are maligning me'. Supply ἐστί with ἔργον: 'this is their duty, and it is your duty not to be persuaded (to do) what is unjust', lit. 'such things as are not just', μή being 'generic'. τοῦτο, accusative of respect with πειθομένοις (or possibly governed by ποιεῖν understood): 'if you are persuaded by me in this, it is possible for you to ...'; ἔστιν = ἔξεστιν. τούτου φάρμακον ... ἴασις, 'the remedy for this (i.e. for this change of mind) is to punish me on a future occasion (αὖθις, i.e. at a second trial), but there is no remedy for (τοῦ) your being persuaded by the prosecution (τούτων) and doing ...'; οὐδὲ ... διαφέρων, 'and the time interval (is) not long', lit. 'the time that intervenes'. For ἐν ᾧ we should say 'after which'. οὔ τοι ... βουλευομένων; 'the case is not a matter for haste but for careful consideration', lit. 'not of men hurrying but of men deliberating well'. γνωρισταί, δικασταί, δοξασταί, κριταί, perhaps best made into verbs: 'make a survey of the case today, sit in judgment on it later; form an opinion on the truth today, give your decision about it later', lit. 'be enquirers into the case now, be judges of it then ...'.

65

ἀνδρός, governed by καταμαρτυρῆσαι: 'to give false evidence against a man who is on trial (φεύγοντος) on a capital charge'. τὸ παραχρῆμα μόνον, 'only for a moment'. The ὥστε after πείσωσιν is not translated. Greek generally uses an ordinary prolative infinitive after πείθειν. ἅμα ... ἀπόλωλεν, 'his chance of obtaining vengeance (against his false accusers) is lost together with his life', lit. 'with his body'. οὔτε, 'not even', and ἐὰν καί, 'even if'. τί ἔσται πλέον, 'what good will it be to ...', if a man's friends or relatives could prove that the prosecution had obtained a verdict of murder by bringing false evidence, they could avenge him by charging the prosecutors with murder; it would have to be a private suit brought by an individual against the person accused of the crime, which is the reason why a slave-owner who killed one of his slaves generally went unpunished, there being nobody sufficiently interested to bring a prosecution against the guilty person.

66

ἐν τῇ τοῦ φόνου δίκῃ, 'in the trial for murder', before the court of the Areopagus at which Euxitheus might be accused if he was acquitted on this occasion; for this and for 'the customary oath', see the notes on 60. κατὰ . . . νόμους, 'according to the established laws'; κεῖμαι is used as the perfect passive of τίθημι. ἐμοὶ . . . ἀπωλόμην, 'I shall have no grounds for complaining (λόγος) that I was illegally sentenced to death'. ἐάν τι πάσχω, a common Greek and English 'euphemism' (avoidance of an unpleasant expression) for death or other misfortune: 'if anything happens to me', or here 'if the worst happens to me'. ταῦτα, the request comes in the last two words of the speech. οὔτε . . . παρείς, 'neither asking you to set aside your sacred duty', as jurymen, to be true to their oaths; lit. 'neither setting aside . . .'. καὶ . . . ἔνεστι, 'my salvation too depends upon . . .'. πειθόμενοι . . . βούλεσθε, 'believe whichever of these arguments that you wish and . . .'.

EURIPIDES, *ION*

The Greek theatre provided no programme or list of characters, and so Euripides used his prologues as a means of informing the audience of the background of his plays and of any changes in the mythological stories that he might be making. This was especially necessary in *Ion*, because the story was probably unfamiliar to most Athenians and the details of the plot quite unknown to them. This Prologue is spoken by Hermes, a son of Zeus and the messenger and servant of the gods; he takes no further part in the play.

l. 1. Atlas was a Titan who, for having taken part in the war of the Titans against Zeus, was condemned to support the heavens on his shoulders, here said to be made of bronze, somewhere in the far west. Perseus turned him into stone by showing him the Gorgon's head and he was identified with Mount Atlas in North Africa. The line in the manuscripts ends with νώτοις οὐρανόν, which breaks the metrical rule that the fifth foot must be an iambus (∪ –), not a spondee (– –), if it contains a caesura (break between two words); Elmsley's correction removes this metrical irregularity. ὁ . . . ἐκτρίβων, 'who bears the (weight of the) sky . . . upon his brazen shoulders', lit. 'wears away the sky', though it was his shoulders that were being worn away by the weight of the heavens.

l. 2. θεῶν . . . οἶκον, in apposition to οὐρανόν. θεῶν is repeated in this line, perhaps accidentally. μιᾶς, genitive of origin: 'begat Maia from one of (the daughters of) the gods', whose name Hermes does not mention; some ancient writers call her Pleione. 'μ' = ἐμέ; the first ε is 'prodelided', the second is 'elided'.

l. 5. τήνδε γῆν, accusative of goal of motion without a preposition. ἵνα, 'where'. The navel, i.e. central point, of the earth was said to be marked by a conical stone placed at the meeting-place of two eagles sent by Zeus; this was in the temple of Apollo at Delphi.

l. 6. Φοῖβος ὑμνῳδεῖ, in classical times a priestess of Apollo called the Pythia sat on a tripod in the shrine of the temple and in a frenzy chanted unintelligible words in answer to questions asked by those who consulted the oracle; the priests interpreted these replies according to their judgment of the needs of the situation and wrote them down in hexameter verse for the visitors' benefit; the advice was often good and generally ambiguous, in case events turned out contrary to what the priests expected.

l. 7. τά must be taken with μέλλοντα as well as with ὄντα, 'proclaiming (lit. 'prophesying') things that are and things that are still to be'.

l. 8. γάρ, this is the 'introductory γάρ', often used at the beginning of a narrative and not to be translated except perhaps as 'now'. ἔστιν . . . πόλις, 'there is a city of no small fame', lit. 'not unknown', like St Paul's description of Tarsus as 'no mean city'; this use of understatement to give emphasis is called 'litotes' or 'meiosis'.

l. 9. χρυσολόγχου, referring to the gilded point of the spear of the bronze statue of Athena Promachos, which was placed on the Acropolis at

Athens during Euripides' lifetime; the genitive is possessive, 'called (the city) of . . .'.

l. 10. οὗ, 'where'. ἔζευξεν . . . βίᾳ, 'joined . . . (to himself) in love by force'; γάμος and γαμεῖν are several times used in this play for the irregular union of Phoebus and Creüsa. Erectheus, the father of Creüsa, was the grandson of Erichthonius who was the fourth of the early kings of Athens (see page 62). Ἐρεχθέως is here scanned ∪ – – ; see l. 83 (n).

l. 11. ἔνθα . . . καλοῦσι, 'where stand the northern rocks which the lords . . . call the "Long Cliffs" ', lit. 'where the lords . . . call the northern rocks the "Long Cliffs" '. ὑπό is 'at the foot of', and 'the hill of Pallas in (lit. 'of') the land of the Athenians' is the Acropolis, at the north-western side of which there are some caves; Creüsa was said to have met Apollo in one of these caves, later called the cave of Apollo and Pan, and afterwards to have abandoned her new-born baby in it. 'The lords of the Attic country' probably means only the citizens of Athens.

l. 14. ἀγνώς, here feminine: 'unknown to her father'. τῷ . . . φίλον, 'for (such) was the will of the god', lit. 'it was dear to the god', i.e. Phoebus.

l. 15. γαστρὸς διήνεγκ' ὄγκον, 'she bore to the very end the burden in her womb'. ὡς is 'when'.

l. 17. ταὐτόν = τὸ αὐτό, 'the same'; this combination of two words into one is called 'crasis' (mixing); κἀκτίθησιν in the next line is another example.

l. 18. ἐκτίθησιν, historic present: 'she cast him out to die'; ὡς with a future participle expresses a purpose. The 'exposure' of an unwanted infant was common in ancient Greece.

l. 19. ἀντίπηγος, the cradle was made of wicker-work (πλεκτόν in l. 37), like the 'ark' in which Pharaoh's daughter found Moses (Exodus, II, 3). ἐν is slightly misplaced.

l. 20. νόμον σώζουσα, 'preserving the custom', which is explained in ll. 21–26, i.e. of giving golden snakes as an ornamental amulet or charm to an infant. γηγενοῦς, it was the proud boast of the Athenians that their ancestor Erichthonius was 'earth-born' and not an immigrant settler; hence αὐτόχθονα in l. 29. The story is told in ll. 83–92.

l. 21. Ἐριχθονίου, an anapaest (∪ ∪ –) is allowed in the second foot in a proper name not divided between two feet. 'The daughter of Zeus' was Athena.

l. 22. φρούρω, φύλακε, δισσώ, and δράκοντε are dual: 'after putting beside him (Erichthonius) two snakes, watchers to guard his body, gave him to ... to keep safe'; δίδωσι is another historic present, and σῴζειν infinitive of purpose after a verb of giving.

l. 23. 'The Aglaurid maidens' were the daughters of Cecrops, the first king of Athens, by his wife Aglaurus; for their story, see the note on l. 88.

l. 24. ὅθεν ... τέκνα, 'whence it is the custom for the descendants of Erechtheus there (i.e. at Athens) to bring up their children in (the protection of) golden snakes', which brought them good luck; we shall see in l. 476 that the snakes formed a necklace for the infant Ion.

l. 26. ἦν ... χλιδήν, 'the fine garment which she wore as a maiden'; when still a girl Creüsa had begun to weave a dress for herself which she 'fastened round' her new-born son before abandoning him; it is called ὕφασμα in l. 462 and played an important part in the recognition scene, when she remembered and described the pattern that she had woven.

l. 27. ὡς θανουμένῳ, 'as to one doomed to die'; not quite the same as in l. 18.

l. 28. ἐμέ and τάδε are both governed by αἰτεῖται (another historic present).

l. 32. αὐτῷ σὺν ἄγγει, 'with the cradle itself', or 'cradle and all'. οἷς ἔχει, 'relative attraction' for ἃ ἔχει: 'which he is wearing'.

l. 33. Δελφῶν, depending on χρηστήρια, but we say 'to my oracle at Delphi'.

l. 34. πρὸς αὐταῖς εἰσόδοις, 'at the very entrance'.

l. 35. τὰ ἄλλα ἡμῖν μελήσει, 'all else will be my care'; it is common in poetry to find ἡμεῖς used instead of ἐγώ. For ὡς εἰδῇς we might say 'let me tell you', instead of 'that you may know it'.

l. 38. κρηπίδων ἔπι, when a preposition follows the noun that it governs, usually at the end of a line of poetry, it has a paroxytone accent (on the last syllable but one), instead of an oxytone (on the last syllable). κρηπῖδες means the platform at the top of the steps that led up to the temple, on which the columns were built; Euripides imagines the pre-historic temple of Apollo to be similar to the fourth-century building of which the ruins can still be seen. In l. 39 κύτος means 'lid', and in l. 40 ὁρῷθ' = ὁρῷτο, optative in a purpose clause.

l. 41. κυρεῖ ... ἐσβαίνουσα, 'the priestess chanced to be entering ... when the sun was driving out on its circular course', genitive absolute.

l. 44. εἴ τις, verbs of wondering are followed by εἰ meaning 'that'; 'she was surprised that any . . . should dare to cast down the child she bore in secret (lit. 'her secret birth-pang') at the temple . . .'; ἐς is misplaced, like ἐν in l. 19.

l. 46. διορίσαι πρόθυμος ἦν, 'she wanted to remove him'.

l. 47. οἴκτῳ . . . 'κπεσεῖν, 'she gave up her cruel purpose out of pity — and the god was working (with her) for the child, so that he was not flung out of . . .'; τῷ παιδί is dative of advantage, and ἐκπεσεῖν (the ἐ- is 'prodelided') is a consecutive clause with ὥστε omitted (or perhaps as though it were in a clause of preventing, 'to prevent him from being flung out', with the 'redundant' (unnecessary) μή, as after e.g. εἴργειν).

l. 49. τὸν . . . Φοῖβον, 'she did not know that Phoebus was his father', lit. 'the one who begat him'; but μητέρα is the direct object of οἶδεν, 'nor did she know the mother from whom he was born', with ἧς as genitive of origin.

l. 52. νέος . . . τροφάς, 'while he was young he . . . around the altars that fed him', both literally because the priests and their attendants ate food offered at the altars, and metaphorically because the temple was his home.

l. 53. ὥς, 'when'. δέμας is accusative of respect, 'he became a man in strength', lit. 'with respect to his body'; or it may be the subject, 'when his body grew to maturity'.

l. 54. σφ' ἔθεντο, 'made him'.

l. 55. πάντων, 'of all his treasures'.

l. 56. καταζῇ . . . βίον, 'he has always lived a holy life until the present time (δεῦρο)'; σεμνὸν βίον is a 'cognate' accusative, used after an intransitive verb when the noun repeats the meaning contained in the verb.

l. 57. ἡ τεκοῦσα, 'the mother of . . .', lit. 'she who gave birth to . . .'.

l. 58. συμφορᾶς τοιᾶσδ' ὑπό, 'because of the following events'; for the position and accent of ὑπό, which is generally used with people, not things, see the note on l. 48.

l. 59. ἦν . . . κλύδων, 'a sea of war arose (lit. 'was') between . . .'; 'the followers (lit. 'sons') of Chalcodon', who was a king in the island of Euboea, were the Euboeans.

l. 61. ὃν . . . συνεξελών, 'joining in and helping to end this war'.

l. 62. γάμων Κρεούσης ἀξίωμα, 'the honour of marriage with Creüsa'.

l. 63. Αἰόλου, genitive of origin: 'an Achaean, sprung from Aeolus, son of Zeus'. The ancestry of Xuthus is confused in the different versions of the legend; see page 62. In the closing lines of *Ion* (not included in this book) Achaeus is the name of a son of Xuthus and Creusa, but here 'an Achaean' means one living in Achaea in Thessaly; in later times Achaea was the name of a district in the northern Peloponnese, of which Euripides says that Xuthus' son Achaeus was to be king. Homer applies the name 'Achaeans' to all the Greeks.

l. 64. χρόνια σπείρας λέχη, 'though he has lived in wedlock for a long time'.

l. 65. καὶ Κρέουσα, 'as also is Creüsa'. ὧν οὕνεκα, 'for this reason'.

l. 67. ἔρωτι παίδων, 'in their longing for children'. τὴν τύχην . . . ὡς δοκεῖ, 'guides their destiny to this end, and has not forgotten the affair, as some think'; λέληθεν is probably impersonal, with αὐτόν as the object, lit. 'it has not escaped his notice, as it seems (to have done)'.

l. 69. εἰσελθόντι . . . τόδε, 'when he enters this oracular shrine'. αὐτοῦ refers to Phoebus and κείνου to Xuthus: 'he will say that the child (lit. 'he', σφε) is sprung from him', genitive of origin. In l. 71 δόμους is accusative of goal of motion.

l. 73. γνωσθῇ Κρεούσῃ, 'may be acknowledged by Creüsa', dative of the agent, or perhaps 'may be made known to Creüsa'; the recognition scene in fact took place at Delphi, not at Creüsa's home in Athens.

l. 73. κρυπτοὶ γενῶνται, 'may remain (not 'become') secret'. ἔχῃ, 'may possess'.

l. 74. Ἴωνα . . . θήσεται, 'he will cause him to be called by the name of Ion, as founder . . .', lit. 'to be called Ion in respect of his name', accusative of respect, as also in l. 77. The Greek colonies on the Aegean coast of Asia Minor were founded by Ionian Greeks from the mainland of Greece who claimed descent from Ion. For the supposed origin of the name, see the note on l. 226; Ion had previously been nameless.

l. 76. πόθεν γῆς, 'from what country', lit. 'whence of the earth', partitive genitive.

l. 77. χρεών, supply ἐστί, 'by what name must we call you?'; for ὄνομα, see the note on l. 74. This line has seven short syllables in succession, i.e. two tribrachs (∪ ∪ ∪) followed by an iambus (∪ –).

l. 80. ὦ . . . θαυμάζω, 'O you who dwell in . . . and are descended (lit. 'nourished') from noble ancestors, how I honour you'; the nameless foundling does not know that this ancestry is also his.

l. 82. τοσαῦτα . . . οὐ πέρα, 'so far indeed (καί) am I fortunate, but no farther'; τοσαῦτα is accusative of respect, and the first person plural is used instead of the singular, like ἡμῖν for ἐμοί in l. 36.

l. 83. ἀληθῶς goes with ἔβλαστεν in l. 85; we should say 'in heaven's name, is it true, as the story is told by men, that . . .', but Creüsa interrupts Ion's question, perhaps because he is slow to complete it out of respect for her; he then goes on 'that your ancestor (πατήρ), the grandfather of your father, was sprung from the earth?' θεῶν is scanned as a monosyllable by what is called 'synizesis' (so also in l. 127), and βροτοῖς is dative of the agent.

l. 84. τί χρῆμα = simply τί, 'what'. In this scene Creüsa four times addresses her son as ξένε, and Ion his mother as 'lady' (γύναι); this is called 'dramatic irony', because the audience has already learned of their relationship from Hermes in the Prologue.

l. 85. ἐκ γῆς, in l. 20 Erichthonius is called γηγενοῦς, 'earth-born'. The line of descent was said to be Erichthonius, Pandion, Erechtheus, Creüsa; πατήρ either means 'your ancestor', or it may be used as a title of respect with πρόγονος, 'the venerable grandfather of your father'.

l. 86. For the scansion of Ἐριχθόνιος, see the note on l. 21. γε in 'stichomythia', i.e. conversation of one line each between two speakers, often means 'yes'. τὸ γένος, 'my high birth'.

l. 87. ἦ . . . ἐξανείλετο, 'did Athena really (καί) raise him up . . . ?'

l. 88. ἐς παρθένους γε χεῖρας, 'yes (γε), into her virgin hands, though she did not give birth to him'. The story was that Gē, the Earth-goddess, gave birth to Erichthonius, a son by Hephaestus, and at once gave the infant to the virgin goddess Athena, who put him in a chest and entrusted it to the three daughters of Cecrops and Aglaurus, with orders not to look inside it; two of them disobeyed and were driven mad and threw themselves down from the Acropolis.

l. 89. ὥσπερ . . . νομίζεται, 'as is usually shown in paintings'.

l. 90. σῴζειν, infinitive of purpose, depending on the historic present δίδωσι in l. 89; 'yes, to the daughters . . . , to keep him (safe) unseen'.

l. 91. ἤκουσα . . . τεῦχος, 'I have heard that the maidens opened . . .'.

l. 93. τί δαὶ . . . λόγος, 'what then of the next tale? Is the story true or false?', lit. 'what then (is) this? (Is) the story a true thing or in vain?'

l. 94. καὶ γὰρ . . . σχολῇ, 'for indeed I have plenty of time', lit. 'I am not in a difficulty with leisure'.

l. 96. ἔτλη . . . κτανεῖν, 'he brought himself (lit. 'endured') to kill . . . as victims for his country'; Erechtheus sacrificed his youngest daughter (youngest except for the infant Creüsa) in order to win the victory in a war against Eleusis, and the elder sisters volunteered to die with her. In l. 98 ἦν is 'I was', another form of ἦ.

l. 99. χάσμα . . . χθονός, 'did the earth gape open and conceal . . .', lit. 'did a chasm in the earth conceal . . . ?'; Erechtheus killed Eumolpus of Thrace in this war, so Eumolpus' father, Poseidon, struck the earth with his trident and caused Erechtheus to be swallowed up in the chasm·

l. 100. We should make πληγαί singular: 'a blow from the sea-god's trident'; ποντίου is feminine, agreeing with τριαίνης.

l. 101. Μακραὶ . . . κεκλημένος, 'is there a place there called the Long Cliffs?'; see the note on l. 11.

l. 102. ὥς . . . τινος, 'how you remind me of something', i.e. of how she was seduced by Phoebus in a cave under the Acropolis and abandoned her son there.

l. 103. σφε is either singular or plural and refers to Μακραί or to χῶρος.

$\overset{-\;\smile\smile}{Πύθιος}$ makes an anapaest ($\smile\;\smile\;-$) in the third foot, which is unusual even for a proper name when it is divided between two feet (see the note on l. 21); it may perhaps be scanned as a trochee ($-\;\smile$) if the last two syllables are pronounced as one, by 'synizesis', as θεῶν became one syllable in l. 83. When lightning-flashes were seen on Mount Parnes, in N.W. Attica, on three nights and three days in any month by watchers in Athens, an embassy was sent to Delphi because Apollo had honoured the Athenians by showing them his lightning. But the place of observation at Athens was not the Long Cliffs, according to Strabo in the first century B.C., unless the custom had changed since Euripides' time.

l. 104. τιμᾷ; τί τιμᾷ; 'honour it? how does he honour it?'; Creüsa is indignant and cannot forget her old wrong. (The reading of the text is uncertain here.) ὤφελον is used to express a wish for the past: 'I wish I had never seen them', i.e. the Long Cliffs.

l. 105. τοῦ θεοῦ τὰ φίλτατα, 'the god's dearest haunt', because the cave in the Long Cliffs was the oldest place of the worship of Apollo in Athens.

l. 106. οὐδέν . . . τινά, 'it is nothing; I share with the cave the knowledge of a deed of shame', i.e. her seduction by Apollo there. Ion tactfully changes the subject at this point.

l. 109. εὐγενῆ . . . τινά, 'he must have been someone of noble birth'.

l. 111. ἔσχεν, 'did he win as a wife . . .'.

l. 112. Εὔβοι'. . . πόλις, 'there is a city-state near Athens, called Euboea', which is in fact the name of the island, not of a town in it.

l. 113. ὅροις ὑγροῖσιν, 'by the limits of the sea'.

l. 114. Κεκροπίδαις κοινῷ δορί, 'in alliance (lit. 'with allied spear') with the sons of . . .'.

l. 115. ἐπίκουρος ἐλθών, 'coming as an ally'. σὸν . . . λέχος, 'he won your hand'.

l. 116. φερνάς . . . λαβών, 'yes, taking it (my hand in marriage) as the dowry of war . . .'.

l. 117. σὺν ἀνδρί, 'with your husband'. χρηστήρια, accusative of goal of motion.

l. 118. Trophonius was an Arcadian seer who had an oracular cave fifteen miles from Delphi; he was consulted by visitors who wanted to get 'a second opinion' on their problem. Xuthus' visit to him is merely a device of Euripides to let Creüsa speak to Ion alone.

l. 119. πότερα . . . χάριν, 'as a sightseer or for the sake of . . .'; when used as a preposition χάριν generally follows the genitive case that it governs.

l. 120. θέλων, it is common in 'stichomythia' for a sentence to continue grammatically from a previous line of the same speaker, as in ll. 83–85; here the main verb is ἐκστρέφει in l. 118, '(he is visiting the cave of Trophonius) wishing to hear the same reply (lit. 'one word') from him . . .'.

l. 121. ὕπερ governs καρποῦ, as the accent shows (see the note on l. 38): 'about the produce of the earth . . . ?'; Ion wonders whether Xuthus and Creüsa are consulting the oracles about a failure of the crops in their country.

l. 122. ἔχοντε, nominative dual of the participle with concessive sense: 'though we have been married a long time'; notice the combination of plural and dual here.

l. 123. The negatives οὐδὲ . . . οὐδέν intensify and do not cancel each other: 'have you never been a mother at all?', to which Creüsa replies that Phoebus knows whether she is childless or not (lit. 'knows my child-lessness'), letting Ion think that she has had no children.

l. 125. τἄλλα, accusative of respect: 'how (ὡς) unhappy you are, though fortunate in everything else'.

l. 126. ὡς . . . ὤλβισα, 'how happy I consider your mother to be'; τὴν τεκοῦσαν is a participle that normally governs an object, as in 142 (σε), but here is used as a noun with σου depending on it; or perhaps σου is genitive of cause, 'I consider the (i.e. your) mother happy because of you'. This is another instance of 'dramatic irony'.

l. 128. Supply εἶ as the verb: 'are you an offering made by a city or sold (to the god) by some (former owner)?'

l. 129. οὐκ οἶδα ... κεκλήμεθα, 'I know nothing except this one thing: I am called (the servant) of Apollo'; until Xuthus later called him Ion he had no legal name, being a slave. Notice the use of the first person plural for the singular here and in l. 130, where ἡμεῖς = ἐγώ.

l. 131. ὡς μὴ ... ἔφυν, '(yes), because I know not who bore me and from what (father) I am sprung'; εἰδότα agrees with σε in l. 130, or rather with ἐμέ understood from σε. μή combines with the εἰ- of εἰδότα to form one syllable (by 'synizesis'); it is used instead of οὐ in a 'generic' sense, 'the sort of person who does not know'. ὅτου, from ὅστις.

l. 132. τοισίδε = τοῖσδε, local dative without ἐν. The second syllable of κατά is lengthened before the στ that follows: 'in a house', meaning within the temple precincts.

l. 133. ἅπαν ... ὕπνος, 'the whole (temple) of the god (is) a home for me, whenever sleep ...'; he means that he sleeps anywhere in the temple, not in a room of his own.

l. 134. παῖς ὤν, 'when you were a boy'. ναόν, accusative of goal of motion.

l. 135. βρέφος ... εἰδέναι, 'those who seem to know say that (I was) an infant'; although he uses the masculine plural Ion means the Pythian priestess who found him and brought him up.

l. 136. Δελφίδων, with τίς: 'which of the Delphian women'.

l. 137. οὐπώποτ' ... με, 'I never knew a mother's breast, and she who brought me up ...'; the sentence is continued in l. 139, after Creüsa's interruption, which the 'stichomythia' (in which each actor speaks one line) requires, '(was) the priestess; I regard her as my mother'.

l. 138. ὡς ... νόσους, 'for being unhappy I have found unhappiness (in you)'.

l. 140. We should make the participle the main verb: 'what means of livelihood do you have now that you have come to (be) a man?', lit. 'having obtained what ... have you arrived at ...'.

l. 141. ἔφερβον, see the note on l. 52. οὑπιὼν (= ὁ ἐπιών, by 'synizesis') ... ξένος, 'and chance strangers as they came from time to time (ἀεί) (gave me presents)'; ὁ ἐπιών, like ὁ τυχών, means 'anyone who chances to come'.

l. 142. Supply ἦν with τάλαινα, 'unhappy was she who gave you birth'; see the note on l. 126.

l. 143. ἀδίκημα ... ἴσως, 'perhaps I was born (as the result of) a wrong done to some woman'.

l. 144. ἔχεις ... ἤσκησαι, 'but you have some means of livelihood, for you are well equipped...', to which Ion replies 'yes, I am dressed in clothes provided by the god ...', i.e. provided by the priests of the temple.

l. 146. οὐδ' ... γονάς, 'were you not eager for an enquiry, to find out your parentage?', lit. 'did you not rush into an enquiry ...'; ἐξευρεῖν is infinitive of purpose.

l. 147. γάρ in dialogue often means 'yes, for ...' or 'no, for ...', sometimes with some explanatory words omitted, as here: 'yes, (I was eager, but in vain,) for I have no clue'.

l. 148. Creüsa now begins to speak of 'another woman', though she means herself. σῇ μητρὶ ταῦτ' = τὰ αὐτά, 'the same (misfortune) as your mother'.

l. 149. εἰ ... χαίροιμεν ἄν, 'if she could help me in the task (of finding my mother), I should be glad'.

l. 150. The antecedent of ἧς is ἐκείνη understood: 'the woman for whose sake I came ...'.

l. 151. ποῖόν τι χρῄζουσα, 'desiring what?' ὡς, 'for'.

l. 153. λέγοις ἄν, a polite imperative; 'speak on'. τἄλλα, accusative of respect: 'I shall serve you in everything else'. A πρόξενος at Delphi did not carry out the same duties as a πρόξενος in other Greek cities, for which see the note on Thucydides 19, 5; at Delphi he entertained visitors from all states and acted as sponsor in bringing them to the oracle. One of Ion's duties was to assist the official πρόξενος and perhaps show visitors round the temple and its precincts.

l. 154. αἰδούμεθα, she is naturally ashamed to tell her story to a strange young man, even though she is pretending that it concerns another woman.

l. 155. οὐ ... οὐδέν, a double negative: 'then you will effect nothing'. Supply ἐστί with ἡ θεός, 'that goddess (i.e. shame) is one that hinders action', lit. 'slow', because those who are ashamed of something are slow to act. The word αἰδώς, 'shame', is understood from αἰδούμεθα, and is personified as a goddess; θεός here is feminine, as also is ἀργός, which is an adjective of two terminations.

l. 156. Φοίβῳ ... ἐμῶν, 'one of my friends says that she was united in love with Phoebus', to which Ion replies in horror, 'what, a mortal woman (lit. 'one born a woman') with ...'.

l. 158. καὶ ... γε, 'yes, and ...'. πατρός depends on the adverb λάθρα.

l. 159. οὐκ ἔστιν ... αἰσχύνεται, 'it is impossible; she is ashamed of a wrong done by a man'; Ion loyally implies that Creüsa is blaming Phoebus for a deed done by some man.

l. 160. οὔ φησιν αὐτή, 'she herself says that this is not so'. ἄθλια, 'other woes too'.

l. 161. τί χρῆμα δράσασα, 'in what way', lit. 'having done what thing?'

l. 163. ὁ ἐκτεθεὶς παῖς, 'the child who was cast out'. 'στιν = ἐστιν. εἰσορᾶν φάος, 'to see the light' is a commonly used equivalent for 'to be alive'; the opposite is ἐκλιπεῖν φάος, as in l. 330.

l. 164. οὐκ . . . οὐδείς, another double negative. ταῦτα καί, 'this too'.

l. 165. The negative in an εἰ-clause is μή, but οὐκέτ' ἔστι is used here because the phrase is regarded as one word, 'he is dead', lit. 'he is no longer (alive)'.

l. 166. ἐλπίζει obviously does not mean 'she hopes': 'she thinks that wild beasts killed him, poor (infant)'.

l. 167. ποίῳ . . . τεκμηρίῳ, lit. 'using what proof', i.e. 'by what proof did she come to this conclusion', lit. 'discover this'.

l. 168. ἵνα, 'to the place where'.

l. 169. The στ of σταλαγμός makes the preceding syllable long.

l. 170. οὔ φησι, 'she says that there was not'. πολλά is adverbial: 'many times'.

l. 171. χρόνος . . . διαπεπραγμένῳ, 'how long is it since the child was killed?': lit. 'what time (is it) for the child having been killed?'; a similar phrase appears in ll. 439–440.

l. 172. εἶχ' ἄν, the elision of ε in the third person singular before ἄν is said to be rare; if the text is correct it means 'if he were alive, he would be the same age as you', lit. 'he would have the same measure of manhood to you'.

l. 173. τίκτει, historic present: 'did she not bear . . . ?', to which Creüsa replies 'the god wrongs her (i.e. in not letting her have another child) and she (is) unhappy in not being a mother (again)'.

l. 175. τί δ' εἰ, 'what if . . . ?', i.e. what would happen if . . . ?

l. 176. τὰ κοινά, accusative of respect: 'he acts unjustly in rejoicing alone in what should be shared (with the mother)'; Creüsa means that Phoebus knows that his son is alive but she does not, though both parents ought to have the pleasure of their son's company.

l. 177. προσῳδός, supply ἐστι: 'her misfortune is in harmony with mine'; he refers to the imaginary mother, who is really Creüsa. τὠμῷ = τῷ ἐμῷ, by 'synizesis'.

l. 178. The accusatives σέ and μητέρα are ambiguous; μητέρα is probably the subject of ποθεῖν and σέ the object: 'I expect that your unhappy mother longs for you'.

l. 179. οὗ 'λελήσμεθα, 'which I had forgotten'; the ἐ of the pluperfect ἐλελήσμεθα is 'prodelided', like the ἐ of ἐστιν in l. 163.

l. 180. ὁ θεὸς . . . χαιρέτω, 'greetings to the god! may he receive the first part of my salutations', lit. 'may the god rejoice having received the first-fruits of . . .'.

l. 181. σύ τε, supply χαῖρε: 'and greetings to you too, lady'. τε instead of δέ is used here after μέν.

l. 182. χρόνιος ἐλθών, 'by coming so late'.

l. 183. οὐδέν, accusative of respect; 'not at all, but you have come at a time of anxiety for me', lit. 'to (my) anxiety', so that she did not at once return Xuthus' greeting.

l. 184. λέξον, aorist imperative, followed by an indirect question τί . . . φέρεις, which itself has an indirect question, ὅπως . . . , '(saying) how offspring of children shall be produced for us', depending on it.

l. 186. οὐκ ἠξίωσε, 'he (i.e. Trophonius) did not think it right to anticipate . . .'.

l. 187. δ' οὖν, 'at any rate'. εἶπεν is followed by an indirect statement after the colon, 'that neither I nor you will return childless'; Xuthus will have Ion as his adopted son and Creüsa will find her own son at last.

l. 189. The mother of Phoebus was Leto. εἰ γάρ with the optative expresses a wish for the future: 'may we go away successfully, and may the dealings that we two have previously had with regard to (ἐς) your son turn out more happily'. The words are intentionally ambiguous; to Xuthus νῷν (the dual dative of ἐγώ) means himself and his wife and the συμβόλαια are the sacrifices that they have made to Phoebus, but to Creüsa νῷν means herself and Phoebus and the συμβόλαια her long-past intimacy with him.

l. 193. ἡμεῖς . . . μέλει, 'I (speak for him) with regard to things outside (the shrine), but others take charge of what is within', lit. 'to others there is a care for things within'.

l. 195. ἀριστῆς, nominative plural of ἀριστεύς, in apposition to οἵ: 'even the noblest . . . whom the lot has appointed'. Five of the Delphian nobles were chosen by lot, each of whom in turn acted as spokesman, προφήτης, for the god, while the temple-slave Ion received visitors outside. For the 'tripod' of Apollo, see the note on l. 6.

l. 196. ἐχρήζομεν, probably referring to Xuthus alone, in spite of the change from the singular ἔχω before.

l. 197. στείχοιμ' ἄν, hardly more than a future indicative: 'I shall go'.

l. 198. χρηστήριον ... κοινόν, 'a general victim for strangers has been slain', lit. 'has fallen'; if the sacrifice was favourably received, as it was on this occasion, the oracle could then be consulted, in order drawn by lot, unless Xuthus' high rank gave him precedence.

l. 200. αἰσία γάρ, 'for (it is) a lucky day'.

l. 201. ἀμφί, 'at'. δαφνηφόρους, probably agreeing with κλῶνας; Creüsa would sit at the altar, holding branches of bay as a suppliant, while Xuthus consulted the oracle.

l. 202. εὐτέκνους ... ἐνεγκεῖν, 'pray to the gods that I may bring away an oracle that promises children'.

l. 205. νῦν ἀλλά, usually ἀλλὰ νῦν, 'now at last'. τὰς πρίν, 'his former...'; πρίν is made into an adjective by the article.

l. 206. ἅπας ... φίλος, 'he could not be wholly friendly...', because he treated her so badly in the past, but she will receive from him ὅσον χρῄζει, 'as much as he is willing (to give)'. θεός in l. 207 is scanned as a monosyllable, as also in ll. 200, 211, 213, and 223.

ll. 208–234. In these lines the metre becomes trochaic (see page 65) instead of iambic. In l. 208 γάρ can be omitted, or taken as '(I say this,) for (it is) a fitting prelude to my words'.

l. 209. Ion is surprised at being thus addressed by a stranger and replies somewhat coolly 'I am well', instead of returning Xuthus' greeting with another χαῖρε. εὖ φρόνει, imperative, 'restrain yourself', lit. 'think well'. δύ' ὄντ' = δύο ὄντε, dual with a plural verb: 'both of us (lit. 'being two') will be happy'.

l. 210. δὸς ... ἀμφιπτυχάς, 'allow me to clasp (or 'kiss') your hand and embrace your body'.

l. 211. μέν in a question sometimes implies doubt: 'are you really in your senses?', an echo of εὖ φρόνει in l. 209. θεοῦ τις βλάβη, 'some spite of heaven'.

l. 212. τὰ φίλταθ' ... ἐφίεμαι, 'now that I have found what is dearest to me I do not want to lose it'.

l. 213. The -α of στέμματα is lengthened before the ρ- of ρήξῃς.

l. 214. κοὐ ῥυσιάζω ... φίλα, 'and I am not a robber, but I am finding my own dear one', neuter plural, like φίλτατα in l. 212.

l. 215. οὐκ ἀπαλλάξῃ, a question used as a command: '(will you not) depart, before you receive ...'. εἴσω governs πλευμόνων; Ion aims an arrow at Xuthus; he carried bow and arrows to keep birds away from the temple and perhaps because Phoebus was the god of archery.

l. 216. ὡς τί, supply ποιήσων: 'why do you flee from me?', lit. 'as about to do what ...'. γνωρίσας, 'now that you have recognised your (nearest and) dearest'.

l. 217. οὐ φιλῶ, either 'I am not accustomed', or 'I refuse'.

l. 218. πίμπρη, imperative; 'burn (me)'. ἔσῃ = ἔσει, the future of εἰμί.

l. 219. ποῦ ... ἐμοί, 'how (lit. 'where') can you be ...? (is it) not ridiculous (lit. 'laughter') for me to ...?'

l. 220. τρέχων ... ἄν, 'as it proceeds, my story will (lit. 'would') reveal to you my (meaning)'.

l. 222. ὅς ... ἐμόν, 'Apollo, who brought you up, though you are my son'.

l. 223. μαρτυρεῖς σαυτῷ, 'you are (the only) witness to your story', lit. 'to yourself'; to which Xuthus replies 'no, but (γε) I heard ...', lit. 'having learnt'.

l. 224. αἴνιγμα, oracular replies often intentionally contained a 'riddling answer' by which the enquirer was 'deceived' (ἐσφάλης), but Xuthus says that if that is so 'then I cannot hear properly'.

l. 225. The answer (λόγος) of Phoebus is contained in the indirect statement made by Xuthus in his three half-lines beginning τὸν συναντήσαντα and ending πεφυκέναι, which are interrupted by Ion's two half-lines, though their syntax is not affected by the intervening questions, which themselves continue the syntax of Xuthus' statement: 'that the person who met me ... when I came out of this temple ... was my own son'.

l. 226. τίνα συνάντησιν, a 'cognate' accusative, for which see the note on l. 56, depending on συναντήσαντα: 'met you in what meeting?' ἐξιόντι agrees with μοι in l. 225; later in the play (not included in this book) Xuthus names his supposed son Ἴων because they met when he was coming out, ἐξιών, from the temple.

l. 227. συμφορᾶς τίνος κυρῆσαι, 'had met with what fortune?'

l. 228. γεγῶτ' and ὄντα agree with παῖδ' ἐμόν in l. 227: 'born your son, or just a gift?', to which Xuthus, regarding Ion as really his son and also a gift from Phoebus who has brought father and son together, replies 'a gift, but begotten by me'.

l. 229. πρῶτα . . . σόν, 'was it I then whom you first met?' ξυνάπτειν πόδα almost suggests our phrase 'to stumble upon'.

l. 230. ἡ τύχη, 'this good fortune'. δύο μίαν θαυμάζομεν, 'we both marvel at the same good fortune'.

l. 231. οὐκ ἔχω φράσαι, I cannot say'.

l. 232. τοῦτο, accusative of respect: 'being delighted at this news (i.e. that he had a son) I did not ask that other question', i.e. who the mother was. κεῖν' = κεῖνο.

l. 233. γῆς . . . μητρός, 'then I am sprung from mother Earth'; knowing that Xuthus had married Creüsa, who was descended from the earth-born Erichthonius (l. 85), Ion half jokingly suggests that his unknown mother is also the earth, but the non-Athenian Xuthus does not accept the story of his wife's parentage, still less his son's.

l. 234. πῶς . . . σός, 'how then could I be your son?' Xuthus does not know the answer, but with an almost pathetic faith in the oracle is content to 'refer the question to Phoebus'.

l. 235. The ἐ of ἐστιν is 'prodelided', as in l. 163. ἵνα . . . ᾖς, '(I ask this) so that you may no longer be . . .'; the old servant at first hopes to be able to help Creüsa find her son.

l. 237. ὁ κακός, 'that cruel god', cruel because of his treatment of Creüsa.

l. 238. Ἅιδου, the first syllable is ᾳ, not αι; iota subscript is not placed below a capital letter but after it.

l. 239. οὐ γὰρ δὴ σύ γε, 'for surely it was not you', but Creüsa replies 'yes, it was I'; when a woman uses the first person plural she makes the gender masculine, hence σπαργανώσαντες; see also l. 413.

l. 241. The final syllable of οὐδέ is lengthened before the ξ of ξυνῄδει: 'did no one even share with you the secret of your son's exposure?'

l. 242. The verb is ξυνῄδει again: 'yes, but it was only my misfortune and concealment (that shared my secret)'; the article makes λανθάνειν into a noun, like τὸ δυστυχεῖν in l. 256.

l. 244. πῶς . . . ἔπη, 'how indeed? (I did it) after uttering from my mouth many piteous words'.

l. 245. τόλμης, genitive of cause: 'you (were) cruel because of your hardness of heart, but the god (was) more (cruel) than you'; σέθεν = σου, genitive of comparison.

l. 246. The main clause of the conditional sentence is omitted: 'yes, (you would have thought me cruel) if you had seen the child . . .'.

l. 247. Some verb like βουλόμενον must be understood from διώκοντ' and taken before πεσεῖν: 'trying to find your breast or (wishing) to nestle (lit. 'fall') in your arms?'

l. 248. ἐνταυθ'. . . ὤν, 'yes, in the place where he was not and so was suffering . . .', lit. 'there, where not being he was suffering . . .'.

l. 249. σοὶ . . . ἐσῆλθεν, 'with what intention (ἐς τί) did the idea occur to you to . . . ?'

l. 250. ὡς . . . σῴζοντα, accusative absolute, generally used only with impersonal verbs; ὡς suggests 'with the idea that the god would save . . .', the present being used for the future.

l. 251. ὡς, an exclamation: 'how terribly'. In l. 252 τί is 'why?'

l. 254. τὰ θνητὰ . . . μένει, 'such (is) human fortune; nothing remains in the same state'.

l. 255. μή . . . ἀντεχώμεθα, 'let us then no longer continue in (lit. 'cling to') our lamentations'.

l. 256. ἀπορία τὸ δυστυχεῖν, 'misfortune (is) helpless', lit. 'helplessness'.

l. 257. τὸν . . . θεόν, 'take vengeance on the god who first . . .'.

l. 258. πῶς . . . ὑπερδράμω, 'how am I . . . to overcome what is stronger (than myself)?' κρείσσω = κρείσσονα, neuter plural, and ὑπερδράμω is a 'deliberative' question in the subjunctive.

l. 261. τόλμησον, aorist imperative: 'then dare (to do) what you can, (that is) to kill . . .'.

l. 262. εὐνὰς τὰς τότε, 'our former love'; in English we sometimes speak, for example, of 'the then king'. αἰδούμεθα = αἰδοῦμαι. ἐσθλός, 'kind to me'.

l. 263. σὺ . . . πεφηνότα, 'then you (must kill) the youth who has appeared to supplant (ἐπί) you'; the servant suggests that Ion will take Creüsa's place in Xuthus' affections.

l. 264. εἰ γάρ, a wish, 'O that it might be possible; how I should like (to do it)!'

l. 265. ξιφηφόρους, used 'proleptically', i.e. anticipating the action contained in the word, like 'they shot him dead'; here, 'by arming your attendants with swords', lit. 'so that they are equipped with swords'. The syntax of the line is continued from l. 265, where πῶς implies a main verb 'how shall I do it?'

l. 266. στείχοιμ' ἄν, almost equivalent to a future: 'I shall go (and do it)'; so also in l. 271.

l. 267. θοινᾷ, present tense but referring to the future: 'where he intends to feast . . .'.

l. 268. ἐπίσημον ... ἀσθενές, 'murder will out (lit. 'is a conspicuous thing', hence the neuter gender) and slaves are weak (supporters)'; τὸ δοῦλον denotes a class of people.

l. 269. φέρε ... τι, 'come then, now suggest some plan yourself'.

l. 270. δόλια καὶ δραστήρια, 'a subtle and effective scheme'.

l. 271. ἀμφοῖν τοῖνδε, dative dual, with another optative with ἄν used instead of a future: 'I shall assist you if it is (lit. 'in') both of these', i.e. if the scheme is both subtle and effective.

l. 273. οἶδ' ... θεοῖς, 'I know it, the one which the Giants fought (lit. 'set up') against the gods at Phlegra'. In this version of the story of the fight between gods and giants Gē (Earth) created a monster called Gorgon to help her sons. Athena killed the monster and took from her the 'aegis', the skin on her breast which was like a corselet fringed with snakes, and wore it as her own breastplate. Like the Gorgon Medusa, slain by Perseus, this one had blood which could do both harm and good. In other versions of the legend Athena's aegis had the head of Medusa in the middle of it.

l. 275. ἦ is interrogative, and σύμμαχον and πόνον are in apposition to Γοργόνα in l. 274; '(do you mean) as an ally for her sons and (to be) a trouble for the gods?' Euripides makes the old servant uncertain of the details of the story, so that the 'stichomythia' (line-by-line dialogue) can be kept up and Creüsa have an excuse for telling him and at the same time the audience this version of the legend. In l. 276 ἡ Διός is 'the daughter of Zeus'.

l. 278. κλύω, historic present. The μῦθος is explained in l. 279: 'that Athena wears the skin of this (monster) upon her breast'. The last syllable of ἐπί is lengthened before the στ- of στέρνοις.

l. 279. ἦν ... ὀνομάζουσι, 'the one that men call ... ?'

l. 280. θεῶν depends on δόρυ, and ὅτ' = ὅτε: 'it obtained this name when she rushed to (help) the spears of the gods', against the giants. Euripides derives the name αἰγίς from ἀίσσειν, 'to rush', not from αἴξ, 'goatskin', which is its usual derivation. θεῶν is again scanned as a monosyllable.

l. 281. τί ... βλάβος, 'what harm then (is) this to ... ?'

l. 282. Creüsa begins to say 'do you know about Erichthonius, or ...', intending to continue with 'or shall I tell you the story?', but she remembers that the old servant must know the history of the family that he serves and ends with 'of course you do', lit. 'why are you not likely (to know it)?'

l. 283. πρῶτον ὑμῶν πρόγονον, 'to be the first ancestor of your family'.

l. 284. The object of δίδωσι (historic present) is δισσούς σταλαγμούς in l. 286.

l. 285. Creüsa is reluctant to come to the point, so the servant, who has not heard this part of the family history before, prompts her by saying '(gave him) what? you (are going to) add words that hesitate (to come)'. προσφέρεις here has a future meaning.

l. 286. For the accent on ἄπο, which governs Γοργοῦς, see the note on ἔπι in l. 38.

l. 287. ἰσχὺν ... φύσιν, 'what power do they have upon the life ... ?', lit. 'having what power upon the nature ...'. ἔχοντας agrees with σταλαγμούς in l. 286, which is divided into τὸν μὲν ... τὸν δέ in l. 288, still governed by δίδωσι in l. 284: 'the one (drop) ... , the other ...'.

l. 289. ἐν τῷ = ἐν τίνι, 'in what (did she place them when) fastening them to the child's body?', lit. 'on his body (genitive governed by καθάψασα) about the child'.

l. 290. χρυσοῖσι δεσμοῖς, 'in a golden bracelet'. ὁ δέ, this is the old demonstrative use of the article, which is very common in Homer; 'and he', i.e. Erichthonius, who as an old man passed on the bracelet and its contents to his grandson Erectheus, son of Pandion. Creüsa inherited it from Erechtheus and wore it (αὐτό in l. 292) on her wrist (χερός can be omitted after καρπῷ). In l. 291 ἐς σ' ἀφίκετο means 'it came to you', i.e. by inheritance.

l. 293. πῶς κέκρανται, 'how is the ... carried into effect?'

l. 294. The antecedent of ὅστις (= ὅς) is σταλαγμός, understood from σταλαγμούς in l. 286: 'the drop of blood that flowed from the hollow vein at her slaying', and the verbs are ἀπείργει and ἔχει in l. 296; the 'hollow veins' are the two large veins that carry the blood circulating in the body back to the heart.

l. 295. τί τῷδε χρῆσθαι, 'to use it how?'; the infinitive depends on κέκρανται in l. 295, or it may depend on χρή understood: 'how must one use it?'

l. 296. τροφὰς ἔχει βίου, 'nourishes life', lit. 'has the nourishment of life'.

l. 297. ἀριθμός, like our 'item' or 'article in a list'; lit. 'what does the second item do?', i.e. 'what is the effect of the second object among those that you mention?' ὧν = ἐκείνων οὕς, 'of those which', an instance of what is called 'relative attraction', just as in English 'a list of what I want' means 'a list of the things which I want'.

l. 298. This Gorgon, like Medusa, had hair consisting of poisonous snakes.

l. 299. αὐτόν, referring to the second drop of blood: 'do you carry it mingled together (lit. 'into one', i.e. mixed with the first drop) . . .'.

l. 300. ἐσθλόν, 'the good'; we might expect the article with each of these adjectives when they are used as nouns. The bracelet evidently had two separate compartments.

l. 301. πάντα ὅσων σε δεῖ, 'everything that you need'; δεῖ here takes an accusative and a genitive.

l. 302. τούτῳ, 'with this poison'. ὁ κτείνων, 'the slayer'. In her blind desire for revenge on the supposed interloper Creüsa is willing to endanger the life of the old servant, though no doubt he deserved death for having suggested the murder first of Xuthus, then of Ion.

l. 303. The verb is κτενῶ understood: 'where and how (lit. 'having done what') shall I kill him?' σὸν . . . ἐμόν, '(it is) your (task) to order, mine to dare (to do the deed)'.

l. 304. δῶμα τοὐμόν (=τὸ ἐμόν), accusative of goal of motion.

l. 305. οὐκ εὖ, 'not wisely'. καὶ . . . ψέγεις, '(I say this,) for indeed you find fault with my (plan)', and so he can find fault with hers.

l. 306. ἆρ' . . . ἐσέρχεται, 'did you suspect (from ὑφοράω) this thing that occurs to me too?'

l. 307. δόξεις, 'you will be thought', lit. 'will seem'. κεἰ μὴ κτενεῖς, 'even though you are not the actual murderer'.

l. 308. ὀρθῶς, 'true'. φασι, 'men (always) say that . . .': the legend of the wicked stepmother is universal; see also l. 380.

l. 309. αὐτοῦ, 'here', at Delphi. ἀρνήσῃς, future indicative: 'where you will deny the murder', plural used for singular.

l. 310. τῷ χρόνῳ, 'by (shortening) the time', instead of waiting until the party returned to Athens. τῆς ἡδονῆς depends on προλάζυμαι.

l. 311. καὶ . . . λαθεῖν, 'yes, and you will conceal from your husband (the fact that you know) what he is eager to conceal from you', i.e. that Ion is Xuthus' son by another woman, as the old servant had falsely told her; the Chorus knows, from Xuthus' own statement, that this is not true, but they keep the truth from Xuthus. It was unusual for the Chorus to play so important a part in the plot of a play, even if only by keeping silent, as here. The -ε of σε is lengthened before the σπ- of σπεύδει.

l. 312. οἶσθ' οὖν ὃ δρᾶσον, 'do you know what you must do?', an illogical idiom, lit. 'do you know what — do it' (aorist imperative), equivalent to οἶσθα τί σε χρὴ δρᾶν.

l. 313. Ἀθάνας, '(the gift) of Athena'; the bracelet was called χρυσοῖσι δεσμοῖς in l. 290.

l. 314. ἐλθὼν . . . πόσις, 'going (to the place) where my husband is making a sacrifice in secret'. Creüsa has been told by the Chorus (in a part of the play not included in this book) that Xuthus intends to offer a birth-sacrifice for his newly-found son at the banquet which is to take place in a specially erected tent, but she does not know that he has now decided to perform the ceremony by himself on the summit of Mount Parnassus, while Ion prepares the tent and the feast. Xuthus is waiting for a suitable moment to tell Creüsa that Ion is his son, and is therefore making the birth-sacrifice in secret, λάθρα. ἡμῖν is dative of (dis)advantage, which here is almost equivalent to a possessive genitive, 'my husband'; so also τῷ νεανίᾳ in l. 317, 'pour it out and let it fall into the drink of the young man'.

l. 320. κλεινὰς Ἀθήνας, accusative of goal of motion. αὐτοῦ, 'here'.

l. 321. ἐπεὶ . . . κοινόν, 'when they came to (the time for) the flutes and the bowl that mixes drink for all'; the flutes provided music for the 'paean' (sacred song) when the eating was over and the triple libations (see the note on l. 336) were poured out in honour of the gods before the 'serious' drinking began. The guests' cups were filled with wine and water mixed in the κρατῆρα κοινόν, lit. 'the general mixing-bowl', for wine was seldom drunk 'neat' in ancient Greece and Rome. There were several mixing-bowls, as we see from l. 339, because of the large number of guests, though the singular is used here.

l. 322. χρεών, supply ἐστιν ὑμᾶς, 'you must . . .', spoken to the slaves, of whom the narrator was one. It was customary to provide larger cups for the after-dinner drinking, so that, as the old slave says in l. 324, 'these guests should more quickly come to joyousness of heart'.

l. 325. ἦν . . . μόχθος, 'there was a bustle of (slaves) bringing . . .'.

l. 326. χρυσέας, pronounced as a spondee (– –) by 'synizesis', and sometimes written χρυσᾶς (see χρυσοῖσι in l. 290). For ὁ δέ, 'and he', i.e. the old servant, see the note on l. 290. ἐξαίρετον agrees with τεῦχος in l. 328; 'taking a special cup . . . gave it to him, brimming over (πλῆρες), after dropping into the wine . . .'.

l. 327. δή shows that the compliment was a mere pretence: 'as though indeed he were doing a favour to . . ', instead of intending to murder him.

l. 329. The antecedent of ὅ, which is φάρμακον δραστήριον, is inside the relative clause and should be taken as the object of βαλών: 'the deadly poison which men say his mistress gave to him so that her newly-found son . . .'. Notice the 'dramatic irony' of παῖς ὁ νέος; Creüsa wants to kill her supposed stepson, whom the audience knows to be her real son. ἐκλείπειν φάος, 'to die', is the opposite of εἰσορᾶν φάος, 'to be alive', as in l. 163.

l. 331. ᾔδειν, third singular of the past tense of οἶδα. The bustle (μόχθος, l. 325) made by the slaves bringing in larger cups enabled the old servant to poison Ion's cup unnoticed. ἔχοντι παιδί is dative of reference where we might expect a genitive absolute: 'as the newly-revealed (πεφηνότι) son was holding the drink-offering . . . , one of the slaves spoke a word of evil omen'. At the critical moment of a sacrifice or drink-offering silence was kept by all present, to avoid the possibility of someone's uttering a word of ill-omen, such as happened on this occasion, for this would necessitate the renewal of the ceremony from the beginning. Notice that δέ is the fourth, instead of the usual second, word here.

l. 334. ὁ δ' . . . τραφείς, 'and Ion, as one who had been brought up in a temple and among scrupulous seers', so that he too was scrupulous in observing all the sacred rites.

l. 335. οἰωνὸν ἔθετο, 'took it (i.e. the βλασφημίαν uttered by a slave) to be a (bad) omen'. The object of ἐκέλευσε is 'the servants'.

l. 336. τὰς . . . θεοῦ, 'the first drink-offering to the god', i.e. to Zeus the Saviour; there were three libations, one to Zeus and Hera, one to the Heroes, and one to Zeus the Saviour, so this was really the third part of the triple libation; Ion poured (δίδωσι) the contents of his cup out on to the ground without drinking the wine at all, in order to cause the ceremony to be started all over again. There are several historic present tenses in this narrative. In l. 337 λέγει means 'ordered', with the dative.

l. 338. ἐκ δ'ἐπίμπλαμεν = ἐξεπίμπλαμεν, from ἐκπίμπλημι; this is an instance of 'tmesis', the 'cutting' of a compound word into its two original arts; see also l. 348, and the note on Homer, Odyssey XXI, l. 21, where it is explained that the Homeric use is not really the same as the later Attic use. ἐξεπίμπλαμεν is followed by a genitive: 'we filled . . . with water and Bybline (perhaps 'Thracian') wine'.

l. 340. ἐν τῷδε μόχθῳ, 'while this was going on', lit. 'during this work'.

l. 342. ἄτρεστα, adverbial accusative, 'fearlessly'; one of Ion's duties was to scare away birds from the temple precincts, or even shoot them with bow and arrows, but doves seem to have been specially privileged and not molested. ὡς δέ, 'and when (the guests) . . .'.

l. 343. ἐς αὐτὸ . . . εἷλκον, 'they dipped their beaks into it, eager for the drink, and drew it up . . .'.

l. 346. ἥ . . . γόνος, 'but the one that settled where the newly-found son had poured away (his wine)'; the antecedent of ἥ is ἐκείνη understood. Ion is never named in this speech but is described by the narrator in several different phrases (ll. 327, 330, 332, 346, 353, 362).

l. 348. ἐκ δ' ἐκλαγξ' = ἐξέκλαγξε, another instance of 'tmesis', as in l. 338. ὄπα is a 'cognate' accusative (see the note on l. 56) used with an intransitive verb: 'uttered a loud cry'.

l. 349. ἀξύνετον, another adverbial accusative: 'making unintelligible screams'; a μάντις could interpret the ordinary cries of birds, but a strange or unintelligible sound was a bad omen.

l. 352. γυμνὰ . . . ἧχ' (= ἧκε, from ἵημι), 'shot out his arms, bared from his cloak, across the table', or 'bared his arms . . . and shot them out . . .', to seize the old servant who was standing on the other side of the table.

l. 354. τίς . . . ἔμελλε, 'who (lit. 'who of men') was intending to . . .'.

l. 355. σὴ (ἦν) ἡ προθυμία, 'yours was the eagerness (to serve me with wine)'.

l. 356. χειρὸς σῆς, governed by πάρα, as the accent shows; see also ὑπο in l. 364.

l. 357. We should make πρέσβυν in l. 358 the object of ἐρευνᾷ: 'he began to search the old man, seizing his aged arm, to catch him red-handed in possession (of the poison)', lit. 'having (it)'.

l. 359. ὤφθη . . . μόγις, 'he was detected (lit. 'seen', from ὁράω) and being compelled (to speak) unwillingly (lit. 'with difficulty') revealed . . .'.

l. 361. συλλαβών, 'taking with him'.

l. 363. κοιράνοισι, no doubt the same as the Δελφῶν ἀριστῆς of l. 195, called 'princes of Delphi' in l. 367; they now formed a summary court of justice to decide this case at once.

l. 364. τῆς Ἐρέχθεως . . . θνήσκομεν, 'I am (lit. 'we are') being murdered by the (daughter of) Erechtheus', whom as a native of Delphi he calls 'the foreign woman', though he will soon find out that he himself is an Athenian by birth.

l. 367. ὥρισαν . . . οὐ ψήφῳ μιᾷ, 'decided by many votes (lit. 'not by one vote') that my mistress should die, flung down from a cliff'.

l. 368. ὡς gives the reason for her sentence of death: 'for trying to slay (lit. 'slaying'; see the note on l. 377) the temple-servant and planning murder . . .'; sacrilege in the precincts of Apollo's temple was itself a serious crime, quite apart from the attempted murder.

l. 369. The double consonant ζ in ζητεῖ causes the preceding short syllable to become long.

l. 370. τὴν . . . ὁδόν, 'the woman who has hastened wretchedly along a wretched path', i.e. the path of murder. ὁδόν is accusative of ground traversed.

l. 371. ἐπίσχες, ὦ παῖ, 'restrain yourself, my child'; Ion is angrily upbraiding Creüsa for trying to murder him. The Pythian priestess who brought up the motherless foundling addresses him as παῖ and he calls her μῆτερ in l. 375. χρηστήριον, an adjective agreeing with τρίποδα, for which see the note on l. 6.

l. 372. The ὑπερ- of ὑπερβάλλω governs θριγκοῦ τοῦδε, and the βάλλω governs πόδα: 'I, the priestess . . . according to (lit. 'preserving') the ancient custom of the tripod, chosen out from . . . , set foot outside this threshold', which was a low wall that marked the boundary of the inner temple.

l. 375. μοι, dative of advantage, here almost equivalent to a possessive genitive: 'my dear mother, though (περ) you did not bear me'.

l. 376. ἀλλ' οὖν . . . πικρά, 'well then, let me so be called; the name (is) not unpleasant to me'.

l. 377. ὡς . . . ἥδε, 'how this woman tried to kill me'; he points to Creüsa standing at the altar where she has fled for refuge. Notice this meaning of the imperfect ἔκτεινεν; the same tense is used in l. 453, ἔκτεινες, and the present participle has the same meaning in ll. 368 and 379.

l. 378. καὶ . . . ἁμαρτάνεις, 'you too are doing wrong in being harsh (towards her)'.

l. 379. οὐ . . . ἀνταπολλύναι, 'ought I not to kill in return those who try to kill me?'

l. 380. The accent distinguishes προγονοῖς, 'stepsons', from προγόνοις, 'ancestors': 'wives (are) always hostile to . . .'; see the note on l. 308.

l. 381. ἡμεῖς, supply δυσμενεῖς ἐσμεν: 'we stepsons are hostile . . . because we suffer evil (from them)'; Ion includes himself with all ill-treated stepchildren, though it is possible that ἡμεῖς = ἐγώ, 'I too am hostile . . .'.

l. 382. μὴ ταῦτα, supply λέξῃς. λείπων, 'when you leave'; the main verb, ἐλθέ, is in l. 384. πάτραν, and Ἀθήνας in l. 384, accusative of goal of motion.

l. 383. χρεών, supply ἐστι; 'what must I do on your advice?', lit. 'being advised'.

l. 384. καθαρὸς . . . καλῶν, 'go to . . . with clean hands (καθαρός), attended by (ὕπο) good omens'.

l. 385. καθαρὸς (ἐστί) . . . κτάνῃ, 'anyone who (lit. 'all whoever') slays . . . has clean hands'.

l. 386. μὴ σύ γε, supply ποιήσῃς τόδε; the σύ is emphatic. οὓς ἔχω λόγους, 'the story which I have (for you)'; the priestess is going to give Ion the relics of his infancy before he leaves Delphi, but she has no idea that in so doing she will also reveal the secret of his birth.

l. 387. λέγοις ἄν, 'speak on'; a polite request, as in l. 153, but in ll. 197, 266, and 271 the optative with ἄν was hardly more than a future indicative. εὔνους . . . λέγῃς, 'whatever you say you will say it because you love me', lit. 'being well-disposed (to me)'.

l. 388. χερὸς . . . ἐμαῖς, 'clasped in my arms', lit. 'in the embrace of my hand'; χερός is singular used for plural, and sometimes means 'arm' instead of 'hand'.

l. 389. ἐν στέμμασιν, 'covered with garlands', which had been placed upon the chest by Creüsa when she abandoned it, to beg for pity from whoever found it, or perhaps by the priests to show that it was now the property of Apollo's temple. In l. 390 ἔλαβον is 'I found'.

l. 391. ὁ μῦθος . . . νέος, 'it is a strange story that has been brought forward (by you)'; Ion has heard some of it before, but not the part about the cradle in which he was found.

l. 392. γάρ, 'yes, for I was keeping them secret', lit. 'in silence'. αὐτά means either 'the full facts' or 'these relics'. Notice the mixture of singular and plural in εἶχον and δείκνυμεν, which must be translated as 'I reveal them'.

l. 393. ἡμᾶς is governed by ἔκρυπτες, τόδε by ἔκρυπτες and by λαβοῦσα: 'why did you conceal this from me, when you found it long ago?'

l. 394. σε ἔχειν λάτριν, 'to have you as his servant'.

l. 395. τῷ = τίνι, 'in what (way)', i.e. 'how'.

l. 396. πατέρα . . . ἐκπέμπει, 'by naming your father he is sending you away . . .'.

l. 397. ἐκ κελευσμῶν ἢ πόθεν, 'in obedience to his orders or for what reason?'

l. 398. ἐνθύμιόν μοι τίθησι, 'suggested (lit. 'made (it) in the mind') to me', followed by Ion's interruption in l. 399, 'to do what?', and by σῶσαι in l. 400, 'to keep this thing that I found until the present time'.

l. 401. The object of ἔχει is τί κέρδος: 'what good does it bring to me — or what harm?' Ion is afraid that he may turn out to be the son of a slave-girl, as he says in l. 428.

l. 403. μητρὸς ζητήματα, 'as clues to find my mother', objective genitive.

l. 404. ἐπεί γε, 'yes, because . . .'. οὔ, i.e. οὐκ ἐβούλετο.

l. 405. ἥδ' ἡμέρα, vocative, but we must either omit ἥδε ('O day of . . .') or say 'Oh, this (is) a day of happy revelations'. In l. 406 αὐτά is 'these relics' and ἐκπόνει is imperative.

l. 407. πᾶσαν γ' ἐπελθών, 'yes, (I shall search for her) traversing the whole of . . .', to which the Pythia replies 'you must (lit. 'will') decide that for yourself', i.e. he must make up his own mind where to start the search; or perhaps 'you will discover the facts (of your birth) for yourself'.

l. 410. ἅ . . . ἐβουλήθη, '(the relics) which he wanted me, though unbidden, to . . .'; in l. 398 the Pythia said that Phoebus merely suggested to her that she should keep them.

l. 411. ὅτου (from ὅστις) οὕνεκα, 'for what reason'. οὐκ ἔχω, 'I do not know'.

l. 412. ᾔδει . . . κεκρυμμένα, 'no mortal man knows that I have these relics or where they were hidden'; for the gender of ἔχοντας when a woman is speaking, see the note on l. 240.

l. 414. ἴσον, adverbial: 'I embrace you as though I were your mother', lit. 'equally as having borne you'; or 'I bid farewell to you', repeating the meaning of χαῖρε; ἀσπάζομαι has both meanings. The priestess leaves the stage at this point.

l. 415. ὡς, 'how', in an exclamation. δάκρυ, singular used for plural.

l. 416. ἐκεῖσε . . . με, 'turning my thought to the time (lit. 'thither') when (ὅθ' = ὅτε) my mother . . .'.

l. 417. κρυφαῖα, adverbial accusative plural with νυμφευθεῖσα: 'after she had been secretly united in love'.

l. 418. μαστὸν οὐχ ὑπέσχεν, 'did not feed me at (lit. 'did not offer') her breast'. ἀνώνυμος, see the notes on ll. 74 and 226.

l. 419. θεοῦ, scanned again as a monosyllable. οἰκέτην, here used as an adjective.

l. 420. τά must be taken with τοῦ δαίμονος also, as in l. 7: 'the (actions) of the god (are) kindly, but (those) of fortune (are) unkind'; in l. 404 ὁ δαίμων meant Apollo, not fortune.

l. 421. χρόνον ὅν, accusative of duration of time: 'all the time when I ought to have been lying softly . . . and getting some enjoyment in life'; τι is adverbial accusative, and βίου is genitive of reference, or perhaps depends directly on τερφθῆναι.

l. 423. τροφῆς, governed by ἀπεστερήθην, with φιλτάτης μητρός possessive genitive: 'I was deprived of the care of a loving mother'.

l. 424. τλήμων . . . χαρμονάς, 'my mother also (χή = καὶ ἡ) is wretched, for . . . having lost the pleasure of (bringing up) her son'.

l. 427. ἀνάθημα . . . βούλομαι, 'as an offering, so that I may not find out any of the things that I do not want (to find out)'; ὧν = ἐκείνων ἅ, another instance of 'relative attraction', for which see the note on l. 297. Still fearing that he may be the son of a slave Ion now intends to dedicate the cradle to Apollo so that it can never be opened to reveal the secret of his parentage.

l. 428. με τυγχάνει τεκοῦσα, 'chances to be my mother'.

l. 429. εὑρεῖν . . . ἐᾶν, '(it is) worse to find (such) a mother than to keep silent and let her be', i.e. let her remain unknown; σιγῶντα agrees with ἐμέ understood in the accusative and infinitive depending on κάκιον (ἐστί).

l. 430. τήνδε, i.e. τὴν ἀντίπηγα, but he interrupts himself with καίτοι τί πάσχω, 'and yet what am I doing?', lit. 'what do I suffer', almost like our 'what's the matter with me?' He changes his mind again and goes on with 'I am opposing the will . . .'.

l. 433. The impersonal verbal adjective ἀνοικτέον is active and governs an object, with ἐμοί understood as dative of the agent: 'I must open this (chest) and I must be bold'.

l. 434. ὑπερβαίην ἄν, the main verb of a conditional sentence with the εἰ-clause omitted (sometimes called a 'potential' optative): 'I could never overstep my fate (lit. 'what is fated')', with something like 'even if I were to try' understood.

l. 435. τί . . . κεκεύθατε, 'why have you been hiding from (lit. 'for') me?'; the perfect of κεύθω is sometimes intransitive.

l. 436. σύνδετα, the fastenings that kept the cradle shut. τἀμὰ φίλα, 'my dear tokens'; they were dear to Ion because they had belonged to his mother and might now reveal who he was.

l. 437. ἰδού, an interjection, not the aorist imperative middle of ὁράω, which is ἰδοῦ: 'behold, how (ὡς) by some miracle . . .'.

l. 439. πλεγμάτων, either 'the garlands', mentioned in l. 389, or the 'plaited work' of the cradle. ὁ δ' . . . τοῖσδε, 'since then a long time has passed over these . . .'; lit. 'the time in the middle (is) long for these . . .'; a similar phrase appears in l. 171.

l. 441. Creüsa in sanctuary at the altar has been listening to the conversation between the Pythia and Ion, and has been watching intently the opening of the cradle. She can now no longer restrain herself and breaks in with 'what revelation of things unhoped for do I indeed see?'

l. 442. σίγα, imperative. The rest of the sentence is unfinished because of Creüsa's interruption; Ion says 'you know that often in the past also to me . . .', perhaps intending to go on 'you have been hostile', but Creüsa breaks in with 'I will not be silent' (lit. 'my affairs (will) not (be) in silence'); do not bid me (be quiet)'.

l. 444. οὗ, 'in which', lit. 'where'. The ἐ- of ἐξέθηκα is prodelided.

l. 445. Creüsa hesitates at the end of l. 444 and then continues 'you, yes, I exposed you, my son . . .'; for μοι, see the note on l. 375. In l. 446 κεἰ = καὶ εἰ, 'even if'.

l. 447. λάζυσθε, addressed to the Delphian attendants who have accompanied Ion on to the stage. He thinks that Creüsa is out of her mind to leave 'the (protection of the) images' on the altar at which she has taken refuge: 'she was mad to rush forward . . .', lit. '(being) mad she leapt .'

l. 449. σφάζοντες οὐ λήγοιτ' ἄν, an imperative: 'kill me and spare not', lit. 'you would not (i.e. 'must not') cease killing'. ὡς, 'for'.

l. 450. καὶ τῆσδε . . . κεκρυμμένων, 'both this cradle and you and your secret possessions', or 'your hidden relics'.

l. 451. Supply ἐστί with τάδε: 'is not this monstrous? I am being seized (by her) by guile'; Creüsa embraced him at l. 449, but he thinks it is all part of a trick to escape justice.

l. 452. σοῖς φίλοισιν, dative of the agent, with the plural used for the singular: 'you are found (to be) a loved one by one who loves you'.

l. 453. ἐγὼ φίλος σός, an indignant question: 'what, I loved by you?' κᾆτα = καὶ εἶτα, 'and then you tried to kill me . . . ?'; for the imperfect, see the note on l. 377.

l. 454. παῖς γ' ... φίλτατον, 'yes, (you are) my son, if this is (what is) dearest to parents'.

l. 455. παῦσαι, aorist imperative middle: 'stop weaving (your cunning) webs'. λήψομαι καλῶς, 'I shall easily (lit. 'well') catch you out', i.e. convict her of falsely claiming to be his mother.

l. 456. ἱκοίμην, a wish: 'may I come to this (test)', because she now knows that Ion is her son.

l. 457. κενόν, supply ἐστι. στέγει πλήρωμά τι, 'does it contain something within it?', lit. 'does it cover something that fills it?' Creüsa must describe the contents of the cradle.

l. 458. σά γ' ἔνδυτα, 'yes, your clothes'.

l. 459. τὸ ὄνομα ... εἰσιδεῖν, 'will you give a description (lit. 'say the name') of them before you see them?'

l. 460. καὶ ἐὰν μὴ φράσω γε, 'yes, and if I do not describe them ...'.

l. 461. ὡς ... τόλμα σου, 'for your confidence is very strange', lit. 'has something strange'.

l. 462. σκέψασθε, plural, addressed to the Chorus or Ion's attendants. The antecedent of ὅ, ὕφασμα, is inside the relative clause: 'look at to garment which I wove when I was a girl'.

l. 463. ἐστί must be understood both with ποῖόν τι and with ὑφάσματα: 'what is it like (lit. 'something of what sort')? Many are the garments woven by girls'.

l. 464. οἷον ἐκδίδαγμα, 'a sample as it were, (or 'a sampler') of ...', like the needlework samplers made by Victorian girls, but this one was large enough to be wrapped round the new-born Ion; it is called χλιδήν in l. 26 and was intended to be a dress for herself when finished.

l. 465. ἔχον, agreeing with ὕφασμα in l. 462: 'with (lit. 'having') what pattern? (I ask this) so that you may not deceive me in this way', by giving a vague description that would not prove anything.

l. 466. Γοργώ, accusative in apposition to μορφήν in l. 465. ἐν μέσοισιν, 'in the middle of ...'.

l. 467. Ion says these words as an aside; he is now nearly convinced.

l. 468. τρόπον, used adverbially: 'in the manner of', with αἰγίδος, 'like an aegis' (see the note on l. 273).

l. 469. θέσφαθ' ὡς εὑρίσκομεν, 'how (true) I am discovering the oracles (to be)', though in fact there had been no oracles referring to the identity of Ion's mother; perhaps the reference is to the words of the Pythia, who in 398 said that it had been suggested to her by Apollo that she should keep Ion's cradle and its contents.

l. 470. παρθένευμα, any work done by a girl, hence 'O work at the loom done by me as a maiden long ago'. Creüsa recognises it, but 471 shows that Ion cannot yet quite believe her, for he asks 'is there anything besides this? or are you making a lucky guess in this alone?'

l. 472. γέννι, scanned as an iambus (∪ –) by 'synizesis': 'an ancient gift, with golden jaws, given by Athena'; the reading of the text is uncertain; it was not only the jaws but the whole serpents that were made of gold; γέννι is singular used for plural.

l. 473. λέγει = ἐκέλευσε: 'who ordered (her people) to bring up their children under the serpents' protection (ἐντρέφειν, lit. 'to bring up among them'), in imitation of Erichthonius of old'; μιμήματα is in apposition to τέκν' ἐντρέφειν; for the golden serpents, see 21–26.

l. 475. The infinitives depend on λέγει in l. 473: 'ordered them to do what, tell me, to make what use of the golden ornaments?'

l. 476. φέρειν, infinitive of purpose: 'as a necklace (plural for singular) for the . . . to wear, my son'.

l. 477. ἔνεισιν οἶδε, 'here they are', plural, referring to the δράκοντες of l. 471. τὸ τρίτον, 'the third thing', in the cradle.

l. 479. In the usual version of the story Athena caused the olive to grow of its own accord on the Acropolis, but Euripides sometimes varies the legends (e.g. the story of the Gorgon in 274–280) and here makes Athena bring the olive to Athens from somewhere else; σκόπελον is governed by the εἰσ- of εἰσηνεγκατο: 'to her own rock', the Acropolis. It would be natural for Creüsa to put an olive-wreath in the cradle, hoping that it would bring the child good luck.

l. 480. ὅς . . . χλόην, 'which, if it is there, never loses its freshness', because it was sprung (γεγώς) from Athena's pure and original olive tree.

l. 482. Ion at last acknowledges Creüsa as his mother. For μοι, 'my', see the note on l. 375. ἄσμενος . . . παρηίδας, 'joyfully I see you and press my lips (lit. 'I have fallen') upon your joyful cheeks': ἀσμένας is an example of 'hypallage' ('transferred epithet'), for it was Creüsa who was joyful, not her cheeks.

l. 484. ἡλίου, genitive of comparison; 'brighter (lit. 'better') than the sun'.

l. 485. συγγνώσεται, 'will pardon me' for her presumption in saying this. ὁ θεός refers to the sun itself, not the sun-god Apollo, for Creüsa would hardly say that Ion outshone his own divine father. χεροῖν, dative dual of χείρ: 'in my arms'.

l. 486. This and the following line are in lyric verse and have the Doric genitives γᾶς (κατὰ γᾶς, 'below the earth'), and Περσεφόνας. μετά governs ἐνέρων as well as Περσεφόνας.

l. 489. ὁ κατθάνων . . . φαντάζομαι, 'I who was dead and am no longer dead am revealed (to you)'.

THUCYDIDES, *THE SIEGE OF PLATAEA*

I

1. μὲν γάρ this can be omitted in English or expressed by the 'inferential' use of 'now' as the first word. The Thirty Years' Peace was made in 446 between Athens and the Peloponnesian allies. The island of Euboea had revolted from Athens a few months earlier in the same year and had been forced to submit by Pericles, and in 432 Potidaea, on the peninsula of Chalcidice in the northern Aegean, an ally of Athens but a colony of Corinth, also revolted, but the Athenians defeated the townsfolk and their Corinthian allies and blockaded the town. In the following year came the first real breach of the Peace, when the Thebans without warning attacked Plataea, a loyal ally of Athens since 519. τέσσαρα καὶ δέκα ἔτη, accusative of duration of time. ἅμα ἦρι ἀρχομένῳ, 'at the beginning of spring', lit. 'together with spring beginning', i.e. early April 431. ὀλίγῳ, dative of measure of difference, πλείους = πλείονες, 'a little more than 300 in number', genitive of comparison. There were eleven 'Boeotarchs' at the head of the Boeotian confederacy, of which Thebes, the chief town, appointed two. Plataea was always at bitter enmity with Thebes. The article followed by the genitive case means 'the son of . . .', which was the usual way of identifying a man in a country that had no surnames. περὶ πρῶτον ὕπνον, 'at about the first sleep', during the third of the five divisions of the night, beginning at about 9 p.m., i.e. between 'lamp lighting' and μέσαι νύκτες, dead of night (later than our midnight). ξὺν ὅπλοις, 'under arms' or 'fully armed' τῆς Βοιωτίας, 'a town of Boeotia'.

2. καὶ οἱ μετ' αὐτοῦ, 'and his party ; the pro-Theban Plataeans were

aristocrats and rich land-owners. ἰδίας ἕνεκα δυνάμεως, 'to obtain power for themselves', lit. 'for the sake of private power'; ἕνεκα often comes after the genitive case that it governs. σφίσιν, indirect reflexive pronoun, referring to the main subject: 'to kill the men among the citizens who were hostile to them', i.e. to Naucleides and his party.

3. ἔπραξαν, 'they arranged', or 'managed'. ὅτι . . . πόλεμος, 'that the war was bound to come', lit. 'would be', referring to the Peloponnesian War, which broke out on about June 30 in this year. τὴν Πλάταιαν, the object of προκαταλαβεῖν, and μήπω is used instead of οὔπω because the genitive absolute clause in which it stands is part of the clause of wishing introduced by ἐβούλοντο: lit. 'the war not yet being established (as) open', i.e. 'before the war had openly broken out'. ᾗ καὶ . . . προκαθεσ-τηκυίας, 'for this reason also they more easily made a secret entrance (lit. 'escaped notice entering'), because no watch had previously been set', at the gates and on the walls.

4. θέμενοι . . . ὅπλα, 'grounding arms in the market-place', lit. 'into the market-place'; this is called the 'pregnant' use of a preposition, meaning that they brought their arms into the market-place and grounded them in it, like our 'he put his hands in his pockets'. τοῖς μὲν . . . ἔχεσθαι, 'they did not take the advice of those who had invited them in, to get to work at once'; ὥστε is sometimes used after a verb of persuading without any change of meaning from the simple infinitive. ἰέναι ἐς, with hostile intent, i.e. 'to attack'. In γνώμην ἐποιοῦντο the imperfect means 'they came to a decision' after consultation. κηρύγμασι χρήσασθαι ἐπιτηδείοις, 'to make (lit. 'use) a conciliatory announcement'. κατὰ τὰ πάτρια, 'according to the ancestral custom of . . .', which is even mentioned in Homer (Iliad II, 504), where Plataea is a member of the Theban confederacy. τίθεσθαι . . . ὅπλα, depending on ἀνεῖπεν: 'proclaimed that they should ground arms beside them'. ῥᾳδίως, i.e. 'quickly'.

2

1. ὡς ᾔσθοντο, 'when they perceived that . . .', followed as usual by a participle. νομίσαντες . . . ἐσεληλυθέναι, 'thinking that far more had entered the city (than had actually come in)'; πολλῷ is dative of measure of difference, like ὀλίγῳ in 1, 1. τοὺς λόγους, 'the proposals'. ἄλλως τε καὶ ἐπειδή, 'especially as'. The subject of ἐνεωτέριζον is 'the Thebans', and the double negative οὐδένα οὐδέν intensifies, instead of cancelling,

the negative: 'were offering no violence at all to anyone', lit. 'were doing nothing new', which is a 'euphemism' (avoidance of an unpleasant word) that occurs also in 5, 2, μηδέν νεώτερον ποιεῖν.

2. πράσσοντές πως ταῦτα, 'while they were engaged in some such negotiations'; the indefinite adverb πως makes the statement vague. ἐνόμισαν . . . κρατήσειν, 'they thought that if they attacked they would easily overcome them'; the participle is equivalent to a conditional clause inside the indirect statement, the nominative being used because the subject of all three verbs is the same. τῷ πλήθει . . . οὐ βουλομένῳ ἦν . . . ἀφίστασθαι, 'the majority . . . did not wish to revolt . . .', lit. 'it was to the majority not wishing to . . .'; this use of the dative of advantage occurs in Homer, *Odyssey* XXI, 209 (note).

3. ἐδόκει ἐπιχειρητέα εἶναι, 'they thought they ought to make the attempt', the impersonal use of the neuter plural of the verbal noun (like the Latin gerundive), with a dative of the agent, αὐτοῖς, understood. ξυνελέγοντο . . . παρ' ἀλλήλους, 'they began to join forces with (lit. 'to') one another by digging through . . .'; the party-walls of the houses were made of dried clay bricks or lath and plaster and could easily be broken through from house to house. ἵν' ἀντὶ τείχους ᾖ, 'to serve as a barricade'; ᾖ is singular because the subject is something like 'the obstruction thus made'. ᾗ, an adverb: 'as each thing seemed likely to be useful for the present (need)'.

4. ὡς ἐκ τῶν δυνατῶν, 'as (well as could be expected) from their present resources'. Supply πάντα as the subject of ἦν. φυλάξαντες . . . περίορθρον, 'waiting for (the time when it was) still night and just before dawn'. ὅπως . . . γίγνωνται, 'so as not to attack them in the daytime (when they would be) more confident and so that they (i.e. the Thebans) should not be on equal terms with them'; the subject of προσφέρωνται is the Plataeans, of γίγνωνται the Thebans. ἥσσους = ἥσσονες: 'that the enemy being more terrified . . . should be at a disadvantage owing to their own knowledge of the city', lit. 'should be inferior to their own knowledge throughout the city'; ἐμπειρίας is genitive of comparison. προσέβαλόν τε, Thucydides often used τε as the second word in a new sentence to mean 'and so'.

3

1. οἱ δ' . . . ἠπατημένοι, 'but when they (the Thebans) realised that they had been tricked'; οἱ is here used in the old demonstrative sense of

the article, which is very common in Homer but is used in Attic almost only with δέ to mean 'and he' or 'and they', and in οἱ μὲν ... οἱ δὲ ..., 'some ..., others ...', see also πρὸ τοῦ in 8, 2. ἠπατημένοι is the participle used instead of the infinitive after a verb of perception, in the nominative because the subject of both verbs is the same. ἐν σφίσιν αὐτοῖς = ἐν ἑαυτοῖς, but we should say simply 'they began to rally', or 'began to close their ranks'. ᾗ with the optative is indefinite, and ἀπεωθοῦντο is middle: 'wherever the Plataeans charged they drove them back'.

2. This long sentence should be split up into shorter sentences, e.g. the three genitives absolute down to βαλλόντων could be made into main verbs, the second sentence could end at διὰ τῆς πόλεως, and ὄντες and ἔχοντες could be made main verbs for the third sentence. When ἔπειτα follows a μέν clause (δὶς μέν) the δέ that normally balances the μέν is often omitted. πολλῷ ... προσβαλόντων, 'they themselves attacked with a great uproar'. For κραυγῇ ... χρωμένων we should say 'were shouting and screaming', lit. 'using shouts ...'. βαλλόντων, 'pelting (the enemy) with ...'; κεράμῳ is collective singular used for the plural; Pyrrhus, king of Epirus, was killed in 272 B.C. at Argos by a tile flung down from a roof-top by a woman during some street-fighting. οἱ πλείους, the limited, not the main, subject of ἔφυγον: 'being ignorant, most of them, ...', but we are taking this as a main verb and saying 'most of them were ignorant of the roads (and the way) by which they had to escape', lit. 'be saved'. χρή is present because the indirect question introduced by the interrogative adverb ᾗ keeps the tense of the direct question; ἄπειροι is followed first by an objective genitive, τῶν διόδων, and then by an indirect question. The town of Plataea was built at the foot of Mount Cithaeron and in spring its streets, which, like those of most Greek towns, were unpaved, were evidently deep in mud (πηλῷ) caused by the heavy rain that fell in the night and by the flood water running down from the mountain. τελευτῶντος ... ἦν, 'these events took place at the end of the month' (genitive absolute), 'when there was no moon. The Attic lunar months were different from ours; there was a new moon in the early morning of 7 April 431, so that the Attic month Elaphebolion must have begun at sunset on 6 April, and as the attack was made at the end of the previous month, Anthesterion, the date of the attack must have been about 4 April. ἐμπείρους ... διώκοντας, 'and they were being pursued by men who knew the roads', lit. 'having pursuers acquainted (with the roads)'. οἱ πολλοί, 'most of them'.

3. πύλας, plural because they were double gates, made fast when closed by a bar placed across both leaves. ᾗ, an adverb, 'by which'. στυρακίῳ . . . μοχλόν, 'by thrusting (lit. 'having used') the spike of a spear into the bar instead of the pin'; the wooden bar was 'locked' by an iron pin that was thrust through it into a socket in the timber of the gate; it could be removed only by a special 'key' that fitted into the head of the pin, below the surface of the bar, and drew it out (see the note on Homer, *Odyssey* XXI, 46, for the way in which a room-door was barred on the inside and could be bolted and unbolted with a special 'key' outside the door.) μηδὲ ταύτῃ, 'not even by this way', an adverb; μή instead of οὐ because this consecutive clause has an infinitive instead of an indicative.

4. ἐς τὸ ἔξω, 'over', lit. 'to the outside'. The first subject, οἱ μέν τινες αὐτῶν, is limited by οἱ πλείους, 'most of them', and the second subject, οἱ δέ ('others'), by οὐ πολλοί, 'a few of them'. κατὰ πύλας ἐρήμους, 'at an unguarded gate', not the one by which they had entered. λαθόντες, both with διακόψαντες and with ἐξῆλθον, 'cut through the bar and escaped unnoticed'. We should translate the genitive absolute γυναικὸς δούσης as 'being given an axe by a woman'. αἴσθησις ταχεῖα ἐπεγένετο, 'they were soon noticed', lit. 'swift perception happened'; this explains why only a few escaped. ἄλλοι . . . πόλεως, 'others in different parts of the city'; πύλεως depends on the adverb ἄλλη.

5. τὸ πλεῖστον . . . ξυνεστραμμένον, 'the largest and most compact body', lit. 'as much as was the most gathered together', followed by the plural verb ἐσπίπτουσιν, which is historic present. ἦν τοῦ τείχους, 'was next to the wall'. Instead of saying οὗ αἱ θύραι . . . ἔτυχον, 'whose doors happened to be open', Thucydides continues with a main sentence καὶ αἱ θύραι . . . αὐτοῦ; so also in 7, 1. πύλας τὰς θύρας, the article distinguishes between the object and the complement.

6. εἴτε . . . εἴτε, used here instead of the double interrogative πότερον . . . ἤ; 'took counsel whether to set fire . . . and burn them to death just as they were, or to treat them in some other way'; the aorist subjunctives are indirect deliberative questions, which would be subjunctive also in the direct question ('are we to . . . ?'), ἔχουσιν in the subordinate clause keeps the original tense used by the speakers, and τι ἄλλο is adverbial accusative.

7. τέλος, an adverb, 'at last'. ὅσοι . . . περιῆσαν, 'any others of . . . who survived'. ξυνέβησαν, 'came to terms with . . .', followed by a dative and

a prolative infinitive, παραδοῦναι, 'that they should surrender . . .', and an infinitive of purpose, χρήσασθαι, with a change of subject, 'for them to treat in whatever way they wished'; ὅ τι, from ὅστις, adverbial accusative.

8. οἱ μὲν . . . . ἐπεπράγεσαν, 'so the Thebans . . . had fared thus', or 'such was the fate of . . .'

4

1. οὓς . . . παραγενέσθαι, 'who ought to have arrived while it was still night'; this is the first mention of a larger force of Thebans coming to occupy Plataea. εἴ τι . . . ἐσεληλυθόσι, '(to help them) in case anything turned out badly for the party that had entered the town'; εἰ προχωροίη is the indirect form of ἐὰν προχώρῃ; the Thebans' own words, or thoughts, were 'we shall help them if anything goes wrong'. ἅμα with the genitive absolute ἀγγελίας ῥηθείσης implies 'as soon as the news was told to them', i.e. by the few who managed to escape. ἐπεβοήθουν, the imperfect means 'hurried to the rescue'.

2. σταδίους ἑβδομήκοντα, accusative of extent of space; about eight miles. τὸ ὕδωρ . . . τῆς νυκτός, 'the rain that had fallen during the night', mentioned in 3, 2. ἐποίησε. . . . ἐλθεῖν, 'caused them to travel . . .'. ἐρρύη μέγας, 'was in flood', lit. 'flowed big', because of the water that came down from Mount Cithaeron, as well as because of the rain.

3. τε, 'and so', as in 3, 4. τῶν ἀνδρῶν, divided into τῶν μέν and τῶν δέ: 'when some of the men had been killed and others were held prisoner alive'.

4. τοῖς . . . Πλαταιῶν, 'against those of the Plataeans who were outside . . .'. καὶ . . . καί, 'both . . . and'. κατασκευή, any kind of farm property such as livestock and wagons. οἷα . . . γενομένου, 'such as (would be found) when trouble had happened unexpectedly . . .'; the accent shows that οἷα is neuter plural, not feminine singular. ἐβούλοντο . . . ἀντὶ τῶν ἔνδον, 'they wanted to have any that they could seize, to exchange them for their own people inside the town', lit. 'if they seized anyone, they wanted (him) to be (ὑπάρχειν) for them instead of . . .'. ἤν = ἐάν, 'if indeed any of them happened to have been taken alive'; the use of εἰ with the optative and ἤν with the subjunctive in the same sentence is unusual.

5. οἱ μέν, 'the Thebans'. ἔτι διαβουλευομένων, 'while the Thebans were still deliberating', or 'making plans'. τοιοῦτόν τι, 'something like this'. δείσαντες . . . ἔξω, 'fearing for their own people outside the city'. λέγοντες,

this could have been λέγοντα agreeing with κήρυκα, as in 19, 2; the nominative plural is used also in 5, 2. δράσειαν, the optative represents the aorist indicative of direct speech: 'saying that the Thebans had not acted justly in what had been done, in trying to seize their (σφῶν) city in time of peace'. ἔλεγον here = ἐκέλευον: 'they told them not to injure anything outside the city'. εἰ δὲ μή . . . ἀποκτενεῖν, 'otherwise (i.e. if they did not obey this order), the Plataeans said that they would retaliate by putting to death the Theban prisoners whom they had in their possession alive', lit. 'that they themselves too would kill their (i.e. the Thebans') men'; ἔχουσι is present because a relative clause in indirect statement retains the tense used by the speaker. Supply αὐτῶν or τῶν Θηβαιῶν with ἀναχωρησάντων in the genitive absolute; 'they said that when the Thebans had withdrawn . . . they would give back these prisoners'. It may be necessary to insert 'the Plataeans' or 'the Thebans' at various places when translating indirect statement if 'they', 'them', or 'their' causes ambiguity.

6. μέν in a new sentence is usually accompanied by οὖν, γάρ, or δή. ταῦτα λέγουσι, 'give this version of the story'. αὐτούς, 'the Plateans', is the subject of ἐπομόσαι. οὐχ ὁμολογοῦσι . . . ὑποσχέσθαι ἀποδώσειν, 'do not admit that they promised to give back . . . '; the subject of the infinitives is not expressed because it is the same as the subject of the main verb. λόγων . . . ξυμβαίνωσι, '(say that they agreed to do so) if (ἤν = ἐάν) they could come to some arrangement after discussions had first taken place'. οὔ φασι, 'they deny that they . . .'.

7. δ' οὖν, 'at any rate', i.e. whatever the truth of the matter; it certainly seems foolish for the Plataeans to have killed these prisoners, who would have been hostages to help them to obtain favourable terms when the Thebans came again to attack Plataea. τὰ ἐκ τῆς χώρας, for this 'pregnant' use of a preposition, see the note on ἐς τὴν ἀγοράν in 1, 4; we should say 'their property in the country', which included also families of the farmers living there. πρὸς ὅν . . . προδίδοντες, 'with whom the traitors had negotiated'; the present participle is equivalent to a noun, or it may mean 'those who were trying to betray the city'.

5

1. ἔπεμπον, the imperfect is sometimes used with verbs of 'sending' and 'going', to suggest the discussions and preparations made before

the journey began (see also ἐπέμπετο in Antiphon, 4), but we use the aorist in English. ὑποσπόνδους, a truce to pick up and bury the dead bodies was never refused by the victorious side who were left in possession of the field of battle, so that the enemy dead should not be deprived of the rites that would enable their spirits to rest in peace; the Theban dead would include both those who were killed in the fighting in the town and those who were taken alive and then slaughtered. τὰ ἐν τῇ πόλει ... ἐδόκει αὐτοῖς, 'they arranged affairs ... to meet the present crisis as seemed (best) to them', i.e. they prepared themselves for a siege by strengthening the defences of the city.

2. ἠγγέλθη ... γεγενημένα, 'the news of what had befallen the Plataeans was reported ...'; this does not refer to the message just dispatched, but to the two previous messages that will be mentioned in §3 of this chapter. Βοιωτῶν, depending on ὅσοι: 'they arrested all the Boeotians who were in ...', lit. 'as many of ... as were in ...'. Supply αὐτούς as the object of κελεύοντες: 'telling them to do no harm to the prisoners of the Thebans whom they held', lit. 'to do nothing newer'; for this 'euphemism', see the note on ἐνεωτέριζον in 2, 1, and for the tense of ἔχουσι, see the note on οὓς ἔχουσι in 4, 5. πρίν, since the sentence contains a negative. μηδέν, 'before' = 'until', and takes the normal construction of an indefinite clause: 'until they themselves also had come to a decision ...'.

3. ἅμα ... γιγνομένῃ, 'at the same time as the entry ... took place'. Supply αὐτῶν with the genitive absolute participles νενικημένων καὶ ξυνειλημμένων: 'when they had just been overcome ...'. τῶν ὕστερον, 'of what happened afterwards'. οὐκ εἰδότες, 'not knowing the full facts'. The object of ἔστελλον (imperfect, as explained in the note on ἔπεμπον in §1) is 'the message', mentioned in §2.

4. ἐξεκόμισαν, i.e. to Athens. We shall see in 13 that 400 Plataeans were left to defend the city, with the addition of an Athenian garrison of 80 men, and there were 110 women slaves to prepare food for the defenders. 212 of the men eventually escaped.

6

1. τοῦ ἐπιγιγνομνου θέρους, 'during the following summer', of 429. οὐκ ἐσέβαλον, the annual invasion of Attica to ravage the crops was not made this year, perhaps through fear of the great Plague that had been

raging in Athens. βασιλεύς, there were two kings at Sparta, holding joint hereditary power, but their authority was limited by five 'ephors' who held office for a year; one king was always in command of any expedition abroad.

2. οὐ δίκαια . . . στρατεύοντες, 'you are not doing what is just or worthy either of yourselves or of the fathers from whom you are sprung in invading . . .'. τῶν ἐθελησάντων . . . ἐγένετο, 'who were willing to join in facing the danger of the battle that took place near our city'; this was the great Battle of Plataea, fought in 479 by an allied army of Greeks which included the Athenians and the Plataeans (but not the Thebans, who sided with the Persian invaders) and a large force of Spartans, all under the command of the Spartan regent Pausanias, against a Persian army under Mardonius, who had been left in command of the land forces by King Xerxes after the Greek naval victory at Salamis in 480; the Greek allies defeated the Persians and saved Greece from foreign domination. ἀπεδίδου . . . οἰκεῖν, 'granted to the Plataeans (the right) to dwell in their own land and city, possessing it independently'; the imperfect ἀπεδίδου, suggests the details of the grant, as with ἔπεμπον in 5, 1. Πλαταιεῦσι becomes accusative in ἔχοντας αὐτονόμους because of the fondness of the Greeks for an accusative with an infinitive. Supply 'proclaimed' as the verb for στρατεῦσαι μηδένα; 'proclaimed that nobody should make war upon them unjustly or with a view to enslaving it'; the aorist στρατεῦσαι indicates a single action, as opposed to the continuous action of the present infinitive οἰκεῖν. εἰ δὲ μή, 'otherwise', i.e. if this immunity was not maintained, as in 4, 5. ἀμύνειν still depends on the verb of proclaiming understood from ἀπεδίδου: 'the allies who were present were to defend the Plataeans to the best of their ability'.

3. προθυμίας, governed by ἕνεκα, like ἀρετῆς: 'because of the courage and patriotism that we then showed (γενομένης) . . .'. τὰ ἐναντία, 'just the opposite of this'. τῶν ἡμῖν ἐχθίστων, 'who are our bitterest enemies'. ἐπὶ . . . ἡμετέρᾳ, 'to enslave us', as in §2.

4. μάρτυρας . . . ποιούμενοι, 'calling to witness the gods, both those to whom the oaths were then made and those of your fathers and of our country'. λέγομεν ὑμῖν = κελεύομεν ὑμᾶς. ἐᾶν, from ἐάω with ἡμᾶς understood as the object.

7

1. εἰπόντων Πλαταιῶν, genitive absolute. ἤν = ἐάν, in a conditional clause that refers to the future, so the meaning is 'your words are just,

(but only) if your actions suit your words', lit. 'if you do things similar to your words'. παρέδωκεν has the same meaning as ἀπεδίδου in 6, 2, and αὐτονομεῖσθε and ξυνελευθεροῦτε are imperative: 'just as Pausanias made the grant to you, you yourselves must both (τε) live independently and join in freeing . . .'. ὅσοι, lit. 'as many as', i.e. 'all those who'. τῶν τότε κινδύνων, 'the dangers of that time'. εἰσι νῦν ὑπ' 'Aθηναίοις, 'are now subject to the Athenians'. παρασκευὴ τοσήδε καὶ πόλεμος γεγένηται, 'such great preparations for war have been made', lit. 'such preparation and war'; this is an example of the figure of speech called 'hendiadys' ('one through two') in which two words connected by 'and' are used instead of a compound phrase, e.g. 'nice and warm' means 'nicely warm'. ἕνεκα often follows the word that it governs but here it governs ἐλευθερώσεως, which depends on αὐτῶν καὶ τῶν ἄλλων; this sentence began as a relative clause introduced by ὅσοι but has now become a main sentence in which we have αὐτῶν instead of ὧν; there is a similar change of construction in 3, 5. ἧς, the antecedent is ἐλευθερώσεως: 'best of all (μάλιστα), share in this freedom and yourselves stand by your oaths'. εἰ δὲ μή, 'otherwise'. The antecedent of ἅπερ is ἡσυχίαν ἄγετε: 'remain neutral (lit. 'keep quiet'), a thing which we have . . . requested you to do'. αὐτῶν agrees with the genitive case contained in the possessive pronoun ὑμέτερα, so that τὰ ὑμέτερα αὐτῶν = τὰ ὑμῶν αὐτῶν, 'your own property'. ἔστε . . . ἑτέρων, 'join neither side'. ἀμφοτέρους . . . ἑτέρους, 'both sides as friends but neither side (as allies) for war'.

2. τὰ ῥηθέντα κοινώσαντες, 'after reporting the words of Archidamus'. ἀδύνατα, the plural is often used instead of the singular in such impersonal phrases: 'it was impossible for them . . .'. ἄνευ, 'without consulting . . .' παῖδες . . . εἶεν, we should expect an accusative and infinitive (like δεδιέναι) in a sentence introduced by γάρ in indirect statements, but Thucydides makes it depend on ὅτι, like ἀδύνατα . . . εἴη. παρ' ἐκείνοις, 'in their care', as mentioned in 5, 4. δεδιέναι . . . ἐπιτρέπωσιν, '(they said that) they were afraid for the whole city, in case (μή) when the Lacedaemonians had departed the Athenians might come and not allow them (to remain neutral)'. ἢ Θηβαῖοι . . . πειράσωσι, 'or that the Thebans, claiming that they were (ὡς ὄντες) included in the oath that the Plataeans should receive both sides, might try . . .'; κατά means 'according to the agreement that they should . . .', and πειράσωσιν here is active, instead of the usual middle.

3. ὁ δέ 'and he', i.e. Archidamus. θαρσύνων πρὸς ταῦτα, 'trying to

encourage them with regard to these matters'. ὑμεῖς δέ, we should translate δέ, at the beginning of a speech replying to another speech, as
'then'. The μέν after πόλιν is balanced by the δέ after αὐτοί. δένδρα ἀριθμῷ
τὰ ὑμέτερα, lit. 'your trees in number', i.e. 'the number of your trees',
referring to olive and vine trees. ἄλλο . . . ἐλθεῖν, 'anything else that can
be counted', lit. 'if anything else (is) able to come into number'.
ἕως. . . . ᾖ, 'as long as the war lasts'; this and the three following subjunctives are indefinite: 'when it is over, we shall return to you whatever
we have taken from you, and until that time (μέχρι τοῦδε) we shall keep
it as a trust, working (the land) and paying whatever rent will satisfy
you', lit. 'a rent, whatever is likely to be enough for you'.

8

1. οἱ δέ, 'and they', i.e. the Plataeans' envoys. βουλευσάμενοι . . .
πλήθους, 'after taking counsel with the people'. ἃ προκαλεῖται . . . κοινῶσαι,
'to report to the Athenians the proposals that Archidamus was making';
the tenses of βούλονται and προκαλεῖται are those that were used by the
speakers themselves in their reply to Archidamus. ἦν (= ἐάν). . . ποιεῖν,
'if they could persuade them (to agree), they were willing to carry out
these (proposals)'; ποιεῖν depends on βούλονται. The object of ἐκέλευον is
αὐτόν understood: 'they asked him to give them a truce'. ὁ δέ, 'and
Archidamus'. ἡμέρας, accusative of duration of time: 'for (a certain
number of) days within which it was reasonable that the envoys could
make the journey (to Athens and back)'; the number of days is not
mentioned; the distance to Athens was about 30 miles.

3. ἐν τῷ πρὸ τοῦ χρόνῳ 'in former times'; in πρὸ τοῦ ('before that') the
article is used in its old sense as a demonstrative pronoun, as in Homer
and in the Attic οἱ δέ (e.g. at the beginning of this chapter; see the note
on 3, 1). ἀφ' οὗ 'since the time when'; for the date of the first alliance
between Plataea and Athens see the note on 22, 5. ἐν οὐδενὶ (χρόνῳ), a
double negative with οὔτε: 'the Athenians say that neither in former
times . . . have they at any time abandoned you when you were being
wronged nor will they now allow (it to happen)'. πρός, 'by', or 'in the
name of'. οὓς . . . ὤμοσαν, an example of a 'cognate' accusative, i.e. one
used after an intransitive verb when the noun repeats the meaning
contained in the verb. μηδὲν νεωτερίζειν περί, 'not to forsake . . .', lit. 'to
make no change about . . .'; there is another meaning of this verb in 2, 1.

It is strange that after urging the Plataeans to resist the Lacedae-monians and undergo a siege, in which 80 of their own men were involved, the Athenians abandoned Plataea to suffer whatever fate should befall it, both now and in the winter of 428 when it was eventually captured. Presumably they were themselves too busily engaged with the siege of Potidaea (431–430) and the revolt of Lesbos (428), besides the troubles caused by the Plague at Athens, to send the promised help to their old allies. In fact, it would have been almost impossible to provision and defend a city in hostile territory so close to Thebes — but the Athenians must have realised this before they encouraged the Plataeans to resist.

9

1. ἐβουλεύσαντο . . . ξυμβαίνῃ, 'resolved not to desert . . . but to put up both with seeing . . . , if they had to, and enduring whatever else might happen'; ὁρῶντας and πάσχοντας would normally be nominative because they refer to the subject of the main verb, ἐβουλεύσαντο, but they are influenced by δεῖ, whose object, αὐτούς, is here omitted. ἐξελθεῖν and ἀποκρίνασθαι depend on ἐβουλεύσαντο, but since the subject changes it is now followed by an accusative and infinitive: 'that no one should leave the city any more (ἔτι) but that (the envoys) should reply that . . .'. For ἀδύνατα see the second note on 7, 2.

2. ἐντεῦθεν δή, 'then indeed'. The μέν in πρῶτον μέν has no δέ-clause to follow it; its place is taken by τοσαῦτα in 10, 1. ἐς ἐπιμαρτυρίαν . . . κατέστη, 'began to call upon . . .', lit. 'settled down to a calling upon . . .'. follows by θεῶν καὶ ἡρώων.

2. θεοὶ . . . ἔχετε, 'all you gods . . . who possess . . .'. ἔστε, imperative: 'be witnesses (to the fact) that we did not come against this land unjustly in the beginning (τὴν ἀρχήν, adverbial accusative), but (only) after these Plataeans first abandoned . . .'. παρέσχετε . . . Ἕλλησιν, 'you made it an auspicious place for the Greeks to fight in'; ἐναγωνίσασθαι is an 'epexegetic' (explanatory) infinitive, and the relative clause ἐν ᾗ . . . ἐκράτησαν becomes a main sentence in παρέσχετε αὐτήν (see also 3, 5, and 7, 1). ἤν (= ἐὰν) τι ποιῶμεν, 'if we take any further action', a 'euphemism' (see the note on μηδὲν νεώτερον ποιεῖν in 5, 2) for 'if we attack the city', προκαλεσάμενοι . . . οὐ τυγχάνομεν, 'though we have made many reasonable proposals we have not been successful (in reaching an agreement)': καί is inserted between two adjectives in Greek (like et in Latin) but is

omitted in English. ξυγγνώμονες . . . νομίμως, 'grant that those who first began the evil-doing should be punished for it and that those who are lawfully exacting vengeance may obtain it'; ξυγγνώμονες ἔστε = ξυγχωρήσατε, 'allow', or 'grant'; ἀδικίας depends both on κολάζεοθαι, where it is genitive of cause, and on ὑπάρχουσι; τιμωρίας depends on τυγχάνειν, though in English we make it the object of ἐπιφέρουσι also.

10

1. τοσαῦτα, adverbial accusative: 'after making this (or 'such an') appeal to the gods'. καθίστη, imperfect, meaning 'he began to bring his army into action'. The subject of ἔκοψαν is of course 'the Peloponnesians', of whom the Lacedaemonians were the leaders and provided the main force; the Thebans also served among the Peloponnesian allies. τοῦ μηδένα ἔτι ἐξιέναι, a genitive of purpose used with an infinitive as a purpose clause: 'to prevent anyone from leaving the city in the future', to escape or get supplies. Notice the fairly common omission of δέ when ἔπειτα follows πρῶτον μέν. πρὸς τὴν πόλιν, 'against the wall of the city'. αὐτῶν depends on αἵρεσιν: 'thinking that this would be the quickest way of capturing it (lit. 'them')', and the genitive absolute gives the reason: 'because so great an army was at work'.

2. ξύλα, mountain timber, not δένδρα, olives and vines. ἐκ τοῦ Κιθαιρῶνος, another example of the so-called 'pregnant' use of the preposition, as in 1, 4; they cut down the trees on Mount Cithaeron (about three miles south of Plataea) and brought it from the mountain to the city. The use of the present participle, τέμνοντες, instead of the aorist, is strange, παρῳκοδόμουν . . . τιθέντες, 'they built a framework of timber along (the mound) on each side of it, placing (the logs) at right angles to one another to serve as (ἀντί) walls'. ὅπως . . . διαχέοιτο, 'so that the mound should not spread over a wide area', but should be kept together by the lattice-work of timber. εἴ τι . . . ἐπιβαλλόμενον, 'anything else that was likely to build up the mound when thrown upon it'; μέλλοι is optative in an indefinite clause, lit. 'if anything else was likely to . . .'; ὕλην would be wood generally, such as branches and twigs, while ξύλα were large logs. The object of the mound was to provide a platform for siege-engines and a base from which to make the final assault.

3. διῃρημένοι κατ' ἀναπαύλας, 'being divided into shifts', or perhaps middle, 'dividing up the work into shifts'. τοὺς μὲν . . . τοὺς δέ, 'some . . .

others'. *Λακεδαιμονίων . . . ἠνάγκαζον*, 'the officers of the Lacedaemonians who were in command of the allies of each city, being in joint command (i.e. with the allies' own officers), urged them on . . .'.

4. *αἰρόμενον*, 'becoming higher', lit. 'being raised'. *ξύλινον τεῖχος*, 'a wooden framework', which they 'constructed and placed against their own wall where the mound was being raised against it'; they then 'built bricks into it', to make an additional inner wall. *ἐγγύς* is made into an adjective when used with the article; 'taking (them) away from the neighbouring houses'.

5. *ξύνδεσμος . . . τὰ ξύλα*, 'the timber served to bind them (i.e. the bricks) together'. *τοῦ μὴ . . . . οἰκοδόμημα*, another purpose clause, as in §1: 'to prevent the structure from being (too) weak as it became high(er)'. *προκαλύμματα εἶχε δέρσεις*, 'it had to protect it (lit. 'as coverings') skins . . .'. *ὥστε . . . εἶναι*, 'so that the men who were working at it . . . were both not hit . . . and were in a safe (position)'; the combination of *μήτε* and *τε* is common.

6. *μέγα*, used predicatively; lit. 'the height of the wall was raised big i.e. 'the wall was raised to a great height'. *οὐ σχολαίτερον*, an adverb: 'just as quickly'. *τοιόνδε τι*, 'the following scheme'. *διελόντες . . . τὴν γῆν* 'taking down (part) of the wall where the mound touched it, they drew the earth away (into the city)'; they had to dismantle the lowest part of the original outer wall and of the new inner timber-and-brick wall: only the foot of the mound touched the wall; see the note on *ἐς τὸ μεταξύ* in 12, 3.

11

1. *αἰσθόμενοι*, supply *τοῦτο* as the object. *ἐσέβαλλον ἐς τὸ διῃρημένον*, 'threw it down into the gap thus formed', lit. 'into that which had been removed'. *ὅπως . . . φοροῖτο*, 'so that it (i.e. the part of the mound near the wall, now repaired and strengthened with clay packed in baskets) should not spread and be carried away like the (loose)earth'.

2. *ταύτῃ*, an adverb: 'the Plataeans, being thwarted in this'. *ἐπέσχον* is intransitive and *τοῦτο* accusative of respect, but we should say 'abandoned this plan', lit. 'stopped with regard to this'. *ξυντεκμηραμένοι ὑπὸ τὸ χῶμα*, 'judging (the distance to take it) under the mound'; all they had to do was to dig the mine in a straight line and when the mound began to subside draw the loose earth (*τὸν χοῦν*) into the city. *ἐπὶ πολύ*, 'for a

long time'. ἐπιβάλλοντας, the case shows that the subject of the ὥστε clause is 'the Peloponnesians'; 'so that they made less progress (with the mound than before), although they continued to throw earth on top of it'. The reason is given in the genitive absolute clause, 'because the mound was being drawn away from them from below'; αὐτοῖς is dative of disadvantage. ἐπὶ τὸ κενούμενον 'into the empty space', left by the withdrawal of the earth from underneath, like τὸ διῃρημένον in §1.

3. δεδιότες ... οὕτω, 'fearing that not even so ...'. ὀλίγοι, supply ὄντες. τὸ μέγα ... χῶμα, 'they stopped working at the large structure opposite the mound', i.e. the timber-and-brick addition to the original wall. ἔνθεν ... ἀρξάμενοι, 'starting from each end of it'. ἀπὸ ... τείχους, 'from the (original) low wall'. ἐκ τοῦ ἔντος, 'on the inside'; the Romans used some prepositions in the same way, e.g. *a fronte*, 'in front'. μηνοειδές ... προσῳκοδόμουν, 'they built an additional crescent-shaped (wall running) into the city', so that when the besiegers captured the reinforced wall in front of their mound they would have to cross an open space and build another mound against the new inner wall. τὸ μέγα τεῖχος is the original wall reinforced by the timber-and-brick structure called τὸ μέγα οἰκοδόμημα earlier in this sentence, and τοῦτο is the new crescent-shaped inner wall. δέοι is in the purpose clause and χοῦν is the infinitive of χόω (not the accusative of χοῦς): 'and that the enemy should have to build a mound against it once more and while advancing inwards ... be more exposed to fire from both sides'; not 'more than before' but 'the further they advanced'.

4. ἅμα τῇ χώσει καί, 'at the same time as they built the mound they also ...'. τοῦ μεγάλου οἰκαδομήματος, depending on ἐπὶ μέγα: 'which, being brought up on to the mound shook down a great part of the large structure', lit. 'over a great (part) of ...'. ἄλλας, governed by προσῆγον: 'they brought up other engines at different parts of ...'. ἅς, governed by ἀνείλκον, βρόχους by περιβάλλοντες. δόκους ... τοῦ τείχους, 'fastening large beams by means of long iron chains at each end (of the beams, lit. 'from the cut part at each end') to two poles resting on and extending over the wall'; the Greeks spoke of fastening a thing 'from' another thing, where we say 'to'; δύο is here indeclinable. Insert 'and' before ἀνελκύσαντες, or start a new sentence here: 'hauling them up at an angle (to the battering-ram)'. χαλαραῖς ταῖς ἁλύσεσι, 'by slackening the chains'. οὐ διὰ χειρὸς ἔχοντες, 'not holding them (firmly) in their hands'. ἡ δέ, 'and it', i.e. the beam.

12

1. ὡς, 'since'. τῷ χώματι . . . ἐγίγνετο, 'the counter-wall (i.e. the crescent-shaped inner wall) was being built to oppose the mound'; the ἀντι- in ἀντιτείχισμα governs τῷ χώματι. νομίσαντες . . . τῶν παρόντων δεινῶν, 'thinking that it was impossible to . . . with (ὑπό) their present means of attack', an unusual meaning of δεινά. πρὸς τὴν περιτείχισιν, 'for a blockade', or 'to build a wall round the city'.

2. πρότερον . . . γενομένου, 'first of all (i.e. before starting the blockade) they decided to make an attempt by fire (to see) if, when a wind sprung up, they could . . .'. πᾶσαν . . . .προσαχθείη, 'they contrived every form (of attack) in the hope that (lit. 'if in any way') it could be forced to submit without the expense of a siege'; δαπάνης καὶ πολιορκίας is another example of 'hendiadys', which is explained in the note on παρασκευὴ καὶ πόλεμος in 7, 1. ἐς τὸ μεταξὺ πρῶτον, 'first into the (space) between the . . .'; the mound originally sloped down so that its foot was right up against the bottom of the wall, but the undermining operations of the Plataeans had presumably opened up a gap between mound and wall. ταχὺ πλήρους γενομένου 'as this space quickly became filled up'. τῆς ἄλλης πόλεως depends on ὅσον πλεῖστον: 'they heaped up brushwood as far as they could reach (by throwing it) into the rest of the city also from the top (of the mound)'; the attackers were still outside the original wall and its reinforcing 'large structure', so they could fill up with faggots only the space between this wall and the new crescent-shaped wall.

4. τοσαύτη . . . εἶδεν, 'greater than anybody had ever seen up to that time', lit. 'as great as nobody had seen'. ἤδη . . . αὐτήν, 'sometimes dry branches, rubbing against one another,, lit. 'already timber rubbed against itself'. ὑπ' ἀνέμων would normally be dative of the agent; see also ὑπὸ τῶν παρόντων δεινῶν in §1.

5. τοῦτο, i.e. τὸ πῦρ. τοὺς Πλαταιᾶς . . . διαφθεῖραι, 'came within a very little of destroying the Plataeans who had escaped the other (dangers)', lit. 'it lacked very little to destroy . . .'. ἐντὸς . . . πελάσαι, 'in a large part of the city it was not possible to approach (the fire)', to try to put it out; the inhabitants had to withdraw from a large part of the town on the side where the brushwood was blazing outside the crescent-shaped wall; no doubt many of the houses near the wall caught fire too and could not be approached. πνεῦμα . . . . οὐκ ἂν διέφυγον, 'if a wind had sprung up blowing towards the city, which of course (καί) . . . , the Plataeans would not

have escaped'. νῦν δὲ καὶ τόδε, 'but as it was, this also . . .'. ξυμβῆναι is followed by two clauses in the accusative and infinitive; for παυθῆναι the subject changes to κίνδυνον.

13

1. καὶ τούτου, 'in this attempt also', governed by διήμαρτον. τὸ πλέον, 'the greater part'. διελόμενοι, like διῃρημένοι in 10, 3. but here aorist middle: 'dividing up the space among the different cities', i.e. among the contingents from the various allied cities . ἐντός τε καὶ ἔξωθεν i.e. on each side of the blockading wall, one to stop the inhabitants from escaping, the other to stop a relieving force from attacking the besiegers.

2. περὶ ἀρκτούρου ἐπιτολάς, 'at about the rising of Arcturus', which takes place on September 18. φύλακας . . .τείχους, 'guards over half of the wall'. τὸ ἥμισυ, 'the other half'. τῷ στράτῳ, dative of accompaniment, 'with their army'. κατὰ πόλεις, 'each to his own city'.

3. ἐκκεκομισμένοι ἦσαν, middle, 'had previously sent away', as described in 5, 4. αὐτοὶ . . . τριακόσιοι, 'they themselves were left to endure the siege to the number of 400', or '400 of their own men were left . . .'. The 120 women were slaves, as the mention of δοῦλος in the next section indicates; they were sold to new owners after the siege (22, 2).

4. τοσοῦτοι . . . καθίσταντο, 'such were the total numbers when they began being besieged , lit. 'settled down to the siege . ἐν τῷ τείχει 'within the walls . τοιαύτη . . . κατεσκευάσθη, 'in such a manner was the blockade . . . completed'.

14

1. τοῦ αὐτοῦ χειμῶνος, 'during the same winter , of 428. τῷ σίτῳ . . . ἐπιέζοντο, 'they began to be hard pressed by the failure of their corn-supply'. τιμωρίας, 'of help'; the Athenians had encouraged the Plataeans to resist after the first Theban attack in 431 (5, 4) and still more emphatically when the siege began in 429 (8, 3); reasons why they did not come to relieve the city are given in the note on 8, 3. ἐφαίνετο, 'seemed likely to come'. ἐπιβουλεύουσιν . . . ἐξελθεῖν, 'they themselves and those of the Athenians who were besieged with them made a plan (historic present) first of all that all should leave the city'. ἢν (= ἐὰν) δύνωνται, 'in the hope that they would be able . . .'. We might make the genitive absolute clause into a main sentence: 'those who suggested the attempt to them were Theanetus the son of Tolmides, a seer, and . . .'; ἀνδρὸς

μάντεως go together, and ὃς καί is 'who also was . . .'; the advice of a professional seer or soothsayer (whose duties were to interpret the will of the gods as revealed by the flight of birds and other natural phenomena and by the inspection of the entrails of sacrificial victims) and of a general (a high state official, elected annually) would carry great weight.

2. Notice again the omission of δέ after ἔπειτα when preceded by πρῶτον μέν. οἱ ἡμίσεις, 'half of them'. μέγαν ἡγησάμενοι, 'thinking it to be (too) great'; this translation makes ἀπώκνησαν govern κίνδυνον, 'shrunk from the danger', but ἀπώκνησαν may be intransitive, 'lost heart, thinking the danger too great'. ἐς . . . μάλιστα, 'up to about 220 men'; when ἐς is used with this meaning (like ad in Latin) the phrase can be the subject of a verb as though it were a nominative; here it is the subject of ἐνέμειναν: 'up to about 220 men voluntarily persisted in the attempt to leave the city, (which was carried out) in the following way'; either ἐς or μάλιστα could have been omitted.

3. ἴσας, 'equal in height to . . .'. ξυνεμετρήσαντο ταῖς ἐπιβολαῖς, 'they obtained the measurement by (counting) the layers . . .'. ᾗ . . . αὐτῶν, 'at a point where the enemies' (αὐτῶν) wall on the side facing them (πρὸς σφᾶς) happened not to be completely plastered over'; the bricks were made of clay dug from the ditches (13, 1), shaped to the required size, and dried in the sun; they were plastered over with whitewash made from the lime of Cithaeron to enable them to resist the rain. The blockading wall is thought to have been about a mile in circumference and 100 yards from the city. ἔμελλον . . . ἄλλως τε καί, 'some were likely to make a mistake, but the majority (πλείους = πλείονες) were likely, to get the calculation right, especially as . . .', which is followed by a participle. οὐ πολὺ ἀπέχοντες, 'they were not far away from it'. ῥᾳδίως . . . τείχους, 'since the wall could easily be seen as clearly as they wanted', to enable them to count the layers of bricks; εἰς ὅ seems to be used for ὅσον, 'as much as they wanted'.

4. ἔλαβον, 'they obtained'. πλίνθου, collective singular; even if the bricks were of an unusual size only a very serious under-calculation of the height required for the ladders would have been dangerous.

15

1. ἦν . . . οἰκοδομήσει, 'was built as follows', lit. 'was such in its building'. For μέν alone, see the note on 4, 6. δύο τούς, 'we omit the article

in English. πρός . . . ἐπίοι, 'both on the side facing (lit. 'from') the Plataeans and (on the outer side) in case anyone should come to attack them from Athens'. ἑκκαίδεκα πόδας, accusative of extent. μάλιστα, 'about'.

2. τὸ μεταξὺ . . .ᾠκοδόμητο, 'this intervening space (of) sixteen feet was taken up with quarters assigned to the sentries', lit. 'had been built (with) buildings . . .'; οἰκήματα is internal accusative, and μεταξύ is made into a noun by the article, as in 12, 3. ἦν ξυνεχῆ, 'it was all continuous', referring to the sentries' quarters and the two parallel walls: 'so that it appeared to be one broad wall that had . . .'.

3. διὰ δέκα ἐπάλξεων, 'at intervals of every ten battlements'. διήκοντες . . . αὐτοῦ, 'extending to its inner face and at the same time (lit. 'the same') also (to) its outer (face)'. παρὰ πύργον, 'at the side of each tower'. δι' αὐτῶν μέσων διῇσαν, 'the sentries passed through the middle of them', by a passage on the top of the wall underneath each tower. There was probably a door at ground-level in the outer wall at the foot of each tower, so that the sentries could reach their quarters, which may have had windows on the outer side to give them light and air, and there must have been stairs inside each tower leading from the ground to the top of the wall and from there to the top of the tower.

4. τὰς νύκτας, 'during the night', accusative of extent of time. ὁπότε εἴη, an indefinite temporal clause: 'whenever there was a rain-storm'. ὄντων δι' ὀλίγου, 'which were close together'; we are not told the size of the towers or the distance between them. φυλακὴν ἐποιοῦντο, 'they kept watch'. The remainder of the blockading army, apart from the sentries posted on the wall or off duty in their quarters inside the double wall, were in camp outside the perimeter, with a mobile reserve of 300 men ready for an emergency (16, 7).

16

1. οἱ δέ, 'the Plataeans'. παρεσκεύαστο, impersonal passive, with αὐτοῖς dative of the agent: 'when all preparations had been made by them'. ἡγοῦντο . . . ἦσαν, 'their leaders were those who were also responsible for (suggesting) the enterprise', Theaenetus and Eupompides, named in 14, 1. τὴν τάφρον, the inner of the two encircling ditches, which apparently did not contain much water and was crossed without difficulty; the ditch outside the blockading wall had more water in it and was harder

to cross (17, 4–5). ἔπειτα, again without δέ, though preceded by πρῶτον μέν. ἀνὰ τὸ σκοτεινόν, 'in the darkness'. αὐτῶν are the same as τοὺς φύλακας, so that the two participles in the genitive absolute could have been accusative agreeing with φύλακας: 'because they did not see the Plataeans ... nor hear them since the wind was drowning with its roar the sound of their approach'; ἀντιπαταγοῦντος τοῦ ἀνέμου is another genitive absolute, lit. 'the wind roaring against the sound caused by (ἐκ) the fact that they were approaching'.

2. ἅμα ... ᾖσαν, 'and at the same time they were also advancing at a long distance from one another'. μή goes with κρουόμενα as well as with παρέχοι: 'should not clash together and reveal their presence', lit. 'provide (for the enemy) perception (of them)'. εὐσταλεῖς τῇ ὁπλίσει, 'lightly equipped', lit. 'well prepared in equipment'. τὸν ἀριστερὸν ... πηλόν 'having only the left foot shod in order to get a safe foothold in the mud', lit. 'for the sake of safety against the mud', which seems a strange thing to do, for a bare foot is slippery in mud, but no doubt Thucydides got first-hand information about the escape; they must have taken the other shoe with them, to put on before making the thirty-odd mile journey to Athens.

3. κατὰ μεταπύργιον, 'at one of the spaces between the towers'; the Plataeans probably knew from previous observation that the sentries took shelter inside the towers during bad weather. ἐρῆμοι, feminine, referring to ἐπάλξεις. ξύν, 'armed with ...'. The imperfect ἀνέβαινον means 'proceeded to climb up', because they had to wait their turn, but ἀνέβη is aorist because Ammeas went up without delay; ἀνέβαινον is repeated, with the additional information that 'those who were following' split up into two parties, six climbing by ladders up one tower and six up the next one, leaving the space between to be held by the third wave of escapers. ἔμελλον ... εἶεν, 'they were going to give (them the shields) as soon as they were close to the enemy', indefinite optative.

4. ὡς ἄνω πλείους (= πλείονες) ἐγένοντο, 'when several of them reached the top', of the wall, not of the towers. οἱ ἐκ τῶν πύργων φύλακες, 'the sentries in the towers'; for this 'pregnant' use of a preposition (lit. 'from the towers'), see the note on θέμενοι ἐς τὴν ἀγορὰν τὰ ὅπλα in 1, 4. ἀντιλαμβανόμενος, used without an object: 'as he tried to grasp it'.

5. βοὴ ἦν, 'the alarm was raised'. τὸ στρατόπεδον, 'the blockading garrison', i.e. the sentries on duty who were sheltering in the towers, the guard off duty who were sleeping in the space between the encircling

walls, and the remainder of the troops who were in camp outside; each man now rushed to his appointed post. ὅ τι ἦν, the imperfect indicative is here used in an indirect questisn instead of the normal present indicative or optative: 'they (lit. 'it', i.e. the blockading garrison) did not know what the danger was', followed by a causal genitive absolute, 'because the night was dark and there was a storm (raging)'. οἱ . . . ὑπολελειμμένοι, 'those of the Plataeans who had been left . . .'. ἐκ τοὐμπαλιν (=τοῦ ἔμπαλιν, the article making the adverb into an adjective), 'on the side opposite to the one where . . .': the fugitives escaped from the north-east corner of the city while a demonstration was being made on the south-eastern side, from which was the direct road to Athens; the Peloponnesians naturally thought that they had gone in that direction immediately. ὅπως . . . ἔχοιεν, 'so that the enemy should pay less (lit. 'least') attention to the fugitives'. We might expect οἱ ἑαυτῶν (or σφῶν)) ἄνδρες instead of οἱ ἄνδρες αὐτῶν, since 'the Plataeans' are the subject of προσέβαλον.

6. κατὰ χώραν μένοντες, 'remaining at their posts', on the wall. ἑαυτῶν, plural, referring to the subject of ἐθορυβοῦντο, though the nearest subject is οὐδείς: 'no one ventured to bring help from his own station'. ἐν ἀπόρῳ . . . τὸ γιγνόμενον, 'they were unable (lit. 'were in a difficulty') to guess what was happening'.

7. οἷς . . . δέοι, 'to whom orders had been given to bring aid if any need should arise'; this is the first mention of a mobile reserve of 300 men who were posted outside the wall in case of emergency; 'when they heard the alarm' (πρὸς τὴν βοήν) they hastened to the south-east corner of the town to prevent the supposed escape in the direction of Athens, or to meet a relieving force from Athens, without waiting to hear what had actually happened from the sentries on the wall who had raised the alarm. φρυκτοί . . . πολέμιοι, 'fire-signals to show an enemy attack were raised (to give the alarm) to Thebes', eight miles away to the north.

8. οἱ . . . Πλαταιῆς, 'the Plataeans in the city also'; ἐκ is used here in the same sense as in §4. πρότερον . . . τοῦτο, 'which had been previously prepared for this very purpose'. ᾗ . . . βοηθοῖεν, the change of mood from the subjunctive to the optative in this purpose clause, and the change of subject (from σημεῖα to πολέμιοι understood) is apparently made only for the sake of variety. ἄλλο τι . . . τὸ ὄν, 'thinking that what was going on was different from what was (really) happening'. πρίν is here used with

the optative (instead of the infinitive) because the sentence contains a negative, μὴ βοηθοῖεν: 'until their comrades who were getting away should make good their escape and reach safety'.

17

1. This is a long and involved sentence which can be taken in more than one way, though the meaning is the same however it is taken; Thucydides perhaps did not revise it, because κλίμακας προσθέντες occurs twice and πλείους is used in two different senses. The simplest solution seems to be that οἱ ὑπερβαίνοντες τῶν Πλαταιῶν is the original subject, which has no main verb of its own but is followed by a parenthesis from ὡς οἱ πρῶτοι down to ἄνδρας πλείους, and is then divided into οἱ μὲν . . . εἶργον βάλλοντες and οἱ δ' ἐν τούτῳ . . . ὑπερέβαινον. We can split it up into shorter sentences by taking οἱ ὑπερβαίνοντες as a genitive, omitting ὡς ('when'), and making some of the participles into main verbs, e.g. 'meanwhile of the Plateans who were climbing the walls the first party had gone up and . . . had got possession of each of the towers, and taking their stand there they were themselves guarding the passages to prevent anyone from coming through them to bring help. They were both setting up ladders from the wall against the towers and getting several men up (to the top). Some of them were keeping away from the towers the enemy who were bringing help against them by shooting at them both from below (i.e. from the δίοδοι of the towers) and from above (i.e. from the top of the towers); meanwhile the others, the main body (οἱ πλείους), . . . were crossing over at the space between the towers'. μηδένα δι' αὐτῶν ἐπιβοηθεῖν is equivalent to a purpose clause, which could also be expressed by τοῦ μηδένα . . . ἐπιβοηθεῖν. There must have been an inner stairway in each tower, from the ground to the top of the wall and from there to the top of the tower; if the Plataeans blocked the passage-ways through the two towers the Peloponnesians would not be able to get out on to the wall to oppose the escapers who were crossing between the two towers. The Plataeans needed two sets of ladders, one to climb from the ground to the top of the wall (προσθέντες κλίμακας, near the end of the sentence), and the other to climb from the top of the wall to the top of the towers (κλίμακας . . . τοῖς πύργοις) in case the inner stairs were too well defended; some of the ladders might also be needed for them to get to the ground on the other side, unless they brought ropes for this purpose.

2. ὁ διακομιζόμενος αἰεί, 'each man as he got across', lit. 'he who was being continually taken over'. ἐπὶ τοῦ χείλους i.e. on the inner edge of the outer ditch (13, 1 and 16, 1). Notice the change of number from ἵστατο to ἐτόξευόν τε καὶ ἠκόντιζον. εἴ τις. . . . διαβάσεως, 'whenever anyone came along (outside) the wall to help and tried to prevent the Plataeans from crossing (the wall)', lit. 'became a hinderer of the crossing'; this refers to any of the Peloponnesians encamped outside the blockading walls, who came on the scene before the arrival of the 300 men of the mobile reserve.

3. οἱ ἀπὸ τῶν πύργων . . . καταβαίνοντες, 'the men on (lit. 'from', as in 16, 4) the towers came down, the last ones with difficulty, and . . .'. ἐν τούτῳ, 'meanwhile'. οἱ τριακόσιοι, the mobile reserve mentioned in 16, 7, who had at first run in the wrong direction.

4. ἑώρων . . . σκότους, 'saw them more clearly out of the darkness'. ἐς τὰ γυμνά, 'on their unprotected side', i.e. the right side, which was not protected by a shield. ἐν τῷ ἀφανεῖ, 'in the darkness', because the torches held by the 300 Peloponnesians only revealed them to the Plataeans but cast no light upon the escapers. φθάνουσι . . . τάφρον, 'even the last of the Plataeans crossed the ditch in time', lit. 'anticipated (the enemy) crossing . . .', historic present. χαλεπῶς δὲ καὶ βιαίως, 'but with difficulty and being hard pressed', or 'under pressure'. There must have been bridges, under a strong guard, placed at intervals to allow the besiegers to cross the outer ditch when necessary, but the escapers of course had to wade or swim across.

5. τε γὰρ . . . καί, 'for both . . . and . . .'. οὐ βέβαιος . . . ἐπελθεῖν, 'not strong enough for them to walk upon it'. οἷος . . . μᾶλλον, 'it was just about to thaw (lit. 'more watery), as when there is an east wind'; ἀπηλιώτου is genitive absolute with ὄντος understood; the participle is rarely omitted in a genitive absolute. ἡ νύξ . . . ἐπεποιήκει, 'the night being snowy with the wind from that direction (lit. 'with such a wind') had made the water deep'. The water in the outer ditch was much deeper than in the inner one because of the snow that melted on the northern slopes of Cithaeron, swelled the mountain streams, and filled up the ditch that surrounded the Peloponnesians' blockading wall: hence μόλις ὑπερέχοντες, 'keeping their heads above the water with difficulty'. αὐτοῖς, dative of advantage, sometimes almost equivalent to a possessive genitive: 'their escape also (i.e. as well as the difficulty of the crossing) was brought about mainly (lit. 'more') owing to the . . .'.

1. τὴν ... ὁδόν, 'on the road that led ...'; this accusative of space traversed occurs five times in this chapter. Thebes was about eight miles north-north-east of Plataea, and the shrine of Androcrates, a Plataean hero worshipped as a demi-god, was about two miles north-east of the city. All roads leading out of Plataea would be blocked by the Peloponnesians, so that after crossing the encircling wall and the outer ditch the fugitives must have gone for a short distance across country, keeping the road to the shrine on their right but not going as far as the shrine itself. When they were past the blockading lines they turned to the left on to the main road to Thebes, travelled along it for about three-quarters of a mile, and then turned south-east towards Erythrae and Hysiae, crossed Cithaeron, and came safely to Athens, about 30 miles away. Meanwhile the pursuers had gone straight along the road to the mountain-pass of Oak's Heads and on failing to find the fugitives had returned to Plataea before the escapers began to approach Cithaeron. The fugitives therefore crossed the road from Plataea to Erythrae some time after the pursuers had returned along it. We do not know whether the Plataeans crossed Cithaeron to the east or the west of the Oak's Heads pass; in the map they are shown crossing by the nearer route, to the west of the pass. αὐτούς is the subject of ἂν ὑποτοπῆσαι and refers to the Peloponnesians, and σφᾶς is the subject of τραπέσθαι and refers to the Plataeans: 'thinking that the enemy would be most unlikely to suspect (lit. 'would least suspect') that they had taken (lit. 'turned along') the road that led ...'; ἂν ὑποτοπῆσαι represents in indirect speech the aorist optative with ἄν of direct speech, and φέρουσαν must be supplied with τὴν ἐς τοὺς πολεμίους . διώοντας has no object: 'they saw the Peloponnesians pursuing on the road that leads to ... and then on to Athens'. The long mountain range of Cithaeron, 4623 feet high at the summit, separates Boeotia on the north from Attica on the south and is crossed by two passes; one of them, still called 'Oak's Heads', leads to Athens, for which the pursuers naturally thought the Plataeans were immediately making.

2. ὑποστρέψαντες ... τῶν ὁρῶν, 'turning off (to the right) they went along the way leading to the mountain, towards Erythrae ..., and taking to (λαβόμενοι) the hills. ..'. ἀπὸ πλειόνων, 'out of a larger number'; about 220 started out (14, 2). εἰσὶ ... οἵ, 'some of them'; this is a fixed phrase which retains the present tense even in past time, lit. 'there are some of

them who . . .'. πρὶν ὑπερβαίνειν, 'before trying to climb the wall'. εἷς τοξότης, 'one, an archer'. ἐπὶ τῇ ἔξω ἐτάφρῳ, 'at the outer ditch'; the article makes ἔξω into an adjective.

3. κατὰ χώραν . . . παυσάμενοι, 'gave up the pursuit and went back to their posts', lit. 'having ceased from help were in their position'. οἱ ἐκ τῆς πόλεως Πλαταιῆς again means 'the Plataeans in the city', as in 16, 4 and 8; the idea of motion from the city comes in κήρυκα ἐκπέμψαντες. τῶν . . . ἀπαγγειλάντων, 'when those who had turned back reported to them that . . .'. ἐσπένδοντο . . . νεκροῖς, 'began to ask for a truce to pick up their dead'; see the note on 5, 1. ἐπαύσαντο, 'stopped making this request'.

19

1. ὑπὸ . . . τούτου, 'at about the same time during this summer', of 427. καὶ οἱ Πλαταιῆς, 'the Plataeans also'; in the preceding chapter (III, 51, not included here) Thucydides has been describing the capture by the Athenians of the island of Minoa, opposite Megara; he now goes on to describe the capture of Plataea by the Peloponnesians. πολιορκεῖσθαι, 'to endure a siege'. τοιῷδε τρόπῳ, 'in the following manner'.

2. The subject of προσέβαλλον (notice the absence of μέν and of a connecting particle) is of course 'the Peloponnesians', and οἱ δέ should be translated as 'and the Plataeans'. εἰρημένον . . . αὐτῷ, 'he had received orders from Lacedaemon to this effect', i.e. not to use force, although the besiegers had tried to storm the city in 429. εἰ . . . .'Ἀθηναίοις, 'if peace should ever be made with (lit. 'towards') the Athenians'. ὅσα . . . προσχωρησάντων, 'that the places that each side possessed (having captured them) in the war should be given back, Plataea should not have to be restored on the ground that they (the Plataeans) had willingly gone over (to the Lacedaemonians)'; they therefore wanted the city to surrender voluntarily. ὡς . . . προσχωρησάντων, the genitive absolute with ὡς gives the 'alleged' reason that would be put forward. λέγοντα, we should translate this as 'to say'; Thucydides sometimes uses the present, sometimes the future, participle in such a sentence; in 4, 5 he has λέγοντες. The verb in the apodosis (main clause) of the conditional sentence of which εἰ . . . χρήσασθαι is the protasis ('if'-clause) is κολάσειν, which is indirect statement depending on λέγοντα, though an ὅτι-clause is more usual with verbs of saying; τε and δέ are parallel to one another, but τε can be omitted: 'if the Plataeans were willing . . . and to submit

to their judgment (lit. 'to use them as judges'), the Lacedaemonians would punish the guilty but no one unjustly'.

3. Notice that μέν is again used without a connecting particle (οὖν, γάρ, or δή); οἱ δέ, 'the Plataeans'. ἐν τῷ ἀσθενεστάτῳ, 'in the last stage of weakness'. ἔτρεφον, 'supplied them with food'. ἡμέρας τινάς, accusative of duration of time. ἐν ὅσῳ, 'until', lit. 'during which time'. οἱ . . . ἄνδρες, 'the judges from Lacedaemon, five in number'; we should omit ἄνδρες.

4. ἠρώτων . . . εἰσίν, 'they summoned them and asked them this one question (lit. 'so much alone'), whether they had done any good service to . . . in the present war'; εἰ here introduces an indirect question, and εἰργασμένοι εἰσίν takes two accusatives.

5. οἱ δ' . . . εἰπεῖν, 'they replied with the request that they should be allowed to speak at greater length', lit. 'they said having requested to speak . . .'. σφῶν αὐτῶν (= ἑαυτῶν) is governed by the προ- in προτάξαντες: 'having appointed as advocates for themselves', or it may be partitive genitive, 'having appointed from among themselves . . .'. A πρόξενος was the representative in his own city of members of a foreign state, like a modern consul, whose duty was to entertain visitors from that state and act as spokesman for it if necessity arose; for the more specialized duties of a πρόξενος at Delphi, see the note on Ion, 153. Aieimnestus had commanded the Plataean contingent that fought as allies of the Athenians at Marathon in 490 and as allies of the Lacedaemonians and Athenians at Plataea in 479: in both battles the invading Persians were defeated: Aieimnestus perhaps named his son Lacon, 'the Lacedaemonian', because of this old connection with the Spartans. The article with a proper name in the genitive case means as usual 'the son of . . .'. ἐπελθόντες, 'coming forward', at the conference; this word and the second ἔλεγον in the sentence refer only to the two spokesmen.

20

1. ἀποβλέψατε, aorist imperative. The γάρ can be omitted in translation. ἀποθανόντας, used as the normal passive of ἀποκτείνω. ἐν τῇ ἡμετέρᾳ, supply γῇ. κατὰ ἔτος ἕκαστον, 'every year', on the anniversary of the Battle of Plataea (479). ἐσθήμασι, these garments were probably burned as offerings to the dead. ὅσα . . . ἐπιφέροντας, 'and offering the first-fruits of everything that (ὅσα) our land produced in due season'. Supply ὄντες with εὔνοι: 'being friendly people (offering them) from a friendly land'.

ὁμαίχμοις ποτὲ γενομένοις, 'to those who were once our comrades in arms'. μὴ γνόντες (from γιγνώσκω) is equivalent to εἰ μὴ γνοίτε: 'if you were to make an unjust decision (lit. 'having decided not rightly'), you would be doing the very opposite of this', i.e. your conduct towards the dead Spartans would be the exact opposite of ours.

2. σκέψασθέ τε, 'and so reflect'; τε at the beginning of a new sentence often has this meaning in Thucydides; see also 21, 1. Pausanias was the Spartan regent in command of the allied forces at the Battle of Plataea (6, 2, and note). νομίζων . . τοιούτοις, 'thinking that he was laying them in friendly soil and among friendly (lit. 'such') people'. τὴν Πλαταιΐδα, the article shows that this is the object and that Θηβαΐδα is the complement: 'if you make the land of Plataea into Theban territory'. τί ἄλλο ἢ . . . καταλείψετε, lit. 'what else (will you be doing) than leaving . . .', which is equivalent to an ἆρ' οὐ question: 'will you not be leaving in a hostile (land) and amongst their murderers your fathers . . . deprived of the honours that they now possess?' The Thebans are called the murderers of the Lacedaemonians because at that time they sided with the Persian invaders against their fellow Greeks, including the Lacedaemonians whose allies they now were. ὧν, an example of what is called 'relative attraction', whereby the relative pronoun is drawn out of its correct case, ἅ, to agrees with its antecedent, γερῶν. πρὸς δὲ καί, 'and in addition also'; πρός is an adverb. ἐρημοῦτε, this present indicative among several future tenses is strange: 'you are making desolate the temples of the gods to whom they prayed before they defeated the Persians', lit. 'to whom having prayed they defeated . . .'. θυσίας. . . ἀφαιρήσεσθε, 'you will be taking away their hereditary sacrifices from those who founded and established them', i.e. from the Plataeans, many of whom were now in safety at Athens and hoped to return eventually to their native city.

21

1. τε, 'and so', as in 20, 2. πρέπον, supply ἐστί: 'as befits us and as necessity compels us'. αἰτούμεθα ὑμᾶς πεῖσαι τάδε, 'we beg you to let us persuade you in this'; ἡμᾶς must be understood as the subject of πεῖσαι, lit. 'that we should persuade (you)', with τάδε adverbial accusative. ὅρκους οὓς ὤμοσαν, for this 'cognate' accusative see the note on the same phrase in 8, 2. ἱκέται . . . τάφων, 'we become suppliants at (lit. 'of') the

tombs of your fathers'; πατρῴων is an adjective. ἐπικαλούμεθα ...
παραδοθῆναι, 'we beseech the dead (lit. 'those who have finished their
labours') that we should not become subject to (ὑπό) the Thebans and
that we who were their dearest friends (i.e. the dearest friends of the dead
Lacedaemonians) should not be handed over to those who were then
their bitterest foes', because the Thebans fought at Plataea as allies of
the Persians against the Lacedaemonians. ἀναμιμνήσκομεν, supply ὑμᾶς
as the object: 'we remind you of that day ...'. ᾗ ... ἐν τῇδε, the
relative clause has only a participle, πράξαντες, but no finite verb, for
κινδυνεύομεν is in the sentence beginning νῦν ἐν τῇδε; grammatically
πράξαντες would be ἐπράξαμεν, followed by νῦν δέ: 'upon which we did
most glorious deeds with them, but now upon this day we are in danger
of suffering the most terrible fate'.

2. This long sentence can be split up into several shorter sentences,
e.g. ὅπερ ... μετ' αὐτοῦ, with 'we are doing' understood as a main verb;
παυόμενοι ... ἑλέσθαι; ἐπισκήπτομεν ... παραδοθῆναι; and γενέσθαι ...
διολέσαι, with ἐπισκήπτομεν repeated as the verb. ὅπερ ... μετ' αὐτοῦ
'we are doing what is necessary and most difficult for men in our
position (τοῖς ὧδε ἔχουσι) to do, that is, to put an end to our
arguments (λόγου), because danger to our lives also (is) close at hand
with this ending', lit. 'with it'. παυόμενοι λέγομεν, 'in conclusion we say'.
εἱλόμεθα ... τελευτῆσαι, 'we should have chosen in preference to this to
die of starvation, the most horrible of deaths'. ὑμῖν ... προσήλθομεν,
'we trusted you and surrendered to you', not to the Thebans. δίκαιον ...
ἑλέσθαι, '(it is) just that, if we fail to convince you, you should restore us
to the same (position as before) and allow us to choose ourselves the danger
that may befall us'; the present indicative is used in the conditional clause
εἰ μὴ πείθομεν instead of ἐάν with the subjunctive in a future
condition, and ὑμᾶς must be supplied as the subject of καταστήσαντας
ἑλέσθαι.

3. μή, to be taken with παραδοθῆναι: 'we, the Plataeans, who were then
(γενόμενοι) most eager to help the Greeks (lit. 'with regard to the
Greeks'), beg as suppliants that we should not be given up to ... out
of your hands and out of your good faith'; ὄντες, which occurs twice in
this sentence, need not be translated (lit. 'being'). γενέσθαι ... ἡμῶν,
supply ὑμᾶς as the object of ἐπισκήπτομεν, which can be repeated in
English to make this a separate sentence: 'we beg you to be our saviours
and not, while freeing ... , to destroy us'.

22

1. The long sentence from οἱ δέ down to ἐποιήσαντο οὐδένα can also be split up into shorter sentences by making some of the participles into main verbs, e.g. οἱ δὲ ... πεπόνθασι, with νομίζοντες taken as though it were ἐνόμιζον; διότι... ἐδέξαντο, with διότι translated as 'for'; ἡγούμενοι ... πεποιθέναι, with ἡγούμενοι taken as though it were ἡγοῦντο; and αὖθις ... οὐδένα. νομίζοντες ... ἕξειν 'thought that the question whether they had received any benefit (lit. 'had suffered anything good') ... would be a fair one for them (to ask'); an adverb with ἔχειν is often equivalent to the corresponding adjective with εἶναι, so that ὀρθῶς ἕξειν is the same as ὀρθὸν ἔσεσθαι. This test question was first asked, in a different form, in 19, 4; the answer was bound to be 'no', unless the Plataeans had been traitors to their own city. τόν τε ... καὶ ὅτε, 'both at other times (lit. 'during the other time') ... and afterwards when ... .'. δῆθεν implies that Thucydides did not regard the argument as being justified: 'because, as they said (δῆθεν), they had requested (ἠξίουν) the Plataeans to remain neutral in accordance with the old treaty made by (lit. 'of') Pausanias after the (defeat of the) Persians', at Plataea in 479; τὸν Μῆδον is collective singular. Pausanias granted the Plataeans independence for ever because of their gallantry in the battle (6, 2–4), but apparently he said nothing about their having to remain neutral in any future war among the Greek cities. ὅτε ... ἐκεῖνα, 'afterwards, when the Plataeans had not accepted (the proposals) which the Lacedaemonians offered to them before the city was blockaded, that they should be neutral (κοινούς) according to those (terms)'; this offer was made by Archidamus in 7, 1. ἡγούμενοι ... πεπονθέναι, 'for they thought that they had been released from the treaty (i.e. the treaty of Pausanias to let the Plataeans remain independent) because of their own just intentions and that they had already been treated badly by them'; they had intended to keep the treaty honestly, but the actions of the Plataeans in defending themselves against attack had made this impossible: what would Pausanias have thought of such an argument? τὸ αὐτὸ ... ἐρωτῶντες, the order of words is strange, for τὸ αὐτό is the object of ἐρωτῶντες and must be taken immediately after it; 'bringing each man forward again in turn and asking him the same question, whether ...'. ὁπότε μὴ φαῖεν, 'whenever they said "no"'. From ἀπάγοντες to ἐποιήσαντο the present participles and the imperfect indicative represent repeated

actions, and the aorist participle and aorist indicatives single actions, but we cannot easily bring out the difference in English. ἐξαίρετον . . . οὐδένα, 'they made no exceptions , or 'excepted nobody'.

2. διακοσίων, genitive of comparison: 'no fewer than 200 of the Plataeans themselves'; the numbers at the beginning of the siege (13, 3) were 400 Plataeans, 80 Athenians, and 120 women to make bread (they were already slaves, and were now sold to new owners). Of the 220 who left the city (14, 2) 212 escaped (18, 2), seven turned back and one was captured. At least 200 Plataeans and 25 Athenians were now executed, so that about 43 men were killed during the siege.

3. ἐνιαυτόν τινα, 'for about a year'. Μεγαρέων . . . ἐκπεπτωκόσι 'to some of the Megarians who had been driven out in a revolution'; ἐκπίπτειν is regularly used as the passive of ἐκβάλλειν. ὅσοι . . . περιῆσαν, 'to those of the Plataeans who (lit. 'as many of . . . as') supported their cause and were still alive'; these Plataean traitors had probably taken refuge at Thebes when their city was first attacked in 431; a pro-Theban party is mentioned in 1, 2. ἐνοικεῖν is infinitive of purpose after a verb of giving: 'for them to live in': the subject of ἔδοσαν is 'the Lacedaemonians'. ἐκ τῶν θεμελίων, either with καθελόντες, 'razing it all to the ground to (lit. 'from') its very foundations', or with ᾠκοδόμησαν, 'they built on its foundations'. πρός, 'near'; the inn was intended to house worshippers at the shrine of Hera, which was outside the city and may have been replaced by the new temple now built. διακοσίων . . . πανταχῇ, '200 feet square', lit. 'of 200 feet each way'. πανταχῇ may go with κύκλῳ, 'having rooms all round it', which were in two storeys (κάτωθεν καὶ ἄνωθεν), for the worshippers to sleep in. τοῖς ἄλλοις, with κατασκευάσαντες: 'making couches from the other materials, copper and iron, that were inside the walls'; grammatically ἔπιπλα, with χαλκός and σίδηρος in apposition, should be in the dative case with τοῖς ἄλλοις as the antecedent of ἅ, but they are put inside the relative clause in the nominative case. The couches were perhaps to be used by the worshippers. αὐτῇ, 'for her', i.e. for the goddess. ἐπὶ δέκα ἔτη, 'on a ten years' lease'.

4. σχέδον. . . ἔνεκα, 'it was indeed (καί) almost entirely for the sake of the Thebans that the Lacedaemonians were so bitterly hostile to (lit. 'about') the Plataeans'. ἐς τὸν . . . καθιστάμενον, 'in the war that had then just begun' in 431; αὐτούς is misplaced and should be taken after νομίζοντες.

5. τὰ κατὰ . . . ἐτελεύτησε, 'such was the end of Plataea', lit. 'affairs

at Plataea thus came to an end'. ἐπειδή, 'since the time when': Thucy-dides' dating puts the first alliance of Plataea with Athens in 519, but it was probably ten years later; possibly there is an error in the numerical symbols in the manuscript, so that the sign for ὀγδοηκοστῷ, 'eightieth', was changed into the sign for ἐνενηκοστῷ, 'ninetieth'. The δέ that corresponds to μέν in τὰ μέν comes at the beginning of the next chapter, which is not included in this book.

Vocabulary

ABBREVIATIONS

also pl. means that the word is sometimes used in the plural with a singular meaning.

The future of all verbs is given, but not the other parts if they are of regular formation. The other parts of irregular verbs are given only when they occur in this book.

a, ι, υ are short except when marked long; but in the 1st declension a final -α preceded by ε, ι, ρ is generally long, and -ας in the genitive singular is always long; these long vowels are not marked.

I have tried to include all the words contained in this book, and also all Homeric forms, but if I have missed any (which is very easily done) I apologise.

A

ἆ, *interj.*, alas.

ἀάατος, *-ον*, terrible.

ἀάω, *aor.*, ἄασα, ἀάσθην, infatuate.

ἀγαγεῖν, *aor. infin. of* ἄγω

ἀγαθός, *-ά, -όν*, good, beneficial; *n.*, ἀγαθόν, a good service.

ἀγακλειτός, *-ή, -όν*, renowned.

ἀγακλυτός, *-όν*, famous.

ἀγαπάζομαι, *-άσομαι* love; *part.*, ἀγαπαζόμενος, lovingly.

ἀγαπάω, *-ήσω*, be satisfied.

ἀγαυός, *-ή, -όν*, proud.

ἀγγελία, *-ας, f.*, news, message.

ἀγγέλλω, -ελῶ, ἤγγειλα, -ελκα, -ελμαι, -ἐλθην announce, bring news.

ἄγγελος, -ου, m., messenger.

ἄγγος, ἄγγους, n., cradle, chest.

ἀγήνωρ, -ορος, proud.

ἅγιος, -α, -ον, H. fem., -η, sacred.

ἀγκαλη, -ης, f., arm.

ἀγκυλομήτης, -ου, H. gen., -τέω, of cunning counsel.

ἀγκύλος, -η, -ον, curved.

'Αγλαυρίς, -ίδος, f., an Aglaurid, a daughter of Aglaurus and Cecrops.

ἀγνώς, -ῶτος, m. or f., unknown.

ἀγορά, -ᾶς, f., market-place.

ἄγρει, imperat. used as interj., come now.

ἄγροικος, -ον, rustic; m., yokel.

ἀγρός, -οῦ, m., field; pl., country-side; ἀγρόνδε, to the fields.

ἄγχι, adv. with gen., near.

ἄγω, ἄξω, ἤγαγον or ἦξα, ἤγμαι, ἤχθην, bring, lead; ἄγε, ἄγετε imperat. used as interj., come, come now.

ἀγών, ἀγῶνος, m., trial.

ἀγώνισμα, -ατος, n., plea.

ἀδελφός, -οῦ, m., brother

ἄδην, adv. with gen., enough.

Ἅιδης, -ου, m., Hades, the Underworld.

ἀδικέω, -ήσω, harm, wrong, treat unjustly.

ἀδίκημα, -ματος, n., wrong; as the result of a wrong.

ἀδικία, -ας, f., wrong, injustice.

ἄδικος, -ον, unjust; οἱ ἄδικοι, the guilty; adv., ἀδίκως, unjustly.

ἀδύνατος, -ον, impossible; ἀδύνατά ἐστι, it is impossible.

ἀέθλια, -ων, n. pl., weapons for a contest, war-weapons.

ἄεθλον, -ον, n., prize, contest.

ἀεί, adv., always, continually, from time to time,

ἀείδω, ἀείσομαι, ἤεισα, H., ἄεισα, sing.

ἄειραν, H. for ἦραν, aor. of αἴρω, lift, raise.

ἄεισε, H. for ἤεισε, aor. of ἀείδω.

ἀέκων, -ουσα, -ον, H. for ἄκων, against one's will.

ἀέλπτος, -ον, unhoped for.

ἀεσίφρων, -φρονος, witless, foolish.

'Αθάνα, -ας, H., 'Αθήνη, -ης, the goddess Athena.

ἀθάνατος, -ον, immortal; m. pl., the gods.

'Αθῆναι, -ῶν, f., pl., Athens.

'Αθηναῖος, -α, -ον, Athenian; m. pl., the Athenians.

ἄθλιος, -α, -ον, wretched; n. pl., griefs, woes; adv., ἀθλίως, miserably.

ἀθρόος, -α, -ον, together, in one body.

ἀθύρω, play; part., ἀθύρων, in play.

αἴ, H. conj. for εἰ, if; αἴ κε, H. for ἐάν; αἴ γάρ, would that, O that.

αἰάζω, -άξω, wail, utter cries.

αἰγίς, -ίδος f., aegis, the shield of Athena, made from the skin of the Gorgon's breast.

αἰεί = ἀεί, adv., always, continually.

Αἰείμνηστος, -ου, m., Aieimnestus, a

famous Plataean general, father of Lacon, Plataean spokesman to the Spartans.

αἴθουσα, -ης, f., colonnade.

αἴθοψ, -οπος, gleaming.

αἷμα, -ματος, n., blood.

αἱμάσσω, -αξω, ἥμαξα, stain with blood.

αἴνιγμα, -ματος, n., riddle, riddling answer.

Αἶνος, -ου, m., Aenus, a town in Thrace at the mouth of the Hebrus.

αἶνος, -ου, m., praise.

αἴνομαι, H. imperf., αἴνυτο, take.

αἴξ, αἰγός, c., goat.

Αἴολος, -ου, m., Aeolus, son of Zeus and ancestor of Xuthus.

αἰπόλιον, -ου, n., herd of goats.

αἰπόλος, -ου, m., goatherd.

αἴρεσις, -εως, f., method of capturing

αἱρέω, -ήσω, εἷλον, H., ἕλον, H. imperf., ἥρεε, ἥρηκα, ἥρημαι, ἡρέθην, take, capture; mid., take, choose.

αἴρω, ἀρῶ, ἦρα, ἦρκα, ἦρμαι, ἤρθην, imperf. pass., ἠρόμην, raise, lift; mid. and pass., be raised, rise; aor. part. mid., ἀράμενος, having faced.

αἰσθάνομαι, -θήσομαι, ἠσθόμην, perceive, see.

αἴσθησις, -εως, f., perception, notice; αἴσθησιν ποιεῖν, give an indication; αἴσθησιν παρέχειν, reveal.

αἴσιμος, -η, -ον, right, moderate.

αἰσίως, adv., happily, successfully.

αἴσσω, ἀΐξω, ἦξα, rush, be eager for.

αἰσχρός, -ά, -όν, shameful, horrible; superl., αἴσχιστος.

αἰσχύνη, -ης, f., shame, shameful death.

αἰσχύνω, -υνῶ, ἤσχυνα, disgrace; mid., be ashamed of.

αἰτέω, -ήσω, ἤτησα, also mid., request, ask for, beg.

αἰτία, -ας, f., charge, accusation, cause.

αἰτίασις, -εως, f., charge, accusation.

αἰτιάομαι, -άσομαι, ᾐτιᾱσάμην, accuse.

αἴτιος, -α, -ον, suggester of, responsible for, with gen.

ἀκάματος, -η, -ον, unwearying, never-resting.

ἀκέλευστος, -ον, unbidden.

ἀκεστός, -ή, -όν, remediable, able to be put right.

ἀκεσφόρος, -ον, capable of healing, with gen.

ἀκέων, also ἀκήν, adv., in silence.

ἀκήρατος, -ον, fresh, pure.

ἄκικυς, -υος, weak, feeble.

ἀκοή -ῆς, f., hearsay, report.

ἀκοίτης, -ου, m., husband.

ἄκοιτις, -ιος, f., wife.

ἀκόλουθος, -ου, m., servant, attendant.

ἀκομιστία, -ίας, H., -ίη, -ίης, needy fare.

ἀκοντίζω, -ίσω, ἠκόντισα, throw javelins.

ἀκόντιον, -ου, n., javelin.

ἄκουσα, H. for ἤκουσα, from ἀκούω.

ἀκούσιος, -ον, involuntary.

ἀκούω, -σω, ἤκουσα, H., ἄκουσα, hear, listen to.

ἀκρίβεια, -ας, f., certainty, exact truth.

ἀκρίβῶς, adv., accurately, in detail, fully.

ἄκριτος, -ον, without trial.

ἀκτή, -ῆς, f., shore.

ἄκων, ἄκοντος, m., javelin.

ἀλάομαι, perf., ἀλάλημαι, wander.

ἄλγος, ἄλγους, n., grief, sorrow.

ἄλη, -ης, f., wanderings.

ἀλήθεια, -ας, H., -είη, -ης, f., truth.

ἀληθής, -ές, true, correct; τὸ ἀληθές or τἀληθές, gen. τἀληθοῦς, the truth; adv., ἀληθῶς, truly.

ἀλήτης, -ου, m., wanderer.

ἀλίσκομαι, ἀλώσομαι, ἑάλων, opt., ἀλοίην, be taken, be convicted.

ἄλκιμος, -η, -ον, strong, mighty.

ἀλκτήρ, -ῆρος, m., protector against, with gen.

ἀλλά, conj., but; ἀλλὰ γάρ but, you will say.

ἄλλη, adv., elsewhere.

ἀλλήλους, -ας, -α, H. dat. dual, ἀλλήλοιιν, each other, one another; πρὸς ἄλληλα, together.

ἄλλοθι, adv., in another place, anywhere.

ἄλλομαι, ἀλοῦμαι, ἡλάμην, H. aor., ἄλτο, leap, spring, hurry, rush.

ἄλλος, -η, -ο, H. f. dat. pl. ἄλλησι, other, another; with ἤ, different from; ὁ ἄλλος the rest; ἄλλοι ἄλλη, different people at different places; adv., ἄλλως otherwise,

merely, only; ἄλλως τε καί, especially.

ἀλοίην, aor. opt. of ἀλίσκομαι

ἀλοιφή, -ῆς, f., lard, grease.

ἄλοχος, -ου, f., wife.

ἄλτο, H. 3rd sing. aor. of ἄλλομαι.

ἄλυσις, -εως, f., chain.

ἄλωσις, -εως, f., capture.

ἅμα, adv., at the same time; prep. with dat., at the same time as, together with.

ἄμαξα, -ης, f., wagon.

ἁμαρτάνω, -τήσομαι, ἥμαρτον, H., ἥμβροτον, be wrong, miscalculate; with gen., miss.

ἁμάρτημα, -ματος, n., mistake.

ἁμαρτία, -ας, f., sin, crime, error.

ἀμέγαρτος, -ον, wretched.

ἀμείβομαι, ἀμείψομαι, answer.

ἀμείνων, -ον, comp. of ἀγαθός, better; adv., ἄμεινον, better.

ἀμέρδομαι, H. 2nd sing., ἀμέρδεαι, lack a share of, with gen.

'Αμμέας, -ου m., Ammeas, son of Coroebus, a Plataean leader.

ἀμνημονέω, -ήσω, forget, with gen.

ἄμουσος, -ον, boorish, ill-mannered.

ἀμύμων, -ονος, excellent.

ἀμύνω, ἀμυνῶ, ἤμυνα, H. aor. infin., ἀμύνέμεν, defend, with dat.; mid., resist, defend oneself (against).

ἀμφέθετο, aor. mid., ἀμφέθηκε, aor. act., of ἀμφιτίθημι.

ἀμφήκης, -ες, two-edged.

ἀμφί, prep. with acc. or gen., around, among, upon; with dat., around; adv., round about.

ἀμφίαλος, -ον, sea-girt.

ἀμφιβάλλω, -βαλῶ, ἀμφέβαλον, H., ἀμφίβαλον, place round, grasp.

ἀμφίβολος, -ον, open to attack on both sides.

ἀμφιέλισσα, -ης, f. adj., curved at both ends.

ἀμφίπολος, -ου, c., attendant, servant, maid; ἀμφίπολοι γυναῖκες, women servants.

ἀμφιπτυχή, -ῆς, f., also pl., embrace.

ἀμφιτίθημι, -θήσω, ἀμφέθηκα, -εθέμην, put round, put round the neck of, with acc. and dat.

ἀμφότεροι, -αι, -α, both, both sides.

ἀμφοτέρωθεν, adv., from or on both sides.

ἄμφω, ἀμφοῖν, dual, both.

ἄν, particle used in a main conditional clause, would; in an indefinite clause, ever.

ἄν, = ἐάν, if.

ἀνά, prep. with acc., up, through, in.

ἀναβαίνω, -βήσομαι, ἀνέβην, ἀναβέβηκα, go up, climb up.

ἀναβοάω, -ήσομαι, ἀνεβόησα, shout.

ἀναγιγνώσκω, -γνώσομαι, ἀνέγνων, -έγνωκα, -εγνώσθην, know; read.

ἀναγκάζω, -άσω, compel, urge on.

ἀναγκαῖος, -α, ον, necessary; m.pl., relatives.

ἀνάγκη, -ης, f., necessity, compulsion.

ἀναγνωσθείς, aor. part. pass. of ἀναγιγνώσκω.

ἀνάγομαι, -άξομαι, ἀνηγαγόμην, -ήχθην, put out to sea.

ἀναδίδωμι, -δώσω, ἀνέδωκα, -εδόθην, yield, produce.

ἀνάδοτος, -ον, to be given up.

ἀναθεῖναι, aor. infin. of ἀνατίθημι.

ἀνάθημα, -ματος, n., offering, ornament (of a feast).

ἀναίρεσις, -εως, f., picking up, disposal.

ἀναιρέω, -ήσω, ἀνεῖλον, -ηρέθην, pick up, lift.

ἀναΐσσω, -αΐξω, -ήϊξα, part. ἀναΐξας, leap up.

ἀναίτιος, -ον, guiltless, innocent.

ἀνακαίω, -καύσω, ἀνέκαυσα, kindle.

ἀνακόπτω, -κόψω, shoot back (a bolt).

ἀνακράζω, -άξομαι, ἀνέκραγον, shout out, cry aloud.

ἀνάκτορον, -ου, n., temple, shrine, also pl.

ἀναλαμβάνω, -λήψομαι, ἀνέλαβον, retract, make amends for.

ἀναμιμνήσκω, ἀναμνήσω, ἀνέμνησα, remind of, with acc. and gen.

ἀνανεύω, -σω, throw back the head in dissent.

ἄναξ, ἄνακτος, m., king, prince, lord.

ἀναξύω, -ύσω, scrape up, smooth out.

ἀνάπαυλα, -ης, f., relief, shift, rest.

ἀναπτύσσω, -ύξω, open.

ἀναστρωφάω, -ήσω, turn (tr.).

ἀνατίθημι, -θήσω, ἀνέθηκα, dedicate, ascribe, assign.

ἀναφέρω, ἀνοίσω, ἀνήνεγκα or -ον, refer.

ἀναχωρέω, -ήσω, withdraw, retire.

ἀνδραποδίζω, -ίσω, sell as slaves.

ἀνδράποδον, -ου, n., slave

ἄνδρεσσι, H. dat. pl. of ἀνήρ.

'Ανδροκράτης, -ους, m., Androcrates, a Plataean hero or demi-god.

ἀνεβεβήκεσαν, plup., ἀνέβην, aor., of ἀναβαίνω.

ἀνέβραχεν, aor. (no present tense), roar.

ἀνέγνων, aor. act., ἀνεγνώσθην, aor. pass., of ἀναγιγνώσκω.

ἀνέθεσαν, aor. of ἀνατίθημι.

ἀνεῖπον, aor. (no present tense), proclaim.

ἀνέκραγον, aor. of ἀνακράζω,

ἀνελέσθαι, aor. mid. of ἀναιρέω.

ἀνέλκω, -έλξω, ἀνείλκυσα draw back, strain at.

ἀνέλπιστος, -ον, unexpected.

ἀνέμνησα, aor. of ἀναμιμνήσκω.

ἄνεμος, -ου, m., wind.

ἀνενεγκών, aor. part. of ἀναφέρω.

ἀνέστην, str. aor. of ἀνίστημι, stand up.

ἄνευ, prep. with gen., without.

ἀνεῳγμένος, p.p.p.; ἀνέῳξα, aor., of ἀνοίγνυμι.

ἀνέχομαι, -έξομαι, ἀνεσχόμην, endure, put up with.

ἀνῆκα, aor. of ἀνίημι.

ἀνήκεστος, -ον, irremediable, irrevocable.

ἀνήρ, ἀνδρός, gen. dual ἀνδροῖν; H. dat. pl. ἄνδρεσσι, m., man, husband, master; ἁνήρ, = ὁ ἀνήρ.

ἀνθέξομαι, fut. mid. of ἀντέχω.

ἄνθρωπος, -ου, dual, ἀνθρώπω, m., man; pl., people.

ἀνίημι, -ήσω, -ῆκα, send up.

ἀνίστημι, ἀναστήσω, ἀνέστησα, set up, make to stand; mid. and str. aor., ἀνέστην, -έστηκα, imperf.,

ἀνιστάμην, stand up.

ἀνιστορέω, -ήσω, question, ask.

ἀνοίγνυμι, -οίω, -έῳξα, -εῴγμαι, open; verbal adj. ἀνοικτέον, one must open; aor. part. pass., ἀνοιχθείς.

ἀνόσιος, -α, -ον, sinful.

ἄνοσος, -ον, harmless.

ἄνπερ, = ἐάνπερ.

ἄντα, adv., straight; prep. with gen., before.

ἀνταπόλλῡμι, -ολῶ, -ώλεσα, kill in exchange.

ἀντέχω, ἀνθέξω, ἄντεσχον, hold out, endure; mid. with gen., cling to.

ἀντί, prep. with gen., instead of, to serve as.

ἀντιάω, -άσω, meet with, obtain, with gen.

ἀντιβολέω, -ήσω, meet with, with gen.

ἀντίθεος, -ον, godlike, godly.

ἄντικρυς, adv., right through.

ἀντιλαμβάνομαι, -λήψομαι, ἀντελαβόμην, attain, reach, grasp (gen.).

'Αντίνοος, -ου, m., Antinous, the chief of Penelope's suitors.

ἀντίον, adv., in reply, opposite.

ἀντιπαταγέω, -ήσω, drown with its roar, roar against, with dat.

ἀντίπηξ, -πηγος, f., cradle, chest.

ἀντιτείχισμα, -ματος, n., counterwall.

ἀντοικτείρω, -ερῶ, ἀντῴκτειρα, pity in return.

ἄντρον, -ου, n., cave.

ἀνύτω, ἀνύσω, ἤνυσα, make, accomplish.

ἄνω, *adv.*, up.

ἄνωγα *perf. with pres. sense*, bid, order; *H. plup.*, ἀνώγει, he ordered.

ἄνωθεν, *adv.*, overhead, above, from above, upstairs.

ἀνώνυμος, -ον, nameless.

ἄξαι, *aor. infin. of* ἄγω.

ἄξιος, -α, -ον, worthy (of), *with gen.*; worthy to, *with infin.*

ἀξίωμα, -ματος, *n.*, reputation; reward.

ἀξιόω, -ώσω, request, demand, desire, deign, think it right.

ἄξω, ἄξομαι, *fut. of* ἄγω.

ἀοιδή, -ῆς, *f.*, singing, minstrelsy.

ἀπαγγέλλω, -ελῶ, ἀπήγγειλα, take a message, bring back news.

ἀπαγορεύω, ἀπερῶ, ἀπεῖπον, forbid; be tired.

ἀπάγω, -άξω, -ήγαγον, -ήχθην, lead away, arrest.

ἀπαιδία, -ας, *f.*, childlessness.

ἄπαις, ἀπαιδος, childless.

ἀπαλλάσσω, -άξω, ἀπήλλαξα, relieve of, release from, *with gen.*; *mid.*, depart.

ἁπαλός, -ή, όν, delicate.

ἀπᾱμάω, -ήσω, cut off.

ἀπαμύνομαι, -υνοῦμαι, ἀπημῡνάμην, ward off, defend oneself against.

ἀπανδρόομαι, -ώσομαι, ἀπηνδρώθην, come to maturity, grow up.

ἀπαρχαί, -ῶν, *f. pl.*, first-fruits.

ἅπᾱς, ἅπᾱσα, ἅπαν, all, the whole.

ἀπασπαίρω, struggle convulsively.

ἀπατάω, -ήσω, deceive, trick.

ἀπάτη, -ης, *f.*, deceit.

ἀπειλέω, -ήσω, ἠπείλησα, threaten.

ἀπειλημμένος, *p.p.p. of* ἀπολαμβάνω.

ἄπειμι, -έσομαι, ἀπῆν, be absent.

ἀπείργω, -είρξω, ἀπείρξα *H. aor.*, ἀπόεργαθεν, ward off, keep away, draw aside.

ἀπειρηκώς, weary, worn out, *p.p. of* ἀπαγορεύω.

ἄπειρος, -ον, unacquainted with, *with gen.*

ἀπελέγχω, -ξω, ἀπήλεγξα, prove; prove guilty.

ἀπεμπολάω, -ήσω, dispose of, smuggle away.

ἀπέχω, ἀφέξω, ἄπεσχον, be away (from), *with gen.*

ἀπεωθοῦντο, *imperf. mid. of* ἀπωθέω.

ἀπηλιώτης, -ου, *m.*, east wind.

ἀπηλλάχθαι, *perf. infin. mid. or pass of* ἀπαλλάσσω.

ἀπημπόλα, 3rd *sing. imperf. of* ἀπεμπολάω.

ἀπήνεγκα, *aor. of* ἀποφέρω.

ἀπήχθην, *aor. pass. of* ἀπάγω.

ἀπό, *prep. with gen.* from; ἀφ' οὗ, since the time when.

ἀποβλέπω, -ψω, ἀπέβλεψα, look at.

ἀποδείκνῡμι, -δείξω, ἀποδέδειγμαι, show, prove.

ἀπόδειξις, -εως, *f.*, proof; revelation.

ἀποδίδωμι, -δώσω, ἀπέδωκα, -δόθην, give, give back, grant, restore.

ἀποέργαθον, *H. aor. of* ἀπείργω.

ἀπόθετο, *H.* 3rd *sing. aor. mid. of* ἀποτίθημι.

ἀποθνήσκω, -θανοῦμαι, ἀπέθανον, ἀποτέθνηκα, die, be killed.

ἀποιμώζω, -μώξομαι, ἀπώμωξα, bewail.

ἀποίχομαι, -ήσομαι, imperf., ἀπῳχόμην, have gone, be away; H. part. gen., ἀποιχομένοιο.

ἀποκαυλίζω, -ίσω, break off.

ἀποκλήω, -ήσω, prevent, thwart.

ἀποκνέω, -ήσω, shrink from; lose heart.

ἀποκρίνομαι,-κρινοῦμαι,ἀπεκρινάμην, reply.

ἀπόκρισις, -εως, f., reply.

ἀποκρούομαι, -σομαι, ἀπεκρουσάμην, beat off.

ἀποκτείνω, -κτενῶ, ἀπέκτεινα, kill.

ἀπολαμβάνω, -λήψομαι, ἀπέλαβον, -είλημμαι,-ελήφθην, catch, cut off.

ἀπολείπω, -ψω, ἀπέλιπον, leave, abandon.

ἀπόλλῡμι, -ολῶ, ἀπώλεσα, H., -όλεσα, -ολώλεκα, lose, kill; -ωλόμην, -όλωλα, die, be killed.

'Απόλλων, -ωνος, m., Phoebus Apollo, god of the sun, healing, and prophecy, father of Ion.

ἀπολογέομαι, -ήσομαι, -λελόγημαι, make a defence.

ἀπολύω, -λύσω, loosen, relax; acquit; mid., free oneself from.

ἀπόλωλα, str. perf. of ἀπόλλυμι, have died: ἀπολώλεκα, perf. trans., have killed.

ἀπομισθόω, -ώσω, hire out, lease.

ἀπορία, -as, f., difficulty, helplessness.

ἄπορος, -ον, difficult, impossible; τὸ ἄπορον, difficulty; ἐν ἀπόρῳ εἶναι, be at a loss, be unable.

ἀποσπένδω, -σπείσω, ἀπέσπεισα, pour away.

ἀποσπογγίζω, -ίσω, wipe away.

ἀποστάζω, -άξω, drip, trickle.

ἀποστερέω, -ήσω, deprive of, take away from, with double acc., or acc. and gen.

ἀποτίθημι, -θήσω, ἀπέθηκα, -εθέμην, H. aor. mid., ἀπό . . . θέτο, cast off, put away.

ἀποτίνω, -τίσω, pay back; mid., take vengeance on.

ἀποτρέπω -ψω, ἀπετραπόμην, ἀποτέτραμμαι, ἀπετράπην, turn away, turn back, dissuade; mid. intr., turn away; p.p.p., ἀποτετραμμένος, bitterly hostile.

ἀποτρωπάομαι, H. frequentative of ἀποτρέπομαι, refrain from, with gen.

ἀποφέρω, ἀποίσω, ἀπήνεγκα, take away; bring.

ἀπόφευξις, -εως, f., acquittal.

ἀποχωρέω, -ήσω, withdraw, retire.

ἀποψηφίζομαι, -ιοῦμαι, acquit; vote for the acquittal of, with gen.

ἀπροσδόκητος, -ον, unexpected.

ἅπτω, ἅψω, set fire to; mid. with gen., touch.

ἄπωθεν, adv., afar; with gen., far from.

ἀπωθέω, -ήσω, ἀπέωσα, imperf. mid., ἀπεωθούμην, throw down; mid., repel.

ἀπώλεσα, H., -όλεσα, aor. of ἀπόλλυμι, destroy; plup. intr., ἀπολώλει, had died.

ἀπώμωξα, aor. of ἀποιμώζω.

ἀπώσας, aor. part. of ἀπωθέω.

ἄρα, inferential particle, then, indeed.

ἆρα, interrog. particle.

ἀράμενος, aor. mid. part. of αἴρω, having faced.

ἀραρυῖα, H. f. p.p. of ἀραρίσκω, with pass. meaning, fitted.

ἀργαλέος, -α, -ον, grievous, painful.

Ἄργος, -ους, H. gen., -εος, n., Argos, a town in the northern Peloponnese.

ἀργός, -όν, slow to act, hindering action.

ἀργυρήλατος, -ον, silver, made of silver.

ἀργυρότοξος, -ον, armed with a silver bow.

ἀρετή, -ῆς, f., courage, valour, excellence.

ἀριθμός, -οῦ, m., number; an item.

ἀριθμέω, -ήσω, imperf., ἠρίθμουν, also mid., count.

ἀριστερός, -ά, -όν, left-hand, on the left.

ἀριστεύς, -έως, H. gen., -ῆος, acc. pl. -ῆας, m., noble, chieftain.

ἄριστος, -η, -ον, superl. adj., best.

ἀριφραδής, -ές, clear, easily seen.

ἀρκέω, -έσω, ἤρκεσα, suffice, help, with dat.

ἀρκτοῦρος, -ου, m., Arcturus, a star behind the Bear, rising about September 18.

ἀρνέομαι, -ήσομαι, deny, refuse.

ἀρτάω, -ήσω, fasten, attach.

ἄρτι, adv., recently, just now.

ἀρχαῖος, -α, -ον, ancient.

ἀρχή, -ῆς, f., beginning; rule; the authorities; ἀρχήν, as adv., in the beginning; originally; at all.

Ἀρχίδαμος -ου, m., Archidamus, Spartan king at the siege of Plataea.

ἀρχός, -οῦ, m., leader.

ἄρχω, ἄρξω, also mid., begin.

ἄρχων, -οντος, m., commander; archon (one of the nine chief magistrates at Athens).

ἀσαφής, -ές, unintelligible.

ἀσέβεια, -ας, f., impiety.

ἀσεβέω, -ήσω, ἠσέβηκα, be impious.

ἀσέβημα, -ματος, n., reckless folly, impiety.

ἀσέληνος, -ον, moonless.

ἄσημος, -ον, unknown; οὐκ ἄσημος, famous.

ἀσθένεια, -ας, f., weakness.

ἀσθενής, -ές, weak, feeble; ἐν τῷ ἀσθενεστάτῳ, in the last stage of weakness.

Ἀσιάς, -άδος, f. adj., of Asia; as f. noun, Asia, i.e. Asia Minor.

ἀσκέω, -ήσω, equip, adorn; perf. pass., εὖ ἠσκῆσαι, you are well fitted out.

ἄσμενος, -ον, joyful, happy.

ἀσπάζομαι, -άσομαι, embrace, greet, bid farewell to.

ἀσπίς, ἀσπίδος, f., shield.

ἀστέγαστος, -ον, undecked, open.

ἀστός, -οῦ, m., citizen.

ἀστραπή, -ῆς, f., lightning, also pl.

ἄστυ, ἄστεως, n., city.

Ἀστύμαχος, -ου, m., Astymachus, son of Asopolaus, a Plataean spokesman to the Spartans.

ἀσύνετος, -ον, unintelligible.

ἀσφάλεια, -ας, f., safety.

ἀσφαλής, ές, safe; τὸ ἀσφαλές, safety.

Ἀσωπόλᾱος, -ου, m., Asopolaus, a Plataean, father of Astymachus.

Ἀσωπός, -οῦ, m., Asopus, a river flowing between Thebes and Plataea.

ἀτασθαλίαι, -ῶν, f. pl., reckless folly.

ἄτεκνος, -ον, childless.

ἀτέμβω, injure, insult.

ἄτερ, prep. with gen., without.

ἄτη, -ης, f., sin; burden of folly.

Ἀτθίς, -ίδος, Attic, of Attica, the country of which Athens was the capital.

ἀτῑμάζω, -άσω, dishonour.

ἀτῑμάω, -ήσω, H. imperf., ἀτίμα, dishonour, insult.

ἄτῑμος, -ον, dishonoured; deprived of, with gen.

Ἄτλας, -αντος, m., Atlas, a Titan who bore the heavens on his shoulders.

ἄτρεστος, -ον, unafraid; n. pl. as adv., fearlessly.

ἄτριπτος, -ον, unworn by toil.

ἄττα, voc., old fellow.

Ἀττική, -ῆς, f., Attica, the country of which Athens was the capital.

αὖ, adv., again; moreover, indeed.

αὐδάω, imperf., ηὔδων, address.

αὐδή, -ῆς, f., voice, sound.

αὐθέντης, -ου, m., murderer.

αὖθι, adv., there.

αὖθις, adv., again.

αὐλή, -ῆς, f., courtyard.

αὐλός, -οῦ, m., flute.

αὐτάρ, conj., but.

αὖτε, adv., then.

αὐτίκα, adv., immediately; for example.

αὖτις, H. for αὖθις.

αὐτόθεν, adv., from that very place.

αὐτόθι, adv., here, there.

Αὐτόλυκος, -ου, H. gen., -οιο, m., Autolycus, grandfather of Odysseus.

αὐτόματος, -ον, spontaneous: ἀπ’ αὐτομάτου, of its own accord, spontaneously.

αὑτόν, = ἑαυτόν, reflex. pron., himself; also = ἐμαυτόν, myself; αὐτὸς καθ’ αὑτόν, independently.

αὐτόνομος, -ον, independent.

αὐτός, -ή, -ό, pron., himself, etc., the very; in oblique cases, he, she, it; ὁ αὐτός or αὐτός, αὐτή, ταὐτό or ταὐτόν, the same.

αὐτοῦ, adv., here, there.

αὐτόφωρος, -ον, caught in the act; ἐπ’ αὐτοφώρῳ, red-handed, caught in the act.

αὐτόχειρ, -χειρος, m., perpetrator, murderer.

αὐτόχθων, -χθονος, earth-born.

αὔτως, adv. thus, so; ὡς ... αὔτως, thus.

αὐχήν, -ένος, m., throat.

ἀφαιρέω, -ήσω, -εῖλον, also mid., take away from, with acc. and gen.

ἀφανής, -ές, unseen, unknown, missing; incapable of proof; τὸ ἀφανές, darkness, shadow.

ἀφανίζω, -ιῶ, ἠφάνισα, suppress, get rid of, do away with; set apart; mid., disappear.

ἄφαρ, adv., forthwith, then.

ἀφαρπάζω, -άσομαι, take away.

ἀφῆκα, aor. of ἀφίημι.

ἀφέντες, aor. part. pl. of ἀφίημι.

ἀφίημι, -ήσω, -ῆκα, 3rd pl. imperf., ἀφίεσαν, send away, give up, let go, leave alone.

ἀφικνέομαι, -ίξομαι, -ἱκόμην, arrive, come.

ἀφίσταμαι, ἀποστήσομαι, ἀπεστησάμην or -έστην, revolt (from).

ἄφρων, ἄφρονος, witless, foolish.

'Αχαιϊάδες, f. pl., Achaean women.

'Αχαιΐς, -ίδος, f. adj. Achaean, of Achaea in the Peloponnese.

'Αχαιός, -οῦ, m. an Achaean, one of a people first living in Phthia in Thessaly, later in the Peloponnese: H., 'Αχαιοί, the Achaeans, Greeks.

ἀχεύων, -ουσα, -ον, pres. part., vexing, grieving.

ἄχθομαι, -θέσομαι, be angry with, with dat.

ἄχνυμαι, grieve, intr.

ἄχος, ἄχους, n., vexation, anger, grief.

ἀχρεῖος, -ον, useless, unfit for service; ἀχρειότατος, least efficient.

ἄψ, adv., again.

ἄψομαι, fut. mid. of ἅπτω.

B

βαδίζω, -ιῶ, go.

βαίνω, βήσομαι, ἔβην, H., βῆν, βέβηκα, H. plup., βεβήκειν, go.

βακχεύω, -εύσω, go mad, behave madly.

βάλανος, -ου, f., bolt-pin.

βάλλω, βαλῶ, ἔβαλον, H., βάλον, aor. part. dual, βάλοντε, throw, strike, pelt, let fall.

βαρύς, -εῖα, -ύ, heavy.

βασανίζω, -ιῶ, examine under torture, enquire into.

βασανιστής, -οῦ, m., torturer, examiner.

βάσανος, -ου, m., examination under torture.

βασίλεια, -ας, H., -η, -ης, f., queen.

βασιλεύς, -έως, m., king.

βαστάζω, -άσω, handle.

βέβαιος, -α, -ον, firm, hard.

βεβαιόω, -ώσω, confirm.

βεβήκει, H. 3rd sing. plup. of βαίνω.

βέλος, -ους, n., arrow.

βελτίων, -ονος, comp. adj., better.

βῆ, βῆσαν, H. aor. of βαίνω.

βία, -ας, H., βίη, -ης, dat. pl. βίηφι, f., force, strength.

βιάζομαι, -άσομαι, H., -ήσομαι, compel; force a way out.

βιαίως, adv., by force, after a struggle, under pressure.

βίος, -ου, m., life.

βιός, -οῦ, m., bow.

βίοτος, -ου, m., means of living; wealth.

βλάβη, -ης, f., mischief, harm, spite.

βλάβος, -ους, n., harm.

βλάπτω, -άψω, harm.
βλαστάνω, -τήσω, ἔβλαστον, be born, spring from.
βλασφημία, -ας, f., ill-omened words.
βλέφαρον, -ου, n., eyelid.
βοάω, -ήσω, shout.
βοή, -ῆς, f., shout, uproar; alarm.
βοήθεια, -ας, f., help; pursuit.
βοηθέω, -ήσω, help, bring help to, with dat.
βοιωταρχέω, -ήσω, be a Boeotarch, one of the chief magistrates of Boeotia.
Βοιωτία, -ας, f., Boeotia, a district of Greece just north of Attica.
Βοιωτός, -ου, m., a Boeotian.
βόσκομαι, -ήσομαι, graze, feed.
βουθυτέω, -ήσω, sacrifice oxen.
βουκόλος, -ου, m., oxherd.
βουλεύω, -εύσω, also mid., take counsel, plan, consider, resolve.
βούλησις, -εως, f., wish, intention.
βούλομαι, -ήσομαι, imperf. also ἠβουλόμην, wish; τὸ βουλόμενον, the wish.
βοῦς, βοός, c., ox, cow.
βραδύς, -εῖα, -ύ, slow; comp. adv. βραδύτερον.
βράχε, H. aor., he roared.
βραχύς, -εῖα, -ύ, short; low.
βρέφος, -ους, n., infant, babe.
βροντή, -ῆς, f., thunder, thunderstorm.
βροτός, -οῦ, m., mortal, man.
βρόχος, -ου, m., noose.
Βύβλινος, -η, -ον, Bybline, an adj. used of wine, perhaps Thracian.

βύβλινος, -η, -ον, made of papyrus (used for rope).
βώμιος, -α, -ον, of or at the altar.
βωμός, -οῦ m., altar.

Γ

γαῖα, -ας, H., -ης, f., earth, land, ground.
γάλα, γάλακτος, n., milk, mother's milk.
γαμέω, γαμῶ, ἔγημα, marry; mid. with dat., be married to: γαμεῖν λέχος, win the hand of.
γάμος, -ου, m., marriage, love, also pl.
γᾶς, H. for γῆς, from γῆ.
γάρ, conj., for; in dialogue, yes, for; no, for; καὶ γάρ, for indeed.
γαστήρ, γαστρός, f., stomach; womb.
γε, enclitic particle, at least; in dialogue, yes.
γεγένημαι, γεγόνως or γεγώς, dual γεγένησθον, perf. of γίγνομαι.
γεγήρᾱκα, perf. of γηράσκω.
γέγωνα, ἐγεγώνει, perf. with pres. sense, shout.
γείνομαι, be born; aor. ἐγεινάμην, beget, bear.
γείτων, -ονος, neighbouring.
γελάω, -άσομαι, H. aor., γέλασσα, laugh.
γελόω, H. for γελάω.
γέλως, -ωτος, m., laughter, laughing-stock, joke; something ridiculous.
γενέσθαι, H. indic., γένετο, γενήσεσθαι, aor. and fut. inf. of γίγνομαι.
γενναῖος, -α, -ον, noble.
γένος, -ους, n., birth, high birth.

γένυς, -υος, f., jaw.

γεραιός, -ά, όν, old; m., old man.

γέρας, -αος, gen. pl., γέρων, n., honour, prize.

γέρων, -οντος, m., old man.

γεύομαι, -σομαι, taste, with gen.

γῆ, γῆς, H. gen., γᾶς, f., earth, land, country.

γηγενής, -ές, earth-born; γηγενὴς μάχη, battle of the earth-born giants.

γῆθεν, adv., from the earth as his mother.

γηθέω, -ήσω, H. aor., γήθησα, rejoice.

γῆμαι, aor. infin. of γαμέω.

γηράσκω, -ἀσομαι, ἐγήρᾱσα, γεγήρᾱκα, grow old.

γίγνομαι, γενήσομαι, ἐγενόμην, H., γενόμην, γέγονα, become, be made, be born, arise, be successful, fall (of rain); τὰ γιγνόμενα, the events; τὸ γεγενημένον, what had happened; γεγόνως (with ἔτη), old; γεγώς, spring from, born.

γιγνώσκω, γνώσομαι, ἔγνων, ἔγνωκα, ἐγνώσθην, discover, realize, decide, understand, recognise; pass., become known.

γλαυκῶπις, -ιδος, f. adj., grey-eyed, bright-eyed.

γλυφίς, -ίδος, f., arrow-notch (for the string).

γναμπτός, -ή, -όν, supple.

γνοίην, γνούς, γνῶ, aor. optat., part., and subj., of γιγνώσκω, discover, decide.

γνώμη, -ης, f., plan, intention, suggestion, reason, judgment, sentence; γνώμην ποῖεισθαι, decide.

γνῶναι, aor. infin., γνώσθω, aor. subj. pass., γνώσω, fut., γνώτον, γνώτην, H. aor. indic. dual, of γιγνώσκω.

γνωρίζω, -ιῶ, recognize.

γνωριστής, -οῦ, m., one who makes a survey of.

γονή, -ῆς, f., birth, parentage, also pl.

γόνος, -ου, m., son.

γόνυ, γόνατος, H. dat. pl., γούνασι, n., knee.

γόος, -ου, H. gen., -οιο, m., lamentation.

Γοργώ, -οῦς or -όνος, acc. -ώ or -όνα, f. the Gorgon.

γοῦν, particle, at least, then.

γούνασι, H. dat. pl. of γόνυ.

γραῖος, -α, -ον, aged, of an old man.

γραμματείδιον, -ου, n., short letter, note.

γραφή, -ῆς, f., picture, painting.

γυμνός, -ή, -όν, bare, unprotected, by itself.

γυνή, γυναικός, voc., γύναι, f., woman, lady, wife.

γωρυτός, -οῦ, m., quiver.

Δ

δαί, inferential particle, then.

Δαΐμαχος, -ου, m., Daïmachus, a Plataean, father of Eupompides.

δαίμων, -ονος, m., god; fortune.

δαίνυμαι, δαίσομαι, 3rd sing. imperat., δαινύσθω, feast.

δαίς, δαιτός, f., feast.
δαΐφρων, -φρονος, prudent.
δάκρυ, -υος, n., tear.
δακρυρρέω, -ήσω, weep.
δακρύω, -ύσω, weep.
δάμαρ, -αρτος, f., wife.
δαμάω, -άσω, subdue.
δαπάνη, -ης, f. expense.
δαφνηφόρος, -ον, of laurel or bay.
δέ, particle, and, but, on the other
    hand; H. καὶ δέ, and indeed.
δεδεμένος, p.p.p. of δέω.
δεδιέναι, perf. infin., δεδιώς, part., of
    δείδω.
δέδοικα, perf., of δείδω,
δεδρāκότες, m. pl. p.p. of δράω, do.
δεῖ, δεήσει, impers. with acc., it is
    necessary, one must, one ought;
    with gen., there is need of.
δείδω, δείσω, perf. with pres. sense,
    δέδοικα, δεδιέναι, δεδιώς, fear.
δείκνῡμι, δείζω, show, reveal.
δειλός, -ή, όν, voc. dual, δειλώ,
    wretched.
δεινός, -ή, -όν, terrible, serious; τὸ
    δεινόν, the danger; τὰ δεινά,
    means of attack; τὸ δεινότατον,
    the most terrible fate.
δεῖπνον, -ου, n., feast, also pl.
δείσας, aor. part of δείδω.
δεῖτε, pl. imperat. of δέω, bind.
δέκα, indecl., ten.
δέκατος, -η, -ον, tenth.
Δελφίς, -ίδος, f., a woman of
    Delphi.
Δελφοί, -ῶν, m.p.l., Delphi, the seat
    of the oracle of Phoebus, at the
    foot of Mount Parnassus.

Δελφοί, -ῶν, m. pl., Delphians, in-
    habitants of Delphi.
δέμας, n., body.
δένδρον, -ου, n., tree.
δεξιός, -ά, -όν, right; f., δεξιά, the
    right hand.
δεξιτερός, -ά, -όν, right, right hand.
δέομαι, δεήσομαι, desire, with gen.
δέπας, H. dat. pl., δεπάεσσι, n.,
    cup.
δέραιον, -ου, n., necklace, also pl.
δέρος, -ατος, n., skin.
δέρσις, -εως, f., skin.
δεσμός, -οῦ,, m., chain, link; fasten-
    ing of a door; pl., bracelet.
δεσπόζω, -όσω, be master of, with
    gen.
δέσποινα, -ης, f., mistress.
δεσπότης, -ου, m., master.
δεῦρο, adv., hither; until this time.
δεύτερος, -α, -ον, second.
δέχομαι, δέξομαι, accept, receive.
δέω, pl. imperat., δεῖτε, δήσω, ἔδησα,
    δέδεμαι, bind.
δέω, δεήσω, lack, with gen.; ἐλαχίστου
    ἐδέησε, with infin., very nearly.
δή, particle, indeed.
δῆθεν, adv., indeed (implying a
    falsehood).
δηλήμων, -ονος, m., destroyer.
δῆλος, -η, -ον, clear, evident.
δηλόω, -ώσω, show, prove.
δῆμος, -ου, m., people, democracy;
    the Assembly of the Athenian
    people.
δημοσίᾳ, adv., at the public expense.
δημοσιόω, -ώσω, confiscate for the
    public use.

δήπου, *adv.*, surely.

δηόω, -ώσω, ravage, lay waste.

δηρόν, *adv.*, too long.

δῆτα, *adv.*, then, therefore.

διά, *prep. with acc.*, on account of; *with gen.*, through, all through, by means of, at intervals of.

διαβαίνω, -βήσομαι, διέβην, cross.

διαβάλλω, -βαλῶ, διέβαλον, malign, slander, give false evidence against.

διάβασις, -εως, *f.*, crossing.

διαβατός, -ή, -όν, fordable, able to be crossed.

διαβιβάζω, -βιβῶ, take across.

διαβολή, -ῆς, *f.*, slander, false accusation, prejudice.

διαβουλεύομαι, -εύσομαι, deliberate, take counsel.

διαγιγνώσκω, -γνώσομαι, διέγνων, decide a case.

διαιρέω, -ήσω, διεῖλον, *also mid.*, take down, divide up, remove.

διακινδυνεύω, -εύσω, risk, endanger, run the risk.

διακομίζω, -ιῶ, take across; *pass.*, cross over.

διακόσιοι, -αι, -α, two hundred.

διαλύω -λύσω, disband, dismiss.

διαμαρτάνω, -τήσομαι, διήμαρτον, fail in, *with gen.*

διαμνημονεύω, -εύσω, remember.

διαμπερές, *H.*, διὰ ... ἀμπερές, *adv.*, straight through.

διανέμω, -νεμῶ, διένειμα, *p.p.p.*, διανενεμημένος, assign, apportion.

διανοέομαι, -ήσομαι, *imperf.*, διενοούμην, plan.

διαπειράομαι, -άσομαι, διεπειράθην, try, continue to try.

διαπεραιόομαι, -ώσομαι, *plup.*, διαπεπαιρώμην, cross over.

διαπράσσω, -άξω, διαπέπραγμαι, gain (revenge); kill.

διατείνομαι, -τενοῦμαι, διετεινάμην, exert oneself.

διαφέρω, διοίσω, -ήνεγκα, bear to the end; intervene; differ; *mid.*, *with dat.*, disagree with; διαφέροντά ἐστιν ἤ, is different from.

διαφεύγω, -φεύξομαι, διέφυγον, escape, survive.

διαφεῦξις, -εως, *f.*, escape, means of escape.

διαφθείρω, -φθερῶ, διέφθειρα, -έφθαρμαι, -εφθάρην, kill, destroy.

διάφορος, -ον, at variance with, contradictory, hostile to.

διαχέομαι, -χεοῦμαι, διεχύθην, spread, sink through, collapse.

διαψηφίζομαι, -ιοῦμαι, vote, decide by vote, give a verdict.

διδάσκω, -άξω, tell, inform.

δίδωμι, δώσω, ἔδωκα, ἐδόθην, give.

δίειμι, *fut.* of διέρχομαι.

διέκ, *prep. with acc.*, right through

διέλθω, *aor. subj.* of διέρχομαι.

διελών, διελόμενος, *aor. part.* of διαιρέω

Διέμπορος, -ου, *m.*, Diemporus, a Boeotian, leader of the first attack on Plataea.

διέρχομαι, -ειμι, -ῆλθον, *H.*, διὰ ... ἦλθε, pass, go through.

διέφθαρμαι, *perf. pass.* of διαφθείρω.

διέχω, -έξω, -εσχον, be apart, be distant (from), *with gen.*

δίζημαι, search for, try to win.
διῆκα, aor. of δίημι.
διήκω, -ήξω, extend, intr.
διήνεγκα, aor. of διαφέρω.
διῃρημένος, p.p.p. of διαιρέω.
διῆσαν, 3rd pl. imperf. of διέρχομαι.
Διί, Διός, dat. and gen. of Ζεύς.
δίημι, -ήσω, -ῆκα, H., διὰ . . . ἧκε, shoot through.
διισχυρίζομαι, -ιοῦμαι, stand by, persist in, with dat.
δικάζω, -άσω, give a verdict, decide, pass sentence; δίκη δεδικασμένη, a sentence that has been pronounced.
δίκαιος, -α, -ον, just, righteous; τὸ δίκαιον, justice, also pl.
δικαιόω, -ώσω, grant as a right.
δικαστής, -οῦ, m., judge, juryman.
δίκη, -ης, f., justice; trial, sentence, verdict; δίκη φόνου, trial for murder; δίκας διδόναι, pay the penalty, be punished (for).
δίοδος, -ου, f., road, passage, way through.
διοϊστεύω, -εύσω, shoot an arrow through, with gen.
διόλλῡμι, -ολῶ, -ώλεσα, kill, destroy.
δίομαι, chase.
διόμνῡμι, -ομοῦμαι, -ώμοσα, swear, take an oath.
διορίζω, -ιῶ, -ώρισα, remove.
διορύσσω, -ύξω, H. aor. part., διὰ . . . ὀρύξας, dig, dig through, dig along.
δῖος, -α, -ον, goodly, noble, fair.
διότι, conj., because.
διπλάσιος, -α, -ον, double.

δίπτυχος, -ον, double, two-fold.
δίς, adv., twice.
δισσοί, -αί, -ά, two; dual, δισσώ, -οῖν.
διφθέρα, -ας, f., leather, hide.
δίφρος, -ου, m., seat, chair.
διώκω, διώξω, pursue, try to find; prosecute; ὁ διώκων, the prosecutor.
διωμοσία, -ας, f., oath taken by parties at a trial.
δμώς, δμωός, dual, δμῶε, m., slave, servant.
δοκέω, δόξω, think, seem; seem good; impers. with dat., decide.
δοκός, -οῦ, m., beam.
δόλιος, -α, -ον, guileful, subtle; τὰ δόλια, guile.
δολοφρονέων, -ουσα, -ον, with crafty intent.
δόμεναι, H. aor. infin. of δίδωμι.
δόμος, -ου, H., -οιο, m., house, home; room, temple; δόμονδε, homewards, to his home.
δόξα, -ης, f., idea, thought.
δοξαστής, -οῦ, m., one who forms an opinion.
δοράτιον, -ου, n., short spear.
δόρπον, -ου, n., supper.
δόρυ, δόρατος or δόρος, n., spear.
δός, δότε, aor. imperat. of δίδωμι.
δουλεία, -ας, f., slavery, enslavement.
δουλεύω, -εύσω, serve, be a servant to, with dat.
δούλη, -ης, f., female slave.
δοῦλος, -ου, m., slave; τὸ δοῦλον, slavery.
δουλόω, -ώσω, enslave.

δοῦναι, aor. infin. of δίδωμι.

δοῦπος, -ου, m., noise.

δούς, δοῦσα, δόν, aor. part. of δίδωμι.

δράκων, -οντος, dual, δράκοντε, m., serpent.

δραστήριος, -α, -ον, vigorous, powerful, effective, deadly; τὰ δραστήρια, vigorous action.

δράω, δράσω, do.

δρόσος, -ου, f., dew, water.

δρύϊνος, -η, -ον, made of oak, oaken.

δρῦς, δρυός, f., oak-tree; Δρυός Κεφαλαί, Oak's Heads, a pass on Mount Cithaeron.

δύναμαι, -ήσομαι, ἐδυνήθην, H. imperf., δύνατο, can, be able, be strong; τὸ δυνάμενον, the power.

δύναμις, -εως, f., power, strength; κατὰ δύναμιν, to the best of one's ability.

δύνασις, -εως, f., power, effect.

δυνατός, -ή, -όν, possible, powerful, able; ὡς ἐκ τῶν δυνατῶν, as well as could be expected from their present resources.

δύο, δυοῖν, dual, also indecl., two.

δυοκαίδεκα, indecl, twelve.

δυσμενής, -ές, hostile.

δύστηνος, -ον, unhappy.

δυστυχέω, -ήσω, be unhappy.

δύω, δύσω, ἔδῦν, set, intr.

δώδεκα, indecl., twelve.

δῶκε, H. aor. of δίδωμι.

δῶμα, δώματος, n., also pl., house, home, temple.

δωρέα, -ας, f., gift; τὴν δωρέαν, adv., as a gift.

δώρημα, -ματος, n., gift.

δῶρον, -ου, n., gift.

E

ἕ, οὗ, οἷ, pron., him, her, it; also indirect reflexive, himself.

ἐάν, conj. with subj., if; ἐάνπερ, if indeed.

ἔαρ, ἦρος, n., spring.

ἐᾶσι, H. 3rd pl. of εἰμί, I am.

ἐάω, ἐάσω, εἴᾱσα, allow, let; H. also εἰάω.

ἑβδομήκοντα, indecl., seventy.

ἐγγενής, -ές, native.

ἐγγίγνεται, -γενήσεται, ἐνεγένετο, impers., it is possible.

ἐγγύς, adv., near by, close at hand.

ἐγείρω, ἐγερῶ, ἤγειρα, wake up, tr.; perf., ἐγρήγορα, be awake.

ἔγημα, aor. of γαμέω.

ἐγκάρσιος, -α, -ον, at an angle.

ἐγκαταλείπω, -λείψω, -κατέλιπον, p.p.p., ἐγκαταλελειμμένος, leave behind.

ἔγνων, aor. of γιγνώσκω.

ἐγρήγορα, perf. of ἐγείρω.

ἔγχος, -ους, H. dat., ἔγχεῖ, n., spear.

ἐγχωρέω, -ήσω, agree with; turn out well for; impers., it is possible, it is open.

ἐγχώριος, -α, -ον, of the country.

ἐγώ, ἐμοῦ or μου, I.

ἔδαφος, -ους, n., ground, ground-level.

ἔδοσαν, 3rd pl. aor. of διδωμι.

ἔδω, ἔδομαι, eat up, devour.

ἔδωκα, aor. of διδωμι.

ἕεδνα, -ων, n.pl., bridal gifts (to the bride's family).

ἔειπε, *H. for* εἶπε.

ἐέλδομαι, desire.

ἐέλδωρ, *n,* wish, desire.

ἔζομαι, ἐδοῦμαι, ἐζόμην, sit, settle.

ἔζευξα, *aor. of* ζεύγνυμι.

ἑήν, *H. for* ἥν, *from* ἑός, his.

ἐθελοντής, -οῦ, *m.,* volunteer.

ἐθέλω, -ήσω, *H.* subj., ἐθέλωμι, ἐθέλῃσι, wish, be willing.

ἐθέμην, *aor. mid. of* τίθημι.

ἔθρεψα, *aor. of* τρέφω.

εἶ, *2nd sing. of* εἰμί, I am.

εἰ, *conj.,* if; εἰ δὲ μή, otherwise; εἰ ἄρα, in case; εἰ γάρ, would that: εἰ δ' ἄγε, come now.

εἶδον, *aor. of* ὁράω.

εἴδω, *subj.,* εἰδώς, *part.,* εἰδέναι, *infin., of* οἶδα.

εἶεν, *particle,* very well, even so.

εἴην, *optat. of* εἰμί, I am.

εἰκάζω, -άσω, ἤκασα, guess, reckon, conjecture.

εἴκελος, -η, -ον, like.

εἰκοστός, -ή, -όν, twentieth.

εἰκώς, εἰκός, *part. of* ἔοικα, natural, fair, reasonable, likely, to be expected; κατὰ τὸ εἰκός, probably, τὰ εἰκότα, the probable result; *adv.,* εἰκότως, reasonably, with justice.

εἷλκον, *H.,* ἔλκον, *imperf. of* ἔλκω.

εἷλον, εἱλόμην, *aor. of* αἱρέω.

εἷμα, εἵματος, *n.,* garment, clothes.

εἰμί, ἔσομαι, *H.,* ἔσσομαι, *imperf.,* ἦν, be; ἔστι, sometimes *impers.,* it is possible.

εἶναι, *infin. of* εἰμί, I am.

εἵνεκα, *H., for* ἕνεκα *prep. with gen.,* for the sake of.

εἶμι, *fut. of* ἔρχομαι, *with pres. sense in tenses other than indic.*

εἴπερ, *conj.;* if indeed.

εἶπον, εἶπας, *pl.,* εἴπατε, *H.,* ἔειπε *and* εἴπεσκε, *subj.,* εἴπῃσι (= εἴπῃ), *aor.,* said, spoke.

εἰργάσθαι, *perf. infin.,* εἴργαστο, *plup.,* εἰργασμένος, *p.p.p., of* ἐργάζομαι.

εἴργω, εἴξω, εἶρξα, prevent.

εἴρηκα, *perf.,* εἰρημένος, *p.p.p., of* ἐρῶ; εἰρημένον ἦν, orders had been given.

εἰρήνη, -ης, *f.,* peace.

εἷς, μία, ἕν, one.

εἰς, *prep. with acc.,* to, towards, into; until.

εἰσβαίνω, -βήσομαι, -έβην, go on board.

εἰσβάλλω, -βαλῶ, -έβαλον, throw into.

εἰσβάς. *aor. part. of* εἰσβαίνω.

εἰσελθών, *aor. part. of* εἰσέρχομαι.

εἰσενήνεγμαι, *perf. pass. of* εἰσφέρω.

εἰσέρχομαι, -εῖμι, -ῆλθον, enter.

εἰσηνεγκάμην, *aor. mid. of* εἰσφέρω.

εἰσιδεῖν, *aor. infin.;* εἰσιδέτην, *H. dual aor. indic., of* εἰσοραω.

εἴσοδος, -ου, *f.,* entrance.

εἰσοράω, -όψομαι, -εῖδον, *H. pres. part.,* εἰσορόων, *dual aor.,* εἰσιδέτην, see, look at, *also mid.;* εἰσορᾶν φάος, be alive.

εἰστήκειν, *plup. of* ἵστημι.

εἰσφέρω, -οίσω, -ήνεγκα, -ενήνεγμαι, bring in, introduce; bring ... to, *with double. acc.*

εἴσω, adv. and prep. with gen., within, inside.

εἶτα, adv., then; κᾆτα, = καὶ εἶτα, and then, and yet.

εἴτε ... εἴτε, conj., whether ... or.

εἶτε, 2nd pl. optat. of εἰμί, I am.

εἶχον, imperf. of ἔχω.

εἰῶμεν, H. for ἐῶμεν, subj. of ἐάω.

ἐκ, ἐξ (before a vowel), prep. with gen., from, out of; ἐξ οὗ, since the time when.

ἔκαμον, aor. of κάμνω.

ἕκαστος, -η, -ον, each.

ἑκάτερος, -α, -ον, gen. dual, ἑκατέροιν, each of two.

ἑκατέρωθεν, adv., on or from each side.

ἕκᾱτι, prep. with gen., for the sake of.

ἑκατόμπεδος, -ον, a hundred feet long.

ἑκατον, indecl., a hundred.

ἐκβαίνω, -βήσομαι, ἐξέβην, got out, leave.

ἐκβάλλω, -βαλῶ, ἐξέβαλον, cast out; utter.

ἐκδίδαγμα, -ματος, n., sampler, practice work.

ἐκδίδωμι, -δώσω, ἐξέδωκα, give up.

ἐκεῖ, adv., there.

ἐκεῖνος, -η, -ο, that.

ἐκεῖσε, adv., thither, to that place.

ἔκηλος, -ον, quiet.

ἔκθεσις, -εως, f., exposure (of an infant).

ἐκκαίδεκα, indecl., sixteen.

ἐκκαλέω, -ῶ, ἐξεκάλεσα, H. aor. part.

mid., ἐκ ... καλεσσάμενος, call out, summon.

ἐκκλάζω, -κλάγξω, ἐξέκλαγξα, H., ἐκ ... ἔκλαγξε, cry aloud, intr.; with cognate acc., ἐξέκλαγξ' ὄπα, uttered a cry.

ἐκκομίζω, -κομιῶ, ἐξεκόμισα, take away, send away.

ἐκκυνηγετέω, -ήσω, dog one's steps.

ἐκλαμβάνω, -λήψομαι, ἐξέλαβον, aor. imperat., ἔκλαβε, receive; hear.

ἐκλείπω, -λείψω, ἐξέλιπον, leave, abandon, lose.

ἐκμανθάνω, -μαθήσομαι, ἐξέμαθον, learn, hear.

ἑκούσιος, -α, -ον, willing, voluntary.

ἐκπέμπω, -πέμψω, send out.

ἐκπίμπλημι, -πλήσω, ἐξέπλησα, 1st pl. imperf., ἐκ ... ἐπίμλαμεν, fill up ... with, with acc. and gen.

ἐκπίπτω, -πεσοῦμαι, ἐξέπεσον, ἐκπέπτωκα, used as pass. of ἐκβάλλω, be cast out.

ἐκπλήσσω, -πλήξω, ἐξέπληξα, strike; terrify.

ἐκπονέω, -ήσω, search for.

ἐκπρίασθαι, used as aor. infin. of ἐξωνέομαι.

ἐκσπένδω, -σπείσω, pour away.

ἔκσπονδος, -ον, released from a treaty.

ἐκστρέφω, -ψω, turn aside to, visit.

ἐκσῴζω, -σώσω, save.

ἐκτεθείς, aor. part. pass. of ἐκτίθημι.

ἔκτεινα, aor. of κτείνω.

ἐκτείνω, -τενῶ, ἐξέτεινα, stretch forth.

ἐκτελέω, -τελῶ, ἐξετέλεσα, H. pres.

subj., ἐκτελέωμεν, finish, make an end of.

ἐκτίθημι, -θήσω, ἐξέθηκα, -ετέθην, cast out, expose, leave (an infant) to die.

ἕκτος, -η, -ον, sixth.

ἐκτός, *prep. with gen.*, outside.

ἐκτρέφω, -θρεψω, ἐξέθρεψα, bring up, feed, nourish.

ἔκυσσε, *H. aor. of* κυνέω.

ἐκφέρω, ἐξοίσω, -ήνεγκα *or* -ον, *H. aor. imperat.*, ἐξένεικε, bring out, carry; possess.

ἑκών, ἑκοῦσα, ἑκόν, willing, of one's own accord.

ἔλαβον, *aor. of* λαμβανω.

ἔλαια, -ας, *f.*, olive tree, olive leaf.

ἔλαθον, *aor. of* λανθάνω.

ἐλάσσων, -ον, *nom. pl.*, ἐλάσσους, *comp.*, *adj.*, fewer; *adv.*, ἔλασσον *or* ἔλαττον, less; *superl.*, ἐλάχιστος least.

ἐλαύνω, ἐλῶ, ἤλασα, drive, guide; slash.

ἕλε, *H. aor.*, ἑλεῖν, ἑλέσθαι, *aor. infin. of* αἱρέω.

ἐλεγχείη, -ης, *f.* disgrace.

ἔλεγχος, -ους, *H. nom. pl.*, -εα, *n.*, proof, chance of proving; disgrace.

ἐλέγχω,-ξω,ἤλεγξα,prove, establish; hold an investigation; disgrace.

ἐλευθέριος, -ον, the Deliverer (epithet of Zeus).

ἐλεύθερος, -α, ον, free.

ἐλευθερόω, -ώσω, set free.

ἐλευθέρωσις, -εως, *f.*, freedom.

ἐλέφας, -αντος, *m.*, ivory.

ἐλέω, -ήσω, *aor. pass.*, ἐλεήθην, pity.

ἐλήφθην, *aor. pass. of* λαμβάνω.

ἐλθεῖν, *aor. infin. of* ἔρχομαι.

ἑλικτός, -ή, -όν, woven, made of wickerwork.

ἔλιπον, *aor. of* λείπω.

ἕλκω, ἕλξω, εἵλκυσα, *H. imperf.*, ἕλκον, draw, drag.

Ἑλλάς, -άδος, *f.*, Greece.

Ἕλλην, -ηνος, *m.*, a Greek.

Ἑλληνοταμίαι, -ῶν, *m.pl.*, Hellenotamiae, Stewards of Greece, the ten officials who administered the funds of the Confederacy of Delos.

ἐλπίζω, -ίσω, hope, expect, think.

ἐλπίς, ἐλπίδος, *f.*, hope.

ἔλπομαι, *H. 2nd sing.*, ἔλπεαι, *perf. with pres. sense*, ἔολπα, *plup.*, ἐώλπει, hope, expect.

ἐμβάλλω, -βαλῶ, ἐνέβαλον, throw on, strike with.

ἐμβολή, -ῆς, *f.*, battering-ram.

ἐμεῖο, *H.*, *for* ἐμοῦ, *gen. of* ἐγώ.

ἔμεναι *and* ἔμμεναι, *H. for* εἶναι, *infin. of* εἰμί, I am.

ἐμμενές, *adv.*, unceasingly.

ἐμμένω, -μενῶ, ἐνέμεινα, *aor. imperat.*, ἔμμεινον, persist in making, abide by, *with dat.*; last, last out.

ἔμηνα, drive mad, *aor. of* μαίνομαι.

ἐμός, ἐμή, ἐμόν, my, mine.

ἔμπαιος, -ον, practised in, *with gen.*

ἔμπαλιν, *adv.*, back; *prep. with gen.*, contrary to; ἐκ τοὔμπαλιν (=τοῦ ἔμπαλιν), on the other side.

ἔμπεδος, -ον, steadfast, unimpaired.

ἐμπειρία, -ας, f., knowledge, experience.

ἔμπειρος, -ον, knowing, acquainted with, with gen.

ἐμπίπρημι, ἐμπρήσω, ἐνέπρησα, set fire to.

ἐμπίπτω, -πεσοῦμαι, ἐνέπεσον, fall down.

ἐμπρήσας, aor. part. of ἐμπίπρημι.

ἐμφανής, -ές, visible, openly seen.

ἐν, prep. with dat., in, amongst, during; ἐν τούτῳ, meanwhile; ἐν ὅσῳ, while, until.

ἕν, n. of εἷς.

ἐναγωνίζομαι, -ιοῦμαι, aor. infin., -ίσασθαι, fight in.

ἐναντίος, -α, -ον, opposite to; m.pl., the enemy; τοὐναντίον (=τὸ ἐναντίον), or τἀναντία (=τὰ ἐναντία) the opposite to, with gen. or ἤ.

ἔναξε, aor. of νάσσω.

ἐναραρίσκω, -αρῶ, ἐνῆρσα, H., ἐν . . . ἄρσε, fit in.

ἕνδεκα, indecl., eleven; οἱ ἕνδεκα, the Eleven Police Commissioners at Athens.

ἔνδον, adv., within, at home; οἱ ἔνδον, those inside; prep. with gen., within; ἔνδον αὑτοῦ, in control of himself.

ἔνδυτον, -ον, n., garment; pl., clothes.

ἔνεγκε, H., ἔνεικε, aor. imperat., ἐνείκαι, H. 2nd sing. aor. optat., of φέρω.

ἔνειμι, -έσομαι, -ῆν, H. 3rd pl. imperf., ἔνεσαν, be in, be here.

ἕνεκα, H., εἵνεκα and οὕνεκα, prep.

with gen., often after the noun, for the sake of, on account of, in connection with.

ἐνέμεινα, aor. of ἐμμένω.

ἐνενηκοστός, -ή, -όν, ninetieth.

ἐνένιπε, H. aor. of ἐνίπτω.

ἔνεροι, -ων, m.pl., those in the Underworld, the dead.

ἔνεσαν, H. for ἐνῆσαν, from ἔνειμι.

ἐνεχώρει, imperf. of ἐγχωρέω.

ἐνῆκα, aor. of ἐνίημι.

ἐνῆρσε, aor. of ἐναραρίσκω.

ἐνῆσθα, 2nd sing. imperf. of ἔνειμι.

ἔνθα, adv., there, where; ἔνθα καὶ ἔνθα, this way and that, on this side and that.

ἐνθάδε, adv., there.

ἔνθεν, adv., from there, from which, then, from this side, from that side.

ἔνθετο, H. aor. mid. of ἐντίθημι.

ἐνθυμέομαι, -ήσομαι, consider, remember.

ἐνθύμιος, -ον, in one's mind.

ἐνί, H. for ἐν; ἔνι, H. for ἔνεστι and ἔνεισι, from ἔνειμι.

ἐνιαυτός, -οῦ, m., year.

ἐνίημι, -ήσω, -ῆκα, send in.

ἐνίλλω, -ήσω, wrap . . . up in.

ἐνίπλειος, -ον, filled with, with gen.

ἐνίπτω, -ψω, ἐνένιπον, rebuke.

ἐνίσταμαι, ἐνστήσομαι, str. aor. act., ἐνέστην, take one's stand, stand in the way.

ἕννῦμι, ἕσσω, ἑσάμην, clothe . . . in, with double acc.

ἐνοικέω, -ήσω, -ῴκησα, live in.

ἔνορκος, -ον, bound by oath.

ἔνοχος, -ον, liable to, *with dat.*

ἐνστάς, *str. aor. part. of* ἐνίσταμαι.

ἐντανύω, *H. fut.* -ύω, -ετάνυσα, *H.,* -ετάνυσσα, string (a bow).

ἐνταῦθα, *adv.,* there, in that place; then; on that count.

ἔντερον, -ον, *n.,* gut (used as lyre-string).

ἐντεῦθεν, *adv.,* then, thereupon, from there.

ἐντίθημι, *H.,* ἐν... τίθημι, -θήσω, -έθηκα, -έθέμην, *H. aor. mid.,* ἔνθετο, place, put on board, lay up; suggest.

ἔντος, *adv. and prep. with gen.,* within; τὸ ἔντος, the inside; ἔντος οὐ πολλοῦ χρόνου, recently.

ἔντοσθε, *adv. and prep. with gen.,* within.

ἐντρέφω, -θρέψω, ἐνέθρεψα, bring up among.

ἕξ, *indecl.,* six.

ἐξ, *before a vowel,* = ἐκ; ἐξ οὗ, since the time when.

ἐξάγω, -άξω, -ήγαγον, lead out, lead away, lead on.

ἐξαίρετος, -ον, chosen, special, excepted; ἐξαίρετον ποιεῖσθαι, make an exception of.

ἐξαιρέω, -ήσω, -εἷλον, remove, take out.

ἐξαίρω, -αρῶ, -ῆρα, *H. imperf.,* ἐξῆρεε, raise up.

ἐξαλείφω, -ψω, *p.p.p.,* ἐξαληλιμμένος, plaster over completely.

ἐξαμαρτάνω, -τήσομαι, -ήμαρτον, make a mistake.

ἐξαναιρέω, -ήσω, -εἷλον, *also mid.,* raise up.

ἐξανειλόμην, *aor. mid. of* ἐξαναιρέω.

ἐξανῆκα, *aor. of* ἐξανίημι.

ἐξανίημι, -ήσω, -ῆκα, send up.

ἐξαπιναίως *and* ἐξαπίνης, *adv.,* suddenly.

ἀξάρας, *aor. part. of* ἐξαίρω.

ἐξαρκέω, -κέσω, suffice, be enough.

ἐξαρτύω, -ύσω, arrange, fit out, prepare.

ἐξαῦτις, *adv.,* again.

ἐξεγγυάω, -ήσω, hand over on bail.

ἐξέθηκα, *aor. of* ἐκτίθημι.

ἐξέθρεψα, *aor. of* ἐκτρέφω.

ἐξείης, *adv.,* in turn.

ἔξειμι, *fnt. of* ἐξέρχομαι.

ἐξελέγχω, -ξω, -ήλεγξα, question.

ἐξελθεῖν, *aor. infin.,* ἐξέλθοντε, *nom. dual aor. part. of* ἐξέρχομαι.

ἐξελῶμαι, *aor. subj. mid. of* ἐξαιρέω.

ἐξένεικε, *H. aor. imperat. of* ἐκφέρω.

ἐξέπληξα, *aor. of* ἐκπλήσσω.

ἐξεργάζομαι, -άσομαι, -είργασμαι, finish, complete.

ἐξέρχομαι, -ειμι, *imperf.,* -ῇα, -ῆλθον, *H.,* ἐκ... ἤλυθον, go out, set out.

ἐξερῶ, *fut. (no pres.),* *H.,* -ερέω, will speak, will say.

ἐξεσία, -ας, *f.,* *H. acc.,* -ίην, a mission.

ἔξεστι, -έσται, -ῆν, *impers.,* it is possible, it is permitted, *with dat.*; *acc. abs.,* ἐξόν, it being possible.

ἐξεσώθην, *aor. pass. of* ἐκσῴζω.

ἐξετάζω, -άσω, -άσθην, judge, examine.

ἐξευρίσκω, -ευρήσω, -εῦρον, find out, discover.

ἐξῆα, ἐξῄει, ἐξῆσαν, imperf. of
    ἐξέρχομαι.

ἐξῆρεε, H. imperf. of ἐξαίρω.

ἐξήρτυον, imperf. of ἐξαρτύω.

ἐξιών, part. of ἔξειμι (ἐξέρχομαι).

ἔξοδος, -ου, f., way out, escape,
    sortie.

ἐξόν, acc. abs. of ἔξεστι.

ἐξονομάζω, -άσω, H. imperf., ἐκ . . .
    ὀνόμαζε, speak, speak out.

ἔξοχος, -ον, best; n. pl. as adv., by far.

ἔξω, fut. of ἔχω.

ἔξω, adv. and prep. with gen., outside;
    ἐς τὸ ἔξω, to the outside, out, over.

ἔξωθεν, adv., outside, from outside.

ἐξωνέομαι, -ήσομαι, with ἐξεπριάμην
    used as aor., buy, pay for.

ἕο, H. for οὗ, gen. of him, of himself.

ἔοικα, perf. with pres. sense, be likely,
    be right; part., εἰκώς, likely,
    natural.

ἔολπε, H. perf. with pres. sense of
    ἔλπομαι.

ἑορτή, -ῆς, f., feast, festival.

ἑός, ἑή, ἑόν, H. for ὅς, ἥ, ὅν, his, her,
    its.

ἐπάγομαι, -άξομαι, -ηγαγόμην, invite.

ἐπαγωνίζομαι, -ιοῦμαι, fight in.

ἐπακτός, -οῦ, m., stranger.

ἔπαλξις, -εως, f., battlement.

ἐπαναβιβάζω, -βιβῶ, -ανεβίβασα,
    send up, get up (tr.).

ἐπάρχομαι, -άρξομαι, begin, pour a
    few drops into each cup as a
    libation.

ἐπέδησε, aor. of πεδάω.

ἐπέθηκε, aor. of ἐπιτίθημι.

ἐπεί, conj., when, since.

ἐπείγομαι, -είξομαι, hurry, hasten.

ἐπειδάν, conj. with subj., whenever,
    when.

ἐπειδή, conj., when, since, as.

ἔπειμι, -έσομαι, -ῆν, H. 3rd sing., -ῆεν,
    be upon.

ἔπειμι, fut. of ἐπέρχομαι.

ἔπειτα, adv., then, next; in the
    future.

ἐπεῖχον, imperf. of ἐπέχω.

ἐπελθεῖν, aor. infin. of ἐπέρχομαι.

ἐπεξίεναι, infin. of ἐπέξειμι, fut. of
    ἐπεξέρχομαι.

ἐπεξέρχομαι, -ειμι, -ῆλθον, go out,
    depart.

ἐπεπήγει, 3rd sing. plup. of πήγνυμι.

ἐπεπράγεσαν, 3rd plup. of πράσσω,
    intr.

ἔπερσα, aor. of πέρθω.

ἐπέρχομαι, -ειμι, -ῆλθον, approach,
    come forward, reach, traverse,
    walk on, attack, take pro-
    ceedings; ὁ ἐπιών or οὐπιών, one
    who chances to come.

ἐπερώτημα, -ματος, n., question.

ἔπεσχον, aor. of ἐπέχω.

ἐπεύχομαι, -εύξομαι, pray to, with
    dat.

ἐπέχω, ἐφέξω, ἔπεσχον, stop, wait,
    cease; hold aloof from; reach,
    with gen.

ἐπηγαγόμην, aor. of ἐπάγομαι.

ἐπῆεν, H. 3rd sing. imperf. of ἔπειμι,
    I am upon.

ἔπηλυς, -ήλυδος, m., stranger.

ἐπήν, conj. with subj., whenever,
    when.

ἐπητύς, -ύος, f., kindness.

ἐπί, prep. with acc., to, up to, for; with gen., on, towards; with dat., on, with a view to.

ἐπιάλλω, -αλῶ, -ίηλα, H. aor. infin., ἐπὶ ... ιῆλαι, put on in addition.

ἐπιανδάνω, imperf., ἐπιήνδανε, please, with dat.

ἐπιβάλλω, -βαλῶ, ἐπέβαλον, throw on, heap on.

ἐπιβοάω, -ήσομαι, also mid., call upon.

ἐπιβοηθέω, -ήσω, come to the rescue, come to help, with dat.

ἐπιβολή, -ῆς, f., layer, course (of bricks).

ἐπιβούκολος, -ου, m., oxherd.

ἐπιβουλεύω, -εύσω, plan, make plans against, with dat.

ἐπιβουλή, -ῆς, f., plot.

ἐπιγίγνομαι, -γενήσομαι, ἐπεγενόμην, happen, follow, come on; spring up to assist, with dat.

ἐπιδείκνυμι, -δείξω, prove, show.

ἐπιδέξιος, -α, -ον, from left to right.

ἐπιδευής, -ές, H. m. pl., -έες, inferior to, with gen.

ἐπιδημέω, -ήσω, be in the district, be on the spot.

ἐπιείκελος, -ον, like, similar to.

ἐπιέλπομαι, hope.

ἐπιῆλαι, aor. infin. of ἐπιάλλω.

ἐπιθειάζω, -άσω, appeal to the gods.

ἐπιθέμενος, ἐπιθείς, aor. part. of ἐπιτίθημι.

ἐπιίστωρ, -τορος, having knowledge of, with gen.

ἐπικαλέω, -καλῶ, ἐπεκάλεσα, also mid., call upon, summon.

ἐπικλίνω, -κλινῶ, lay upon; perf. part. mid., ἐπικεκλιμμένος, resting on.

ἐπίκλοπος, -ον, skilled in, with gen.

ἐπίκουρος, -ου, m., ally.

ἐπιλείπω, -ψω, ἐπέλιπον, fail, run short.

ἐπιμαρτυρία, -ας, f., calling to witness.

ἐπινεύω, -νεύσω, H. aor., ἐπὶ ... ἔνευσε, nod to, signal with a nod.

ἔπιον, aor. of πίνω.

ἐπιπαρανέω, -ήσω, heap up in addition.

ἔπιπλα, -ων, n.pl., materials.

ἐπίσημος, -ον, conspicuous; revealed.

ἐπισκήπτω, -σκήψω, order, beg.

ἐπίσταμαι, -στήσομαι, know; part., ἐπιστάμενος, skilled in, with gen.; adv., ἐπισταμένως, skilfully.

ἐπιστέλλω, -στελῶ, ἐπέστειλα, send.

ἐπιστέφομαι, -στεψομαι, fill up with, with gen.

ἐπιστήσας, aor. part. of ἐφίστημι.

ἐπιστρέφομαι, -στρέψομαι, ἐπεστράφην, visit.

ἐπισχεῖν, ἐπίσχες, aor. infin. and imperat. of ἐπέχω.

ἐπισχεσία, -ας, H. acc., -ίην, f., pretext, excuse.

ἐπιτέλλομαι, -τελοῦμαι, ἐπετειλάμην, order, with dat.

ἐπιτήδειος, -α, -ον, fit, capable; conciliatory.

ἐπιτίθημι, -θήσω, ἐπέθηκα, -εθέμην, place on, set on, offer; mid. with dat., attack.

ἐπιτῑμητής, -οῦ, m., assessor.

ἐπιτολαί, -ῶν, f.pl., rising, first appearance.

ἐπιτρέπω, -τρεψω, permit, with dat.; mid., entrust, leave.

ἐπιφέρω, ἐποίσω, -ήνεγκα, bring, bring against; inflict, exact; mid. with dat., rush against.

ἐπιφλέγω -φλέξω, set fire to.

ἐπίφορος, -ον, blowing towards.

ἐπιχειρέω, -ήσω, try, make an attempt; verbal adj., ἐπιχειρητέον, the attempt should be made.

ἐπιχρίω, -χρίσω, anoint, grease.

ἐπιών, part. of ἔπειμι, fut. of ἐπέρχομαι; ὁ ἐπιών or οὑπιών, anyone who chances to come.

ἔπλετο, imperf. of πέλομαι.

ἐποίχομαι, -ήσομαι, ply, perform.

ἕπομαι, ἕψομαι, ἑσπόμην, follow, with dat.

ἐπόμνῡμι, -ομοῦμαι, -ώμοσα, aor. infin., -ομόσαι, confirm by oath, act on oath.

ἐπόρνῡμι, -όρσω, -ῶρσα, H. imperf., ἐπὶ ... ὄρνυε, urge on, incite.

ἔπορον, no pres., give; perf. pass., πέπρωται, it is fated.

ἔπος, ἔπους, H. dat. pl., ἔπεσσι or ἐπέεσσι, word, answer.

ἕπτα, indecl., seven.

ἐργάζομαι, -άσομαι, εἰργασάμην, εἴργασμαι, do, work, work at; farm.

ἔργον, -ου, n., work, task, deed, business.

ἔρεξα, aor. of ῥέζω.

ἐρέουσι, H. for ἐροῦσι, from ἐρῶ.

ἐρεύνα, -ης, f., enquiry.

ἐρευνάω, -ήσω, make a search.

Ἐρεχθεῖδαι, -ῶν, m.pl., descendants of Erechtheus, Athenians.

Ἐρεχθεύς, -έως, m., Erechtheus, sixth king of Athens, father of Creüsa.

ἐρέω, H. for ἐρῶ, and for ἔρομαι.

ἐρῆμος, -η, -ον, deserted, unguarded.

ἐρημόω, -ώσω, make desolate.

ἐριδαίνω, -δήσω, compete with.

Ἐριχθόνιος, -ου, m., Erichthonius, fourth king of Athens, grandfather of Erechtheus.

ἕρκος, -ους, n., barrier; outer wall.

Ἑρμῆς, -οῦ, m., Hermes, son of Zeus and Maia, messenger of the gods.

ἔρομαι, H., ἐρέω, ἐρήσομαι, ἠρόμην, ask, ask for.

ἔρος, -ου, m., desire.

ἔρριψα, aor. of ῥίπτω, throw.

ἐρρύην, aor. of ῥέω.

Ἐρύθραι, -ῶν, f.pl., Erythrae, a village three miles east of Plataea.

ἐρύομαι, fut., ἐρύομαι, εἰρυσάμην, H. aor. infin, ἐρύσσασθαι, string (a bow).

ἔρχομαι, εἶμι, ἦλθον, come, go.

ἐρῶ, H., ἐρέω, perf., εἴρηκα, εἴρημαι, will say; εἰρημένον ἦν, orders had been given.

ἔρως, ἔρωτος, m., love, desire.

ἐρωτάω, -ήσω, imperf., ἠρώτων, ask, question.

ἐς, = εἰς, prep. with acc., to, into, towards, up to.

ἐσάγω, -άξω, -ήγαγον, bring in.

ἐσακοντίζω, -ιῶ, -ηκόντισα, throw javelins.

ἐσάμην, aor. mid. of ἕννυμι.

ἔσαν, H. for ἦσαν, imperf. of εἰμί, I am.

ἐσβαίνω, -βήσομαι, -έβην, go in, enter.

ἐσβάλλω, -βαλῶ, -έβαλον, throw into; make an invasion.

ἐσεληλυθέναι, perf. infin of ἐσέρχομαι.

ἐσέρχομαι, -ειμι, -ῆλθον, -ελήλυθα, aor. imperat., ἔσελθε, imperf., ἐσῄειν, dual, ἐσίτην, go in, go on.

ἔσεσθον, fut. dual, ἔσεται, H. fut., ἔσῃ, 2nd sing. fut., of εἰμί, I am.

ἐσήγαγον, aor. of ἐσάγω.

ἐσηγέομαι, -ήσομαι, suggest, propose (a plan).

ἐσῄειν, H. for ἐσῄει, ἐσῆλθον, aor., εἰσίτην, dual imperf., of εἰσέρχομαι.

ἐσηκόντιζον, imperf. of ἐσακοντίζω.

ἔσθημα, -ματος, n., garment, clothes.

ἐσθίω, ἔδομαι, ἔφαγον, H. infin., ἐσθιέμεν, eat.

ἐσθλός, -ή, -όν, good, kind, faithful, scrupulous.

ἔσκε, H. for ἦν, imperf. of εἰμί, I am.

ἐσκομίζω, -ιῶ, -εκόμισα, bring in.

ἔσοδος, -ου, f., entry, entrance.

ἐσοικοδομέω, -ήσω, build into.

ἔσομαι, H., ἔσσομαι, fut. of εἰμί, I am.

ἔσπεισα, aor. of σπένδω.

ἐσπίπτω, -πεσοῦμαι, -έπεσον, rush or fly into.

ἐσπόμην, aor. of ἕπομαι.

ἐσσάμενος, aor. part. of ἵζομαι.

ἔσσομαι, ἐσσόμενος, H. fut. of εἰμί, I am; οἱ ἐσσόμενοι, future generations.

ἔσσω, fut. of ἕννυμι.

ἔστασαν, 3rd pl. plup., ἑστήκει, H. 3rd sing. plup., ἑστηκέναι, H., ἑστάμεν, perf. infin., ἔστησα, weak aor., ἔστην, str. aor., of ἵστημι.

ἐστεγασμένος, -ή, -όν, decked, having a deck; p.p.p. of στεγάζω, cover.

ἐστί, 3rd sing. of εἰμί, I am; ἔστι, sometimes = ἔξεστι.

ἐστώς = ἑστηκώς, standing, p.p. of ἵστημι.

ἐσφάλην, aor. pass. of σφάλλω.

ἐσφέρω, -οίσω, -ήνεγκα, bring in.

ἐσφορέω, -ήσω, carry in.

ἔσχατος, -η, -ον, furthest.

ἔσχεθον, H. for ἔσχον, aor. of ἔχω.

ἔσω, adv., within.

ἑταῖρος, H., ἕταρος, -ου, m., companion.

ἐτεθνήκει, ἐτέθνασαν, plup. of θνῄσκω.

ἔτεκον, aor. of τίκτω.

ἐτέτακτο, plup. pass. of τάσσω.

ἕτερος, -α, -ον, the other, another, the one ... the other.

ἑτέρωθεν, adv., from the other side.

ἔτι, adv., yet, still, again, any longer.

ἔτλην, aor. of τλάω.

ἑτοῖμος, -η, -ον, ready.

ἔτος, ἔτους, H. dat. ἔτεϊ, n., year.

ἐτραπόμην, aor. mid. of τρέπω.

ἐτύχθην, aor. pass. of τεύχω.

εὖ, adv., well.

Εὔβοια, -ας, f., Euboea, a long narrow island near the east coast of central Greece.

Εὐβοῖς, -ίδος, acc., Εὐβοῖδα, f. adj., Euboean.

εὐγενής, -ές, noble, of noble birth.

εὐερκής, -ές, H. gen., -έος, well-fenced.

εὐθύς, adv., immediately.

εὐκαμπής, -ές, H. acc.,-έα, well-bent, curved.

εὐκλεής, -ές, H. m. acc. pl., εὐκλεῖας, noble, of good repute.

εὐκόσμως, adv., in good order.

εὔκυκλος, -ον, rounded, well-rounded.

Εὔμαιος, -ου, m., Eumaeus, the faithful swineherd of Odysseus.

εὐμενής, -ές, auspicious.

εὐνάω, -ήσω, marry; ηὐνάσθην, be married to, with dat.

εὐνή, -ῆς, f., bed; marriage, love.

εὔνημα, -ματος, n., marriage, also pl.

εὔνους, ουν, kindly, loving, well-disposed, favourable.

ἐϋξεστος, -η, -ον, H. f. dat. pl., ἐϋξέστης, well-polished; also ἐΰξοος, -ον.

εὔορκος, -ον, in accordance with one's oath.

Εὐπείθης, -ους, m., Eupeithes, father of the suitor Antinous.

εὔπεπλος, -ον, fair-robed, beautifully attired.

εὐπηγής, -ές, well-built, sturdy.

Εὐπομπίδης, -ου., m., Eupompides, son of Daimachus, a Plataean general.

εὐπορέω, -ήσω, be happy, be successful.

εὔπτερος, -ον, well-feathered.

εὕρημα, -ματος, n., discovery.

εὑρίσκω, εὑρήσω, εὗρον or ηὗρον, find; mid., bring upon.

Εὐρυκλεία, -ας, f., Eurycleia, old nurse of Odysseus.

Εὐρύμαχος, -ου, m., Eurymachus, (i) one of the suitors of Penelope; (ii) a Theban who arranged the entry of the Thebans into Plataea.

Εὐρυτίδης, -ου, m., Eurytides, son of Eurytus, i.e. Iphitus, a friend of Odysseus.

Εὐρυτίων, -ωνος, m., Eurytion, a centaur who attacked the Lapiths.

Εὐρώπη, -ης, f., Europe.

εὐρώς, -ῶτος, m., decay.

εὐσεβής, -ές, righteous; τὸ εὐσεβές, one's sacred duty.

εὐσταλής, -ές, well-prepared, ready for action.

ἐϋστρεφής, -ές, well-twisted.

εὔτεκνος, -ον, promising children.

εὔτροχος, -ον, well-rounded.

εὐτυχέω, -ήσω, be fortunate.

εὔχομαι, εὔξομαι, pray; declare.

εὖχος, -ους, n., glory, renown.

ἔφαν, H. for ἔφασαν, from φημί.

ἐφάνην, aor. pass. of φαίνω.

ἔφασαν, 3rd pl., ἔφη, 3rd sing., ἔφατο, 3rd sing. mid., aor., of φημί.

ἐφημέριος, -α, ον, of the present day; living only for the day.

Ἐφιάλτης, -ου, m., Ephialtes, an Athenian politician, murdered in 462.

ἐφίεμαι, ἐφήσομαι, -είμην, desire.

ἐφίστημι, ἐπιστήσω, ἐπέστησα, put on top of; keep.

ἐφορμάομαι, -ήσομαι, be eager.

ἔχε, *H. for* εἶχε, *imperf. of* ἔχω.

Ἔχετος, -ου, *m.*, an ogre king in Homer.

ἔχευαν, *H. aor. of* χέω.

ἐχθρός -ά, -όν, hostile, hated; *m.*, an enemy, opponent; *superl.*, ἔχθιστος, bitterest enemy.

ἔχραον, *aor.*, become eager to, *with infin.*

ἔχουν, *imperf. of* χώννυμι (χόω).

ἔχω, ἕξω *or* σχήσω, ἔσχον, *H.*, ἔσχεθον, *imperf.*, εἶχον, *H., 3rd sing.*, ἔχε, *aor. part.*, σχών, σχόμενος, have, hold, restrain, involve, understand, dwell in, be able; *mid. with gen.*, cling to, proceed to; *with adv.*, = εἶναι with adj.; ὧδε ἔχειν, to be in such a position, ὥσπερ ἔχουσι, just as they are.

ἐψιάομαι, *H. infin.*, ἐψιάασθαι, enjoy oneself.

ἐώλπει, *H. plup. of* ἔλπομαι.

ἔωθεν, *adv.*, at dawn.

ἐών, ἐοῦσα, ἐόν, *H. for* ὤν, *pres. part. of* εἰμί, I am.

ἑώρων, *imperf. of* ὁράω.

ἕως, *conj.*, while.

Z

ζεύγνυμι, ζεύξω, *tr.*, join, marry.

Ζευξίδᾱμος, -ου, *m.*, Zeuxidamus, father of the Spartan king Archidamus.

Ζεύς, Ζηνός *or* Διός, *m.*, Zeus, king of the gods.

ζημιόω, -ώσω, punish.

ζητέω, -ήσω, search for; try, desire.

ζήτημα, -ματος, *n.*, search; clue to find, *with gen.*

ζωγρέω, -ήσω, capture alive.

ζώω, ζώσω, *H. part.*, ζώοντες, live.

H

ἦ, *3rd sing. of* ἠμί; *also 1st sing. imperf. of* εἰμί, I am.

ἦ, *adv.*, indeed; *in questions*, really; *also* ἦ καί, ἦ τοι, indeed.

ἤ, *H.*, ἠέ, *conj.*, than, or; ἤ ... ἤ, either ... or; ἤ ... ἤ, whether ... or.

ᾗ, *dat. f. sing. of* ὅς; *as adv.*, wherefore, as, how, where, whereby.

ᾖα, *H. for* ᾖ, *1st sing. imperf. of* εἰμί, I am.

ἠβαιός, -α, -ον, least.

ἥβη, -ης, *f.*, youth, manhood.

ἠγγέλθην, *aor. pass. of* ἀγγέλλω.

ἡγέομαι, -ήσομαι, *with gen.*, lead; *with acc. and infin.*, think.

ἠδέ, *conj.*, and.

ᾔδειν, ᾔδεσαν, *past tense of* οἶδα.

ἤδη, *adv.*, already; sometimes.

ἡδονή, -ῆς, *f.*, pleasure, joy.

ἡδύς, ἡδεῖα, ἡδύ, sweet; ἡδύ, *as adv.*, merrily.

ἠέ, *H. for* ἤ.

ἠελίοιο, *H. for* ἡλίου, *gen. of* ἥλιος.

ἤθελον, *imperf. of* ἐθέλω.

ἤϊεν, *H. for* ᾔει, *imperf. of* εἶμι (ἔρχομαι).

ἧκα, *aor. of* ἵημι.

ἥκιστα, *superl. adv.*, least.

ἠκόντιζον, *imperf. of* ἀκοντίζω, hurl javelins.

ἤκουσα, *aor. of* ἀκούω.

ἥκω, ἥξω, have come.

ἠλακάτη, -ης, f., distaff.

ἤλασα, aor. of ἐλαύνω.

ἤλατο, aor. of ἅλλομαι.

ἥλιος, -ου, H., ἠελίοιο, m., sun.

Ἦλις, Ἤλιδος, f., Elis, a district in the north-west Peloponnese.

ἤλυθον, H. aor. of ἔρχομαι.

ἧμαι, part., ἥμενος, sit.

ἦμαρ, ἤματος, n., day.

ἤμαξα, aor. of αἱμάσσω.

ἤμβροτον, H. aor. of ἁμαρτάνω.

ἡμεῖς, ἡμῶν, pl., we; often = ἐγώ, I.

ἡμέρα, -ας, f., day.

ἡμέτερος, -α, -ον, our; my.

ἠμί, imperf., ἦν, ἦ, = φημί, speak, say.

ἡμίονος, -ου, c., mule.

ἤμισυς, -εια, -υ, half.

ἦν, imperf. of εἰμί, I am; ἐξῆν, it was possible.

ἤν, = ἐάν, if.

ἥν, acc. fem. sing. of ὅς, who, and of ὅς, his.

ἠνδραπόδισα, aor. of ἀνδραποδίζω, enslave.

ἤνεγκα, aor. of φέρω.

ἡνίκα, conj., when.

ἦξα, aor. of ἀΐσσω.

ἠξίωσα, aor. of ἀξιόω.

ἥξω, fut. of ἥκω.

ἠπατημένος, p.p.p. of ἀπατάω.

ἤπειρος, -ου, H. gen., -οιο, f., mainland.

ἠπιστάμην, imperf. of ἐπίσταμαι.

Ἥρα, -ας, f., Hera, wife of Zeus.

Ἡραῖον, -ου, n., temple of Hera.

Ἡρακλῆς, -έους, H. acc., -ῆα, m., Heracles, son of Zeus and Alcmena.

ἦρεε, H. imperf. of αἱρέω.

ᾑρεῖτο, imperf. pass. of αἱρέω.

ἠρεύνων, imperf. of ἐρευνάω.

ἠριθμοῦντο, imperf. of ἀριθμέω.

ἤρκεσα, aor. of ἀρκέω.

ἡρόμην, aor. of ἔρομαι.

ᾑρόμην, imperf. pass. of αἴρω.

ἦρος, ἦρι, gen. and dat. of ἔαρ.

Ἡρώδης, -ου, m., Herodes, an Athenian who was murdered at Methymna in Lesbos.

ἡρῷον, -ου, n., shrine of a hero or demi-god.

ἥρως, -ωος, m., hero, demi-god.

ἠρώτων, imperf. of ἐρωτάω.

ᾖσαν, 3rd pl. imperf. of εἶμι (ἔρχομαι).

ἠσεβήκως, p.p. of ἀσεβέω.

ᾐσθόμην, aor. of αἰσθάνομαι.

ἤσκησαι, 2nd sing. perf. pass. of ἀσκέω.

ἥσσων, -ον, nom. pl., ἥσσονες or ἥσσους, comp. adj., inferior to, at a disadvantage; adv., ἧσσον, less.

ἡσυχάζω, -άσω, remain quiet, be neutral, make no movement.

ἡσυχία, -άς, f., quiet, quietness; ἡσυχίαν ἄγω, keep quiet, remain inactive.

ᾐτιᾱσάμην, aor. of αἰτιάομαι.

ἥτις, f. of ὅστις.

ἤτριον, -ου, n., warp (of woven cloth).

ηὐνάσθην, aor. pass. of εὐνάω.

ηὗρον, aor. of εὑρίσκω.

ἤ ὖτε, conj., as, like.

ἠφάνισα, aor. of ἀφανίζω.

ᾗφι, H. dat. f. sing. of ὅς, his.

ἧχ', = ἧκε, aor. of ἵημι.

ἦψα, aor. of ἅπτω.

ἠῶθεν, adv., at dawn, tomorrow morning.

Θ

θάλαμος, -ου, m., room; θάλαμονδέ, to her room.

θάλασσα, -ης, f., sea.

θάλλω, θαλῶ, flourish, be fresh.

θάλπω, θαλψω, warm.

θαμβέω, -ήσω, be amazed (at).

θανάσιμος, -η, -ον, deadly, causing death.

θάνατος, -ου, m., death.

θανεῖν, aor. infin., θανοῦμαι, fut., of θνήσκω.

θάπτω, θάψω, ἐτάφην, bury.

θαρσαλέος, -α, -ον, bold, confident.

θαρσύνω, -υνῶ, encourage.

θᾶσσον, comp. adv., more quickly.

θάσσω, sit.

θαυμάζω, -άσομαι, be surprised, wonder (at).

θαυμαστός, -ή, -όν, wonderful, strange.

θεά, -ᾶς, f., goddess.

Θεαίνετος, -ου, m., Theaenetus, son of Tolmides, a Plataean sooth-sayer.

θεᾱτής, -οῦ, m., spectator.

θεήλατος, -η, -ον, sent by a god; n., divine miracle.

θεῖναι, θείς, θέντες, aor. infin. and part. of τίθημι.

θεῖον, -ου, n., sulphur.

θεῖος, -α, -ον, H. gen., -οιο, godlike, goodly.

θέλω, -ήσω, aor. imperat. θέλησον, short form of ἐθέλω, wish.

θεμέλιος, -ου, m., foundation.

θέμεν, H. for θεῖναι, θέτο, H. for ἔθετο, θέμενος, aor. part. mid., of τίθημι.

θεοειδής, -ες, H. acc., -έα, godlike, goodly.

θεομανής, -ές, maddened by the gods, mad.

θεός, -οῦ, m., god, often scanned as a monosyllable; also f., goddess.

θέρος, -ους, n., summer.

θές, aor. imperat. of τίθημι.

θεσπίζω, -ιῶ, ἐθέσπισα, prophesy, foretell.

θέω, θεύσομαι, run.

Θῆβαι, -ῶν, f. pl., Thebes, chief city of Boeotia.

Θηβαΐς, -ΐδος, f. adj., Theban.

Θηβαῖος, -α, -ον, Theban; m.pl., the Thebans.

θηητήρ, -ῆρος, m., admirer; expert.

θῆκε, H. for ἔθηκε, aor. of τίθημι.

θήκη, -ης, f., tomb.

θῆλυς, -εια, -υ, female; θήλεια ἵππος, brood mare.

θήρ, θηρός, m., wild beast.

θησαύρισμα, -ματος, n., treasure.

θήσομαι, fut. mid. of τίθημι.

θνήσκω, θανοῦμαι, ἔθανον, τέθνηκα, die, be killed.

θνητός, -ον, mortal; τὰ θνητά, mortal affairs.

θοινάτωρ, -ορος, m., feaster.

θοινάω, -ήσω, feast.

θορυβέομαι, -ήσομαι, be excited, be confused.

θόρυβος, -ου, m., uproar, clamour.

θοῶς, adv., quickly.

Θρᾷξ, Θρᾳκός, m., a Thracian, living on the northern shores of the Aegean.

θριγκός, -οῦ, m., wall; kerb.

θρόνος, -ου, m., seat, chair of state.

θυγάτηρ, -ατρός, f., daughter.

θυμέλη, -ης, f., altar, hearth, sanctuary, also pl.

θυμός, -οῦ, m., heart, soul, spirit.

θυοσκόος, -ου, m., one skilled in sacrificing.

θύρα, -ας, H., -ή, gen. pl., -έων, f., door; θύραζε, out of doors, to the door, out.

θύρετρον, -ου, n., door.

θύρωμα, -ματος, n., door.

θυσία, -ας, f., sacrifice.

θύω, θύσω, sacrifice, offer a sacrifice.

θυώδης, -ες, H. acc., -έα, sweet-scented, fragrant.

θώραξ, -άκος, m. cuirass, breastplate.

I

ἴασις, -εως, f., cure, remedy.

ἰδέα, -ας, f., way, method.

ἰδεῖν, aor. infin., ἴδε, H. for εἶδε, aor. indic., of ὁράω.

ἴδιος, -α, -ον, private, one's own; τὸ ἴδιον, private revenge; ἰδίᾳ, as adv., independently.

ἰδού, interj., behold!

ἰέναι, infin. of εἶμι (ἔρχομαι).

ἱερός, -ά, -όν, H.f., -ή, sacred, holy; m., a temple-servant; n., temple; n. pl., sacrifices, divine rites.

ἰζάνω, settle down.

ἵζομαι, εἰσάμην, ἐσσάμενος, dedicate, found.

ἰῆλαι, see ἐπιάλλω.

ἵημι, ἥσω, ἧκα, send, shoot out; mid., ἵεμαι, desire.

Ἰθάκη, -ης, f., Ithaca, an island off the west coast of Greece, the home of Odysseus.

ἰθύνω, -υνῶ, ἴθυνα, set straight.

ἱκανός, -ή, -όν, sufficient, satisfactory.

ἱκάνω, = ἱκνέομαι, come, reach.

Ἰκάριος, -ου, H., -οιο, m., Icarius, father of Penelope.

ἱκέτης, -ου, m., suppliant.

ἱκνέομαι, ἵξομαι, ἱκόμην, come, reach.

ἱλήκω, H. 3rd sing. subj., ἱλήκῃσι, be gracious, be kind.

ἱμάς, ἱμάντος, m., strap.

ἵμεναι, H. for ἰέναι, infin. of εἶμι, go.

ἵνα, conj., where, to the place where; with subj. or opt., that, in order that.

ἰοδόκος, -ον, holding arrows.

ἰός, ἰοῦ, m., arrow.

ἰός, ἰοῦ, m., poison, venom.

ἱππεύω, -εύσω, ride; drive a chariot.

ἱππόβοτος, -ον, H. gen., -οιο, pasturing horses.

ἵππος, -ου, c., horse, mare.

ἴς, ἰνος, f., strength; ἴς Τηλεμάχοιο, mighty Telemachus.

ἴσασι, 3rd pl. of οἶδα.

ἰσοπλατή, -ές, of the same size as, with dat.

ἴσος, -η, -ον, equal, as high as; impartial, favourable; ἐξ ἴσου, on equal terms, equally; ἴσον or ἶσον, as adv., equally.

ἴστε, pl. imperat. of οἶδα.

ἴστημι, στήσω, ἔστησα, set up, place; ἴσταμαι, imperf., ἱστάμην, str. aor., ἔστην, ἔστηκα, H. infin., ἑστάμεν, 3rd pl. plup., ἔστασαν, p.p., ἑστώς, ἐστάθην, stand.

ἱστορέω, -ήσω, ask, enquire.

ἱστός, -οῦ, m., loom (for spinning), also pl.

ἰσχυρός, -ά, όν; strong.

ἰσχύς, -ύος, f., power, strength.

ἰσχύω, -ύσω, be strong, be vigorous.

ἴσχω, = ἔχω, have, possess.

ἴσως, adv., perhaps.

Ἴφιτος, -ου, m., Iphitus, son of Eurytus, a friend of Odysseus.

ἴψ, ἴπος, m., a worm that eats horn and wood.

Ἴων, Ἴωνος, m., Ion, son of Apollo and Creüsa.

K

κ', before a vowel, = κε, would; ever.

κἀγώ, = καὶ ἐγώ.

κἀβάκχευσε, = καὶ ἐβάκχευσε.

καθαιρέω, -ήσω, -εῖλον, take away, destroy.

καθάπαξ, adv., once for all.

κάθαπερ, adv., just as.

καθάπτω, -άψω, fasten.

καθαρός, -ά, -όν, pure, with clean hands.

καθέζομαι, imperf., καθεζόμην, sit.

καθελών, aor. part. of καθαιρέω.

κάθες, aor. imperat. of καθίημι.

καθέστηκα, καθεστώς, perf. of καθίσταμαι.

καθεωρώμην, imperf. pass. of καθοράω.

κάθημαι, imperf., ἐκαθήμην, sit.

καθίζω, -ιῶ, ἐκάθισα, sit upon; make (an army) encamp.

καθίημι, -ήσω, -ῆκα, pour in; dip.

καθίστημι, καταστήσω, κατέστησα, place, set, establish, make, restore; mid., arrange; καθίσταμαι, κατέστην, καθέστηκα, begin, settle down, be established; ὁ καθεστώς, the present.

καθοράω, κατόψομαι, -εῖδον, see; pass., be visible.

καί, conj., and, also, even; καὶ ... καί, both ... and; καὶ γάρ, for indeed; H., καὶ μέν, καὶ δέ, = καὶ μήν, and indeed.

καινός, -ή, -όν, new, new-found.

καίτοι, conj., and yet.

καίω, καύσω, ἔκαυσα, H., ἔκηα, imperat., κῆον, light (a fire).

κἀκεῖ, = καὶ ἐκεῖ, there too.

κἀκείνῳ, = καὶ ἐκείνῳ.

κἀκέλευσα, = καὶ ἐκέλευσα.

κακίζομαι, -ιοῦμαι, 2nd sing. pres. indic., κακίζῃ, become a coward.

κακοδαίμων, -μονος, unfortunate; crazy.

κακός, -ή, -όν, bad, evil; unkind; n., trouble, mischief, a grudge; superl., κάκιστος, basest, most worthless.

κακόω, -ώσω, ill-treat.

κἀκτίθησι, = καὶ ἐκτίθησι.

κάλαμος, -ου, m., reed.

καλέω, καλῶ, ἐκάλεσα, call.

κάλλιπε, H. for κατέλιπε, aor. of καταλείπω.

καλός, -ή, -όν, H., κᾱλός, good, fair;

n. as adv., sweetly; *adv.*, καλῶς, well; it is well.

κἄμέ, = καὶ ἐμέ, *from* ἐγώ.

κάμνω, καμοῦμαι, ἔκαμον, κέκμηκα, toil, be tired, be in difficulties; οἱ κεκμηκότες, those who have finished their labours, the dead.

καμπύλος, -η, -ον, curved, bent.

κἄν, = καὶ ἐν; κἄν, = καὶ ἐάν, even if; κἄνπερ, = καὶ ἐάνπερ, even if.

κἄπί, = καὶ ἐπί.

κάρᾱ, *indecl. n.*, head.

καρπός, -οῦ, *m.*, fruit, produce.

καρπός, -οῦ, *m.*, wrist.

καρτερόθῡμος, -ον, stout-hearted.

κασιγνήτη, -ης, *f.*, sister.

κασίγνητος, -ου, *m.*, brother.

κᾆτα, = καὶ εἶτα, and then, and yet.

κατά, *prep. with acc.*, according to at, down, throughout, by, opposite to, on account of; *with gen.*, against, down from.

καταβαίνω, -βήσομαι, κατέβην, go down, descend.

καταβάλλω, -βαλῶ, κατέβαλον, throw down, dislodge.

καταγιγνώσκω, -γνώσομαι, κατέγνων, *part.*, καταγνούς, condemn; *with* θάνατον, condemn to death.

καταγώγιον, -ου, *n.*, inn.

καταδείδω, -δείσω, κατέδεισα, be greatly afraid.

καταζάω, *infin.*, -ζῆν, live, go on living.

καταθείομεν, *H. for* -θῶμεν, *aor. subj.*, καταθέσθαι, *aor. infin. mid.*, *of* κατατίθημι.

καταθνήσκω, -θανοῦμαι, κατέθανον,

part. and infin., κατθανών, die, be killed.

κατακαίω, -καύσω, burn, *tr.*

κατακούω, -ακούσομαι, hear.

κατακτείνω, -κτενῶ, κατέκτεινα, *str. aor.*, -έκτανον, kill.

καταλαμβάνω, -λήψομαι, κατέλαβον, *p.p.p.*, κατειλημμένος, seize, capture.

καταλέγω, -λέξω, tell.

καταλείπω, -λείψω, κατέλιπον, *H. 3rd sing.*, κάλλιπε, *dual part.*, κατά ... λιπόντε, leave, leave behind.

καταμαρτυρέω, -ήσω, give evidence against, *with gen.*

κατανοέω, -ήσω, notice, perceive.

καταποντόω, -ώσω, throw into the sea, throw overboard.

κατασείω, -σείσω, shake down, throw down.

κατασκευάζω, -άσω, prepare, array, complete, make.

κατασκευή, -ῆς, *f.*, property, gear, farm-equipment, furniture.

καταστήσας, *aor. part. of* καθίστημι.

κατασχεῖν, *aor. infin. of* κατέχω.

κατατίθημι, -θήσω, κατέθηκα, *H. aor. imperat.*, κάτθετε, put aside, put down.

καταφανής, -ές, clear, known.

καταψεύδομαι, -ψεύσομαι, tell lies against, falsely accuse, *with gen.*,

καταψηφίζομαι, -ιοῦμαι, condemn, *with gen.*

κατέγνωστο, *3rd sing. plup. perf. of* καταγιγνώσκω.

κατεδοῦμαι, *fut. of* κατεσθίω.

κατέθηκα, *aor.* of κατατίθημι.

κατείβω, *2nd dual,* -είβετον, shed.

κατειλημμένος, *p.p.p.* of καταλαμβάνω.

κατεῖπον, *aor.* (*no pres.*) speak, declare, name; incriminate, *with gen.*

κατέκτανον, *str. aor.* of κατακτείνω.

καθεσθίω, -έδομαι, -έφαγον, eat up.

κατέστην, *str. aor.* of καθίστημι.

κατηγορέω, -ήσω, bring an accusation against, charge, *with gen.*

κατηγορία, -ας, *f.*, accusation, charge.

κατήγορος, -ου, *m.*, accuser, denouncer.

κατθανεῖν, κατθανών, *aor. infin. and part.* of καταθνήσκω.

κάτθετε, *H. for* κατάθετε, *aor. imperat.* of κατατίθημι.

κατόπιν, *adv.*, behind, after.

κατόπισθε, *adv.*, behind.

κάτωθεν, *adv.*, below, from below.

κε, κεν, *H. for* ἄν, *in main conditional clause,* would; *with subj.,* ever.

κεδνός, -ή, όν, trusty.

κείατο, *H. 3rd pl. imperf.* of κεῖμαι.

κεῖμαι, κείσομαι, *imperf.*, ἔκειτο, ἐκεῖντο, *H.*, κεῖτο *or* κέσκετο, *pl.*, κείατο, lie; *also used as pass.* of τίθημι, *hence* κείμενος, established.

κειμήλιον, -ου, *n.*, treasure.

κεῖνος, -η, -ο, = ἐκεῖνος, -η, -ο, that; he.

κεκαδήσω, *H. fut.* of χάζω.

κεκλῆσθαι, κεκλημένος, *perf. infin. and p.p.p.* of καλέω.

κέκλυτε, *H. aor. imperat. pl.* of κλύω.

κεκμηκώς, *p.p.* of κάμνω.

κεκορυθμένος, -η, -ον, equipped, armed, *p.p.p.* of κορύσσω.

κέκρανται, *3rd sing. perf. pass.* of κραίνω.

κεκρασπέδωται, *perf. pass.* of κρασπεδόω.

Κεκροπίδαι, -ῶν, *m.pl.*, descendants of Cecrops., *i.e.* Athenians.

Κέκροψ, -οπος, *m.*, Cecrops, the first king of Athens.

κεκρυμμένος, *p.p.p.* of κρύπτω.

κεκτημένος, *p.p.* of κτάομαι.

κέλευσμα, -ματος, *n.*, order, instruction.

κελεύω, -εύσω, *also* κέλομαι, order.

κενός, -ή, -όν, empty.

κενόω, -ώσω, make empty; τὸ κενούμενον, the empty space.

κεραία, -ας, *f.*, pole.

κεραμίς, -ίδος, *f.*, tile.

κέραμος, -ου, *m.*, tile, tiles.

κεράννῡμι, κεράσω, ἐκράθην, mix, combine.

κέρας, κέρᾱτος *or* κέρως, *H.pl.*, κέραα, *n.*, horn (of a bow).

κέρδος, -ους, *n.*, gain, profit, advantage.

κερκίς, -ίδος, *f.*, weaver's shuttle, *hence* weaving, woven work.

κέσκετο, *H. for* ἐκεῖτο, *from* κεῖμαι.

κεύθω, κεύσω, ἔκυθον, hide, conceal, *tr.*; *perf. intr.*, κέκευθα.

κευτυχῶμεν, = καὶ εὐτυχῶμεν.

κεφαλή, -ῆς, *f.*, head; face.

κεχρημένος, needing, eager for, *with gen.*, *p.p.p.* of χράομαι.

κῆον, *H. aor. imperat.* of καίω.

κῆρ, κῆρος, *n.*, heart.
κήρυγμα, -ματος, *n.*, proclamation.
κῆρυξ, -υκος, *m.*, herald; squire.
Κιθαιρών, -ῶνος, *m.*, Cithaeron, a mountain range separating Boeotia from Attica.
κινδῡνεύω, -εύσω, be in danger (of), risk.
κίνδῡνος, -ου, *m.*, danger.
κλαίω, κλαύσομαι, ἔκλαυσα, *H. imperf.*, κλαῖον, κλαῖε, *imperat. dual,* κλαίετον, weep, weep for.
κλαυθμός, -οῦ, *m.*, weeping.
Κλεόμβροτος, -ου, *m.*, Cleombrotus, father of the Spartan regent Pausanias.
κλεινός, -ή, -όν, famous.
κλέπτω, κλέψω, steal, seize, hide.
κληΐς, -ῗδος, *f.*, key; bolt.
κληρόω, -ώσω, choose by lot, appoint by chance.
κλήω, κλήσω, *H. aor. mid. imperat.,* κλήϊσαι, close, bar.
κλῖμαξ, -μακος, *f.*, ladder, stairway.
κλίνη, -ης, *f.*, couch.
κλίνω, κλινῶ, ἔκλῖνα, lean, *tr.*
κλύδων, -ωνος, *m.*, wave; κλύδων πολέμιος, wave of war.
κλύω, κλύσω, *H. aor. imperat. pl.,* κέκλυτε, hear.
κλών, κλωνός, *m.*, branch, twig.
κοῖλος, -η, -ον, hollow.
κοινός, -ή, -όν, common, shared, allied, party (of a wall); neutral.
κοινόω, -ώσω, report, make known.
κοινωνός, -οῦ, *m.*, accomplice, partner, sharer in, *with gen.*
κοιρανέω, -ήσω, *H. pres. indic.,*

κοιρανέουσι, rule, be king.
κοίρανος -ου, *m.*, ruler, noble.
κολάζω, -άσω, punish.
κολλητός, -ή, -ον, *H. f. dat. pl.,* κολλητῇσιν, well-fastened.
κόλλοψ, -οπος, *m.*, peg (for a lyre).
κομίζω, -ιῶ, ἐκόμισα, -ίσθην, take care of, carry; *pass.*, make a journey.
κόπτω, κόψω, cut down.
κόρη, -ης, *f.*, girl, daughter.
Κόροιβος, -ου, *m.*, Coroebus, a Plataean, father of Ammeas.
κορώνη, -ης, *f.*, hook used as door-handle; bow-tip.
κουρέω, -ήσω, adorn, dress.
κοὐ, = καὶ οὐ; κοὐδείς, = καὶ οὐδείς.
κούρη, -ης, *f.*, girl, daughter.
κουρίδιος, -α, -ον, of one's marriage.
κοῦρος, -ου, *m.*, boy, page; *comp. adj.,* κουρότερος, younger.
'κπεσεῖν, = ἐκπεσεῖν.
κραδίη, -ης, *H. for* καρδία, *f.*, heart.
κραθείς, *aor. part. pass. of* κεράννῡμι.
κραίνω, κρανῶ, *3rd sing. perf. pass.,* κέκρανται, accomplish, carry into effect.
κραναός, -ή, -όν, rocky.
κρασπεδόω, -ώσω, *perf. pass.,* κεκρασπέδωμαι, surround with a border (of).
κρᾶτα, *acc.,* κρατός, *n.,* (*no nom.*), head.
κρατερώνυξ, -υχος, strong-hoofed.
κρατέω, -ήσω, *3rd pl. plup.,* ἐκεκρατήκεσαν, overpower, be master of, control, *with gen.*

κρατήρ, -ῆρος, H., κρητήρ, m., mixing-bowl.

κράτος, -ους, n., power, authority, victory.

κραυγή, -ῆς, f., shouting.

κρείσσων, -ον, n. pl., κρείσσω, stronger, better; more welcome.

Κρέουσα, -ης, f., Creüsa, daughter of Erechtheus and mother of Ion.

κρήδεμνον, -ου, n., veil, also pl.

κρηπίς, -ῖδος, f., platform, floor, also pl.

κρητήρ, -ῆρος, m., H. for κρατήρ.

κρίνω, κρινῶ, ἔκρῑνα, judge, put on trial.

κριτής, -οῦ, m., judge.

Κρονίων, -ονος, m., son of Cronus, i.e. Zeus.

Κρόνος, -ου, m., Cronus, son of Uranus and father of Zeus.

κρούω, κρούσω, strike.

κρυπτός, -ή, -όν, secret, hidden.

κρύπτω, κρύψω, p.p.p., κεκρυμμένος, hide, conceal, swallow up.

κρύσταλλος, -ου, m., ice.

κρυφαῖος, -α, -ον, secret, in secret.

κτανεῖν, str. aor. infin. of κτείνω.

κτάομαι, κτήσομαι, p.p., κεκτημένος, obtain.

κτείνω, κτενῶ, ἔκτεινα, str. aor., ἔκτανον, kill.

κτῆμα, -ματος, n., possession.

κτίζω, κτίσω, establish.

κτίστωρ, -ορος, m., founder.

κτυπέω, -ήσω, H. imperf., ἔκτυπε, make a noise, thunder.

κτύπος, -ου, m., noise, sound.

κυδάλιμος, -η, -ον, noble, renowned.

κύκλος, -ου, m., circle; κύκλῳ, all round; in his course.

κυνέω, -ήσομαι, H. imperf., κύνεον, aor., ἔκυσσα, kiss.

κυρέω, -ήσω, happen to be, with part.; meet, with gen.

κύτος, -ους, n., cradle, chest; lid.

κύων, κυνός, c., dog.

κῶας, n., fleece, sheepskin.

κωλῡτής, -οῦ, m., one who hinders.

κῶμος, -ου, m., flock, flight (of birds).

κώπη, -ης, f., handle.

Λ

λάβε, H. for ἔλαβε, λαβεῖν, λαβών, aor. infin. and part., of λαμβάνω.

Λᾱερτιάδης, -ου, H., -εω, m., son of Laërtes, i.e. Odysseus.

λάζυμαι, seize.

λαθεῖν, aor. infin. of λανθάνω.

λάθρᾱ, adv., secretly; with gen., unknown to.

λαθραῖος, -α, -ον, secret, born in secrecy.

λαιμός, -οῦ, m., throat, lips.

Λακεδαιμόνιοι, -ων, m. pl., the Lacedaemonians, Spartans.

Λακεδαίμων, -μονος, f., Lacedaemon, Sparta.

Λάκων, -ωιος, m., Lacon, son of Aieimnestus, Plataean 'proxenus' to the Spartans.

λαμβάνω, λήψομαι, ἔλαβον, ἐλήφθην, take, seize, obtain; mid. with gen., take to.

λαμπάς, -πάδος, f., torch.

λαμπρός, -ά, -όν, glorious; τὰ

λαμπρότατα, most glorious deeds.
λανθάνω, λήσω, ἔλαθον, λέληθα, λέλησμαι, *1st pl. plup.*, ἐλελήσμεθα, escape notice, be unseen by, conceal from; *mid. with gen.*, forget, τὸ λανθάνειν, secrecy.
λᾱός, -οῦ, *m.*, people.
λάτρις, -ιος, *m.*, servant, lackey.
λέγω, λέξω, say, order.
λείβω, λείψω, pour out.
λειμών, -ῶνος, *m.*, meadow.
λείπω, λείψω, ἔλιπον, leave.
λέληθα, *perf.* 'λελήσμεθα, *plup. mid.*, *of* λανθάνω.
λέξον, *aor. imperat. of* λέγω.
Λεοντιάδης, -ου, *m.*, Leontiades, father of the Theban Eurymachus.
λευκός, -ή, -όν, white.
λέχος, -ους, *n.*, bed; marriage; γαμεῖν λέχος, win the hand of; χρόνια σπείρας λέχη, after being married a long time.
λήγω, λήξω, cease, cease from, *with gen. or part.*
λήσω, *fut. of* λανθάνω.
ληφθείς, *aor. part. pass.*, λήψομαι, *fut. of* λαμβάνω.
Ληώδης, -ου, *m.*, Leodes, son of Oenops, one of Penelope's suitors.
λιγέως, *adv.*, shrilly, loudly.
λίθινος, -η, -ον, made of stone.
λίθος, -ου, *m.*, stone.
λιμήν, λιμένος, *m.*, harbour.
λιμός, -οῦ, *m.*, hunger, starvation.
λιπαρός, -ά, -όν, shining.
λιποίμην, *aor. mid. opt.*, λιπόντε,

nom. dual. aor. part., of λείπω.
λίσσομαι, beg.
λογισμός, -οῦ, *m.*, calculation, count.
λόγος, -ου, *dual*, λόγω, λόγοιν, *m.*, word, story, speech, proposal, argument, theory; *pl.*, discussions.
λοιβή, -ῆς, *f.*, libation, drink-offering.
Λοξίας, -ου, *m.*, Loxias, a name of Apollo.
Λυκῖνος, -ου, *m.*, Lycinus, an acquantance of Herodes and Euxitheus.
λῡμαίνομαι, -οῦμαι, ill-treat.
λύω, λύσω, loosen, open; *mid.*, ransom, obtain the release of.

M

'μ', =ἐμέ, *acc. of* ἐγώ.
μαθών, *aor. part. of* μανθάνω.
Μαῖα, -ας, *f.*, Maia, daughter of Atlas and mother of Hermes.
μαίνομαι, μανοῦμαι, *perf.*, μέμηνα, be mad; *aor. act.*, ἔμηνα, drove mad.
μακάριος, -α, -ον, happy.
μακρός, -ά, -όν, *H. f. acc.*, -ήν, long; αἱ Μακραί, the Long Cliffs, at Athens; *comp. adv.*, μακρότερα, at greater length.
μάλα, *adv.*, much; *comp.*, μᾶλλον, more; *superl.* μάλιστα, very much, most, best of all; about; ὡς μάλιστα, as much as you like; generally.
μανθάνω, μαθήσομαι, ἔμαθον, learn, discover.

μαντεῖον, -ον, n., oracular shrine.

μάντευμα, -ματος, n., oracle.

μαντεύομαι, -εύσομαι, consult an oracle (about); give an oracular response.

μαντευτός, -ή, -όν, given by an oracle.

μάντις, -εως, m., seer, soothsayer.

μαρτυρέω, -ήσω, be a witness (to), bring evidence; impers. pass., evidence is given.

μαρτυρία, -ας, f., evidence.

μάρτυς, -υρος, m., witness.

μαστός, -οῦ, m., breast; μαστὸν ὑπέχειν, offer the breast, feed an infant.

ματήν, adv., in vain; spoken idly.

μάχαιρα, -ας, f., dagger, knife.

μάχη, -ης, f., battle.

μεγάθυμος, -ον, great-souled.

Μεγαρεύς, -έως, m., a Megarian, from Megara, a town near the Isthmus of Corinth.

μέγαρον, -ου, H., -οιο, n., hall, room, also pl., μέγαρονδέ, to the hall.

μέγας, μεγάλη, μέγα, large, high; n. as adv., μέγα, very; μέγαλα, loudly; ἐπὶ μέγα, over a large part; superl., μέγιστος.

μέγεθος, -ους, n., greatness, violence.

μεθίημι, -ήσω, -ῆκα, H. 3rd pl. imperf., μέθιεν, let go; intr., relax, cease from, with gen.

μεθίστημι, μεταστήσω, μετέστησα, turn aside, tr.; mid. and str. aor. act., μετέστην, intr.

μέθυ, -υος, n., wine.

μεθύω, be drunk.

μείγνῡμι, μείζω, mix, mingle; aor. infin. pass., μιγῆναι, be united in love, marry.

μειλίχιος, -α, -ον, gentle.

μεῖναι, aor. infin. of μένω.

μέλαθρον, -ου, n., hall, house, also pl.

Μελάνθιος, -ου, H., -οιο, m., Melanthius, the disloyal goatherd of Odysseua.

μέλας, μέλαινα, μέλαν, H. f. gen. pl., μελαινάων, black.

μέλει, -ήσει, impers. with dat., it is a care to, it concerns; also with gen. of the thing.

μελιηδής, -ές, honey-sweet.

μέλλω, -ήσω, be about to, intend, be likely to; hesitate.

μέλος, -ους, H. dat. pl., -εσσι, n., limb, arm.

μέμηκα, perf. of μαίνομαι; οἱ μεμηκότες, the mad.

μέμνημαι, (perf.), μεμνήσομαι, remember, with gen.

μέν, particle, usually followed by δέ, on the one hand, but often omitted in translation; also = μήν; H., καὶ μὲν δή, and indeed.

μενεαίνω, desire greatly.

μένος, -ους, n., strength.

μένω, μενῶ, ἔμεινα, remain, stay.

μέριμνα -ης, f., anxiety.

μερίς, -ίδος, f., part; some.

μέρος, -ους, n., part.

μέσος, -η, -ον, middle; ἐν μέσῳ, in the middle.

Μεσσήνη, -ης, f., Messene, a district of Sparta.

Μεσσήνιοι, -ων, m.pl., Messenians, from Messene.

μετά, prep. with acc., after; with gen., with, with the help of; with dat., among; μεθ' ἡμέραν, by day.

μέτα, =μέτεστι, 3rd sing. indic. of μέτειμι.

μεταβαίνω, -βήσομαι, μετέβην, move across.

μεταγιγνώσκω, -γνώσομαι, μετέγνων, part., μεταγνούς, change one's mind.

μεταμέλει, -ήσει, impers. with dat. and gen., repent of, change one's mind about.

μετανοέω, -ήσω, change one's mind.

μεταξύ, adv. and prep. with gen., between; τὸ μεταξύ, the space between.

μεταπίπτω, -πεσοῦμαι, μετέπεσον, change, intr.

μεταπύργιον, -ου, n., space between two towers.

μετασχών, aor. part. of μετέχω.

μεταστῆναι, str. aor. infin of μεθίστημι.

μεταυδάω, -ήσω, imperf., -ηύδα, speak.

μετάφημι, μετέφην, speak among, with dat.

μεταχωρέω, -ήσω, depart.

μετέειπε, H. for μετεῖπε.

μέτειμι, -έσομαι, -ῆν, be present; μέτα, =μέτεστι: also impers., there is a share of, with gen.

μετεκβαίνω, -βήσομαι, μετεξέβην, go from one ship to another.

μετέκβασις, -εως, f., a move to another ship.

μετέχω, μετασχήσω, μετέσχον, take a share in, with gen.

μετέωρος, -ον, aloft; τὸ μετεώρον, the top.

μέτρον, -ου, n., measurement, measure, size, length.

μέτωπον, -ου, n., face, face of a wall.

μεῦ, H. for μου, gen. of ἐγώ.

μή, conj. used with subj., opt. and infin., not, that . . . not.

μηδέ, adv., not even, and . . . not (used like μή).

μηδείς, μηδεμία, μηδέν, nobody, nothing, no (used like μή).

μηδέτερος, -α, -ον, neither of two (used like μή).

Μῆδος, -ου, m., a Mede, a Persian, usually pl.; μετὰ τὸν Μῆδον, after the defeat of the Persians.

Μηθυμναία, -ας, f., the territory of Methymna, in Lesbos.

μηκέτι, adv., no longer (used like μή).

μῆλον -ου, n., sheep.

μήν, μηνός, m., month.

μήν, particle, indeed.

μηνοειδής, -ές, crescent-shaped.

μηνυτής,-οῦ, m., informer.

μηνύω, -ύσω, lay information, reveal, make public.

μήποτε, adv., never (used like μή).

μήπω, adv., not yet (used like μή).

μήρια, -ων, n. pl., thigh-pieces.

μήτε . . . μήτε, conj., neither . . . nor; μήτε, and . . . not (used like μή).

μήτηρ, μητρός, H., μητέρος, f., mother.

μητρυιά, -âs, f., step-mother.
μηχανάομαι, -ήσομαι, plup., ἐμεμηχάνητο, H. pres. subj., μηχανόωντο,
plot, make a plot.
μηχανή, -ῆς, f., trick, device, daring
scheme; siege-engine.
μηχάνωμα, -ματος, n., plot, device.
μία, f. of εἷς.
μιγῆναι, aor. infin. pass. of μείγνυμι.
μίμημα, -ματος, n., imitation, also pl.
μιν, H. for αὐτόν, -ήν, -ό, him, her, it.
μνᾶ, μνᾶς, f., mina, 100 drachmas,
about £4 in silver, but with a
very much higher purchasing
power.
μνάομαι, 3rd pl., μνῶνται, 3rd sing.
imperat., μνάσθω, court, woo;
desire, plan.
μνῆμα, -ματος, n., memorial.
μνήμων, -ον, mindful; μνήμων εἰμί,
remember.
μνηστήρ, -ῆρος, H. dat. pl., -ήρεσσι,
m., suitor.
μογέω, -ήσω, toil.
μοῖρα, -ας, f., fate, destiny.
μολεῖν, aor. infin. (no present), come,
go.
μόλις, adv., with difficulty.
μολπή, -ῆς, f., dancing.
μόνος, -η, -ον, alone, only.
μόρσιμος, -ον, sent by fate.
μορφή, -ῆς, f., figure, pattern.
μοχλός, -οῦ, m., bar.
μόχθος, -ου, m., hard work, bustle.
μῦθέομαι, -ήσομαι, say, speak, tell a
story.
μῦθος, -ου, m., word, story; suggestion.

Μυκήνη, -ης, f., Mycenae, capital
of King Agamemnon, in Argos
(northern Peloponnese).
μύνη, -ης, H. dat. pl., -ῃσι, f., excuse.
Μυτιλήνη, -ης, f., Mytilene, the
chief town of Lesbos.
μυχοίτατος, -η, -ον, superl., innermost, in the farthest corner.
μῶν, interrog. particle, surely not?

N

ναί, adv., yes; indeed.
ναιετάω, H. part., ναιετάων, dwell
in; also in pass. sense, ναιετάων,
situated, placed.
ναίω, dwell, live.
νᾱός, -οῦ, m., temple, also pl.
νάσσω, νάξω, stamp down.
Ναυκλείδης, -ου, m., Naucleides, a
Plataean who admitted the
Thebans into Plataea.
ναῦς, νεώς, H., νεός, νηῶν, νηυσί,
f., ship.
νεᾱνίας, -ου, m., young man, youth.
νέεσθαι, H. infin. of νέομαι.
νεῖκος, -ους, n., enmity, feud.
νείμω, aor. subj. of νέμω.
νεκρός, -οῦ, m., corpse, dead body.
νεμεσσάω, -ήσω, H. imperf., νεμέσσα,
and νεμέσα, aor., νεμέσσησα, be
angry (with).
νέμω, νεμῶ, ἔνειμα, give; mid., possess, inhabit.
νεογνός, -όν, and νεογονός, -όν, new-
born.
νέομαι, H. infin., νέεσθαι, go.
νέος, -α, -ον, young, new, newly-
found; violent; comp., νεώτερος,

too young; μηδὲν νεώτερον ποιεῖν, do no violence.

νεός, H. for νεώς, gen. of ναῦς.

νευρά, -ᾶς, H., -ή, -ῆς, f., bow-string.

νεώς, -ώ, m., temple.

νεωτερίζω, -ιῶ, make a (political) change, take violent action, do harm.

νηί, dat. of ναῦς.

νηλεής, -ές, H. dat., νηλεῖ, pitiless.

νημερτής, -ές, H. acc., -έα, sure, for certain.

νήπιος, -α, -ον, speechless, young; foolish; m., an infant.

νῆσος, -ου, f., island.

νηυσί, H. dat. pl. of ναῦς.

νῑκάω, -ήσω, conquer, overcome: pass. with gen., submit to.

νιν, him, her, it (= αὐτόν, -ήν, -ό).

νοέω, H. 2nd sing., νοόεις, -ήσω, know.

νομεύς, -έως, H. acc. pl., -ῆας, m., shepherd.

νομίζω, -ιῶ, ἐνόμισα, think; νομίζε-ται, it is customary; νομιζόμενος, customary.

νόμιμος, -η, -ον, lawful, customary; τὰ νόμιμα, customary gifts; adv., νομίμως, lawfully.

νόμος, -ου, m., law, custom.

νοσέω, -ήσω, be ill, be weak, suffer, be unhappy.

νόσος, -ου, f., illness, suffering, unhappiness.

νοστέω, -ήσω, return, intr.

νοσφίζομαι, -ιοῦμαι H. aor. part., νοσφισσάμενος, depart, leave.

νοτερός, -ά, -όν, rainy; χειμὼν νοτερός, rain storm.

νουθετέω, -ήσω, advise, order.

νοῦς, νοῦ, H., νόος, νόου, m., mind, attention; νοῦν ἔχω or προσέχω, pay attention; νοῦν δίδωμι, turn one's thoughts.

νύκτωρ, adv., in the night.

νυ, H. for νυν.

νυμφεύω, -εύσω, marry; pass., be married.

νῦν, νῡνί, adv., now; νῦν δέ, but as it is; νῦν ἀλλά, now at last.

νυν, νῦν, enclitic adv., well then, then, now.

νύξ, νυκτός, f., night.

νωμάω, -ήσω, H. aor., νώμησα, serve out, handle.

νῷν, of us two, gen. and dat. dual of ἐγώ.

νῶτον, -ου, n., back, shoulder, also pl.

Ξ

'ξέθηκα, = ἐξέθηκα, aor. of ἐκτίθημι.

ξεῖνος, -ου, H. for ξένος, m., friend, guest, stranger.

ξεινοσύνη, -ης, f., friendship.

ξεναγός, -οῦ, m., commander of allies or auxiliaries.

ξένος, -ου, m., friend, guest, stranger.

ξέω, ξέσω, H. aor., ξέσσα, plane.

ξιφηφόρος, -ου, armed with a sword.

ξιφίδιον, -ου, n., dagger.

ξίφος, -ους, n., sword.

ξόανον, -ου, n., statue of a god at an altar.

Ξοῦθος, -ου, m., Xuthus, son of

Aeolus and husband of Creüsa.

ξυγγενής, -ές, related; m., kinsman.

ξυγγνώμων, -ον, indulgent; with εἰμί, grant that, with dat. and infin.

ξυγκαλέω, -καλῶ, ξυνεκάλεσα, call together.

ξυγχωρέω, -ήσω, agree.

ξύλινος, -η, -ον, made of wood, wooden.

ξυλλαμβάνω, -λήψομαι, ξυνέλαβον, -είλημμαι, seize, arrest; with gen. and dat., help . . . in.

ξυλλέγομαι, -έξομαι, come together.

ξύλον, -ου, n., wood, timber, also pl.

ξυμβαίνω, -βήσομαι, ξυνέβην, happen; make terms with, come to an agreement with, with dat.

ξυμβάλλω, -βαλῶ, ξυνέβαλον, H. 3rd pl. dual, ξυμβλήτην, meet.

ξύμβασις, -εως, f., agreement.

ξυμβῆναι, aor. infin. of ξυμβαίνω.

ξυμβλήτην, H. 3rd pl. dual aor. of ξυμβάλλω.

ξυμμαχέω, -ήσω, be in alliance, be allied.

ξυμμαχία, -ας, f., alliance.

ξυμμαχίς, ίδος, f. adj., allied; as noun, allied city.

ξύμμαχος, -ου, m., ally.

ξυμμετρέομαι, -ήσομαι, ξυνεμετρησάμην, calculate, get the measurements of.

ξυμμέτρησις, -εως, f., measurement.

ξύμπας, -πασα, -παν, all, the whole; n. as adv., τὸ ξύμπαν, entirely.

ξυμπολιορκέω, -ήσω, join in besieging.

ξυμφορά, -ᾶς, f., chance, fortune, misfortune.

ξύμφορος, -ον, useful.

ξύν, prep. with dat., with; ξὺν ὅπλυις, fully armed.

ξυναίρω, -αρῶ, -ῆρα, aor. mid. infin.. -άρασθαι, join in facing: mid., take part in.

ξυνάπτω, -άψω, join together; ξυνάπτειν πόδα, meet.

ξύνδεσμος, -ου, m., a binding together.

ξυνέβην, aor. of ξυμβαίνω.

ξυνειλημμένος, ξυνέλαβον, p.p.p. and aor. of ξύλλαμβάνω.

For the present tense of verbs beginning ξυνεβ-, ξυνεκ-, ξυνελ-, ξυνεμ-, ξυστ-, ξυνεχ-, see ξυμβ-, ξυγκ-, ξυλλ-, ξυμμ-, ξυνεστ-, ξυγχ-.

ξυνελευθερόω, -ώσω, join in freeing.

ξυνεστραμμένος, p.p.p. of ξυστρέφομαι; imperf., ξυνεστρεφόμην.

ξυνεχής, -ές, continual, continuous; adv., ξυνεχῶς, continuously.

ξυνεφίσταμαι, ξυνεπιστήσομαι, join in commanding; p.p., ξυνεφεστώς, being in joint command.

ξυνήδη, imperf. of ξύνοιδα.

ξυνθείς, aor. part. of ξυντίθημι.

ξυνίστωρ, -ορος, m., witness.

ξύνοιδα, -είσομαι, imperf., -ήδη, share knowledge of, know; ξυνειδὼς αὑτῷ, being aware in one's own mind, having a guilty conscience.

ξυνόμνῡμι, -ομοῦμαι, -ώμοσα, make a sworn alliance (with), join in swearing.

ξυντεκμαίρομαι, -αροῦμαι, -ετεκμη-
ράμην, calculate, guess.
ξυντίθημι, -θήσω, -έθηκα, construct,
put together.
ξυντυγχάνω, -τεύξομαι, -έτυχον,
happen, befall; ὁ ξυντυχών, that
may befall.
ξυστρέφομαι, -στρέψομαι, imperf.,
ξυνεστρεφόμην, perf., ξυνέσ-
τραμμαι, gather together, rally.
ξυνώμοσα, aor. of ξυνόμνυμι.
ξυνώμοτος, -ον, confederate; τὸ
ξυνώμοτον, the sworn con-
federacy.

O

ὁ, ἡ, τό, dual, τώ, H. gen., τοῖο; in H.
a demonstrative pronoun, he, she, it;
or a relative pronoun, who, which;
in Attic Greek the definite article,
the; ὁ δέ, and he; οἱ μὲν ... οἱ δέ,
some ... others.
ὀγδοήκοντα, indecl., eighty.
ὄγκιον, -ου, n., chest.
ὄγκος, -ου, m., burden.
ὅδε, ἥδε, τόδε, this; he, she, it.
ὁδός, -ου, f., road, way, journey.
ὀδούς, ὀδόντος, m., tooth, tusk.
ὀδύρομαι, -οῦμαι, weep, lament, be
angry.
Ὀδυσσεύς, -έως, H. also Ὀδυσεύς,
-ῆα, -ῆος, -ῆϊ, m., Odysseus, son
of Laërtes, husband of Penelope,
and king of Ithaca.
ὅθεν, adv., whence, wherefore.
οἱ, dat. of ἕ; also = αὐτῷ, -ῆ.
οἶδα, εἴσομαι, imperf., ᾔδη or ᾔδειν,
know.

οἴκαδε, adv., homewards.
οἰκέτης, -ου, m., slave, servant; adj.,
of a slave.
οἰκέω, -ήσω, live in.
οἴκημα, -ματος, n., building, room.
οἰκίον, -ου, n., house.
οἰκδομέω, -ήσω, plup. pass., ᾠκοδόμητο, build, build over.
οἰκοδόμημα, -ματος, n., building,
structure.
οἰκοδόμησις, -εως, f., building,
method of building.
οἴκοθι, adv., at home.
οἶκος, -ου, m., house, home; room;
οἰκόνδε, to her room.
οἶκτος, -ου,m., pity, sorrow, lamentation.
οἰκτρός, -ά, -όν, pitiful, piteous.
οἶμαι, contracted form of οἴομαι,
think.
οἴμοι, interj., alas.
οἰνηρός, -ά, -όν, of wine, wine-.
οἰνοβαρείων, H. pres. part., being
heavy with wine.
οἶνος, -ου, m., wine.
οἰνοχοεύω, pour wine.
οἰνοχόος, -ου, m., cup-bearer.
Οἶνοψ, -οπος, m., Oenops, father of
the suitor Leodes.
οἷο, H. gen. of ὅς, his.
οἴομαι, H., ὀΐομαι, -ήσομαι, imperf.,
ᾠόμην, think.
οἷος, -α, -ον, H. f., -η. as, such as;
οἷός τέ εἰμι, be able.
οἶος, -η, -ον, alone.
ὄϊς, οἰός, c., sheep.
οἰστός or ὀϊστός, -ου, m., arrow.
οἶσθα, 2nd sing. of οἶδα.

οἴσω, *fut. of* φέρω.

οἴχομαι, -ήσομαι, go away, be gone.

ὀίω, *H. for* οἴομαι, think.

οἰωνός, -οῦ, *m.*, omen, (*lit.*, bird).

ὀλβίζω, -ιῶ, ὤλβισα, reckon happy.

ὄλβος, -ου, *m.*, wealth, happiness, prosperity.

ὄλεθρος, -ου, *m.*, death, destruction.

ὀλίγος, -η, -ον, few, small; δι' ὀλίγου, close together; ὀλίγῳ, (by) a little.

ὄλλῡμι, ὀλῶ, ὤλεσα, *mid.*, ὠλόμην, *H. aor. act.*, ὄλεσσα, *mid.*, ὀλόμην, destroy; *mid.*, die.

ὀλολῡγή, -ῆς, *f.*, cheering, screaming.

ὀμαιχμος, -ου, *m.*, comrade in arms, ally.

ὁμαρτέω, -ήσω, walk together.

ὁμῑλέω, *H. 1st pl.*, ὁμῑλέομεν, -ήσω, assemble.

ὅμῑλος, -ου, *m.*, company.

ὄμνῡμι, ὀμοῦμαι, ὤμοσα, swear.

ὁμοβώμιος, -ον, worshipped at the same altar.

ὅμοιος, -α, -ον, similar to, consistent with; *adv.*, ὁμοίως, similarly, in the same way.

ὁμοκλέω, -ήσω, *H. imperf.*, ὁμόκλεον, chide, rebuke.

ὁμολογέω, -ήσω, admit, confess.

ὀμφαλός, -οῦ, *m.*, navel, centre.

ὄν, *n. pres. part. of* εἰμί, I am; τὸ ὄν, what actually happens.

ὧδε, to his (*acc. of* ὅς, his, *with* -δε).

ὄνειρον, -ου, *n.*, dream.

ὄνησις, -εως, *H.*, -ιος, *f.*, benefit, advantage.

Ὀνητορίδης, -ου, *m.*, Onetorides, a Theban, father of Diemporus.

ὄνομα, -ματος, *n.*, name, description.

ὄνομαι, ὀνόσομαι, say insultingly.

ὀνομάζω, -άσω, call, name.

ὀξύς, ὀξεῖα, ὀξύ, sharp.

ὄπα, *acc. of* ὄψ (*not used in nom.*) voice, cry.

ὀπάζω, ὀπάσσω, give.

ὀπάων, -ονος, *m.*, attendant.

ὄπις, *acc.* ὄπιν *or* ὄπιδα, *f.*, vengeance.

ὁπλίζω, -ιῶ, ὤπλισα, arm.

ὅπλισις, -εως, *f.*, equipment.

ὅπλον, -ου, *n.*, cable, rope; *pl.*, arms; ξὺν ὅπλοις, fully armed, under arms.

ὁπλότερος, -α, -ον, *comp. adj.*, younger,

ὁπόθεν, *adv.*, from which, from where.

ὅποι, *adv.*, whither, where.

ὁπόσος, -η, -ον, how great; *pl.*, how many.

ὁπότε, *conj.*, whenever, when, since.

ὅπου, *conj.*, where, when.

ὅππῃ, *conj.*, where, whither.

ὀπτήρ, -ῆρος, *m.*, eye-witness.

ὄπωπα, *perf. of* ὁράω; *H. plup.*, ὀπώπει.

ὅπως, *conj.*, how, that, in order that.

ὁράω, ὄψομαι, εἶδον, ὄπωπα, *H. plup.*, ὀπώπει, see, detect.

ὄργανον, -ου, *n.*, craftsman's work.

ὀργή, -ῆς, *f.*, anger.

ὀργίζομαι, -ιοῦμαι, ὠργισάμην, be angry.

ὀρέγομαι, -ξομαι, reach up.

ὀρθός, -ή, -όν, straight, right,

proper; to one's full height: adv.,
ὀρθῶς; μὴ ὀρθῶς, wrongly; superl.,
ὀρθότατα, with full certainty;
ὀρθῶς ἔχω, be fair.
ὁρίζω, -ιῶ, ὥρισα, separate; bound;
decree.
ὀρίνω, dual, ὀρίνετον, aor. ὤρῑνα, stir
up.
ὅρκιος, -α, -ον, invoked by oath, by
whom one swears.
ὅρκος, -ου, m., oath.
ὁρμάω, -ήσω, rush, start.
ὁρμέω, -ήσω, lie at anchor.
ὁρμίζομαι, -ιοῦμαι, ὡρμισάμην, come
to anchor.
ὄρνις, ὄρνῑθος, c., bird.
ὄρνῡμι, ὄρσω, ὦρσα, rouse, stir up,
incite; mid., arise; pres. imperat.,
ὄρνυσθε.
ὅρος, -ου, m., boundary, limit.
ὄρος, -ους, n., mountain.
ὄροφος, -ου, m., roof.
ὀρρωδία, -ας, f., fear, alarm.
'Ορτίλοχος, -ου, m., Ortilochus, a
Spartan friend of Odysseus.
ὀρύσσω, ὀρύξω, dig.
ὄρφνη, -ης, f., darkness, night.
ὅς, ἥ, ὅ, relative pronoun, who, which;
also H. demonstrative, that.
ὅς, ἥ, ὅν, H. gen., οἷο, his, her, its.
ὅσιος, -α, -ον, righteous, just; adv.,
ὁσίως, justly; τὰ ὅσια, human
rights.
ὅσος, -η, -ον, H., ὅσσος, as much as;
pl., as many as; n., as adv., as far
as; ἐν ὅσῳ, while, until.
ὄσσε, dual, ὔσσων, ὄσσοις, n., the two
eyes.

ὅστις, ἥτις, ὅτι, m., gen., ὅτου, dat.,
ὅτῳ, whoever, who; ὅτου εἵνεκα,
for what reason: ὅτῳ τρόπῳ, in
what way.
ὅταν, conj. with subj., whenever,
when.
ὅτε, conj., when, since.
ὅτι, n. of ὅστις; conj., that; because.
ὅτου, ὅτῳ, gen. and dat. of ὅστις.
ὅττι, H. for ὅτι, that; because.
οὐ, οὐκ, οὐχ, οὐχί, adv., not; οὔ, no.
οὗ, gen. of ὅς; also adv., where.
οὖας, οὔατος, n., ear.
οὐδαμοῦ, adv., nowhere.
οὐδέ, conj., and . . . not, nor, not
even; οὐδὲ μὲν οὐδέ, never, never.
οὐδείς, οὐδεμία, οὐδέν, nobody,
nothing; no.
οὐδέπω, adv., not even yet.
οὐδέτερος, -α, -ον, neither of two.
οὐδός, -οῦ, m., threshold.
οὐκέτι, adv., no longer.
οὔκουν, adv., not indeed.
οὐλή, -ῆς, f., scar.
οὖν, adv., therefore, then; δ'οὖν, at
any rate.
οὔνεκα, = ἕνεκα, prep. with gen., for
the sake of; ὧν οὔνεκα, wherefore;
as conj., because.
οὗπερ, adv., where.
οὐπιών, = ὁ ἐπιών, part. of ἔπειμι
(ἐπέρχομαι), anyone who chances
to come.
οὔποτε, adv., never.
οὔπω, adv., not yet; οὐπώποτε,
never yet; never.
οὔτε, adv., and . . . not; οὔτε . . . οὔτε,
neither . . . nor.

οὔτις, οὔτι, no one.

οὗτος, αὕτη, τοῦτο, also οὑτοσί, this, here in court; τοῦτο μὲν ... τοῦτο δέ, on the one hand ... on the other, not only ... but also, either ... or.

οὕτω, οὕτως, also οὑτωσί, adv., thus.

οὐχ, οὐχί, adv., not.

ὀφείλω, -ήσω, H. aor., ὄφελλον, owe; aor. ὠφέλον, with infin., a wish for the past, would that.

ὄφις, ὄφεως, m., snake, serpent.

ὄφρα, conj. with indic., until; with subj., in order that.

ὀφρύς, -ύος, f., eyebrow.

ὀχεύς, -έως, H. acc. pl.,-ῆας, m., bolt.

ὀχέω, -ήσω, H. part., -έων, carry.

ὀχθέω, -ήσω, be vexed, be annoyed.

ὄχθος, -ου, m., hill.

ὄψ, not used in nom., ὀπός, acc. ὄπα, voice, cry.

ὄψις, -εως, f., sight, eyes; ὄψιν προσβάλλω, set eyes on, with dat.

Π

πάγχρυσος, -ον, golden, all golden.

παθεῖν, aor. infin. of πάσχω,

πάθος, -ους, n., suffering, misfortune.

παιδεύομαι, -εύσομαι, spend one's childhood.

παιδνός, -οῦ, m., boy, lad.

παῖς, H., πάϊς, παιδός, c., child, boy, son, girl, daughter.

πάλαι, adv., long ago, formerly.

παλαιός, -ά, -όν, old, ancient.

παλάμη, -ης, H. dat. pl., -ῃσι, f., hand.

πάλιν, adv., again.

παλίντονος, -υν, springy, that springs back.

Παλλάς, -άδος, f., Pallas Athena, goddess of wisdom and war.

πάλος, -ου, m., lot, chance.

πανουργέω, -ήσω, commit a crime; οἱ πανουργοῦντες, criminals.

πανταχῇ, adv., everywhere, all round, each way.

πάντῃ, adv., everywhere.

πανστρατίᾳ, dat. used as adv., in full force.

πάνυ, adv., much, very much.

πάρ, H. for παρά.

παρά, prep. with acc., to, past, along, contrary to, besides, after; with gen., from; with dat., among, near, with.

παραβαίνω, -βήσομαι, παρέβην, transgress, disregard.

παραβάλλω, -βαλῶ, παρέβαλον, throw down, pile up side by side.

παραβοηθέω, -ήσω, bring help, come to help.

παραγίγνομαι, -γενήσομαι, παρεγενόμην, arrive.

παράγω, -άξω, παρήγαγον, lead forward.

παραδίδωμι, -δώσω, παρέδωκα, aor. infin. act., παραδοῦναι, p.p.p., -δεδόμενος, hand over, surrender.

παραζεύγνῦμι, -ζεύξω, set beside.

παρακαταθήκη, -ης, f., a trust, deposit.

παράκειμαι, imperf., παρεκεῖτο, lie beside.

παράκοιτις, -ιος, f., wife.

παραλαμβάνω, -λήψομαι, παρέλαβον, remove, take from.

παρανίσχω, imperf., -ῖσχον, raise as a counter-signal.

παρανόμως, adv., illegally.

παράπαν, with τό, adv., at all.

παρασκευάζομαι, -άσομαι, 3rd sing. plup. pass., παρεσκεύαστο, p.p.p., παρεσκευασμένος, prepare, make preparations.

παρασκευή, -ῆς, f., preparations, previous arrangements; expedition.

παρασχήσομαι, fut. mid. of παρέχω.

παρατίθημι, -θήσω, -έθηκα, H., πὰρ ... θῆκε, H. pres. imperat., πὰρ ... τίθει, set before, place beside.

παραχρῆμα, adv., immediately; ἐν τῷ παραχρῆμα, by immediate action; εἰς τὸ παραχρῆμα, immediately; for the moment.

παρέδομεν, 3rd pl. aor. of παραδίδωμι.

παρέθηκα, aor. of παρατίθημι.

παρειαί, -ῶν, f. pl., cheeks.

πάρειμι, -έσομαι, be present; impers., πάρεστι, it is possible.

παρείς, aor. part. of παρίημι.

παρελθεῖν, aor. infin. of παρέρχομαι.

παρέλκω, -έλξω, -είλκυσα, draw out.

παρέξομαι, fut. mid. of παρέχω.

παρέρχομαι, -ειμι, -ῆλθον, go by, pass by, be over.

παρεσκευασμένος, παρεσκεέαστο, p.p.p. and plup. pass. of παρασκευάζομαι.

παρέστην, str. aor. of παρίστημι.

παρέχω, παρασχήσω or παρέξω, -έσχον, provide, make; mid., produce.

παρήγαγον, aor. of παράγω.

παρηΐς, -ΐδος, f., cheek.

παρθένος, -ου, f., maiden, virgin; adj., maiden.

παρθένευμα, -ματος, n., work done by a maiden.

παρίημι, -ήσω, -ῆκα, part., -είς, relax, loosen, set aside.

παρίστημι, παραστήσω, παρέστησα, set aside; str. aor., παρέστην, stand beside.

Παρνησόνδε, to Mount Parnassus, near Delphi.

πάροδος, -ου, f., way through, passage.

πάροιθε, prep. with gen., before.

παροικοδομέω, -ήσω, -ῳκοδόμησα, build ... alongside.

πάρος, adv., before, formerly.

παρών, pres. part. of πάρειμι; τὰ παρόντα, the present need.

πᾶς, πᾶσα, πᾶν, all, the whole.

πάσσαλος, -ου, m., peg.

πάσχω, πείσομαι, ἔπαθον, πέπονθα, suffer, be treated.

πατήρ, πατρός, m., father.

πάτρα, -ας, f., native land.

πάτριος, -α, -ον, ancestral, hereditary; of one's fathers; τὰ πάτρια, the ancestral custom.

πατρίς, -ίδος, f. adj., native, of one's father; as f. noun, native land.

πατρῷος, -ον, of one's fathers, ancestral.

Παυσανίας, -ου, m., Pausanias, regent of Sparta during the Persian Wars.

παύω, παύσω, dual imper. mid.,

παύεσθον, aor. pass., ἐπαύσθην, stop, check; mid., cease from.

πάχος, -ους, n., thickness.

παχύς, -εῖα, -ύ, H. f. dat., παχείῃ, thick, broad, strong.

πεδάω, -ήσω, bind.

πέδιλα, -ων, n.pl., sandals.

πέδον, -ου, n., ground, earth, place.

πείθω, πείσω, aor. mid., ἐπιθόμην, πέποιθα, ἐπείσθην, persuade; mid. and πέποιθα, trust, obey, take the advice of, with dat.

πεῖρα, -ας, f., attempt, enterprise.

πειράω, -άσω, usually mid., with aor., ἐπειράθην, try, make an attempt; H. fut., -ήσομαι, aor. infin. mid., -ήσασθαι, 3rd sing. subj., -ήσεται, opt., -ησαίμην, try, make trial of, with gen.

πειρητίζω, make trial of, with gen.

Πειρίθοος, -ου, H. -οιο, m., Pirithous, king of the Lapithae.

πελάζω, πελάσω or πελῶ, ἐπέλασα, approach, come near.

πέλεια, -ας, f., dove, pigeon.

πέλεκυς, -εως, H., acc., pl., -εας, m., axe.

πελεμίζω, -ίξω, H. aor., πελέμιξα, cause to tremble.

πέλομαι, 3rd sing. imperf., ἔπλετο, be.

Πελοποννήσιοι, -ων, Peloponnesians, living in the Peloponnese in southern Greece.

πέμπτος, -η, -οι, fifth.

πέμπω, -ψω, ἐπέμφθην, send.

πέντε, indecl., five.

πεπλός, -οῦ, m., robe, raiment.

πεπνῦμένος, -η, -ον, part. used as adj., wise.

πέποιθα, perf. of πείθομαι, trust, believe, with dat.

πέπονθα, perf. of πάσχω.

πέπρᾱγα, perf. (intr.) of πράσσω, fare.

πέπρωται, 3rd sing. perf., it is fated; p.p.p. πεπρωμένος, fated; from ἔπορον (no pres.), give.

πεπυσμένος, p.p.p. of πυνθάνομαι.

περ, enclitic particle used to strengthen an adj.; with part., although.

πέρᾱ, adv., beyond, further; comp. περαιτέρω, more, further.

περαίνω, -ανῶ, ἐπέρᾱνα, finish, complete.

περαιόομαι,-ώσομαι ἐπεραιώθην, cross.

πέρθω, πέρσω, sack, ravage.

περί, prep. with acc., about, around; with gen., about, concerning; with dat., for, concerning.

περιβάλλω, -βαλῶ, -έβαλον, throw round, throw over.

περίβολος, -ου, m., encircling line; circumference.

περίειμι,-έσομαι, imperf.,-ῆν, survive.

περιέχω, -σχήσω, -έσχον, surround.

περιῆσαν, 3rd pl. imperf. of περίειμι.

περίκειμαι, -κείσομαι, H. imperf., περίκειτο, lie round, enclose.

περιοράω, -όψομαι, -εῖδον, allow.

περίορθρον, -ου, n., dawn, just before dawn.

περίπτυγμα, -ματος, n., covering.

περισταυρόω, -ώσω, build a stockade round.

περιτειχίζω, -ίσω, build a wall round, invest.

περιπείχισις, -εως, f., circumvallation, the building of a wall round a besieged city.

περιφρουρέω, -ήσω, besiege.

περίφρων, -φρονος, prudent.

Περσεφόνα, -ας, f., Persephone, wife of Hades and queen of the Underworld.

πεσών, aor. part. of πίπτω.

πετάννῡμι, πετάσω, open (tr.); H. aor. pass., πετάσθησαν, they flew open.

πέτρα, -ας, f., rock.

πετρορριφής, -ές, hurled down from a rock.

πεφηνώς, having appeared, newly-revealed, intr. p.p. of φαίνω.

πέφνε, H. aor. (no pres.), he killed.

πεφοβημένος, p.p.p. of φοβέω.

πέφῡκα, be born from, be sprung from; be; perf. intr. of φύω, beget.

πῇ, adv., whither; πῃ, anywhere.

πήγνῡμαι, πήξομαι, plup., ἐπεπήγειν, freeze, intr.

πηλός, -οῦ, m., mud, mire.

πῆμα, πήματος, n., trouble, woe, mischief.

Πηνελόπεια, -ας, H. dat., -είῃ, f., Penelope, daughter of Icarius and wife of Odysseus.

πῆχυς, -εως, m., bridge or centre-piece of a bow.

πιέζομαι, -έσομαι, be hard pressed, be in difficulties.

πιθήσας, H. aor. part., trusting in, with dat.

πιθόμενος, aor. mid. part. of πείθω.

πικρός, -ά, -όν, bitter, unpleasant.

πίμπλημι, see ἐκπίμπλημι.

πίμπρημι, imperat., πίμπρη, πρήσω, set fire to, burn.

πινυτός, -ή, -όν, wise.

πίνω, H. infin., πῑνέμεν, πίομαι, ἔπιον, drink.

πιπράσκω, πράσω, ἐπράθην, sell.

πίπτω, πεσοῦμαι, ἔπεσον, fall; be sacrificed.

πίσσα, -ης, f., pitch.

πιστεύω, -εύσω, trust, believe, with dat.

πίστις, -εως, f., good faith.

πιστός, -ή, -όν, faithful, trusty.

πιστόομαι, -ώσομαι, aor. pass. imperat. dual, πιστωθῆτον, be persuaded.

πιφαύσκομαι, declare, foretell.

πλαγκτός, -ή, -όν, vagabond, perhaps crazy.

πλανάομαι, -ήσομαι, wander.

Πλαταιά, -ᾶς, f., Plataea, a town of Boeotia eight miles south of Thebes, friendly to Athens.

Πλαταιῆς, -ῶν, m.pl., the Plataeans.

Πλαταιίς, -ίδος, f.adj., Plataean.

πλέγματα, -ων, n.pl., wreaths; plaited work.

πλειστάκις, adv., with ὡς, as often as possible.

πλεῖστος, -η, -ον. superl. of πολύς, most, greatest: περὶ πλείστου εἶναι be of the greatest value or importance.

πλείων, πλεῖον, also πλέων, πλέον, comp. of πολύς, more, greater; τί πλέον, what good is it? τὸ πλέον, the majority; οἱ πλείονες, οἱ πλέους, most of them.

πλεκτός, -ή, -όν, woven, wicker.

πλέκω, πλέξω, weave a web.
πλέον, n. of πλέων, = πλεῖον, more.
πλεύμων, -μονος, m., lung.
πλέω, πλεύσομαι, imperf., ἔπλεον, ἔπλευσα, sail.
πληγή, -ῆς, f., blow, stroke.
πληγείς, aor. pass. of πλήσσω.
πλῆθος, -ους, n., mass, majority; people.
πλήν, adv., except.
πληρής, -ές, full, brimming.
πληρόω, -ώσω, fill.
πλήρωμα, -ματος, n., something that fills.
πλησίος, -α, -ον, near, next; n. as adv., with gen., near.
πλήσσω, πλήξω, ἐπλήγην, strike.
πλινθεύομαι, -εύσομαι, make bricks.
πλίνθος, -ου, f., brick.
πλοῖον, -ου, n., boat, ship.
πλοῦς, πλοῦ, m., voyage, good weather for sailing; πλοῦν ποιοῦμαι, make a voyage.
πνεῦμα, -ματος, n., wind.
πόθεν, adv., whence, from where; for what reason; ποθέν, from some place.
ποθέω, -ήσω, long for.
ποιέω, -ήσω, H. fut. infin., ποιησέμεν, also mid., make, cause, do; τὰ πεποιημένα, what had been done.
ποιητός, -ή, -όν, H. m. gen., -οῖο, built, constructed.
ποῖος, -α, -ον, what sort of? what?
πολεμέω, -ήσω, make war on, oppose, with dat.
πολέμιος, -α, -ον, hostile, of war; to

show an enemy attack; m., the enemy.
πόλεμος, -ου, m., war; πολεμόνδε, to the war.
πολιορκέω, -ήσω, besiege; pass., stand a siege.
πολιορκία, -ας, f., siege.
πολιός, -ά, -όν, grey.
πόλις, -εως, H. dat. pl., πολίεσσι, city, state.
πολίτης, -ου, m., citizen, fellow-citizen.
πολλάκις, adv., often.
πολλόν, H. for πολύ, much.
πολυδάκρῦτος, -ον, H. gen., -οιο, tearful.
πολυκλήϊς, -εσσα, -εν, with many banks of oars.
πολύκμητος, -ον, well-wrought.
πολύς, πολλή, πολύ, H.n., πολλόν, much, many, far; πολλά, often; πολύ, much; ἐπὶ πολύ, over a wide area; πολλῷ, (by) far.
πολύτλας, gen., -τλαντος, much-enduring.
πολύφρων, -φρονος, wise.
πολυχειρία, -ας, f., a large number of workers.
πονηρός, -ά, -όν, bad, wicked.
πόνος, -ου, m., labour, toil, trouble, suffering.
πόντιος, -α, -ον, of the sea.
πόποι, with ὦ, exclamation of disgust, surprise, or fear, for shame, indeed, good heavens.
πορεύομαι, -εύσομαι, march, travel.
πόροι, opt. of ἔπορον.
πόρρω, adv., far.

πόσις, -ιος, m., husband.

ποσσί, H., for ποσί, dat. pl. of πούς.

ποταμός, -οῦ, m., river.

ποτέ, enclitic particle, at any time, ever.

Ποτείδεία, -ας, f., Potidaea, a town on the Chalcidican peninsula in the north Aegean.

πότερος, -a, -ον, which of the two.; πότερα, adv. introducing a double question.

ποτιδέγμενος, H. aor. part of προσδεχομαι, expecting.

πότμος, -ου, m., fate., destiny.

πότνια, -ας, f., lady.

πότον, -ου, H., -οιο, n., drink.

ποῦ, adv., where; που, somewhere; I think.

πούς, ποδός, H. dat. pl., ποσσί, m., foot.

πρᾶγμα, -ματος, n., affair, business.

πρᾱθείς, aor. part. pass. of πιπράσκω.

πράσσω, -ξω, do, manage; negotiate, make terms; intr., with perf., πέπρᾱγα, fare; εὖ πράσσειν, be happy.

πρέπει, impers., it is fitting; part., πρέπον (ἐστί), it is right; f., πρέπουσα, fitting.

πρέσβυς,-εως, m., old man; ambassador, envoy; as comp. adj., πρεσβύτερος, older.

πριάμενος, used as aor. part. of ὠνέομαι, buy.

πρίν, conj. with infin., before; in a negative sentence, until; as adv., formerly, first; ὁ πρίν, the former, the first, as adj.

πρό, prep. with gen., before, in front of, rather then; πρὸ τοῦ, before this time, previously.

προάγω, -άξω, -ήγαγον, induce, compel.

προαπολείπω, -ψω, προαπέλιπον, abandon first, desert, fail.

προαπόλλυμαι, -ολοῦμαι, -ωλόμην, die first, be executed too soon.

πρόβατον, -ου, n., sheep.

προβλώσκω, -μολούμαι, go out.

πρόγονος, -ου, m., grandfather.

προγονός, -οῦ, m., stepson.

προδίδωμι, -δώσω, προῦδωκα, betray, desert; οἱ προδίδοντες, the traitors.

προέσθαι, aor. infin. mid. of προίημι.

προέχω or προὔχω, -σχήσω, προέσχον, project; mid., make a proposal, offer; τὸ προέχον, the projecting part, the head.

προθῡμία, -ας, f., eagerness, will; patriotism.

προθῡμος, -ον, eager, willing.

πρόθυρον, -ου, n., porch.

προῆκα, aor. of προίημι.

προϊδών, aor. part. of προοράω.

προίημι, -ήσω, -ῆκα, send forth; abandon.

προκαθίστημι, -καταστήσω, -κατέστησα, place beforehand; perf., προκαθέστηκα, be placed beforehand.

προκαλέομαι, -έσομαι, προὐκαλεσάμην, request, challenge, propose.

προκάλυμμα, -ματος, n., covering, protection.

προκαταγιγνώσκω, -γνώσομαι, -κατ-ἔγνων, condemn in advance, *with gen.*; *with* φόνου, for murder.

προκαταλαμβάνω, -λήψομαι, -κατέλαβον, seize.

προλάζυμαι, anticipate, enjoy earlier, *with gen.*

προλαμβάνω, -λήψομαι, προὔλαβον, anticipate, forestall.

προμνηστῖνοι, -αι, -α, *pl.*, one by one.

προνοέομαι, -ήσομαι, προὐνοησάμην, plan beforehand.

πρόνοια, -ας, *f.*, design, intention, forethought.

προξενέω, -ήσω, be a public host; help, serve.

πρόξενος, -ου, *m.*, representative of one state living in another state; public host.

προοράω, -όψομαι, -εῖδον, foresee, see.

προοφείλω, -ειλήσω, *imperf. pass.*, προωφειλόμην, owe previously.

πρόρρησις, -εως, *f.*, proclamation.

πρός, *prep. with acc.*, to, towards, against, with regard to, to suit, facing, near; *with gen.*, on the side of, in favour of, in the direction of; *with dat.*, near, in addition to; *as adv.*, in addition.

προσάγω, -άξω, -ήγαγον, *aor. part. pass.*, -αχθείς, bring forward, reduce, win over.

προσάπτω, -άψω, fasten to, wrap round.

προσαυδάω, -ήσω, *3rd sing. imperf.*, -ηύδα, address.

προσβαίνω, -βήσομαι, -ἔβην, *H. aor.*

mid., -βήσετο, approach, ascend, set foot on.

προσβάλλω, -βαλῶ, -ἔβαλον, attack, *with dat.*; ὄψιν προσβάλλω, set eyes on.

προσβολή, -ῆς, *f.*, attack.

πρόσβορρος, -ον, northern, facing north.

προσέειπε, *H. for* προσεῖπε.

προσέθεσαν, *aor. of* προστίθημι.

προσεῖπον, *H.*, -έειπε, *aor.* (*no pres.*), I addressed.

προσέμειξα, *aor. of* προσμείγνυμι; *imperf.*, προόσέμισγον.

προσεπεξευρίσκω, -ευρήσω, -εὗρον, devise further.

προσέρχομαι, -ειμι, -ῆλθον, approach, *with dat.*

προσέχω, -σχήσω, -ἔσχον, turn towards; νοῦν προσέχω, pay attention to.

προσηύδα, *3rd sing. imperf. of* προσαυδάω.

προσήκει, *imperf.*, -ῆκε, *impers. with dat.*, it concerns; οἱ προσήκοντες, relations.

προσθείς, *aor. part. of* προστίθημι.

πρόσθεν, *adv.*, formerly; ὁ πρόσθε χρόνος, the former time.

προσιέναι, *infin. of* πρόσειμι (προσέρχομαι).

προσκηδής, -ές, *H. gen.*, -έος, loving, affectionate.

προσκλίνω, -κλινῶ, -ἔκλῑνα, lean against, *tr.*

προσμείγνῡμι, -μείξω, *imperf.*, -ἔμισγον, -έμειξα, reach, come to grips with.

προσοικοδόμεω, -ήσω, *imperf.*, -ῳκοδόμουν, build in addition.

προσπέμπω, -ψω, send to.

προσπίπτω, -πεσοῦμαι, -έπεσον, charge, attack, touch, *with dat.*; strike against.

προσποιέω, -ήσω, win over.

προστίθημι, -θήσω, -έθηκα, *part.*, -θείς, place against.

προσφέρω, -οίσω, -ήνεγκα, add; *mid.*, attack, *with dat.*

πρόσφημι, -φήσω, -έφην, speak to, address.

πρόσφθεγμα, -ματος, *n.*, greeting, salutation.

πρόσφορος, -ον, suitable; τὰ πρόσφορα, his rightful place.

προσχώννῡμι, also προσχόω, -χώσω, *imperf. pass.*, -εχοῦτο, -έχωσα, pile up, build a mound.

προσχωρέω, -ήσω, come over (to).

πρόσχωσις, -εως, *f.*, mound.

πρόσω, *adv.*, hither.

προσῳδός, -όν, in harmony with, agreeing with.

προτάσσω, -τάξω, appoint as advocate for.

προτείνω, -τενῶ, προύτεινα, offer.

πρότερος, -α, -ον, former, first; *n.*, with or without τό as *adv.*, previously.

προτίθημι, -θήσω, προύθηκα, προύτέθην, put forward, offer.

προύκαλεσάμην, *aor.* of προκαλέομαι.

προύνοησάμην, *aor.* of προνοεόμαι.

προύτέθην, *aor. pass.* of προτίθημι.

πρόφασις, -εων, *f.*, excuse, reason, motive.

προφερής, -ές, *superl.*, προφερέστατος, excellent.

προφέρω, -οίσω, -ήνεγκα, also *mid.*, put forward, appeal to.

προφητεύω, -εύσω, speak on behalf of, *with gen.*

προφῆτις, -εως, *f.*, interpreter, priestess.

προχωρέω, -ήσω, advance; turn out well.

προωφείλετο, *3rd sing. imperf. pass. of* προοφείλω.

πρῶτος, -η, -ον, first; ἀπὸ πρώτης, from the first; *n.*, πρῶτον, as *adv.*, first.

πτηνός, -ή, -όν, winged.

πτωχός, -οῦ, *m.*, beggar.

Πυθάγγελος, -ου, Pythangelus, a Boeotarch, Theban leader of the attack on Plataea.

πυθέσθαι, *aor. infin. of* πυνθάνομαι.

Πῡθικός, -ή, -όν, Pythian, Delphic, Delphian.

Πύθιος, -α, -ον, Pythian, Delphic; *m.*, Apollo, the Pythian god.

πῡθόχρηστος, -ον, revealed by the Pythian (Delphic) oracle.

πύκα, also πυκινῶς, well, firmly.

πύλη, -ης, *f.*, gate; *pl.*, double gates.

Πύλος, -ου, *f.*, Pylos, a town in S.W. Greece.

πυνθάνομαι, πεύσομαι, ἐπυθόμην, πέπυσμαι, learn about, hear.

πῦρ, πυρός, *n.*, fire.

πύργος, -ου, *m.*, tower.

πυρφόρος, -ον, incendiary.

πω, *enclitic particle*, yet.

πῶμα, πώματος, *n.*, drink; wine.

πώποτε, *adv.*, never yet.
πῶς, *adv.*, how? πως, for some
reason; οὔ πως, not at all.

Π

ῥά, *H. enclitic particle like* ἄρα, then,
indeed, therefore; straightway.
ῥᾴδιος, -α, -ον, easy; *comp.*, ῥᾴων,
adv., ῥᾷον; *superl.*, ῥᾷστος.
ῥάκος, -ους, *H. pl.*, -εα, *n.*, rag.
ῥέζω, ῥέξω, do, perform.
ῥέω, ῥεύσομαι, ἐρρύην, flow.
ῥήγνῡμι, ῥήξω, ἔρρηξα, break, tear.
ῥηθείς, *aor. part. pass. of* ἐρῶ, will
say; τὰ ῥηθέντα, what has been
said.
ῥηϊδίως, *H. adv.*, *of* ῥᾴδιος; *superl.*
ῥήϊτατα.
ῥῆξαι, *aor. infin. of* ῥήγνῡμι.
ῥῆσις, -εως, *H.*, -ιος, *f.*, talk conversation.
ῥίπτω, -ψω, ἔρριψα, *infin.*, ῥῖψαι,
throw.
ῥίς, ῥῑνός, *f.*, nostril.
ῥύμη, -ης, *f.*, rush.
ῥῡσιάζω, -ασω, seize, carry off by
force.
ῥῡτήρ, -ῆρος, *m.*, one who draws, a
drawer.

Σ

σανίς, -ίδος, *H. dat. pl.*, -ίδεσσι, *f.*,
floor, platform.
σαφής, -ες, clear; τὸ σαφὲς, the
truth.
σαυτόν, -ήν, reflexive pronoun,
yourself.
σαώσεαι, *H. 2nd sing. fut. mid. of*
σῴζω.

σβέννῡμι, σβέσω, *aor. infin.*, σβέσαι,
quench.
σέθεν, = σοῦ, *poetic gen. of* σύ.
σείω, σείσω, shake, *tr.*
σέλας, -αος, *H. dat.*, σέλᾳ, *n.*, light.
σεμνός, -ή, -όν, holy, righteous.
σέσωκα, *perf. of* σῴζω.
σηκός, -οῦ, *m.*, cave.
σῆμα, -ματος, *n.*, sign, indication.
σημαίνω, -μανῶ, ἐσήμηνα, reveal, tell.
σημεῖον, -ου, *n.*, sign, trace, clue,
signal.
σθένος, -ους, *H.*, -εος, *n.*, strength.
σίδηρος, -ου, *m.*, iron.
σιγάω, -ήσω, be silent.
σιγή, -ῆς, *f.*, silence.
σῑτοποιός, -όν, to prepare food, to
bake bread.
σῖτος, -ου, *m.*, bread, food.
σιωπή, -ῆς, *f.*, silence.
σκέπτομαι, -ψομαι, *aor. imperat.*,
σκέψασθε, consider, reflect.
σκηνή, -ῆς, *f.*, tent, *also pl.*
σκόπελος, -ου, *m.*, cliff.
σκοπέω, -ήσω, consider.
σκοπός, -οῦ, *m.*, mark, target.
σκοτεινός, -ή, -όν, dark; τὸ σκοτεινόν,
darkness.
σκότος, -ους, *n.*, *also* -ου *m.*, darkness.
σμῑκρός, -ά, -όν, small, a little.
σός, σή, σόν, your (*sing.*).
σπάργανα, -ων, *n.pl.*, swaddling-
clothes.
σπαργανόω, -ώσω, wrap up.
σπείρω, σπερῶ, ἔσπειρα, sow; beget;
ὁ σπείρας, the father; χρόνια
σπείρας. λέχη, after being married
a long time.

σπένδω, σπείσω, H. aor. σπεῖσα, pour away wine; pour a libation; mid., make a truce; ask for a truce.

σπέρμα, -ματος, n., seed; offspring.

σπεύδω, -εύσω, hasten, be eager.

σπονδή, -ῆς, f., libation, drink-offering; pl., truce, treaty; peace.

σποράδην, adv., scattered about, here and there.

σπουδή,-ῆς,f., trouble, pains.

στάδιον, -ου, n., pl. also m., stade (202 yards), furlong.

σταθείς, standing, aor. part. pass. of ἵστημι.

στάθμη, -ης.f., carpenter's line.

σταθμός,-οῦ,m., door-post, pillar.

σταλαγμός, -οῦ, m., drop.

στάσις, -εως,f., revolution.

στέαρ, στέατος, n., fat, lard.

στεγάζω, -άσω, cover in; deck.

στεγανός, -ή, -όν, roofed.

στέγη, -ης,f., tent.

στέγος, -ους, n., house, home.

στέγω, -ξω, cover, conceal.

στειλειή, -ῆς,f., axe-socket, hole for the handle of an axe.

στείχω, -ξω, go.

στέμμα, -ματος, n., garland.

στένω, groan.

στέρνον, -ου, n., breast, chest.

στέφανος, -ου, m., wreath, garland.

στῆ, H. for ἔστη, str. aor. of ἵστημι.

στῆθος, -ους, H. dat. pl., -εσσι, n., bosom, chest.

στῆσε, H. for ἔστησε, weak aor. of ἵστημι.

στίβος, -ου, m., path.

ὅτιν, = ἔστιν, 3rd sing. of εἰμί, I am.

στολή, -ῆς,f., equipment, armour.

στόμα, -ματος, n., mouth.

στοναχή, -ῆς, f., groaning.

στονόεις, -εσσα, -εν, grief-laden, causing grief.

στράτευμα, -ματος, n., army, host.

στρατεύω, -εύσω, send or make an expedition.

στρατηγέω, -ήσω, be a general.

στρατόπεδον,-ου,n., garrison; camp.

στρατός, -οῦ, m., army.

στρεβλόω, -ώσω, torture on the rack.

στυγέω, -ήσω, hate.

στυγερῶς, adv., miserably.

στυράκιον, -ου, n., spike in the butt of a javelin (for fixing it in the ground).

σύ, σοῦ, dual, σφώ, σφῷν, H., σφῶιν, pl., ὑμεῖς, you.

συβώτης, -ου, voc., -α, m., swineherd.

συγγίγνομαι, -γενήσομαι, συνεγενόμην, be with.

συγγιγνώσκω, -γνώσομαι, συνέγνων, forgive, with dat.

συγγνώμη, -ης,f., forgiveness.

σύγγονος, -ου, c., brother, sister.

συγγράφω, -ψω, write.

συγκεράννῦμι, -κεράσω, fut. pass., συγκραθήσομαι, mingle; produce.

συγχωρέω,-ήσω, agree with, accept, with dat.

συζεύγνῦμι, -ζεύξω aor. pass., συνεζύγην, join; marry.

συλλαμβάνω, -λήψομαι, συνέλαβον, -ελήφθην, arrest, take with one-self.

συμβολαίον, -ου, n., contract; pl., dealings.

σύμβολον, -ου, n., token, relic.

σύμβουλος, -ου, counsellor, confederate.

σύμμαχος, -ου, m., ally; as adj., supporting.

συμμείγνῡμι, -μείξω, mix.

συμπλέω, -πλεύσομαι, imperf., συνέπλεον, συνέπλευσα, sail with.

σύμπλους, -ου, m., fellow voyager.

συμπονέω, -ήσω, take part in, labour at together.

συμφέρω, συνοίσω, -ήνεγκον, bring together; be useful, be expedient, with dat.; mid., agree with, confess; τὸ σύμφερον, what is expedient.

συμφορά, -ᾶς, f., fortune (good or bad), event.

σύν, prep. with dat., with.

συναγωνίζομαι, -ιοῦμαι, help, with dat.

συναναιρέω, -ήσω, -εἷλον, part., -ελών, help to pick up.

συναντάω, -ήσω, meet, with dat.

συνάντησις, -εως, f., meeting.

συναποκτείνω, -κτενῶ, -απέκτεινα, join in killing.

συνάντομαι, imperf., -ηντόμην, meet, with dat.

σύνδετον, -ου, n., fastening.

συνεζύγην, aor. pass. of συζεύγνῡμι.

συνέθεσαν, 3rd pl. aor. of συντίθημι.

συνειδείην, opt. of σύνοιδα.

σύνειμι, -έσομαι, imperf., -ῆν, be in the company of; οἱ συνόντες, αὐτῷ, his companions.

συνεκσῴζω, -σώσω, join in saving, come to the rescue.

συνεξαιρέω, -ήσω, -εἷλον, part., -ελών, help in ending.

συνέπλεον, imperf. of συμπλέω.

συνεργός, -ον, working with.

συνήντετο, imperf. of σύνάντομαι.

σύνοιδα, -είσομαι, -ήδη, be aware of; σύνοιδα ἐμαυτῷ, I am conscious of; σύνοιδέ μοι, he shares my (guilty) secret.

συντίθημι, -θήσω, -έθηκα, devise.

συνών, part. of σύνειμι.

σῦς, συός, c., pig; m., boar.

συφορβός, -οῦ. m., swineherd.

σφαγή, -ῆς, f., slaughter; wound.

σφάγιον, -ου, n., victim, sacrifice.

σφάζω, -ξω, kill.

σφάλλω, σφαλῶ, ἔσφηλα, ἐσφάλην, deceive.

σφε, m. and f. acc. sing. and pl., him, her, them.

σφεῖς, σφᾶς, σφῶν, σφίσι, m. and f.pl., they.

σφέτερος, -α, -ον, his, her, their.

σφι, H. dat. of σφεῖς, =αὐτοῖς.

σφίσι, dat. of σφεῖς; in Attic Greek, indirect reflexive; σφίσιν αὐτοῖς, =ἑαυτοῖς.

σφοδρα, adv., very much.

σφῶϊν, H. dat. pl. dual of σύ.

σχέδον, adv., almost; σχέδον τι, almost.

σχέτλιος, -α, -ον, cruel.

σχολαῖος, -α, -ον, slow; comp. adv., οὐ σχολαίτερον, just as quickly.

σχολή, -ῆς, f., leisure.

σχόμενος, σχών, aor. mid. and act.

part. of ἔχω; σχόντες αἰτίας, facing charges.

σῴζω, σώσω, H. 2nd sing. fut. mid., σαώσεαι, save, keep; face; pass., reach safety.

Σωσίας, -ου, m., Sosias, one of the Hellenotamiae (Treasurers of Greece) in about 430.

σωτήρ, -ῆρος, m., saviour.

σωτηρία, -ας, f., safety, means of safety.

σωφρονέω, -ήσω, be wise; be in one's senses.

T

ταλαεργός, -όν, hard-working.

ταλαιπωρέω, -ήσω, suffer hardship.

ταλαίπωρος, -ον, unhappy.

τάλᾱς, τάλαινα, τάλαν, unhappy.

τἀληθές, τἀληθοῦς, =τὸ ἀληθές, τοῦ ἀληθοῦς, the truth.

τἄλλα, =τὰ ἄλλα, the other things.

τἀποκτεῖναι, =τό ἀποκτεῖναι, aor, infin. of ἀποκτείνω.

τἀμά, =τὰ ἐμά.

ταμίας, -ου, m., steward.

τἀναντία, =τὰ ἐναντία, the opposite.

τανυστύς, -ύος, f., stringing (of a bow).

τανύω, -ύσω, or -ύω, H., aor., τάνυσσα, string.

τἄρα =τοι ἄρα, then.

ταρσός, -οῦ, m., basket.

τάρφθη, H. aor. pass. of τέρπω.

τάσσω, τάξω, 3rd sing. plup. pass., ἐτέτακτο, arrange, give orders.

ταῦρος, -ου, m., bull.

ταύτῃ, adv., by this way, in this direction.

ταὐτομάτου, =τοῦ αὐτομάτου, spontaneously.

ταὐτόν, =τὸ αὐτό, n. of ὁ αὐτός, the same.

ταφείς, aor. part. pass. of θάπτω.

τάφος, -ου, m., tomb.

ταφός, -οῦ, m., amazement.

τάφρος, -ου, f., ditch.

τάχος, -ους, n., speed; κατὰ τάχος, quickly.

ταχύς, -εῖα, -ύ, H. m. pl., -έες, swift; comp., θάσσων, superl., τάχιστος; n. as adv., ταχύ, and τάχα, swiftly.

τε, enclitic particle; in H. it makes a statement general; also, and; in Attic Greek, and; τε ... καί, both ... and; in Thucydides sometimes, and so.

τέγος, -ους, H., -εος n., roof.

τεθνάμεν, H. for τεθνάναι, =τεθνηκέναι, perf. infin. of θνήσκω; τεθνεώς, =τεθνηκώς, perf. part.

τεῖχος, -ους, n., wall, also pl.; barricade.

τεκμήριον, -ου, n., clue, sign, proof.

τέκνον, -ου, n., child.

τέκτων, -τονος, m., carpenter.

τεκών, aor. part. of τίκτω; ὁ τεκών, the father; ἡ τεκοῦσα, the mother; οἱ τεκόντες, the parents.

τέλεος, -α, -ον, completed, complete.

τελευταῖος, -α, -ον, last; τὸ τελευταῖον, at the end.

τελευτάω, -ήσω, finish, with acc. or gen; intr., come to an end; die.

τελέω, τελέσω, perf. pass., τετέλεσμαι,

bring to pass, accomplish, put an end to.

τέλος, -ους, n., end; binding effect; διὰ τέλους, to the end, continually; as adv., τέλος, at last.

τέμνω, τεμῶ, ἔτεμον, cut, cut down, ravage.

τέρας, τέρατος, or τέραος, n., sign, portent, monster.

τέρπω, -ψω, aor. pass., ἐτέρφθην, H., τάρφθην, delight, tr., mid., be glad, take pleasure in, have one's fill of, with gen.

τέσσαρες, -α, four.

τέταρτος, -η, -ον, fourth; n. as adv., for the fourth time.

τετελεσμένος, p.p.p. of τελέω.

τετρακόσιοι, -αι, -α, four hundred.

τετυγμένος, τετύχθω, p.p.p. and imperat. of τεύχω; τετυκέσθαι, aor. infin. mid.

τευ, H. for τινός, gen. of τις.

τεύξομα, fut. of τυγχάνω.

τεῦχος, -ους, n., chest, ark.

τεύχω, -ξω, H. aor. mid., τετυκόμην, τέτυγμαι, made, do, build.

Τηλέμαχος, -ου, m., Telemachus, son of Odysseus and Penelope.

τηρέω, -ήσω, wait for, watch for.

τῆσι, H. for ταῖς, dat. f. pl. of ὁ, ἡ, τό.

τίθημι, θήσω, ἔθηκα, H., θῆκα, infin. θέμεν, ἐθέμην, H. 3rd sing., θέτο, place, set, put, lay down, plan, make; mid., cause, reckon; ground (arms).

τίκτω, τέξω, ἔτεκον, beget; give birth to; ὁ τεκών, the father; ἡ

τεκοῦσα, the mother; οἱ τεκόντες, the parents.

τῑμάω, -ήοω, honour.

τῑμωρέω, -ήσω, avenge, get vengeance on; support one's case.

τῑμωρία, -ας, f., vengeance, punishment; help.

τῑμωρός, -ου, m., champion, defender.

τίς, τί, who?, what?, τί, why?; τῷ, how?

τις, τι, H. gen., τευ, anyone, any, someone, some.

τιταίνομαι, bend (a bow).

τιτύσκομαι, take aim.

τλάω (not used in pres.), τλήσομαι, ἔτλην, dare, have the heart to.

τλήμων, -ον, unhappy; cruel.

τοί. H. nom. pl. of ὁ, ἡ, τό, they; also as a relative pronoun, who.

τοι, enclitic particle, then, therefore, wherefore, also τοίγαρ, τοίνυν.

τοῖν, gen. or dat. dual of ὁ, ἡ, τό.

τοῖος, -α, -ον, such.

τοιόσδε, τοιάδε, τοιόνδε, such, as follows.

τοίσδεσι, τοίσιδε, =τοῖσδε, dat. pl of ὅδε.

τοιοῦτος, -αύτη, -οῦτο, such.

τοῖχος, -ου, m., wall.

τόλμα, -ης, f., boldness; daring deed; hardness of heart.

τολμάω, -ήσω, dare, venture; verbal adj., τολμητέον, one must be bold.

Τολμίδης, -ου, m., Tolmides, father of Theaenetus, a Plataean.

τομή, -ῆς, f., end of a beam (the cut piece).

τόμια, -ων, n.pl., sacrifices when oaths were taken, hence oaths.

τοξεύω, -εύσω, shoot an arrow; aim at, desire, with gen.

τόξον, -ου, n., oftenpl., bow; archery; arrow.

τοξότης, -ου, m., archer.

τόσος, -η, -ον, H., τόσσος, so great, so loud; n. as adv., so much.

τοσόσδε, -ήδε, -όνδε, H., τοσσόσδε, so much, as great as this.

τοσοῦτος, -αύτη, -οῦτο, H., τοσσοῦτος, so great; n.as adv., so much, as much.

τότε, adv., then, later; οἱ τότε, the former; τοτὲ μὲν . . . τοτὲ δέ, at one time . . . at another.

του, = τινός, gen. of τις.

τοὐμόν, = τὸ ἐμόν.

τοὔμπαλιν, = τοῦ ἔμπαλιν, with ἐκ, on the other side.

τοὐναντίον, = τὸ ἐναντίον, the opposite.

τοὔνομα, = τὸ ὄνομα.

τοῦτο, n. of οὗτος.

τράπεζα, -ης, f., table.

τραπέσθαι, τραπόμενος, aor. infin. and part. mid. of τρέπω.

τραφείς, aor. part. pass. of τρέφω.

τρέπω, τρέψω, turn, tr.: mid., with aor. ἐτραπόμην. turn, intr.; turn pale; take (a road).

τρέφω, θρέψω, ἐτράφην, feed, supply with food; bring up; breed; pass., be descended from.

τρέχω, δραμοῦμαι, ἔδραμον, run, proceed.

τρίαινα, -ης, f., trident.

τριακόσιοι, -αι, -α. H., τριηκόσιοι, three hundred.

τριακοντούτης, -ες, lasting thirty years.

τρίβω, τρίψω, ἐτρίφθην, rub, rub together.

τριηκόσιοι, H., for τριακόσιοι.

τρίπους, -ποδος, m., tripod, stool of the Pythian priestess at Delphi.

τρίς, adv., three times.

τρίτος, -η, -ον, third.

τριφθείς, aor. pass. part. of τρίβω.

τρόπος, -ου, m., way, manner; acc. as adv. with gen., like.

τροφή, -ῆς, f., food, nurture, nourishment, means of livelihood, also pl.; βώμιοι τροφαί, the altars that fed him.

τροφός, -οῦ, f., nurse.

Τροφώνιος, -ου, m., Trophonius, a Boeotian seer who had an oracular cave 15 miles from Delphi.

τροχός, -οῦ, m., ball; wheel (for torture).

τρυφάω, -ήσω, lie snugly.

τρώω, hurt, damage.

τυγχάνω, τεύξομαι, ἔτυχον, H., ἐτύχησα, happen, wth part.; obtain, with gen.; meet, with dat.; be right, be successful.

τύχη, -ης, f., destiny, chance, fortune, fate.

τυχεῖν, τυχών, H., τυχήσας, aor. infin. and part. of τυγχάνω.

τώ, m. nom. dual of ὁ, ἡ, τό.

τῷ, = τίνι, dat. of τίς; also how?

τὠμῷ, = τῷ ἐμῷ.

Υ

ὑγρός, -όν, watery, flowing, of the sea.

ὑδατώδης, -ές, watery, slushy, about to melt.

ὕδωρ, ὕδατος, n., water; rain.

ὑετός, -οῦ, m., rain.

υἱός, -οῦ and υἱέος, H. dat. pl., υἱάσι, m., son.

ὕλη, -ης, f., wood, timber, dry branches

ὑμεῖς, ὑμῶν, H., ὕμμες, ὑμέᾱς, ὑμείων, you, pl. of σύ, dual, σφώ, H. dat., σφῶϊν.

ὑμέτερος, -α, -ον, your.

ὑμνωδέω, -ήσω, chant.

ὑπάγω, -άξω, -ήγαγον, draw away.

ὑπαείδω, ὑπαείσομαι, H. aor, ὑπὸ ... ἄεισε, sing.

ὑπάρχω, -άρξω, 3rd sing. plup. mid., -ῆρκτο, exist, be; with gen., begin.

ὑπεῖδον, aor. of ὑφοράω.

ὑπεναντίος,-ου,m.,opponent,enemy.

ὑπέρ, prep. with gen., over, beyond; concerning.

ὑπερβαίνω, -βήσομαι, -εβην, aor. opt., -βαίην, cross over, climb over; overstep.

ὑπερδραμεῖν, aor. infin., of ὑπερτρέχω.

ὑπερέχω, -σχήσω, -έσχον, keep one's head above water.

ὑπερήμερος, -ον, liable to imprisonment or distraint for debt.

ὑπερηνορέων, -οντος, proud.

ὑπερτείνω, -τενῶ, -έτεινα, project over.

ὑπερτρέχω, -δραμοῦμαι, -έδραμον, overcome.

ὑπερφίαλος, -ον, proud, noble; adv., -ως, exceedingly.

ὑπέρχομαι, -ειμι, -ῆλθον, come over, creep over.

ὑπερῷον, -ου, n., upper room, also pl.

ὑπέχω, ὑποσχήσω, ὑπέσχον, offer; undergo, bear; face (a charge).

ὑπῆλθον, aor. of ὑπέρχομαι.

ὑπηρέτης, -ου. m., assistant.

ὑπῆρκτο, 3rd sing. plup. mid. of ὑπάρχω.

ὑπισχνέομαι, ὑποσχήσομαι, ὑπεσχόμην, promise.

ὕπνος, -ου, m., sleep.

ὑπό, prep. with acc., under; with gen., by, because of; with dat., subject to; adv., beneath.

ὑποδέομαι, -δήσομαι, perf., -δέδεμαι put on (shoes); p.p.p., ὑποδεδεμένος, shod, wearing shoes on, with acc.

ὑποζύγιον, -ου, n., beast of burden; ox.

ὑπολαμβάνω, -λήψομαι, ὑπέλαβον, reply; aor. part., ὑπολαβών, in reply.

ὑπολείπω, -ψω, ὑπέλιπον, p.p.p., ὑπολελειμμένος, leave behind, also mid.

ὑπονείφω, snow a little; past. part., ὑπονειφομένη, with νύξ, a snowy night.

ὑπόνομος, -ον, underground; m., a mine.

ὑπόσπονδος, -ον, under a truce.

ὑποστρέφω, -ψω, turn round, intr.

ὑποσχεῖν, aor. infin. of ὑπέχω.

ὑποσχέσθαι, aor. infin. of ὑπισχνέομαι.

ὑποτοπέω, -ήσω, suspect.

ὑπότροπος, -ον, coming back.

ὑπουργέω, -ήσω, help.

ὗς, ὑός, H. dat. pl., ὑέσσι, c., pig.

Ὕσιαι, -ων, f.pl., Hysiae, a village four miles S.E. of Plataea.

ὕστατος, -η, -ον, superl. adj., last.

ὑστεραῖος, -α, -ον, of the next day; τῇ ὑστεραίᾳ, on the next day.

ὕστερος, -α, -ον, later, following; ὁ ὕστερος, the second man; n. as adv., ὕστερον, afterwards, since then; too late.

ὑφαίνω, ὑφανῶ, ὕφηνα, weave.

ὕφασμα, -ματος, n., web, weaving, woven work.

ὑφέλκω, -ξω, -είλκυσα, imperf., -εῖλκον, draw away.

ὑφίσταμαι, ὑποστήσομαι, ὑπεστησάμην, undertake.

ὑφοράω, -όψομαι, ὑπεῖδον, suspect.

ὑφορβός, -οῦ, m., swineherd.

ὑψηλός, -ή, -όν, high, lofty.

ὕψος, ὕψους, n., height.

Φ

φαεινός, -ή, -όν, shining.

φαῖεν, 3rd pl. opt. of φημί.

φαίνομαι, φανοῦμαι, πέφηνα, ἐφάνην, appear, seem, turn out to be: clearly be, with part.; act., φαίνω, show.

φάκελος, -ου, m., faggot, bundle of wood.

φανερός, -ά, -όν, clear, open, evident, visible.

φαντάζομαι, -τάσομαι, appear, be revealed.

φάος, φάους, n., light; εἰσορᾶν φάος, be alive; ἐκλιπεῖν φάος, die.

φαρέτρα, -ας, H., -η, -ης, f., quiver.

φάρμακον, -ου, drug, remedy; poison, also pl.

φάσαν, φάτο, H. for ἔφασαν, ἔφατο, aor. act. and mid. of φημί; φάσθαι, aor. infin.; φασί, 3rd pl. pres. indic.

φάσκω, say, declare; τὸ μὴ φάσκειν, his denial.

φάσμα, -ματος, n., vision, revelation.

φάτις, -εως, f., saying; name.

φείδομαι, φείσομαι, ἐφεισάμην, spare, with gen.

φερνή, -ῆς, f., dowry, also pl.

φέρβω, feed.

φέρω, οἴσω, H. imperf., φέρον, ἤνεγκα, bear, pay, lead (of a road); mid., win, gain; imperat., φέρε, come now, well then.

φέρτερος, -α, -ον, comp. adj., better.

φεῦ, interj., alas.

φεύγω, φεύξομαι, ἔφυγον, flee; abandon, lose, avoid; be on trial, be accused: ὁ φεύγων, the accused man.

φημί, φήσω, ἔφην, H., 3rd pl., φάσαν, mid., ἔφατο, H., φάτο, say; οὔ φημι, infin., μὴ φάναι, say no, deny.

φθάνω, φθήσομαι, ἔφθασα or ἔφθην, anticipate, do in time, do before.

φθέγγομαι, φθέγξομαι, speak, say.

φθονέω, -ήσω, be jealous of, with dat.

φιάλη, -ης, f., goblet, cup.

φιλέω, -ήσω, love; be accustomed to.

φίλημα, -ματος, n., embrace, kiss.

φιλία, -ας, f., friendship; terms.

φίλιος, -α, -ον, friendly.

φίλος, -η, -ον, H., gen., -οιο, dear; H., with parts of the body, one's own; superl. φίλτατος; τὰ φίλτατα, the things held most dear; φίλον ἐστί μοι, I wish; m., a friend.

φλαῦρος, -α, -ον, damaging, compromising.

Φλέγρα, -ας, f., Phlegra, in Chalcidice (north Aegean coast), scene of the fight between the gods and the giants.

φλέψ, φλεβός, f., vein.

φλόξ, φλογός, f., flame, conflagration.

φοβερός, -ά, -όν, fearful, full of fear.

φοβέω, -ήσω, frighten; mid., with aor. ἐφοβήθην, fear; p.p.p. πεφοβημένος, terrified.

Φοῖβος, -ου, m., Phoebus Apollo, god of the sun, healing, and prophecy, father of Ion.

φοινῑκόεις, -εσσα, -εν, purple.

φοινῑκοσκελής, -ές, red-legged; red.

φονεύς, -έως, m., murderer.

φόνος, -ου, m., murder, death, also pl.

φορά, -ᾶς, f., rent.

φορέω, -ήσω, H. 3rd sing. inperf., φόρει, bring, carry, take away.

φορμηδόν, adv., crosswise, at right angles to one another.

φόρμιγξ, -μιγγος, f., lyre.

φράζω, φράσω, tell, say, describe.

φρενόω, -ώσω, instruct.

φρήν, φρενός, f., heart, soul, wit, senses, also pl.

φρονέω, -ήσω, H. pres. part., φρονέων, think; εὖ φρονέω, be in one's senses; restrain oneself; with acc., support the cause of.

φροῦδος, -η, -ον, gone, departed; φροῦδος ἦ, I departed.

φρουρέω, -ήσω, guard, keep safe.

φρουρός, -οῦ, dual, φρουρώ, m., guard, watcher; pl., garrison.

φρυκτηρα, -ας, f., beacon-fire.

φρυκτός, -οῦ, m., fire-signal.

φυγεῖν, or. infin. of φεύγω.

φυλακή, -ῆς, f., guard, garrison, station.

φύλαξ, -ακος, dual, φύλακε, m., guardian.

φυλάσσω, -άξω, guard, watch for.

Φυλείδης, -ου, m., Phyleides, a Theban, father of Pythangelus.

φύσις, -εως, f., nature, life.

φύω, φύσω, ἔφῡσα, beget; intr., ἐφῦν, πέφῡκα, be born, be sprung from he.

φωνέω, -ήσω, speak.

φώς, φωτός, m., man, hero.

φῶς, φωτός, n., light, daylight.

X

χ', = κε, would; ever.

χάζω, κεκαδήσω, deprive of.

χαίρω, χαιρήσω, rejoice, be glad; be well; imperat., χαῖρε, hail, greetings; farewell.

χαλαρός, -α, -ον, loose, made slack.

χαλεπαίνω, -πανῶ, ἐχαλέπηνα, be angry.

χαλεπός, -η, -ον, H. gen. -οίο, difficult; bitter; adv., with difficulty.

χάλκεος, -α, -ον, brazen, bronze.

χαλκοβαρής, -ές, bronze-weighted.

χαλκός, -οῦ, m., bronze; a sword.

Χαλκωδοντίδαι, -ων, m.pl., sons of Chalcodon, a king in Euboea, hence Euboeans.

χαμάζε, adv., to or on the ground.

χανδόν, adv., greedily.

χαρίζομαι, -ιοῦμαι, ἐχαρισάμην, please, do a favour to, with dat.

χάρις, χάριτος, f., favour; χάριν πράσσειν or φέρειν, do a favour.

χαρμονή, -ῆς, f., joy, enjoyment.

χάσμα, -ματος, n., chasm, gaping hole.

χεῖλος, -ους, n., lip, beak; edge.

χειμάζομαι, -άσομαι, be storm-tossed.

χειμέριος, -α, -ον, stormy.

χειμών, -ῶνος, m., winter; storm.

χείρ, χειρός or χερός, dual, χεῖρε, χεροῖν, dat. pl., χερσί, H., χείρεσσι, f., hand; διὰ χειρός, in one's hand, firmly; ἐς χεῖρας ἰέναι, come to close quarters.

χειροποίητος, -ον, made by the hand of man.

χείρων, -ον, comp. adj., inferior.

χελῑδών, -όνος, f., swallow.

χερμάδιον, -ου, n., stone.

χέρας, χερσί, χεροῖν, acc. and dat. pl. and dual of χείρ.

χέω, χεῶ, ἔχεα, pour.

χή, = καὶ ἡ.

χηλή, -ῆς, f., claw.

χηλός, -οῦ, m., chest.

χθόνιος, -α, -ον, in or of the Underworld.

χθών, χθονός, f., land.

χιτών, -ῶνος, m., tunic.

χλαῖνα, -ης, f., cloak.

χλιδή, -ῆς, f., adornment; fine garment.

χλόη, -ης, f., freshness; green leaves.

χόλος, -ου, m., anger.

χορδή, -ῆς, f., string (of a lyre).

χοῦς, χοῦ, m., mound; the loose earth of a mound.

χόω, infin., χοῦν, imperf., ἔχουν, raise, heap up; see χώννῡμι.

χράομαι, χρήσομαι, use, treat, meet with, make, submit to, with dat.; p.p., κεχρημένος, eager for, needing, with gen.

χράω, = χρῄζω, be eager, desire.

χρεία, -ας, f., need, necessity; business relationship.

χρεῖος, -ους, n., debt.

χρή, χρήσει, imperf., ἐχρῆν or χρῆν, it is necessary, one must, one ought, impers. with acc.; also with acc. and gen., one has need of; part., χρεών, with ἐστι, = χρή.

χρῄζω, desire, be eager.

χρῆμα, -ματος, n., thing; pl., money; τί χρῆμα, what?, why?

χρήσασθαι, aor. infin. of χράομαι.

χρηστήριον, -ου, n., oracle, oracular shrine; victim.

χρηστήριος, -α, -ον, oracular, prophetic.

χρηστός, -η, -ον, good, kindly.

χρόνιος, -α, -ον, long-lasting, for

long time; late; long ago; χρόνια
σπείρας λέχη, after being married
for a long time.

χρόνος, -ου, m., time, also pl.

χρύσειος, also χρύσεος, -η, -ον, and
χρῦσοῦς, -ῆ, -οῦν, golden, gold.

χρῡσήλατος, -ον, golden, of beaten
gold.

χρῡσήλογχος, -ον, with a golden
spear.

χρῡσός, -οῦ m., gold.

χρῡσοφύλαξ, -ακος, c., guardian of
gold.

χρύσωμα, -ματος, n., golden decora-
tion; golden bracelet.

χρώς, χρωτός, m., flesh; complexion,
colour.

χῶμα, -ματος, n., mound.

χώννῡμι, χώσω, ἔχωσα, (infin., χοῦν,
imperf., ἔχουν, from χόω), raise,
heap up, build.

χώρα, -ας, H., -η, -ης, f., land,
country, place; κατὰ χώραν, at
one's post.

χωρέω, -ήσω, come, go, advance.

χωρίον, -ου, n., place; part, space.

χωρίς, adv., separately.

χῶρος, -ου, m., place.

χῶσις, -εως, f., building of a mound.

Ψ

ψαύω, ψαύσω, touch, with gen.

ψέγω, ψέξω, find fault with, dis-
approve of.

ψευδής, -ές, false; n.pl., ψευδῆ, lies.

ψεύδω, ψεύσω, deceive; defraud.

ψηφίζομαι, -ιοῦμαι, ἐψηφισάμην,
vote, decide, give a verdict (on).

ψῆφος, -ου, f., vote.

ψῑλός, -ή, -όν, light-armed.

ψόφος, -ου, m., noise.

ψῡχή, -ῆς, f., soul, spirit, life.

Ω

ὤ, interj., Oh.

ὦ, interj., with voc., O.

ὦ, 1st sing. subj. of εἰμί, I am.

ὧδε, adv., thus, as follows.

ὠδίς, -ῖνος, f., birth-pain, hence
child.

ᾤετο, imperf. of οἴομαι.

ὠκύς, -εῖα, -ύ, swift; H. adv., ὠκά,
swiftly.

ὤλβισα, aor. of ὀλβίζω.

ὠλένη, -ης, f., arm.

ὤλεσα, ὠλόμην, aor. act. and mid. of
ὄλλυμι.

ὤμοι, interj., alas.

ὦμος, -ου, H. gen. and dat. dual,
ὤμοιϊν, shoulder; hand.

ὠμός, -ή, -όν, cruel, harsh.

ὤμοσα, aor. of ὄμνῡμι.

ὠμότης, -ητος, f., cruelty, cruel
purpose.

ὤν, οὖσα, ὄν, pres. part. of εἰμί, I am.

ὠνέομαι, -ήσομαι, with ἐπριάμην used
as aor., buy.

ὥρα, -ας, H., -η, -ης, f., time, right
time.

ὡραῖος, -α, -ον, in due season.

ὡρισμένος, p.p.p. of ὁρίζω.

ὥρμησα, aor. of ὁρμάω.

ὡρμισάμην, aor. of ὁρμίζομαι.

ὤρμουν, imperf. of ὁρμέω.

ὥς, and ὧς, adv., thus, so.

ὡς, adv. and conj., as, when, how,

because, on the ground that;
with subj. or opt., in order that;
with superl., as . . . as possible:
ὡς . . . αὕτως, thus; *as prep.
with acc.*, to; *also* = ὥστε, so
that.

ὥσπερ, *adv.*, just as.

ὥστε, *conj.*, so that, with the result
that, so as to.

ὠφέλεια, -ας, *f.*, help, benefit;
chance of safety.

ὠφελέω, -ήσω, help, benefit, be of
use.

ὠφέλιμος, -η, -ον, useful.

ὤφελον, *str. aor. of* ὀφείλω, *used with
infin. in a wish for the past*, would
that.

ὤφθην, *aor. pass. of* ὁράω.